ECONOMIC LIBERALISATION AND INSTITUTIONAL REFORMS IN SOUTH ASIA

Recent Experiences and Future Prospects

Edited by

DILIP DUTTA

ATLANTIC PUBLISHERS AND DISTRIBUTORS

Published for
THE CENTRE FOR SOUTH ASIAN STUDIES
FACULTY OF ECONOMICS
THE UNIVERSITY OF SYDNEY
SYDNEY, NEW SOUTH WALES,
AUSTRALIA

Published by
ATLANTIC PUBLISHERS AND DISTRIBUTORS
B-2, Vishal Enclave, Opp. Rajouri Garden, New Delhi-27
Phones : 5413460, 5429987

Sales Office
4215/1, Ansari Road, Darya Ganj, New Delhi-110 002
Phones : 3273880, 3285873, 3280451
Fax : 91-11-3285873
E-mail : info@atlanticbook.com
Web : www.atlanticbook.com

ISBN 81-7156-847-5

Typeset at
APD Computer Graphics, Delhi

Printed at
Mehra Offset Press, Delhi

PREFACE

The origin of the idea to publish this book goes back to May 1996, when the Centre for South Asian Studies was established at the University of Sydney, Australia. The Centre and the University's Department of Economics jointly organised an international conference on South Asian Development in 1997 and Beyond : Its Relevance for Australia during 12-14 September 1997. The conference was organised around three themes : (i) promotion of knowledge and understanding of South Asian countries in Australia; (ii) close examination of the strengths and weaknesses of economic and political institutions of the South Asian countries and (iii) focusing on the possibility of Australian technology transfer through different commercial links and aid projects. The papers presented at the conference were assessed by independent referees, who recommended publication of a select group of papers focusing on the second theme. As no paper, covering the same theme on Bhutan, was presented at the conference, it remains unrepresented in this publication.

In organising the conference and bringing out this publication, I received valuable assistance from a number of individuals, including my colleagues and students. Although I cannot acknowledge all of them by name, I must gratefully acknowledge the support of Associate Professor Debesh Bhattacharya, Director of the Centre for South Asian Studies and co-organiser of the conference. Generous financial support from the Australian Agency for International Development (AusAID) is also acknowledged. Without its support, it would have been impossible to invite several eminent scholars and experts from the South Asian countries to attend the conference in Sydney. Financial support from Professor Bill Schworm, Head of the Department of Economics at the University of Sydney, for the publication of this Volume is also appreciated.

I sincerely thank all the paper contributors, the chairpersons and panel members involved in various sessions at the conference, and all other participants who had directly or indirectly assisted in making the conference a success. Last but not the least, I hope that this Volume will be useful to academics, policy makers, development practitioners and administrators.

—Editor

LIST OF CONTRIBUTORS

Meena Acharya, General Secretary, T.P. Acharya Memorial Foundation, Kathmandu, Nepal.

Nasiruddin Ahmed, Director, Prime Minister's Office, Dhaka, Bangladesh.

Prema-Chandra Athukorala, Senior Fellow, Australia South Asia Research Centre, The Australian National University, Canberra, Australia.

B.B. Bhattacharya, Professor in Economics, Institute of Economic Growth, Delhi University, New Delhi, India.

Biplab Dasgupta, Professor in Economics, Calcutta University and Member of Parliament, India

Dilip Dutta, Senior Lecturer in Economics, University of Sydney, Sydney, Australia.

R.N. Ghosh, Senior Honorary Research Fellow, Department of Economics, The University of Western Australia, Nedlands, Perth, Australia.

B.S. Ghuman, Professor and Chairperson, Department of Public Administration, Panjab University, Chandigarh, India.

Akhtar Hossain, Senior Lecturer in Economics, University of Newcastle, New Castle, Australia.

Amir Mahmood, Lecturer in Economics, University of Newcastle, New Castle, Australia.

Peter Mayer, Professor in Politics, University of Adelaide, Adelaide, Australia.

Binayak Ray, Visiting Fellow at the Department of Political and Social Change at the Australian National University, Canberra, Australia.

Kishore Sharma, Lecturer in Economics, Charles Stuart University, Wagga Wagga, Australia.

M.A.B. Siddique, Director, Centre for Migration and Development Studies, University of Western Australia, Perth, Australia.

Rehman Sobhan, Director, Centre for Policy Dialogue, Dhaka, Bangladesh.

CONTENTS

1

Introduction

DILIP DUTTA

In the course of a long historical, cultural and linguistic heritage, the peoples of South Asia have shared many common values. There are various analyses of and approaches to the long historical process of socio-economic development underdevelopment in the region of South Asia[1]. Since the post-Second World War decolonisation wave, the newly independent nations including those in South Asia have been striving to achieve economic development in general and modernisation in particular. Under-development and uneven development have been the common features of many developing societies, and the countries in South Asia are no exception.

Generally speaking, countries in the region not only are internally segmented and differentiated by different socio-economic-technological environments, but also have different socio-economic interest groups/classes. A common differentiation of a socio-economic system that is often referred to in the literature on development economics is dualism[2]. Using this

---

1. Recent summaries and reviews of various such analyses of and approaches to the historical process of socio-economic development/underdevelopment in the region of South Asia can be found in Alavi (1989) and Subrahmanyam (1996), amongst others.

2. In Dutta (1991), the present author has an elaborate analysis of various concepts of dualism such as economic dualism, organisational or institutional dualism, and general or structural-functional dualism as used in literature on development economics and other social sciences.

concept of 'dualism' in a systemic and structural sense, this implies that two different, although interacting, socio-economic-technological environments — the traditional or unorganised segment (predominantly agricultural and pre-capitalistic) and the modern or organised segment (predominantly industrial and capitalistic) — co-exist within the geographical boundary of a nation guided by the State authority. Each and every country's socio-economic system in the region is, by and large, dualistic, although in varied degrees. It is expected that the activities, organisations and institutions of both segments, under the guidance of the State authority in each of these countries, would lead to gradual transformation from their traditional nature to a predominantly modernised one.

Compared to the achievements attained by their nearest low and middle-income neighbours of East and Southeast Asia, achievements by South Asian countries have been far less than potential, especially over the last three decades[3]. It is becoming more and more evident that large sections of their population have been unable to actively participate in the modernisation process of industrialisation and urbanisation, and still lack the capacity to afford even the minimum subsistence needs for food, shelter, health and education. Various sources could easily testify to this precarious situation in the region. In a recent publication on Human Development in South Asia, Haq (1997, p. 2) finds :

> South Asia is fast emerging as the poorest, the most illiterate, the most malnourished, the least gender-sensitive — indeed, the most deprived region in the world.

This grim picture of the region is certainly not without many country specific achievements. For instance, compared to other countries in the region, Sri Lanka, even at a low level of income, has achieved higher development in the social sector, especially in education and health levels. Similarly, India's achievement of

3. See Table 1.3 : ***South Asia compared with East Asia*** in Haq (1997, p. 14).

maintaining a constitutional and representative democracies, since the Independence, is well recognised.

In response to the worsening fiscal deficits and balance of payment crises[4], most of the South Asian countries, earlier or later over the past decade or so, have been compelled to adopt the strategy of comprehensive economic liberalisation[5] and, therefore, various institutional reforms. While economic liberalisation implies a move toward decentralised market mechanisms, institutional reforms allow for required changes in the underlying norms and rules of not only a country's economic system, but also its societal system in general. Since the economic system is closely interlinked with the socio-cultural and politico-legal dimensions of a society, institutional reforms must indeed be country specific.

The recent focus on institution and institution building in the literature on Economic Development is unquestionably very pertinent — especially during the process of economic liberalisation that has been taking place in many developing countries including those in the South Asia region. Various policy reforms such as delicensing of industries, elimination of subsidies, privatization of the state-owned enterprises, deregulation and internationalisation of the financial sector, elimination of restrictions on international trade, etc. require either significant restructuring of the existing institutions or completely designing new institutions. These policy reforms and the accompanying institutional restructuring and innovations are meant to make the modern segment economically efficient and then to easily integrate it into the global market system, while the traditional segment is usually left to absorb trickle down effects. However, poverty-

4. For a short review on the question of centrality of crisis as a requirement for reform to take place, see Peter Mayer's paper in this Volume.

5. In their review on the post-1985 liberalisation episodes, Dean, Desai and Riedel (1994) record 1991 as the year of comprehensive liberalisation in Bangladesh and India, while 1988 and 1987 are recorded for the same in Pakistan and Sri Lanka respectively. Nepal's comprehensive liberalisation follows India's and it, therefore, takes place after 1991.

stricken rural masses of the traditional segments in South Asian countries have gradually become politically active and, therefore, cannot be expected to remain passive and silent spectators in the drama of an unpredictable trickle down process any longer. Pressures are mounting on individual governments for the adoption of an appropriate course of action so that the masses of their respective traditional segments can also actively take part in the nation building process. Consequently, policy measures for sustainable growth as well as social sector development are very much high priority on the agenda of all the governments in South Asia. Any noticeable progress in social sector development and, thereby, in poverty alleviation is yet to be witnessed in the region.

On regional front, over the years, various country groups and trade associations[6] have emerged in order to foster co-operation and competition among the participating countries. Similarly, seven South Asian nations (Bangladesh, Bhutan, India, Maldives, Nepal, Pakistan and Sri Lanka) have formed the South Asian Association for Regional Cooperation (SAARC). Although the idea of forming a regional grouping was first mooted in November 1980, the Charter establishing the SAARC was not adopted until December 1985. The objectives, principles and general provisions, as written in the SAARC Charter, are as follows :

Objectives

- To promote the welfare of the peoples of South Asia and to improve their quality of life;
- To accelerate economic growth, social progress and cultural development in the region and to provide all individuals the opportunity to live in dignity and to realise their full potential;

6. To name a few important such country groups and trade associations, one can mention Association of Southeast Asian Nations (ASEAN), Asia-Pacific Economic Co-operation (APEC), Commonwealth of Independent States (CIS), European Union (EU), North American Free Trade Agreement (NAFTA), Organisation of Petroleum-Exporting Countries (OPEC), etc.

- To promote and strengthen collective self-reliance among the countries of South Asia;
- To contribute to mutual trust, understanding and appreciation of one another's problems;
- To promote active collaboration and mutual assistance in the economic, social, cultural, technical and scientific fields;
- To strengthen cooperation with other developing countries;
- To strengthen cooperation among themselves in international forums on matters of common interests and
- To cooperate with international and regional organizations with similar aims and purposes.

Principles

- Cooperation within the framework of the Association is based on respect for the principles of sovereign equality, territorial integrity, political independence, non-interference in the internal affairs of other states and mutual benefit.
- Such cooperation is to complement and not to substitute bilateral or multilateral cooperation.
- Such cooperation should be consistent with bilateral and multilateral obligations of the member states.

General Provisions

- Decisions at all levels in the SAARC are taken on the basis of unanimity.
- Bilateral and contentious issues are excluded from its deliberations.

The key component of the SAARC's functions, the Integrated Program of Action (IPA), has identified a number of core areas of cooperation, each covered by a Technical Committee. Over the years, there has been a steady increase in the number of such core areas, currently including agriculture, communication, education, environment, health and population activities, meteorology, prevention of drug trafficking and drug abuse, rural development, science and technology, tourism, transport and women in development. Although the Association has emerged as a major instrument in facilitating interaction among member countries on a wide range of issues of common concern, lack of cooperation in the core economic areas on any significant scale remains a concern to all. However, the decision, made at the Sixth SAARC Summit in Colombo in October 1991, for establishing a South Asia Preferential Trading Arrangement (SAPTA) became a concrete step towards co-operation in the vital area of trade. Subsequently, the agreement on SAPTA was signed in Dhaka in April 1993 during the Seventh SAARC Summit, and came into force on 7 December 1995 when all member States met the necessary conditions. Under this Agreement, the gradual reduction and eventual elimination of tariffs within the SAARC countries is envisaged. SAPTA is thus considered to be a step towards the creation of the South Asian Free Trade Area (SAFTA). In the Declaration of the Tenth SAARC Summit in Colombo on 31 July 1998, the Heads of State or Government have reiterated the importance of achieving SAFTA as mandated by the Ninth SAARC Summit.

> To this end they decided that a Committee of Experts, in consultation with Member States, be constituted with specific Terms of Reference (TOR) to work on drafting a comprehensive treaty regime for creating a free trade area. The Heads of State or Government expressed the view that such a treaty must incorporate, among other things, binding time-frames for freeing trade, measures to facilitate trade, and provisions to ensure an equitable distribution of benefits of trade to all states, especially for smaller and least developed countries, including mechanisms for compensation of revenue loss. They emphasised the importance of finalising the text of the regulatory framework by the year 2001....... The Heads of State or Government agreed that the benefits of economic liberalization would be more extensive

and better balanced through the promotion of trade-creating joint ventures, investment and trade in services such as tourism.

Over the years, for more than a decade, all countries in South Asia have been making stronger efforts to achieve higher and sustained economic growth as well as institutional development on two fronts — at individual government levels and also jointly through the SAARC. One of the three themes of the international conference on South Asian Development in 1997 and Beyond : Its Relevance for Australia held at the University of Sydney during 12-14 September 1997 was to closely look at the institutional strengths and weaknesses of these efforts made and the prospects ahead. This Volume selects a total of 13 papers focussed on this theme and presented to the conference. One missing gap in the Volume is our inability, even after much effort, to include a chapter covering the same theme on Bhutan[7]. Most of the papers had several revisions and the present Volume has been the result of a serious reviewing process undertaken by an independent distinguished assessor.

Part I, Towards Building a South Asian Community and Regional Trade Block, focuses on the role that the SAARC as an institution may actively play in building a South Asian community as well as a regional trade block. Drawing on extensive experience as an academic and active development planner, Rehman Sobhan reviews the areas the SAARC will need

7. Bhutan, a landlocked economy, has vaery close economic links with India. Because the local currency, the ngultrum (Nu), is pegged to the Indian Rupee at par, inflation is strongly influenced by price changes in India. Not only Bhutan's external trade is predominantly with India, but also it receives substantial budgetary support from India as well as grants to finance investment projects. After India's liberalisation in 1991, Bhutan has adopted policy of careful macroeconomic management and a number of structural reforms. As the *Asian Development Outlook* (1997, p. 120) observes, substantial progress in structural reform has been made with the corporatisation of the postal service, introduction of auctions of government securities and the conversion of the Unit Trust of Bhutan into the country's second commercial bank. "Preparatory work has been carried out with regard to tariff reform, liberalizing foreign exchange and FDI regulations, strengthening the legal framework, and deregulating interest rates (*ibid.*)."

to address in order to build an economic community. He argues that the SAARC has not been the pace-setter for forging ties among the countries in South Asia, rather it has moved forward with extreme caution[8], haunted by the memories of their divisive history. Observing that particular governments within South Asia perpetuate tensions with their neighbours for mere political interest, he warns that such political opportunism tends to establish a symbiotic link between confrontational politics at home and within the region. He also believes that the largest country in the region, India, needs to make a special effort to tackle various problems carried over from history so that its smaller neighbours have little reason to be apprehensive and distrustful of its intentions.

Biplab Dasgupta questions the mainstream economists' belief that world trade is voluntary, free and competitive. He, instead, shows that the world market is heavily loaded in favour of stronger economies. According to Dasgupta, within the framework laid down by the World Trade Organization (WTO) in 1995, there is little prospect for economic development of less developed countries (LDCs) without their coming together and collectively demanding a renegotiation of the world trade structure. Referring to the South Asian Free Trade Area (SAFTA) proposed by the SAARC, Dasgupta argues that such an organisation is not only feasible and mutually beneficial, but also has many significant political and security pay offs. For survival in the world market and, therefore, sustained economic development of the countries in South Asia, there is, Dasgupta asserts, no alternative to SAFTA. Within this context, he also examines Indo-Bangladesh trade and economic relations of recent years.

Part II, Economic Liberalisation and Institutional Reforms : Country Studies, contains papers that highlight varied degrees of political stability and rates of economic progress in some of the South Asian countries due to their structural and institutional constraints. It is, therefore, argued that needs for and effects of

8. Such caution can be evident from the Principles under the SAARC Charter, which have been reproduced in this Introduction.

economic liberalisation are country specific. Akhtar Hossain analyses the importance of institutional and organisational development for economic and political stability in Bangladesh. He argues that in an otherwise underdeveloped feudal society, high economic growth with equity is crucial in establishing socio-political stability. High economic growth, in turn, requires the presence of macroeconomic stability, which depends on measures that include the development and the establishment of economic and social institutions and organisations. Hossain concludes that simultaneous development of economic, social and political institutions and the establishment of democratic political organisations would create a mechanism for modern economic growth to take place.

B.S. Ghuman tests the hypothesis that as the State vacates space for market forces in the economic decision making sphere, economic benefits have a tendency to concentrate in a few areas having locational advantages. Ghuman finds that the Indian experience in economic liberalisation supports this hypothesis, because gains of liberalisation in the field of industry have accrued mainly to select states with added advantages such as proximity to ports, higher stage of industrialisation, vigorous implementation of economic reforms, well developed infrastructural facilities, etc.

R.N. Ghosh and M.A.B. Siddique focus on the fact that organised sectors of the Maldivian economy have recently experienced shortage of labour, especially in the tourism and service sector. In spite of that, there is still a large pool of unemployed and underemployed workers in the unorganised sectors, such as in fisheries. Many of these marginal and unemployed workers are women, living in remote islands away from the Male atoll. Poor educational facilities in the Maldives further contribute to the problem of relative under-representation of the Maldivians in the growth-oriented sectors of the economy. They argue that suitable institutional reforms embracing better vocational training, better transport between islands, safer and culturally more acceptable work environment for women, and similar measures, would likely release a large untapped supply of labour and help overcome the current tight labour market situation. Nevertheless, the dependence on expatriate labour would continue in the foreseable future.

Meena Acharya provides an overview of the state of the Nepalese economy since the mid eighties when economic stablilisation and restructuring programs started and also refers to the recent period of political volatility after the overthrow of the old Panchayat System in 1990. As the process of economic liberalisation is accelarated during the nineties, she notes that the deteriorating terms of trade for agriculture, accelerated erosion of wage earnings due to inflationary pressures, created by both external liberalisation and adjustment of administered prices, have generated disenchantment among the peasants and working class population. Superimposition of market economy on feudalistic socio-economic structure has created vast opportunities for graft and profiteering. On the positive side, the politicisation of rural masses has, according to Acharya, increased the mobilisation of the rural population by NGOs for development work and grievance settlement. This positive development is expected to complement the diversion of resources to rural areas following the acceptance of the Agricultural Prospective Plan in the Ninth Plan Approach.

After providing a critical assessment of the recent economic and institutional reform process in Pakistan, Amir Mahmood outlines the necessary conditions and challenges that need to be addressed if the country is to achieve a sustainable rate of economic growth with an improvement in the standard of living. Mahmood argues that such conditions must include a stable political climate, governance issues, investment in the public infrastructure, improved ethnic and sectarian harmony, improvement in law and order, eradication of institutional corruption, and a shift from defence spending to investment on human resources.

Prema Chandra Athukorala reviews the key elements of the market-oriented reforms initiated in Sri Lanka since 1977 and then examines patterns of industrial growth, export orientation, and factor productivity growth. This chapter has an indepth analysis of how export-oriented foreign direct investment had played an important role in transforming Sri Lanka's classical, primary commodity-dependent economy into a 'new exporting country' (NEC). Athukorala also draws attention to the importance of concomitant liberalisation of both trade and investment policy regimes in determining the outcome of liberalisation reforms in small, trade dependent countries like Sri Lanka. The upsurge in political instability and its adverse effect on foreign investment inflow in Sri Lanka has also been touched in his concluding remarks.

Part III, Liberalisation Experiences and Issues : Sectoral Studies, highlights specific effects of economic liberalisation on major sectors in some South Asian countries. Although most papers in Part II have covered various sectors together, papers in this part focus on some individual sectors more intensively, such as Bangladesh's external sector, India's financial and State-owned public sectors and Nepal's manufacturing sector.

Nasiruddin Ahmed argues that significant steps have been taken during the 1990s to liberalise Bangladesh's trade regime in order to solve the problem of persistent trade deficit. The primary objective of trade liberalisation policies has been to move towards a liberalised trade regime with flexible exchange rate management. Trade liberalisation is expected to have a positive effect on export and thereby on economic growth by removing anti-export bias and making exports more competitive in international markets. This is being done mainly by correcting an overvalued exchange rate and creating incentives for expanding the tradeable sector. By reducing the bias against exports, trade policy reform is expected to be very effective in spurring investment, both domestic and foreign, in export-oriented sectors. Similarly, by reducing the level of quantitative restrictions on imports and permitting increased import of raw materials, intermediate and capital goods, trade liberalisation is likely to contribute to higher economic growth.

Although economic reform has deregulated the Indian economy quite significantly, especially the external sector, the financial sector has not been deregulated to that extent. B.B. Bhattacharya argues that, in spite of decline in the degree of India's financial repression since 1991, the health of the financial system remains quite critical. He stresses that the Indian financial system can neither withstand open competition from foreign financial institutions, nor continue in its present form. The compulsions of the fiscal system may, however, prevent real reform in the financial sector. Unless fiscal deficit stabilises at a more sustainable level, the government may not grant full autonomy to the financial sector. On the other hand, a lure for capital inflows from abroad could also endanger the system and produce the same kind of debacle witnessed in Mexico in 1994 and more recently in South East Asia.The emerging financial scenarios in India, therefore, do not appear to be very bright. The situation could be improved through a better regulatory mechanism. This would require a kind of political will, which at the moment appears to be missing in India.

Peter Mayer provides a chronological detail of India's experience of divestment of its public sector enterprises (PSUs) or what is commonly known as state-owned enterprises (SOEs). Mayer argues that, contrary to the SOEs reform studies by World Bank staff and many others, the reform of India's SOEs follows a different model, a dialectical one. He identifies two key players in India's disinvestment process. One was the Standing Conference of Public Enterprises (SCOPE) that represented India's SOEs. In its public rhetoric, SCOPE has welcomed economic liberalisation and pressed for reforms that would allow a greater role of market-forces in the running of SOEs. The other unlikely key player was the United Front (UF) government, which took power after the 1996 elections. Following the recommendations made by the Disinvestment Commission (DC), the UF government announced divestment of nine firms (dubbed 'navaratnas' or nine jewels) in early July 1997. According to Mayer, this transformation has taken place in the absence of the compulsion of economic crisis and has been undertaken by a fragile coalition government, dependent upon parties of the left unsympathetic to the dilution of public ownership.

Kishore Sharma investigates the consequences of liberalisation on the structure of manufacturing industries in Nepal. This is, as he argues, important because doubts that liberalisation may not solve the problems of less developed countries (LDCs) remain strong, due mainly to the low supply elasticities and the early stage of industrialisation. His analysis shows that despite low supply elasticities and the early stage of industrialisation, liberalisation reforms are conducive to bringing some changes in the structure of manufacturing output, trade-orientation and productivity growth in a LDC like Nepal.

Part IV, Government Performance and Administrative Reform, is concerned with the quality and effectiveness of government administration. Binayak Ray, after highlighting general symptoms of poor governance and, therefore, corruption, argues that governance issues need to be examined within the context of intra- and inter-relationships between various components of the state apparatus, including government, and the community. In his case study of India, he considers administrative reform issues in conjunction not only with constitutional, bureaucratic and judicial reform issues, but also with issues related to political pluralism. For good governance, Ray reiterates, amongst others, five mantras of the anti-corruption drive, namely, monopoly regulation, official transparency and accountability, detection of and penalties for corruption. Although Ray focuses on India, his analysis could be applicable to other South Asian countries as well.

While much can be learnt from the experience of our low and middle-income neighbours of East and Southeast Asia, South Asia's policy design and pattern of growth and development will remain to be unique not only at the regional level, but also at an individual country level. There is no doubt, however, that commitment to human development and equity will continue to be an essential ingredient of sustainable economic growth as well as stable socio-political development.

REFERENCES

Alavi, H. (1989), 'Formation of the Social Structure of South Asia under the Impact of Colonialism,' in H. Alavi and J. Harriss (eds.), *South Asia*, London : Macmillan.

Asian Development Outlook (1997), Asian Development Bank, Oxford University Press.

Dutta, D.K. (1991), 'Socio-Economic Analysis of Dualistic Economies : A review of Methodological Alternatives,' *Journal of Interdisciplinary Economics*, Vol. 3.

Haq, M.H. (1997), *Human Development in South Asia* 1997, Karachi : Oxford University Press.

Dean, J.M., S. Desai and J. Riedel (1994), 'Trade Policy Reform in Developing Countries Since 1985 : A Review of the Evidence,' World Bank Discussion Papers, No. 267, Washington, D.C. : The World Bank.

SAARC in Brief (1995), SAARC Secretariat, Kathmandu, Nepal.

SAARC *Summit Declarations*, SAARC Secretariat, Kathmandu, Nepal, (Various Issues).

Subrahmanyam, S. (1996), 'Institutions, agency and economic change in South Asia : A survey and some suggestions,' in B. Stein and S. Subrahmanyam (eds.), *Institutions and Economic Change in South Asia*, New Delhi : Oxford University Press.

PART I

TOWARDS BUILDING A SOUTH ASIAN COMMUNITY AND REGIONAL TRADE BLOCK

2

The Future of SAARC : Towards Building a South Asian Community

REHMAN SOBHAN

Introduction : A Role for SAARC

The South Asian Association for Regional Cooperation (SAARC) is now more than a decade old institution. Whilst many would argue that it could have achieved more, as many would also recognise that the very fact that the seven countries of South Asian are assembled together in a regional association is a remarkable achievement, given their inherited and indeed continuing divisions. However, as SAARC enters the 21st century it needs to keep itself abreast of both the concerns of civil society as well as the compulsions of globalisation. In this paper we will review the areas where SAARC will need to chart a course for defining the future of South Asian cooperation and the attendant implications of these initiatives. It is arguable that SAARC has not been the pace-setter for forging ties within South

Asia, even though its creation visualised that the regional organisation would play a catalytic role in building a South Asian community. Rather, SAARC has moved forward with extreme caution, haunted by the memories of their divisive history which tends to inhibit decisive action to stimulate cooperation.

The constraints within SAARC on taking bold decisions has left it to the forces of civil society in South Asia, acting through the market mechanism, to set the tempo for forging the course of economic relations. This market driven process has contributed to the emergence of imbalances in the level and pattern of intercourse, originating from the prevailing structural asymetries as between the South Asian economies. The resultant growth in imbalances in economic transactions involving both goods and labour is creating tensions between the member governments, which is influencing the formal process of cooperation within SAARC. Initiatives to promote cooperation tend to thus move foreward in fits and starts with no guiding design behind it, based on a series of negotiated compromises between the member states.

It is argued here that SAARC as an institution needs to now chart its future in a more purposeful manner, taking into account the attendant changes in the objective realities of South Asia, both as a result of the forces of globalisation as well as the dynamics of civil society. The task before SAARC as an institution is to identify the areas where SAARC's members will each stand to gain from cooperation, whether at the regional or sub-regional level, within South Asia. This will involve estimating the costs and benefits of cooperation in order to identify priorities for regional cooperation and to indicate areas where positive sum gains from such cooperation are apparent.

The charting of a more purposeful future for South Asia, which needs to be addressed by SAARC, may be discussed under the following heads :

(a) Building an economic community.

(b) Developing the infrastructure for cooperation.

(c) The political implications of building a South Asian community.

Building an Economic Community

Asyemtrical economic relations

Over the last decade or so the move towards economic liberalisation in every country in South Asia has given greater play to an assertion of market forces in governing the level and pattern of economic transactions in each country. This interplay of market forces has played a significant role in accelerating the evolution of an economic community within South Asia. The move towards economic liberalisation within the South Asian region has enhanced the movement of goods, labour and capital across regional boundaries, both at the formal and informal level. Bhutan, Bangladesh, Nepal and Sri Lanka have, for all practical purposes, become free trade areas for exports from India. This means that market forces are now guiding private trade with India, even where residual import restrictions remain on the statute books. Even though Bangladesh has substantially liberalised its import regime, particularly since 1991, it retains both tariffs and non-tariff barriers on certain varieties of textile imports. These barriers have been totally unsuccessful in containing the illegal imports of such products across Bangladesh's land borders with India. Import of *sarees* for example, remains one of the few banned imports. However, the Bangladesh market is flooded with sarees of all varieties smuggled in from India, to the point where the domestic handloom industry, which is most affected by such free imports, operates on the assumption that unless it can compete with Indian imports it cannot survive. Needless to say, many textile enterprises, particularly the smaller ones, have been driven to the wall. The same situation is faced by the tobacco, cosmetics, food processing, sugar and cement industry and, indeed, many other local industries whose production and investment decisions are increasingly predicated on the reality of an open market with India.

As India's exports become globally more competitive in terms of both price and quality, its comparative advantage in accessing the markets of its neighbours is likely to increase exponentially. The opportunity for Bangladeshi traders or manufacturers to bring in products across the border, legally or if need be illegally, at short notice, is advantageous for a variety of reasons not the least being the economies in inventory costs. Over the last decade Bangladeshi traders have been competing with each other to obtain wholesale agencies for Indian exporters to the Bangladesh market, whose products are now being advertised on local billboards and the electronic media. Such a situation is also prevalent in Sri Lanka, Nepal and Bhutan. In the latter two countries, the bulk of the consumer goods in their stores tend to be of Indian origin and the Indian rupee is in common usage in all retail establishments. Pakistan appears to be the only member of SAARC which has managed to sustain a protective and discriminatory trade regime against Indian imports, though this has not been entirely successful as may be seen by the widespread use of Indian products which are competitive in the Pakistan market. India's market access within South Asia is growing at a pace where South Asia is emerging as one of India's fastest growing markets in its global trade. India's official exports within SAARC have tripled between 1990 and 1995 from US $ 487 million to $ 1.5 billion and SAARC's share of India's global exports have increased from 2.7 per cent to 5.1 per cent. If unofficial trade is included, these figures could double. Today Indian producers and exporters are formulating their corporate strategies on the basis of open market access to all of their neighbours.

Promoting trade liberalisation within South Asia

Attempts to formally accelerate trade within South Asia to some extent, appears to be lagging behind the realities of the market place. Policies of import liberalisation, initiated as part of the World Bank's structural adjustment reforms (SAR), have emerged as the dominant influence on South Asia's trade relations. The decision at the Dhaka Summit meet of SAARC in 1994 to initiate a South Asia Preferential Trading Agreement (SAPTA) did not formally come into effect till the end of 1995. Following this accession by all members to the provisions of SAPTA, two rounds of negotiations have been concluded amongst the various member countries whereby various members have provided import concessions to all SAARC members for a variety of commodities. At last count, India had provided preferential concessions to 513 commodities on offer by Bangladesh as exports. This involves a removal of all non-tariff barriers (NTBs), as well as a 50 per cent reduction on the prevailing tariffs set by India on these items. The concessions affect most of Bangladesh's principal exports in the world market. India's offer to Bangladesh is made on the basis of the latter's priviliged status as a least developed country, entitled to special concessions under the provisions of the rules of the World Trade Organisation (WTO). Bangladesh's principal export industries such as readymade garments, leather goods and ceramics can now reconstruct their corporate plans, taking into account their ready access to the Indian market. Such a prospect could transform their entire horizon for future expansion.

The Search for market access in India

As far as Bangladesh, Sri Lanka, Nepal and Bhutan are concerned, concessions offered by them to India for imports under SAPTA are something of an irrelevance since they retain few NTB's , their global tariff regime is already low and their capacity to protect their borders against illegal imports is weak. The principal policy objective of these four smaller economies of South Asia has so far been to obtain equivalent access to the Indian market, comparable to the access available to India to enter its neighbour's markets. This position derives from a general acceptance by successive governments that they cannot today effectively protect their domestic market from Indian exports through effective policing of their borders. This is not a very satisfactory way to embrace a regime of import liberalisation, since it originates in an acceptance of weak state capacity as a foundation for policy rather than the policy itself determining the role of that state. Without involving ourselves in the merits of such an approach to statecraft we may assume that these South Asian countries have now decided to make a virtue out of necessity and within SAARC, constitute the vanguard for the demand for seeking a rapid dismantling of trade barriers by India.

This approach thus does not limit itself to a commodity-based set of concessions offered to their exports by India under the provisions of SAPTA, but seeks a comprehensive withdrawal of all import restrictions by India on imports from the smaller SAARC countries. This demand for ready access to the Indian market has been most strongly articulated by Bangladesh and Sri Lanka. Bangladesh has for the last few years requested India to provide a unilateral removal of all trade barriers restricting Bangladesh's exports to India. This involves removal of quantitative restrictions (QR) and other NTBs, as well as the elimination of tariffs so as to put Bangladesh on par with Nepal and Bhutan in obtaining access to the Indian market. Bangladesh, at this stage, offers no corresponding concessions to India on the grounds that Bangladesh's economy is less evolved and furthermore, India already has a ready access to Bangladesh's market both at the formal and informal level. In contrast, Sri Lanka has, in recent years, pressed India for a bilateral fast-track approach to trade liberalisation. Sri Lanka, which already has the most liberalised trading regime in South Asia, has proposed to India that both countries should mutually offer each other major tariff concessions which would, in a short span of time, establish a free trade area between India and Sri Lanka.

The argument underlying Bangladesh and Sri Lanka's position states that the present approach of incremental concessions under SAPTA only benefits commodities under production in these countries. Since their production base remains narrow, scope for deriving significant benefits from SAPTA remain limited. However, a trade regime which provides for unrestricted access to the Indian market for all goods produced in these respective countries will enable domestic, regional and international investors targetting these two countries to make their investment decisions on the assumption that they have free access not just to the local market, but to the entire Indian market. Such a set of expectations would transform the business perspective of prospective domestic and foreign investors towards Sri Lanka and Bangladesh, who in the normal course of events, could not expect their own markets to attract too many investors. Such a perspective seeks to transform India's larger and more diversified economy from a threat to its smaller neighbours, to an area of opportunity.

Within such a perspective, India's smaller neighbours would hope to use Indian's large and now accessible market opened to its South Asian neighbours, as a key element in transforming their development structures. Areas of economic activity which had hitherto remained unfeasible because of the limitations of the domestic market in Nepal or Bangladesh, could now be contemplated as new growth centres stimulated by Indian, Japanese, Thai or Malaysian investments, who would see earning opportunities for their investments serving a market of over a billion people. This broadening of development horizons for these smaller economies would contribute towards a diversification of the economy, development of the infrastructure, upgradation of technologies and expansion of employment opportunities, all of which would give a broader constituency of people in each country a stake in the positive outcomes from South Asian cooperation.

The Dynamics of State driven attempts at cooperation : The Indo-Bangladesh experience

Once upon a time, when governments used to exercise more command over their economies than they do today, greater faith was placed in such programmes of cooperation originating in bilateral inter-governmental agreements between public sector agencies, committed to providing market guarantees. In 1972, just after the liberation of Bangladesh, the Bangladesh Planning Commission, in the course of bilateral discussions with the Indian Planning Commission, argued about the need for enhancing and diversifying Bangladesh's export capacities to ensure a more balanced pattern of trade between India and Bangladesh. It was then envisaged by the Bangladesh Planning Commission that, under the prevailing patterns of trade, a regime of liberalised trade between Bangladesh and India would lead to a build-up of trade surpluses in favour of India, because of its more diversified and mature economy. It was argued by the Bangladeshis that such a perpetuation of unbalanced trade would generate political tensions within Bangladesh, because of popular perceptions that India was using Bangladesh as a captive market and the Bangladesh economy would continue to be underdeveloped, undiversified and dependent on India for most of its manufactured imports. Such a pattern of economic relations would be economically unsustainable because Bangladesh would run into balance of payments constraints and would also tend to be politically unsustainable, as it would fuel Bangladeshi pathologies over domination by and dependence on India. Since Bangladesh had just emerged as an independent country, to escape from the syndromes of domination and dependency which had governed their relations with Pakistan, there was a presumption that Bangladeshis would remain no less sensitive to exchanging dependency on Pakistan for dependency on India.

The Bangladesh Planning Commission thus proposed that three major industrial projects be set up in Bangladesh, targetted to market all or a part of their output in India. It was envisaged that three industrial projects, drawing upon Bangladesh's then abundant natural gas, would include a urea fertiliser plant, a sponge iron plant using iron ore imported from India and a cement plant using limestone from deposits in Meghalaya located across Bangladesh's North-eastern borders. For each of these projects, India would provide buy-back guarantees for an agreed period of time to provide for a secure market to justify such capital intensive investments.

Feasibility studies were completed for all three projects, which were approved in principle at the summit meeting of Indira Gandhi and Sheikh Mujibur Rahman in New Delhi in May 1974. All three projects became casualties of the change of regime in

Bangladesh following the assasination of Sheikh Mujibur Rahman in August 1975. The projects were thus put into cold storage. However, over the next 20 years, as relations between India and Bangladesh periodically thawed, these three projects were resurrected at various bilateral summit meetings as ancient symbols signifying opportunities for cooperation. But such exercises came to nothing. During the 1980's, attempts by the private sector to revive the sponge iron project briefly tantalised the business community, but this too came to naught since even today such large investments remain difficult to contemplate without some form of state involvement.

The failure to materialise any significant project which could be expected to enhance and diversify the country's capacity to export to India, condemned Bangladesh to two decades of accumulating imbalance in its trade with India. As forecast by the Bangladesh Planning Commission when it prepared a policy paper on this subject in 1972, a market driven trade regime exposed Bangladesh to a progressive increase in export penetration by India, whilst leaving Bangladesh with little to export in return in the absence of any investment effort dedicated to reach India. As Bangladesh accelerated the pace of its global trade liberalisation, India's exports to Bangladesh also accelerated since they were best positioned to avail of the market openness of its neighbours. Furthermore, in the absence of any move within SAARC to coordinate monetary and exchange rate policies, over the past few years the Indian Rupee has depreciated significantly against the Bangladesh Taka, which has made Indian exports to Bangladesh particularly competitive compared to rival suppliers.

Between 1985 and 1996, Bangladesh has built up a cumulative trade deficit with India of US $ 3,105 million. US $ 2,626 million, or 85 per cent of this deficit, was accumulated in the period 1991-96 when a regime, traditionally vocal about Indian hegemony over Bangladesh, was in power in Bangladesh. The same party, now in opposition today, is highly critical of its incumbent successor regime for permitting Indian goods to flood the Bangladesh market. In practice, however, the previous regime itself initiated a more aggressive strategy of trade liberalisation in 1991, which it bequeathed to its successor regime. Bangladesh is now committed to pay for the resultant acceleration in the trade deficit with India through external earnings generated by its exports of goods and services to the rest of the world. In a global regime of open trade this would be unexceptionable. Indeed, a sizeable part of Bangladesh's $ 2.5 billion exports of ready-made garments (RMG) is based on the importation of yarn and fabric from India. However, in the peculiar environment which governs Indo-Bangladesh relations, a trade deficit with India acquires political significance whilst a similar deficit with China or Thailand is seen as the outcome of the free play of the market. Narrowing this deficit with India thus becomes a political as much as an economic imperative for sustaining Indo-Bangladesh relations.

Market driven cooperation

Aid donors to Bangladesh do not share our own sense of compulsion about the Indo-Bangladesh trade deficit. They thus remain disinclined to support large state projects dedicated to export to India. In the absence of any policy commitments of any support from aid donors for public action to promote large investment projects directed to India, Bangladesh must now depend on the market to attract prospective investments to a secure market in India. It is for this reason that ready access to the Indian market has emerged as a paramount concern in Bangladesh's relations with India.

There is thus still scope for a number of dedicated export projects in Bangladesh targetted to the Indian market. Such projects, conceived as mixed sector joint venture projects, could expect to mobilise capital in the international market if in fact a medium term procurement guarantee could be offered by India to buy the output from such a venture. Such a procurement guarantee is not inconceivable, since India's future imports still remain monopolised by its public sector and Bangladesh remains perhaps the most market competitive source of urea to service eastern India. Now that Bangladesh is itself such a large market for India, it can exercise some leverage in its negotiations for both market access as well as for investment participation by Indian investors in such a project with an assured market. Both the Investment Finance Corporation (IFC), affiliate of the World Bank and its counterpart in the Asian Development Bank (ADB) could be inducted into such a venture if they could be persuaded to move to an ideologically more flexible position. Whilst neo-liberal purists may frown upon market guarantees for such projects, since this interferes with the play of market forces, it must be appreciated that in a highly competitive global capital market venture capital is only likely to reach the least developed countries, such as Bangladesh or Nepal, if some such security of return is guaranteed to prospective external investors.

The Prospects for Sub-regional Cooperation

A South Asian Growth quadrangle

Outside of trade cooperation, scope for cooperation is apparent in a variety of areas of cooperation within South Asia which relate to area specific projects tied to a shared geography and hydrology. Such programmes demand initiatives at a sub-regional level, since physical separation does not always provide for a mutuality of interest which covers all members of a regional entity such as SAARC. Similarly, projects tied to a bilateral market need not be limited to two countries. Thus, Nepal has for many years sought to harness its hydro-electric potential, which is estimated to be in the range of 40,000 mw. The economics of such investments in generating power in Nepal depend heavily on the exportation of electricity to India and beyond to Bangladesh. However, such projects, involving massive investments, can only hope to draw in private foreign capital if there are firm market guarantees by Nepal's neighbours for the purchase of such power.

Nepal's dependence on external markets to justify the optimisation of its natural resources points to the fact that such resources can never remain exclusive to the country which owns them. Projects such as urea fertiliser, sponge iron and cement based on Meghalaya limestone remain natural resource based ventures which need a wider market to yield optimum benefits. Meghalaya and other North Eastern states of India, known as the seven sisters, are abundant in natural resources which include gas, oil and the water resources of the Brahmaputra, which remains one of the world's largest untapped reservoirs for hydro-electric power. However, the potential to use such natural wealth remains limited due to the physical separation of North East India, from the mainland of India. It is arguable that the remoteness of the North Eastern states of India, inhabited by tribal ethnic groups distinct from the inhabitants of the Indian mainland, has condemned this region to remain economically the most backward part of India. This has, in turn, contributed to some element of alienation of the people of these states from the body politic of India which has served to fuel militant insurgencies committed to greater autonomy, if not independence for these regions. If, in fact, a major effort could be made to develop, diversify and enhance the economic opportunities available to these people of the North East, to the point where they would become stakeholders in the future of their region, much of the violence and political instability which has destabilised this region could be contained.

However, the only way the full development potential of the North East region could be realised would appear to lie in closer interaction with Bangladesh, which provides both a market for its natural resources as well as a source of ready supply to meet its market demand and can provide the infrastructure linkages needed to integrate the region with the rest of South Asia. The fact that Bangladesh and India have in their years of separate development made little attempt to design a more holistic development design which could incorporate the needs of the North Eastern states, has been a critical factor in perpetuating their backwardness. Even though quite serviceable transport links by land and air tie the North East to the rest of India, the very presence of Bangladesh as a geographic wedge between the region and the heartland India, has made it appear unattractive to any market driven investment process.

It remains inconceivable that either state or market forces could transcend the diseconomies of moving resources back and forth across the narrow land corridor which links the states of West Bengal and Bihar in mainland India with the North Eastern states, which also remains landlocked, being cut off from the Bay of Bengal by Bangladesh. The foreign trade of these states thus has to move through Calcutta and Haldia, more than 500 miles away by rail, instead of moving through Chittagong port located only 50 miles from the borders of Tripura state.

In such a politico-geographical context, a positive sum game is available to both Bangladesh and India through a programme of cooperation, whereby Bangladesh could reduce its trade imbalances with India by gradually supplementing the mainland of India as the principal source of manufactured exports to the North East, as well as the principal outlet for the productive utilisation of its natural resources. Innumerable joint venture investments bringing together the resources of the North East, Bangladesh's infrastructure and port access, Indian capital and technology, all integrated into plants located in both the North Eastern states and Eastern Bangladesh, could be set up to service this regional market. Chittagong port could expand from a small national port to a regional hub, around which the economies of both Eastern Bangladesh as well as North Eastern India could flourish to the point where the economic prospects of the entire sub-region could be totally transformed within a decade.

If indeed this regional transformation process could be integrated, through the Asian Highway and Asian Railway under implementation by the member countries of the United Nations'(UN) Economic and Social Commission for Asia and the Pacific (ESCAP), with both South East Asia as well as South West China, the prospects for this area defy the imagination. Within this process, Nepal and Bhutan, which have very recently been accorded land transit rights to Bangladesh across Indian territory, could be linked to the growth of this sub-region once the Jamuna Bridge is completed. This major engineering venture across the river Jamuna was designed to link Eastern and Western Bangladesh. The impact of this bridge is, however, likely to reach beyond the boundaries of Bangladesh. The bridge spans the last physical divide between East/South East Asia and South Asia and beyond with Central Asia and Europe. The Jamuna Bridge thus promises to command the same historical potential which was exercised by the bridge over the Boshphorus which links Europe with Asia.

The prospects for promoting sub-regional development in South Asia, bringing together Bangladesh, Bhutan, Nepal and the Eastern region of India, has in recent years appeared on the agenda of the concerned countries and, as well has attracted the attention of multilateral aid agencies such as the World Bank (WB) and Asian Development Bank (ADB), who are each initiating their own studies on the potential of such a growth quadrangle. UN agencies, such as ESCAP, have also recognised the potential of sub-regional cooperation in transforming the most backward parts of South Asian into an area of opportunity. In recent past, at the initiative of Nepal, the four governments of the Eastern region of South Asia, Bangladesh, Bhutan, India and Nepal, have launched the South Asian Growth Quadrangle initiative to explore areas of cooperation within the sub-region.

It is of considerable irony that such efforts to establish a basis for cooperation that could transform some of the most backward regions of Asia have been bedevilled by political controversy, both at the intergovernmental and domestic level. It was thus agreed at SAARC's Male summit in April 1997 that programmes and projects for cooperation, originating from this sub-regional entity, would be reported to SAARC to ensure that the quadrangle programmes would not run contrary to the overriding SAARC agenda for cooperation.

Rebuilding the Infrastructure for Cooperation

To build an economic community, SAARC will need to recreate an infrastructure to sustain such cooperation. Half a century ago South Asia was possessed of a shared social and physical infrastructure, which most regional groupings around the world even today are yet to attain. This infrastructure has been dismantled due to political reasons, since at no point in time, even within the logic of an autarchic development path, did it make economic sense to dismantle physical and social capital serving an entire region. Today, the task faced by SAARC and its member states operating at the regional, sub-regional and bilateral level, is to painfully reconstruct this fractured infrastructure. This task of reconstruction remains a paramount task for SAARC which, as an institution, may again command some comparative advantage because it is best positioned to estimate the externalities or positive sum gains to be derived from such a collective effort. Thus, re-building a trans-South Asian road network becomes immensely more attractive if its gains are computed for the whole region, than as between India and Bangladesh or India and Pakistan. In reviewing the scope for rebuilding South Asia's infrastructure, we will review both the physical as well as the social infrastructure which had been broken up over the last half century.

The Physical Infrastructure

Communications

Some efforts have been made to quantify estimates of the gains from integrating South Asia's transport networks. Such estimates indicate net financial gains of US $ 1,960 million, accruing to all countries in SAARC from providing transit facilities to one another. However, gains in generating externalities for promoting cooperation, which are yet to be quantified, may be much greater. Whilst economic benefits are obvious, the principal obstacle to rebuilding South Asia's land transport links remain political. Thus, domestic political constraints on reaching agreements with a neighbour for providing through traffic facilities have continued to compromise the reconstruction of South Asia's fractured infrastructure. Today, South Asia needs to restore the Grand Trunk Road to its pristine glory when, from the days of Moghul emperor Sher Shah Suri, it connected Bengal with

Afghanistan, but now as part of the much broader concourse of the Asian Highway connecting Asia with Europe. Today, comfortable inter-country travel in South Asia remains the privilege of the more affluent air-travellers, whilst the poorer masses go through the torture of changing vehicles several times to journey from Dhaka to Karachi and expose themselves to untold harassment and monetary exploitation at the border crossings. Most travellers have now concluded that unofficial routes are both quicker and less costly.

SAARC has for some time been trying to work out protocols to ease travel within the region. Some progress has been registered, at least in improving air links. But mass transit across South Asia is hampered by both the physical break in land links, as well as the politically determined constraints to accelerate trans-border traffic. Thus, much needs to be done to restore physical links which atrophied over the years and to develop protocols on customs and immigration to facilitate travel. In each of these areas, progress is hampered by security concerns as well as the underdeveloped infrastructure.

The telecommunication links within South Asia still remain primitive by global standards. But here SAARC has made a difference and scope for accessing the region *via* the airwaves has dramatically improved in the way of links by telephone, fax, e-mail and through the media. Today, some TV channels serving the region are developing programme packages for audiences targetted both to the region and to specific linguistic groups with a transnational audience.

A regional energy grid

Attempts to build a common energy infrastructure with a shared energy grid for gas and power, which links all of South Asia with the energy reserves of Iran and even Central Asia, have been established as technically feasible and economically advantageous for the region. Such an integrated energy market for the region would not only be cost effective in terms of sharing scarcities and surpluses across the region but would generate sufficient commercial synergy to make this into one of the most attractive markets for prospective investors in the energy sector of South Asia.

Thus, notwithstanding the strain in Indo-Pak relations, the private investors in Pakistan's Hubco power plant are exploring possibilities of selling some surplus power to neighbouring regions of India because it is clearly cost effective to do so. In contrast, both North East India and West Bengal, which have temporary local surpluses in their grid, have offered to sell energy for use in adjacent areas in Bangladesh. However, business logic in both these commercial ventures remains constrained by political apprehension to sell power to India from Pakistan and to buy power from India to supply Bangladesh. It would thus appear to be logical to make Bangladesh's key RMG sector heavily dependent on Indian fabrics and their consumption of beef heavily dependent on the nightly smuggling of cattle from India into Bangladesh, but unacceptable to import 100 MW of power into power starved North West Bangladesh. Such is the tortured grammer of domestic politics in South Asia when it pertains to neighbourly relations!

The Social Infrastructure

Apart from the physical infrastructure, significant attractive benefits may be realised through cooperation in the area of social development. Most South Asian countries are today exporters of skilled labour in the form of scientists, doctors, engineers, economists who have become part of the brain drain from the region to service the developed world and the oil rich regions of the Middle East. Unskilled labour at the lower end of the job market also remains a major export from South Asia to these markets. Given the enormous amount of professional resources which are drained out of the region, there is considerable scope for market driven investments in higher education and research institutions as well as in medical centres, designed to service both a regional and even an international market. South Asia is close to enjoying a global comparative advantage in the area of skilled services, since nowhere in the world, except perhaps in

China, can you find world class surgeons performing coronary bypass surgery for under US $ 5,000, or where top flight academics are willing to teach at a professorial level for salaries which will fall within US $ 25,000 per year.

Massive investments in developing centres of excellence in South Asia in the medical, engineering, natural and social sciences could be built around faculties drawn from all the countries as well as their global diaspora, to service students from the region as well as other developing countries. Such centres could provide technological inputs to service national and regional economic development. Such collective enterprises could draw upon both intergovernment as well as private enterprise, because of the attendant economic benefits from such investments. Here again, SAARC can play a role in identifying areas of cooperation in human development, designing institutions of excellence to service the region and estimating the positive sum gains for the region from such collective efforts.

Whilst private enterprise have been much involved in the area of human development in India, especially in the exporting of education and health services within the region, very little investment seems to be in evidence in the other countries of South Asia for developing either their own capacities or to contribute to institutions within the region. Some bilateral ventures, as for example, in developing private hospitals in Nepal and Bangladesh, draw upon Indian capital and technical support. But for any significant breakthrough to be made, a conscious effort is needed at the governmental level, either bilaterally or within SAARC to locate such regional centres of excellence within the less developed countries of the region.

In the absence of a conscious effort by SAARC to promote such centres of excellence, the market will undoubtedly take its own course with a substantial imbalance in trade in services opening up in more advanced countries such as India, in the area of medical services and education. This growing market is opening up scope for domestic private investment in the health and education sector in other SAARC countries, largely to meet local demand, which is currently diverted to India. Such gestures of import substitution hold promise but it will be a long while before such efforts capture a significant share of the regional export market for human development. Though some facilities, such as the Lahore University of Management Science (LUMS), are acquiring a regional reputation and donor agencies offer scholarships to South Asians to avail of its facilities.

However, most private initiatives tend to be exclusive to the better off classes, which serves to perpetuate a class division between those families who can afford to invest in private education, as well as healthcare and those condemned to survive on the declining quality of South Asia's public services. More effort, through SAARC, may be needed to encourage the emergence of facilities whereby less well-off people in South Asia can avail of institutions of excellence designed to serve a South Asian market. The use of charitable foundations and scholarships to enable common people to move across borders to avail of such social services would carry enormous political advantage in integrating South Asia at the level of civil society.

Cooperation in Macro-economic Policies and Planning

Movement in the area of trade cooperation and infrastructure development needs to be eventually backed up by moves towards harmonisation of macro-economic policies. Unilateral and asymmetrical exchange rate adjustments, we have observed, has already placed Bangladesh at a competitive disadvantage, first with India and more recently with Pakistan. Such beggar-my-neighbour policies are clearly disadvantageous to all parties. Similarly, asymmetrical tariff rates encourage illicit trade across borders through re-export from low to higher tariff neighbours. Products such as fertiliser with lower, occasionally subsidised, prices, end up across the border if prices next door are higher. Variations in interest regimes in the region encourage use of trans-border informal capital markets.

In the prevailing conditions of partial market integration, through informal channels in South Asia, national Finance

Ministers are losing control over their domestic monetary system. However, the rather unstructured behaviour of such informal markets is leading to financial distortions in each country. People operate across multiple markets, depending on the sector and the party's own socio-political position in the economy. In such circumstances, there is a clear advantage in some pricing and monetary policies in South Asia mediated through SAARC. However, given the political constraints to such initiatives, at least, for the moment, a beginning may be made through regular meetings of the Governors of the respective Central Banks and of the Finance Ministers of the region.

There is also some advantage through SAARC to initiate a process of consultation amongst Planning, Trade and Industries Ministers. The expansion of trade within South Asia will be served by moves towards economic restructuring within the region, whereby the smaller countries can diversify their economies to better avail of opportunities offered by open access to markets of their larger neighbours. Such a process of economic restructuring need not limit itself to South Asia. The flying geese model of global restructuring, as it applies to the Asian region, suggests that a variety of economic activities are poised to relocate themselves, recently from Japan to South Korea, and more recently from Malaysia to South Asia, to avail of their emerging comparative advantage in more labour intensive economic activities. However, here again South Asia could become bitter rivals in the fight for relocated industries and as suppliers of labour intensive exports. Economic statesmanship of a high order may save South Asia much grief if such a process of regional restructuring could be harmonised drawing upon the institutional mechanisms of SAARC.

Conclusion : The Political Implications of Building a South Asian Community

It is evident that infrastructure development, investment trade and macro-economic policy cooperation within South Asia carry positive sum benefits for all parties. But all such initiatives remain constrained by inherited political inhibitions about cooperation.

Obstacles to trade have tended to be conditioned by past apprehensions of the less developed economies of South Asia that the bigger partners will economically dominate them in a relation of unequal trade. We have observed that rebuilding the physical and human infrastructure of South Asia is constrained by security driven apprehensions, which persuade countries to sacrifice mutual economic benefits. Attempts by SAARC, as a community to promote cooperation, will have to take account of these political relations on the ground, since after all SAARC is made up of governments and not an aggregation of the citizens of South Asia. It is arguable that particular governments within South Asia find it politically convenient at home to perpetuate tensions with their neighbours. Such gestures of political opportunism tend to establish a symbiotic link between confrontational politics at home and within the region. Thus, the route to South Asian cooperation originates in the nature of politics at home.

Inter-state conflicts are not, however, figments of the imagination. There are real issues of political contention among South Asian states. Perceived unreasonable behaviour of some governments do indeed aggravate tensions. Bangladesh has always felt it had been treated unfairly by India over the issue of the Farakka Barrage built by India to divert the waters of the Ganges to flush the port of Calcutta. The actual construction of the project, its ecological and economic impact on Bangladesh as a lower riparian and the subsequent failure to reach a satisfactory agreement on the apportionment of the flow of the Ganges, has been recognised by all shades of opinion in Bangladesh as an indication of a more powerful upper riparian taking advantage of a smaller neighbour. The issue of the Ganges waters has perhaps caused the most damage to cooperative relations between the two countries. The conclusion of a Ganges Water Treaty in December 1997 thus assumes a major significance in creating the basis for further cooperation. But if for any reason there is any deviation from the letter and spirit of the treaty, this is likely to be particularly corrosive to good relations, particularly in Bangladesh.

The Ganges water dispute between India and Bangladesh highlights two issues at the heart of building a South Asian community. These two issues relate to the dominance of the historical legacy which drives most of South Asia's bilateral conflicts and the special problems associated with the disproportionality in the strength of the conflicting parties.

The legacy of history

Virtually, all the major outstanding interstate disputes in South Asia originate in the breakup of an integrated community. Indeed, a number of debilitating domestic political conflicts have similar historic origins. Thus, the Kashmir dispute is itself part of the unfinished agenda of the partition of India. The conflict over the Ganges waters was a similar legacy of the partition of India. Upto 1947, the Ganges-Meghna-Brahmaputra basin was a shared resource for the region. The Farakka barrage was in fact conceived in the 1930s. But within a milieu, where the Ganges was serving an integrated economy, there was no way that such a project could move ahead without taking into account the impact of the project on the lower riparian areas, located in what was then Southern Bengal and the political resistance to such a project from the people of this region, which would not have been without influence in both the state and national legislatures. The dispute over the Indus waters between India and Pakistan, which preceded the Ganges water dispute, was again the direct result of breaking up Punjab's historically integrated water resources and irrigation system between West Punjab, now in Pakistan, and East Punjab in India. It required the intervention of the World Bank and massive external assistance to partition the waters of the Punjab to take account of the international boundary which divided its water system.

A policy for labour flows

Labour movements across international boundaries have become issues of political disputation in South Asia. Once an integrated labour market was fractured, what people deemed to be their natural market for labour and capital flows now became illegitimate because an international boundary had been put in place to interrupt these flows. These boundaries largely victimised ordinary citizens who have reacted by ignoring these boundaries, so that people move on their own volition and goods now largely flow according to the dictates of the market. Efforts by governments in South Asia, whether located in the Ministry of Commerce or the Ministry of Home Affairs, to contain these flows, are deemed to be increasingly ineffective, which erodes the authority of the state and also opens up scope for interstate tensions. Thus, movement of people from Bangladesh into India has become an issue of domestic political debate in India. In Pakistan, where over a million Bangladeshis now live and work under a rather 'grey' status, the Government of Pakistan has not officially made much of an issue over the status of the Bangladeshis working in Pakistan. This may largely owe to the fact that these workers occupy a labour niche in the Pakistan economy, which conforms to the supply and demand situation in Pakistan's labour market. In Bhutan, the position and status of Nepalese residents there, for generations, has become an issue with the government, leading to the expulsion of many Nepalese which has, in turn, fuelled tensions between Nepal and Bhutan.

It is apparent that the issue of labour flows across South Asia's borders is more likely to surface as an issue of political concern if some political party finds there is political gain in exploiting the issue. Since most such immigrants have been socially and economically integrated into the host country, the scope for any party igniting a political conflagration with international dimensions is limited, unless a government or major political party deliberately chooses to provoke such an agitation. Most metropolitan centres, as for example in India, remain a mosaic of ethnic groups co-existing in peace, if not harmony, where a Bangladeshi migrant would be no more distinguishable or less acceptable than a migrant from West Bangal or Bihar or Nepal.

It may not be advisable to indefinitely bank on the good sense of South Asia's political parties to keep the peace with expatriate minorities. In an environment where SAARC is officially committed to establish SAFTA by 2003 and capital flows are also being liberalised, there would be little use in keeping labour flows as the only remaining illicit activity where evading the facts is elevated into an act of state policy. There is, perhaps, no area where the compulsions of civil society are more likely to precipate inter-state conflict than over the issue of movements of people across state boundaries. SAARC thus needs to treat this issue with particular urgency.

India's political vision

In dissolving the political barriers standing in the way of building a South Asian community, the first actions must begin at home where each country will have to address its relations within South Asia, as an issue of external relations rather than domestic politics. It is thus necessary to build a domestic political consensus within each South Asian country, as an essential instrument to support the building of a South Asian community. As part of such a domestic exercise to depoliticise the approach towards South Asian cooperation, the largest country in the region, India, will have to make a special effort to deal with the various pathologies which condition the perspectives of their smaller South Asian neighbours towards India. Problems carried over from history have put most countries into contention with India. Few of these bilateral problems are intractable. But the smaller neighbours of India appear apprehensive and distrustful of the intentions of their larger neighbour. They reckon that India is always inclined to use its size to extract leverage over its weaker neighbours in addressing any bilateral disputes.

Such apprehensions about India's intentions may well be correct in some, if not all cases. But politics is all about bargaining and compromise. Negotiating skills are determined by a nation's capacity to strike the best bargain, which may frequently be sub-optimal. However, if all negotiations are built around suspicion of the intentions of your neighbour and fear that any compromise will expose you to political attack at home, it is no surprise that most such bilateral negotiations in South

Asia have tended to remain deadlocked with old problems lingering on year after year. Any attempt to break out of this deadlock through compromise means that leaders in the smaller countries have to take their political life in their own hands. In the special circumstances of South Asia, India thus carries a heavy responsibility. Indifference to accommodate the concerns of smaller neighbours who are viewed as unreasonable, often ungrateful and driven by domestic political compulsions, is a rather unstatesmanlike approach to regional politics. In such circumstances, more rather than less is expected of India in their contribution towards building a South Asian community.

At a bilateral level, on an issue by issue basis, there may be little compulsion for India to give concessions to a weaker neighbour. In a South Asian context, unilateral gestures of accommodation by India to a particular country do, however, have a payback in making other South Asian countries less neurotic about India's intentions. The so called Gujral doctrine, currently in vogue, is associated with the proclaimed approach of I.K. Gujral, the previous Prime Minister of India, to make unilateral gestures to its neighbours in resolving outstanding disputes. The Gujral doctrine may in practise be less generous than it appears. But as a concept, it reflects a positive approach towards building a climate of accommodation within the South Asia region, originating from the most powerful country in the region accepting the need to forego some of its advantages in the interest of building a more harmonious region.

In practise, such acts of statesmanship from India could yield considerable long term economic and political gains. South Asia has already shown signs of emerging as a major market for India. To sustain the growth of such a market, India needs to invest in the prosperity of its neighbours, both by opening its own market to them, as well as investing in expanding and diversifying the export capacity of the smaller countries. To ensure that such economic rewards are shared and sustained, India has to allay the inherited fears of its neighbours that intimacy in the economic arena does not mean dominance, whether economic or political or indeed, the shelving of ongoing disputes.

Open regionalism

Most South Asian countries remain vulnerable to some domestic sectarian conflict where a neighbour is involved. Usually such external involvements relate to the need to look after the interests of religious or ethnic minorities within the neighbouring country, with whom the intervening country shares some affinity. The present practice has been for such separatist movements to seek sanctuary within a neighbouring country, who may in turn choose to covertly sustain such insurgencies either through logistic support, or by providing arms to the insurgents. How far one country in South Asia will go to support a political resistance ongoing in a neighboring country tends to depend on the tenor of interstate relations.

It may here be argued that the approach to separatist conflicts in South Asia, whether of the Kashmiris, the tribals of N.E. India and Bangladesh, the Tamils in Sri Lanka, the Nepalis in Bhutan, could be constructively addressed within the context of a South Asian community based on open regionalism. If the South Asia region could, in practice, open its borders to free movement of goods, people, capital, and ideas, where local identities, sustained by the opportunity of local self rule, are recognised as legitimate demands, then seeking a particular juridical identity as a state could become less compulsive. If Kashmiris or Nagas or Tamils in Sri Lanka, could govern themselves, whilst at the same time enjoying the freedom to move readily across national boundaries into Pakistan or India or Bangladesh, more creative solutions may emerge through dialogue than may be forthcoming out of acts of armed struggle. Such a perspective could view South Asia as an integrated community, where national flags and identities will continue to be respected. But many of the appurtenances of nationhood associated with the right to work, to trade, to seek capital and human development, will increasingly come to be accessed within a regional context defined by seamless borders.

Such a South Asia that is made up of national borders without boundaries, demands not just statesmanship by India but considerable courage and self confidence from its neighbours. The latter could indeed build up their economies to avail of the access to the Indian market and could negotiate positive sum gains in other areas from India by impressing upon India the positive sum gains associated with acts of statesmanship originating from their larger neighbour. It is in such a context that SAARC, as an institution, has a major role to play. It will not only design the contours of a South Asian community, but also define its place in the world, particularly in the context of its dynamic Asian neighbours.

3

International Institutions for Global Trade : The Case for South Asian Free Trade Association

BIPLAB DASGUPTA

1. Introduction

In light of the South Asian Free Trade Area (SAFTA) proposed by the South Asian Association for Regional Cooperation (SAARC), the main objective of this paper is to present a case in favour of its creation for a variety of reasons. We intend to show that (a) for sheer survival and development of the countries belonging to the region of South Asia there is no alternative to SAFTA, (b) that it is feasible and mutually beneficial and (c) that such an organisation will also have many significant political and military pay offs.

We begin with an examination in Section 2 of the global trade context, within which SAFTA has to operate. In Section 3, we go through the implications of the eighth round of General Agreement on Tariffs and Trade (GATT) negotiations for the less developed countries (LDCs) and offer the view that there is a need for them to stand up collectively and demand renegotiation of the Marakesh Agreement of April 1994 as well as the provisions of the World Trade Organization (WTO) that came into being in January 1995. In Section 4, we look into the trade relations between two South Asian countries, India and Bangladesh, in addition to the political constraints to the establishment of SAFTA. Section 5 summarises the main conclusions of this paper.

2. The Global Trade Context

A major justification for SAFTA is the way in which the world trade system used to operate under GATT and now operates under WTO. The world market is far from free and competitive, and is heavily loaded in favour of the stronger economies. To survive in this hostile environment, the poor and weak countries need to form global trade alliances; and an initial step in this direction, is to form regional trade blocks. The gap between what the rich countries preach and what they actually practise in the world market is enormous. It is, therefore, imperative on the part of the LDCs to take account of what they actually do and to ignore, as far as possible, the sermons they deliver from the altar, as policy choices.

The Principles

The principles, as preached by the developed countries, are as follows :

(1) Trade benefits every participant, though some benefit more than others.

(2) The productivity and efficiency of a country's economy is linked with its outward-orientation. The rate of growth of an economy is positively correlated with its degree of integration with the global economy. In contrast, the inward-looking economies tend to be inefficient and generate low growth.

(3) The theory of comparative advantage determines what a country can produce and export best. For instance, a less developed country is more likely to enjoy comparative advantage in producing and trading in agricultural products and/or some light industries, such as textiles. On the other hand, the industrial countries

are likely to perform better with industrial goods, which are capital and knowledge intensive.

(4) Any barrier to trade in the name of self sufficiency, based on a strategy of import substitution, promotes inefficiency. Import controls and regulations, by making imports costly, make the production of tradeables costlier, thus taking away the comparative advantage in producing them. It imposes heavy welfare costs on consumers, in terms of higher prices of import-substitutes. Further, such controls encourage rent-seeking activities that cause further diversion of resources for an unproductive pursuit, and thus impose further welfare loss on the economy (Krueger, 1990, Chapter 7).

(5) Even if import liberalisation results in the closing down of some lines of domestic production, this is inevitable and is welcome, as it helps to determine which domestic products are or are not in tune with comparative advantage. Armed with this knowledge and the weeding out of inefficient industries, domestic resources could then be diverted to industries that enjoy comparative advantage, thus leading to growth.

(6) Subsidies distort allocation of resources and do not allow the market forces of demand and supply to equalise and thus determine the desirable levels of price and output at which the market is cleared. Any restraint on the free functioning of market forces, particularly by an interventionist state, is problematic per se. There should be no interference with the entry of the multinational companies (MNCs) in the domestic market, or of their capital and remittances. The government should be neutral and non-discriminatory in its attitude towards them.

These principles, whether good or bad, are not followed by a single country today. What happens in practice is described below :

Who Cares for Comparative Advantage?

No country identifies its export items on the basis of its comparative advantage, as given by factor endowments and history. Had this been the case, the rich countries would not have become major players in world food trade. Today countries under the Organisation for Economic Cooperation and Development (OECD) account for 80 per cent of world cereal trade, 55 per cent of which is sold to less developed countries (OECD, 1992, p. 13). Being highly industrialised, the last thing these rich and high-wage countries are suited to produce and export are labour-intensive agricultural goods. Nonetheless, the United States and the European Union have been the two major exporters of wheat for several decades now. This is not due to any comparative advantage they enjoy with regard to these items, but because of the enormous subsidy their governments give to agriculture. The scale of such subsidies is far beyond what the LDCs offer to their own agriculturists. In the early nineties, OECD countries gave an astronomical $ 240 billion worth of agricultural subsidies (Watkins, 1992, p. 70). That huge amount of subsidies was meant for only 3 per cent to 10 per cent of their population who work in agriculture, compared with 60 per cent to 70 per cent engaged in agriculture in LDCs.

In the United States, agricultural subsidies date back to the thirties, while in Europe they began with the Common Agricultural Policy (CAP) of the European Economic Community in 1962. In Europe, a variable levy system ensures that foreign wheat supplies are always dearer than the local supply (Cohn, 1993, p. 25). In both cases, the subsidies originated from the concern for self sufficiency in food in war situations, but later the subsidies went beyond that original intention, prompted largely by agriculturist lobbies, to make their food, butter and milk the cheapest in the world. Use was made of large food surpluses made possible by such generous subsidies, as an instrument of foreign policy, to influence the domestic and external policies of the recipients of PL 480 aid (Cohn, *Ibid.*, p. 22).

In the past, the United States was opposed to making agriculture a subject for GATT negotiations. The Keynesian proposal for an International Trade Organisation (ITO) could not be implemented, even after its charter was finalised in Havana, largely due to opposition from the US agriculturists in the early fifties (Cohn, *ibid.*, p. 21). When the GATT system became operational in 1955, the United States pressured other countries to agree to a waiver that technically permitted it to continue with a highly protectionist policy for agriculture (Low, 1995, p. 24). If today the United States has changed its policy and has been instrumental in forcing agriculture as a subject for the eighth round of GATT negotiations, it is largely because the present level of subsidies is too high, even for this economic giant, tormented as it is by heavy fiscal deficits. And if the United States is no longer willing and/or able to offer subsidies, at least at such high levels, it is keen to see that none of its competitors does. The irony of the recent WTO agreement is that, while it is opposed to agricultural subsidies, it has permitted both the United States and European Union to continue with deficiency payments and compensation payments, on the ground that these are not trade distorting (Watkins, *op. cit.*, p. 122).

Trade Restrictions in the West

While the rich countries are preaching (1) replacement of non-tariff barriers by their tariff equivalents and then, (2) a drastic lowering of tariff levels, they, in practice, throughout the eighties, strengthened non-tariff barriers (NTBs) particularly against LDC exports. Such NTBs take a variety of forms such as Multi-Fibre Arrangement (MFA), Safeguards, Anti-dumping Suits, Countervailing Duties, Voluntary Export Restraint (VER), Voluntary Import Enhancement (VIE), and Super 301, as well as Special 301 that applies to patent agreements.

Voluntary Export Restraint (VER)

One of the worst among these is VER, which is now the core of new protectionism in the West. This is preferred to other non-tariff restrictions because this can be quickly imposed or removed and thereby help in maintaining the mythology of free trade (Bhagwati, 1991, p. 171). In this arrangement a fiction is maintained that a country (*e.g.*, South Korea exporting microwaves or Japan exporting automobiles) is, on its own, restricting exports of a particular product to another country. In practice though, there is nothing voluntary about these arrangements; the arms of the exporting countries are twisted in a variety of ways to make the agreement look voluntary. In several cases, such VERs are preceded by actions under anti-dumping legislation, to coerce the concerned exporting country to submission.

The VER is a preferred instrument of protection for declining, uncompetitive industries, and for agriculture in the United States. Of the 236 VERs in the world today, 60 cover food and agricultural products, 50 cover steel and steel products, 27 cover electronic products, 21 cover non-MFA textile and clothing items, 17 cover automobiles and road transport equipment, 16 cover footwear, 13 cover machine tools and 32 cover others. About 10 per cent of world trade, and a good part of the trade by East Asian countries is covered by VERs. Forty-nine of those operate against Japan and 33 against South Korea, whilst the remaining East Asian countries account for a bulk of 52 such VERs directed against less developed countries (Low, *op. cit.*, pp. 77-78).

The 1994 Marakesh agreement seeks to eliminate VERs under article 11 : 1b. It also proposes to phase out existing grey areas within four years. However, it remains to be seen whether this provision will be given effect. There is a fear that the VER may go underground, taking the form of unwritten market sharing arrangements among private firms. Alternatively, its formal demise may give rise to a growing number of anti-dumping suits or countervailing duties.

Multi-Fibre Arrangement (MFA)

The Multi-Fibre Arrangement came into being as a panic reaction to Japan's entry into GATT, and "in an early example of what has become a traditional method of ensuring opacity and lack of accountability in the twilight zone of GATT legality" (Low, *op. cit.*, p. 107).

Following the Short-Term (1961-62) and the Long-Term (1962-73) Arrangements made as international agreements for regulating trade in textiles and clothing, the Multi-Fibre Arrangement (MFA) came into existence in 1974. In all these agreements the exporting countries have been bound by quota restrictions in the importing countries. The MFA agreement is renewed after every three or four years. MFA participants covered 44 countries in July 1993 (taking European Economic Community as a single country) and accounted for some 80 per cent of world textiles and clothing exports. One of its declared objectives at the time of inception was to restrain low cost export from disrupting the local markets. Shorn off rhetoric, the simple objective was not to allow countries with abundant labour to enjoy their comparative advantage (Jackson, 1993, p. 226; Low, *op. cit.*, pp. 108-109). In each round of agreement, the coverage has been wide-ranging in terms of products, while becoming more restrictive in terms of quotas. As a major consequence of the MFA, it has reduced the LDCs'share in the rich country markets. For example, the LDCs' share in the UK textile market has declined from 32 per cent in 1974 to 25 per cent in 1993, while the share of the EC has increased from 36 per cent to 53 per cent (Watkins, *op. cit.*, pp. 49-51).

Though the Uruguay Round of the GATT agreement provides for the liquidation of MFA by 2005 AD, the provisions for the liquidation of MFA are, unlike other front-loaded time-bound arrangements, back-loaded in the sense that half of the dismantling of MFA would take place only in the very last phase. It remains to be seen whether that too is going to be implemented according to schedule, in view of the stiff resistance within the United States against the disbanding of MFA.

Super 301

What is known as 'super 301' is actually the section 301 of the US Trade Act; the adjective 'super' is added commonly to indicate its power and importance. Section 301 gives the President the broad authority to retaliate against other countries for unreasonable and unjustifiable trade practices affecting the commercial interests of the United States (Low, *op. cit.*, p. 56). Low has described it as "the most overtly political, and least circumscribed statute in terms of remedies and retaliatory possibilities. The negotiation is one-sided as it demands removal of something" (Low, *op. cit.*, p. 87).

The articles under this section further empowers the United States Trade Representative (USTR) to issue notices to countries accused of unfair trade against US exports. The issue of notice is usually followed up by a detailed discussion with the officials of the country concerned, with the objective of removing unfair trade practices. Between 1975 and 1990, 77 such notices were issued, and retaliatory action was taken in 8 cases : 3 against the EC, 2 against Japan, and 1 each against Canada, Brazil and Argentina. The EC was provoked to engage in counter-retaliatory measures in 2 out of 3 cases and Brazil took the case to Court, which led to the withdrawal of the US sanction. The other 69 cases were either dropped or led to trade liberalising settlement (Low, *op. cit.*, pp. 89-91). Subsequently, more cases had been taken up for the same reason.

In all these cases, whatever the United States had done was unilateral. As Hudec pointed out, "Foreign reactions have been sharpened by irritation over the self-righteous tone of the new law. The detailed procedures are structured as a series of public investigations and decisions which makes them appear to be 'trade crimes' trials. Foreign governments have bristled at having their policies 'tried' in this manner and have gone out of their way to ridicule the quasi-judicial appearance of these procedures'' (reproduced in Low, *op. cit.*, p. 90).

The East Asian countries have been relatively more vulnerable to the Super 301 retaliatory trade measures. Their names tend to appear quite frequently in the 'hit list', and they, it seems, generally succumb under pressure, because of political and military compulsions against any determined action from the United States (Low, *op. cit.*, p. 89). In many cases, Super 301 is used in conjunction with some other restrictive measures. One method used by USA is to threaten action under anti-dumping measures, where dumping is defined in such a way that, in effect, it provides protection to inefficient high-cost US industries. Such threat of harassment often compels the country concerned to accept VER as a lesser evil. VER, anti-dumping suits and Super 301 are all used, sometimes separately and sometimes together, to extract maximum trade concessions from the East Asian countries in order to make them accept US exports, including agricultural goods and insurance services (Low, *op. cit.*, pp. 118-124).

There is also an article called Special 301 which relates to intellectual property rights (IPR) and is covered by the trade legislation. It requires the USTR to identify foreign countries that 'deny adequate and effective protection of intellectual property rights, or deny fair and equitable market access to US persons that rely upon intellectual property protection.' It provides the Congress with the sense that IPR protection is vital to the international competitiveness of the United States (Low, *op. cit.*, pp. 64-65).

The expectation that, with the establishment of a multilateral trade dispute settlement machinery under WTO, Super 301 would become redundant has proved to be wrong. Super 301 has not ceased to work. During the Uruguay Round negotiations, the USA insisted that Super 301 would stay, especially to allow private parties a right of complaint and to handle non-GATT issues (Low, *op. cit.*, p. 230).

Voluntary Import Enhancement

One of the objectives of the Super 301 was to force Japan to discuss the issue of market access. It was followed, therefore, by what came to be known as negotiations on Structural Impediments Initiative (SII) (Low, *op. cit.*, p. 92). Though Japan continued to negotiate then, and also afterwards, and even conceded many US demands, the exchanges were often acrimonious and left the Japanese side with a bitter taste in their mouth. This particular policy has been described by Bhagwati (*op. cit.*, p. 179) as Voluntary Import Expansion (VIE), where the word voluntary, as in the case of VER, is safely within quotes. According to this policy, a country agrees to open up its economy to another and specifies the extent of such access.

Another way the United States wished to obtain both greater market access and a lowering of their bilateral trade deficit (then running at $ 50 billion), was by forcing the Japanese to overvalue their currency, thus making their goods relatively more expensive. The 1985 Plaza Accord of G7 countries led to an appreciation in the value of the Yen and a corresponding depreciation in the value of the dollar. The idea of a North American Free Trade Association (NAFTA) was mooted in the same year, again with the same objective of finding a larger market for US goods. In the same year the US filed an 'anti-dumping suit' against Japanese semiconductor industries, which was withdrawn after one year, on the understanding that Japan would allow US companies a 20 per cent share in the Japanese market within five years. Still, in 1988, based on the allegations of US companies, the US government imposed a 100 per cent punitive tariff on selected Japanese electronics imports, such as laptop and desktop computers, colour TVs and power hand tools. Eventually, capitulating under US pressure, the government of Japan maintained that a predetermined share of US companies in Japanese semiconductor industry was uncalled for, and that such a share should be the outcome of free competition (Okuda, 1996, pp. 176-178).

However, one interesting consequence of these pressures and restrictions, in addition to the increase in the wages and prices of Japanese exports, was the shift of a considerable amount of Japanese investment to low wage Southeast Asian countries, which operated under the Original Equipment Manufacture (OEM) arrangement. This shift has been instrumental in changing the industrial landscape of the Southeast Asian region.

The use of various NTBs by the rich countries as mentioned above brings into the following question: how does one determine what is or is not fair trade? It is to be noted that the principle of free trade in the original GATT negotiations has been replaced by the principle of fair trade, where the fairness or otherwise is determined subjectively by the country concerned.

Environmental and Labour Standard Issues

In recent years, following Marakesh agreement, new items, particularly issues relating to environmental and labour standards, have been introduced in global trade negotiations. Attempts have been made to establish a new global regime on investment and competition policy, which appears to have adverse implications for LDC exports.

Following the OPEC's quadrupling of oil prices during the 1970s, it was thought that a rising environmental consciousness would work in favour of the less developed countries, as people in rich countries would increasingly move away from consumption of synthetics and rather favour primary, natural products imported from poor countries. That has not happened; on the contrary, environmental issues are being increasingly used against the less developed countries. The import controls allowed by the Marakesh agreement which seeks to 'protect human, animal or plant life or health' are being increasingly applied to block Third World exports (Schott, 1990, pp. 52-53).

Environmental legislation is dictting specificiations prepared by rich country industrial interests, which the poor country exporters are not usually aware of and can not meet. Ecolabelling is inducing consumers in rich countries to shy away from poor country exports on environmental grounds. There is also the fear that deregulation, and the opening up of the economy to companies with short-term horizons, will lead to environmental degradation and be instrumental for the polluting industries to be located more increasingly in the less developed countries.

One of the most controversial issues has been the attempt to link trade to the pattern of labour use. Rich countries tend to take the view that less developed countries are enjoying a differential advantage over their richer counterparts, in terms of cheap labour costs. To rectify this, rich countries propose uniform and standardised labour market behaviour, including conformity in terms of wages paid and the conditions under which the workmen operate. The opposition from less developed countries puts forward their view that, given the state of their economy, their workers can not expect a wage or working conditions that are comparable with those in the rich countries. There is a strong feeling that this is less a concern for the plight of workers than for reducing the competitiveness of the poor country exports. Some would argue even further and add that the only advantage that less developed countries, bereft of capital, technology and management resources, enjoy is in terms of their relatively low wages, without which they would lose whatever small share of the world market they still hold. Nor would it be possible to raise wages without a corresponding rise in GDP. In recent years, carpet exports from LDCs have been discouraged on the grounds that these are based on the exploitation of child labour.

Another labour issue relates to the international flow of labour. If, in accordance with the Structural Adjustment Policy and the GATT agreement, the mobility of capital and technology, as well as of goods and services is assured, then why should labour, a major input of production, not be equally mobile across international borders? Like commodities and capital, labour too should flow to markets where the demand for labour exceeds its supply. If international capital enjoys national treatment in all countries, why then should foreign labour power too, irrespective of its source, not enjoy the same non-discriminatory treatment vis-a-vis local labour? The fact is there is a clearly visible reticence to extend the idea of mobility of inputs and outputs to labour power. On the contrary, immigration laws have been considerably tightened in the past two decades to contain flow of labour power from the Third World countries. Obviously, a concept that is good, both philosophically and economically, for capital, commodities and so forth, is not good when it comes to poor country labour exports.

Another fallacy is that, alongside the demand for better labour standards in poor countries, rich country multinational corporations (MNCs) have been demanding the dilution of labour laws that protect the interests of workers. Here, the argument is that such labour ligislation makes the downward movement of wages rigid and does not allow the labour market to adjust to the forces of demand and supply. Further, such legislation discourages foreign investment, while the need with respect to poor countries is for more than foreign direct investment in factories and industries. "The overriding tendency (of the World Bank) has been to criticize existing labour laws and regulations, whenever they may raise the cost of labour and otherwise impede the freeer operation of market forces," as one International Labour Organization (ILO) document concludes (Plant, 1994, p. 57). Such a view looks at the problem only from the side of management, as if production is only undertaken by management, ignoring the contribution of the workforce and the sufferings, uncertainties and poverty they undergo to keep the wheels of the industry moving.

One major issue that is seldom discussed, is the distorting impact of MNC management salaries on the overall wage and salary structure in a country. In many cases, MNCs are offering a salary level that is many times the existing one for senior administrators and business personnel. To protect their own management staff from poaching by MNCs, the local firms are often being forced to pay salaries that are completely out of tune with the salaries of lower level staff. In some countries the ratio between the highest salary, that of management, and the lowest, for those working on the shopfloor, is as high as 100 : 1. This is leading to serious unrest in the workforce and is operating as a negative incentive for the majority of workers.

Role of Multinational Corporations (MNCs)

A great deal of what passes as international trade is, from the point of view of a multinational corporation (MNC), given its multinational character, an intra-company affair : a transfer between two affiliates located in two different countries. Towards the end of the seventies, such intra-firm, but international, trade accounted for about 30 per cent of total world trade. These companies are also involved in a great deal of trade amongst themselves : by the early 1980s trade between the 350 largest MNCs amounted to an estimated 40 per cent of global trade. MNCs also dominate technology flows, most of which remain confined within the corporate framework: for the US four-fifths of technology receipts are intra-firm, over 90 per cent for Germany. A handful of MNCs (say six to ten), account for 60-70 per cent of the global production of leading minerals, such as bauxite, copper, iron ore, nickel and zinc as well as major agricultural exports such as tea, coffee or bananas.

Due to the vastness of the MNCs' resources and control over technology, their vertically integrated character, the multinational scope of their operation with numerous affiliates spread over the world as well as their political clout, place the MNCs easily at an advantageous position when bargaining with the LDC governments. The MNCs may deny the host government vital information that might have improved the latter's bargaining position and may even punish a host government for adopting a hostile attitude, by not producing or exporting enough from that source. It may even induce its own government to impose an embargo on the trade of the country, should the host government retaliate by nationalising. Various UN proposals, with regard to greater transparency in MNCs' negotiation with LDC governments for effective bargaining, have not gone very far, largely owing to a lack of enthusiasm, sometimes direct antagonism, on the part of rich country governments.

A major consequence of the structural adjustment programs and the Marakesh agreement has been the freeing of MNCs free from the controls and regulations of host governments and to widen their access to markets that were hitherto closed. By eliminating 'local content requirements' and by insisting on 'national treatment,' the conflict between the global objectives of MNCs and the national objectives of host governments has now been resolved in the former's favour. The reduction of subsidies and the establishment of a global patent regime have also helped them to more effectively penetrate the local economy and maintain their superiority over local producers for a long time to come.

In the context of the recent drive towards globalisation, it is instructive to refer to an OECD document, which analyses, among other things, globalisation process and its impact on less developed countries. It states : "Globalisation represents a new phase in the process of internationalisation and the spread of international production. It refers to a set of emerging conditions in which value and wealth are increasingly being produced and distributed within world-wide corporate networks. Large multinational firms operating in concentrated supply structures are at the hub of these conditions." In addition, it continues, "As a result, in a growing number of industries in manufacturing and services, the prevailing form of supply structure is world oligopoly....As a result of the convergence of computer, communication and control technology, it has now become feasible for MNEs to install captive intra-corporate world-wide information networks, through which management can link production , marketing and R & D facilities around the world. Although many MNEs still locate their strategic R&D near their corporate headquarters, networks offer such firms new opportunities for the internationalisation of R&D, as well as for international sourcing of technological resources" (OECD, 1992, p. 209).

As for the consequences, this document states categorically that, "the first concerns the marginalisation of developing countries within the globalisation process. The second concerns concentration as a world process and whether a global competition policy is needed and how it might be implemented. The third relates to the problems posed by support given by governments to firms engaged in global competition and the need for new rules and codes of behaviour. The fourth relates to standards and norms in a context of rapid and pervasive technological change, corporate concentration and globalisation" (OECD, *ibid.*, p. 209).

Adverse Terms of Trade

For several decades now the global terms of trade has been unfavourable to agricultural exports. Most studies, mainly undertaken by the World Bank, IMF and UNCTAD, indicate not only how terms of trade have been moving against primary exports, but also the fearful prospect of the trend actually persisting until the end of the first decade of the next century. The index of real commodity prices fell by half between 1980 and 1993, and, according to Lewis T. Preston, the past President of World Bank, "Today the real price of many non-oil commodities are the lowest they have been since 1945; in many cases prices are so low that they do not cover production costs. For 1993, the transfer in purchasing power from the developing to the developed countries due to the fall in non-oil commodity prices between 1980 and 1993, was about $100 billion — more than double the net aid flows to developing countries in 1993" (Development Committee, 1994, p. 8). It is not only that the negative terms of trade effect outweighed the positive effect of aid inflow, rather these also accounted for a massive loss of up to 7 per cent of GNP, in case of less developed countries. The document predicted that during the next ten years, commodity prices would increase slightly faster than those of manufactured goods, but, after that, the long run declining trend would again assert itself (*Ibid.*).

The share of food in world trade has declined from 21.4 per cent in 1962 to 9.5 per cent in 1992; and of non-food agriculture from 10.2 per cent to 2.1 per cent. Over the same period, the share of metals and minerals has slided from 7.7 per cent to 2.4 per cent, the share of fuels from 11.4 per cent to 4.3 per cent, and in the case of manufacture, from 49.2 per cent to 81.6 per cent. Even in the case of the less developed countries, the share of food in their exports has drastically declined from 37.3 per cent to 12.1 per cent. Over the past two decades, "the volume of world trade in manufactures has increased twice as fast as the volume of primary commodities.....for each percentage point of increase in world output, trade in manufacturing went up 2 per cent, while trade in primary products rose only 0.6 per cent" (ECLAC, 1994, p. 39).

There is a hope, in many less developed countries, that, at the conclusion of the ten-year period following the establishment of WTO in 1995, as the subsidies given to agriculture in the

USA and Europe are reduced, they would be able to capture a good slice of the world market. Had only a few countries been making such calculations, there could have been a reasonable chance of these expectations being fulfilled. The fact is that practically all the less developed countries have been generously rendered this advice by the World Bank and all of them are making preparations for the day when the partial withdrawal of subsidies will open up huge rich country markets for them. As a consequence, the familiar 'fallacy of composition' has come into play. In this situation, more production and exportation of agricultural commodities, in line with their static comparative advantage, by all the poor countries of the world together, is likely to pull down their prices even further and harm them collectively. There is every likelihood that this secular tendency towards further declines in terms of trade — because of technical and other changes that have reduced the intensity of use of minerals, metals, and agricultural products in the developed countries — would now be reinforced by the scramble for rich country agricultural markets in the first decade of the 21st century. Thus, whatever gains the less developed countries would make in terms of volume is likely to be overweighed by their losses in value terms. For example, during the 1980s, the volume of agricultural exports increased by 2.3 per cent, while their value increased by 1.4 per cent a year (ECLAC, *op. cit.* p. 38, pp. 69-70). On the other hand, whatever the rich countries lose in terms of loss of agricultural exports would be more than made up by their saving in terms of subsidies and the cheapening of the cost of industrial production, because of low prices of agricultural imports.

One of the major complaints of the less developed countries had always been that the terms of trade between rich country exports of industrial goods and poor country exports of primary goods is determined by rich countries, and, always in their favour. The demand for a parity between the two sets of prices has been voiced since the early sixties, but became highly audible during the seventies, following the quadrupling of oil prices and particularly in the context of the debate on the proposed New International Economic Order. The less developed countries had always complained that the world prices for their products did not account for their scarcity value, as the market was dominated by purchasing power. The success they achieved in 1973, by forcing a significant rise in oil prices, did not come about through autonomous interaction of oil prices, rather through the formation and determined cartel action of the oil exporting countries to counter the cartel of the oil companies. The world market, as it works, is incapable of determining prices that are rational in terms of reflecting the scarcity value of specific goods.

The comparative advantages are products of colonial history, when the option of independent economic development was not available and the economy of the colonised country was run for the benefit of the colonial power. Any decision on export items based on comparative advantage would only perpetuate the existing division of labour in world trade.

The East Asian development was feasible because they refused to subscribe to this static concept of comparative advantage and sought to move away from textiles. More significantly, they took a dynamic view and created a comparative advantage for the goods they produced. They established, at the initiative of their governments, and with generous subsidies as well as protection from foreign predators, industries such as steel, heavy chemicals, and ship building. Such a strategy helped them create the industrial infrastructure for the next generation of industries with high income elastic demand, such as electronic goods and computers. The wide array of items they now export also ensures that their economy does not become vulnerable to the collapse of world demand for one item or another. In other words, the most successful group of countries in the past three decades succeeded because they defied the World Bank prescription and discarded the static concept of comparative advantage.

Any trade strategy for South Asia has to be based on these ground realities of rich country domination of the world market and the restrictive trade practices indulged in by the rich countries. One approach can be of South Asia's capitulation to super power domination and remaining content with whatever comes, in the form of export opportunities. Another is to assert South Asia's economic sovereignty, to demand renegotiations of terms under which world trade operates today and to form alliances for the realisation of these.

3. Role of SAFTA as a Regional Trade Block

Regional Bodies as Exceptions to GATT Norms

The case for a regional trade block like SAFTA rests on a number of considerations. First of all, the loophole in GATT agreements, from the very early days, favoured the regional blocks and customs unions. A declared objective of GATT was non-discrimination and universalisation of trade relations, by way of the most favoured nation (MFN) concept. Simply defined, under this concept, the trade concessions agreed upon by any two countries would be automatically extended to other member countries of GATT. The superlative made it clear that there could not be any country more favoured than the GATT members, who were most favoured. If any member chose to make an agreement with another state that provided more concessions than were hitherto available to other members, the former became immediately applicable to all other members. In other words, a member could not discriminate against another member when entering into trade negotiations with a third country.

However, this principle of non-discrimination was subject to an important exception: the regional customs unions were eligible to discriminate in favour of their own members within the region, as against other GATT members. It was never made clear how such concessions given to regional trade bodies was compatible with MFN, but regional economic bodies became an important feature of world trade scene from the early days (Low, *op. cit.*, p. 27). A large number of regional trade bodies have so far taken full advantage of this loophole, from the European Economic Community (EEC) to the North American Free Trade Association (NAFTA) through the Andean Pact, the Central American Common Market (CACM), the Carribean Community (Caricom), the Association of South East Asian Nations (ASEAN), and the Preferential Trade Area for Eastern and Southern Africa (PTAESA). In each case, the members of those regional bodies have been offered tariff concesssions that are not available to other countries.

It has been asked whether such regional groupings are building blocks or stumbling blocks towards the development of a well integrated global market. One argument is that such regional alliances make their individual members economically stronger and more competitive, and, therefore, more willing to accept global integration.

A second argument in favour of SAFTA is that it would improve the collective bargaining strength of its members at global level negotiations. In early GATT negotiations, some concessions were given to poor countries, keeping in mind their backwardness and adverse balance of payments position, in terms of Generalised System of Preference (GSP). But, by the time of the Uruguay Round, the rich countries were insisting that the poor countries should grow out of those. The principle of non-discrimination was overshadowed by the principle of reciprocity. To get something out of the negotiations, one had to give something. Countries not capable of giving anything, no matter what their condition was, were left out of reckoning. If the United States was to concede on MFA, or a reduction in an agricultural subsidy, the LDCs were expected to open up their markets to services and so on (Low, *op. cit.*, pp. 29-30). East Asian and South East Asian countries were willingly taken as partners in world trade negotiations, precisely because these countries were strong enough to respond to offers from the rich countries with counter offers.

Reasons for LDCs' Weak Bargaining Power and Lack of Unity

One major reason for the poor performance of less developed countries in the negotiations, apart from their weak economic power, was the lack of specialised staff and advice. The weak bargaining position of the LDCs was ruthlessly exposed during the Uruguay Round, which continued from 1986 to 1993. Between 1986 and 1991, for five years, the less developed countries showed a certain sense of purpose and unity by resisting the introduction of services and intellectual property rights in the negotiations. But, after the collapse of the Soviet Union in 1991, they seemed to have lost the will to fight the single superpower left in the world stage. Thus, when a draft was prepared by Arthur Dunkel, the Director General of GATT, in December 1991, there was little resistance to it from the LDCs. The discussion on the Dunkel draft dragged on for another two years, though it was supposed to be concluded in a matter of a few months. This was largely because of serious disagreements between North America and Europe, with the LDCs having no role to play in it. "For the most part, developing countries have greeted the GATT Director General's proposals with resignation rather than enthusiasm.... The majority of developing countries have been studiously indifferent to the text,...." (Watkins, *op. cit.*, pp. 131-132).

Besides, unlike the European Union or Cairns Group of agriculturally advanced rich and middle income countries, the LDCs seldom functioned as a group with unity of purpose, or devoted much effort or time to coalition building or lobbying. "LDCs are unsure of what interests they have and/or of how to advance or protect them in agreement. Consequently, they are unable to exercise influence in the negotiations. Uncertainty, combined with political disorganization among the LDCs, erodes whatever bargaining power their markets and potential consumer interests afford them" (Hopkins, 1993, p. 147).

Within the less developed countries there was also a major difference in terms of attitude towards specific issues, for example with respect to agricultural subsidies. Some were net food importers, who were keen to obtain food at the lowest possible price from the world market, no matter what the source was (Hoekman, *op. cit.*, p. 478). They were, naturally, the least interested in maintaining subsidies that served the interests of producers. India in a sense straddled both worlds : it was technically a net food importing country, but its production was near self-sufficiency level and its aspiration was to emerge eventually as a net exporter. While G15 countries led by India and Brazil had one kind of strategy, another group of 20 less developed countries threw in their lot with the West.

Issues Concerning Patent Rights

While GATT agreements on services and investment are detrimental to the interests of LDCs, the most ominous are those relating to patent rights. The GATT agreement on intellectual property rights establishes an international patent regime and expects the member countries to amend their own patent laws in conformity with the latter, within a given time frame. While the developed countries have been asked to change their patent laws within one year of the Marakesh agreement of 1994, the poor countries have been given five years, and, in the case of pharmaceuticals and some other activities, ten years (Schott, *op. cit.*, p. 120). This measure at once closes the option of liberally using foreign technologies and of applying 'reverse engineering techniques' for adapting technologies available elsewhere for indigenous industrial development. Though described as 'piracy' by the rich countries, those using foreign technology in this way were not doing anything illegal, but were following patent laws of their own countries (Lesser, 1991, p. 1). Now, with the internationalisation of patent laws, vigorously monitored by WTO, the path taken by almost all the developed countries of the world in the course of their development, including the newly industrialised East Asian countries, will be denied to the less developed countries of the world of today.

Apart from taking away the option of using foreign technologies as liberally as the East Asians, the new patent regime contains several highly restrictive conditions. One of this extends patent rights to 20 years (from 7 to 14 years in case of the Indian patent law), though, given the very high rate of obsolescence of the modern technologies in today's world, a downward revision to 5-7 years should have been more in order. India has 5 year product patent for foods or medicine and Andean countries for 4 years, renewable for an additional five years (Lesser, *op. cit.*, pp. 15-16). This longer period would allow the rich countries to enjoy the high economic rent of their patented technologies for a very long time. Further, it will virtually rule out indigenous development of technologies in the backward countries and will keep those perpetually dependent on the rich countries for technologies.

> The new GATT agreement eliminates the distinction between 'product' and 'process' patent, and thus denies the poor countries like India the option to acquire a 'process' by paying royalty and then to produce the 'product' at a cheap cost by using local materials and manpower. The industry to be hurt most by this condition is the pharmaceutical industry, which now supplies Indian masses life-saving drugs at a fraction of the cost in rich countries, because the cost of the inputs is low here. As the UN Economic Commission for Latin America and the Caribbean concludes : "The rules on intellectual property are a particular cause of concern, since they may raise the prices of medicines and other patented products in the short run, but may also limit access to new technologies in the longer term" (ECLAC, *op. cit.*, p. 44).

Some have raised the question as to whether intellectual property rights is a 'trade' issue to be covered by GATT negotiations. Until recently, the World Intellectual Property Rights Organisation (WIPRO), established in 1974 following a World Intellectual Property Convention in 1967, was the agency to look after such issues (Lesser, *op. cit.*, pp. 10-11). The main argument for including it in the GATT agenda was that protection of intellectual property rights would enhance trade. By granting and enforcing patent rights internationally, it was argued, owners of patents would no longer be forced to keep details of their inventions secret, since such details would form a part of their patent application, and, thus, the knowledge itself would be disseminated more freely [Deardoff (2), 1993, pp. 436-437]. Such an argument does not account for the fact that patents create monopolies and massive economic rent, and erect barriers to the dissemination of knowledge. Unless patents are judiciously bound by time and space, there is every likelihood that the gains from incentive for innovation, through patents, will be negated by the restriction on the flow of knowledge. Since most such patents originate in rich countries, these restrictions widen global inequality between the rich and poor countries and consequently, deny poor countries the opportunity to move along the learning curve [Deardoff (1), 1993, p. 145]. It is often argued that patents are 'defensive strategy' adopted by rich country corporate interests in order to preserve markets, even without direct investment.

A major issue concerns patent rights on seed varieties. The World Summit of 1993 gave a call for enhancing bio-diversity, but the new patent regime is likely to have the opposite effect. Ever since the conclusion of the Marakesh agreement, there has been a mad rush from the large multinational firms, to collect germplasms of wild plant varieties in the less developed countries and then to patent them. The most talked about has been the patenting of 'neem tree', which is a part of Indian folk culture and whose medicinal and other properties has been known to the Indian people from time immemorial. The irony of such patenting is that neem products, processed by foreign companies, would now have to be purchased by Indians who are accustomed to obtaining it free from nature. Ironically, while the demand for a global patent regime arose from the fear of widespread poaching of rich country innovations, inventions and technology by the poorer ones, the biosphere of the latter is now being plundered by rich country corporate interests under the new regime.

One way of handling this problem is to echo the proposal of the International Undertaking on Plant genetic Resources, an initiative taken by the United Nations' Food and Agriculture Organization (FAO). Accordingly, all germplasm needs to be recognised as a public resource and part of the heritage of mankind. This way, poor countries would at least be able to retain some control over their own plants and other forms of life (Lesser, *op. cit.*, p. 64).

Much depends on the political will of the government of the country concerned. While conforming to the 1994 Marakesh agreement and recasting the domestic patent law in line with the international patent regime, there is some room for maneuver by making skillful use of some of the articles of the agreement. Virtually all patent laws exclude mere ideas or theories; patents are intended to apply to the embodiment of those ideas. The national laws can be so drafted that the flow of ideas is not obstructed. Moreover, India can follow the WIPRO model patent law, that in turn follows the European practice of excluding plants and animals or the method of treatment of human or animal body. Some poor countries already include foodstuffs and medicines in this list of excluded items (Lesser, *op. cit.*, p. 28). Further, under articles 27.2 and 27.3 of the Marakesh agreement, countries may deny patent protection for certain inventions, such as those which involve 'diagnostic, therapeutic and surgical methods for the treatment of humans and animals,' and plants and animals (other than microorganisms) and biological processes (other than microbiological processes) for their production (Schott, *op. cit.*, p. 18). These safeguards could be used by the Indian government to protect Indian species from global patenting, yet this has not been done in the legislation drafted so far.

The Case for South Asian Free Trade Area (SAFTA)

The expression 'South Asia' is of post-colonial origin and refers to a group of countries located in the region that were under British rule for a long time. Areas comprising present day India, Pakistan and Bangladesh constituted British India, while Sri Lanka, Nepal and Bhutan were separately administered by the British (as also Burma, now Myanmar, which is reckoned as a part of Southeast Asia). As these countries were together under the same colonial rule, they shared a common historical experience and were subjected to similar types of economic exploitation. More importantly, from the point of view of this paper, the overwhelming proportion of their economic transactions was conducted within South Asia and the economic activities in various parts developed in a complimentary manner. For example, as between West Bengal (now in India) and East Bengal (now Bangladesh), the latter produced raw jute, while in the former the jute factories were located. Though over the past fifty years a great deal of that complimentarity has been eroded, it is not difficult to identify areas of complimentarity and to take recourse to integrated resource-based planning, taking South Asia as a whole, or a part of it, as the relevant entity.

Until recently, the economic relationship among South Asian countries was underplayed, while some coordination in the fields of culture and sports took place through SAARC. Thus, the region could not take advantage of the loophole in GATT agreements that favoured the regional bodies. SAPTA or South Asian Prefernetial Trade Agreement came much later and only recently is SAFTA or the South Asian Free Trade Association being discussed. If one goes by formal pronouncements, SAFTA should come into being by the early part of the next century. In other words, several decades of possible collective growth through the establishment of a common market has been lost as a result of the unwillingness of the countries concerned to cooperate in a common endeavour.

A second possible use of SAFTA would be as an important step towards building something similar to G77 of the seventies at the world level, that would demand a New International Economic Order (NIEO) and a restructuring of world trade including renegotiation of the WTO agreement. Building on this regional grouping, it would be possible to seek co-operarion with other regional groups and then proceed to a much broader and bigger group of LDCs, which would be able to bargain from a position of strength. While almost all LDCs suffer from oppressive conditionalities attached to structural adjustment and stabilisation programmes and various GATT/WTO agreements, no single country alone can take on the economic might of the OECD, or even of MNCs.

A third use of SAFTA would be in defusing the political and military tension in the area, and, thus, in reducing expenditure on armaments. We will have more to say on this in another Section below :

4. Indo-Bangladesh Relations

Indo-Bangladesh economic relationship had never been smooth in the past. Until 1971, the year of its liberation, the government of Pakistan actively discouraged a close relationship between West Bengal in India and East Pakistan. During this period (from 1947 to 1971) economic complimentarities were ignored and efforts were made to make East Pakistan independent of West Bengal's economic influence. Chittagong emerged as a major port, while modern jute factories were established to process raw jute.

Though the Indian army played an important role in Bangladesh's liberation in 1971, the honeymoon period did not last beyond a year or two. A part of the explanation lies in the fear, typical of small neighbours, of being swamped by a bigger economy and losing economic independence. Though a Joint Economic Commission was set up in 1972, soon afterwards it went into hibernation. A new version of that Joint Economic Commission was floated in 1982, but it only met thrice and hardly resolved any outstanding issue. If that was the official position, contacts among businessmen were also limited; whatever the reason, the West-oriented Indian private sector did not take much notice of economic possibilities that existed in their backyard.

Even in 1982-83, Indian official exports to Bangladesh amounted to a meagre Rs. 325 million, and imports to a pathetic Rs. 39 million. Though trade increased in the nineties, even in 1993-94 the corresponding figures were Rs. 13497 million and

Rs. 561 million, respectively (Dubey, pp. 29-33). While Indian export items were quite large in number, Bangladesh export items were subject to periodic changes. While Newsprint was a major export item from Bangladesh until the early nineties' economic reform in India, fertilisers now account for about half of Bangladesh exports to India.

Economic Co-operation Beginning after 1996

New opportunities for trade talks began only after 1996, when elections brought new governments in both India and Bangladesh. In the case of India, in contrast with the hegemonic attitude of the late 1980s, when India had quarrelled with practically every neighbour, the new government enunciated a new foreign policy, with good neighbourly relations as its cornerstone. In the case of Bangladesh, the new government under Sheikh Hashina discarded anti-India public rhetoric and sought better relations with India. The main stumbling block was the issue of sharing Ganga water. But, once a treaty was signed on this issue towards the end of 1996 and Prime Ministers of both countries undertook goodwill visits to the other, political conditions were created for discussion on possibilities for widening areas of economic cooperation.

Trade Pattern and Imbalances

Whatever the political relationship, the very fact that they are neighbours has encouraged the flow of trade, both legal and illegal, in a wide variety of items . Smuggling flourishes on both sides of the border and provides livelihood to many, while also criminalising the social life. The items exchanged continually change, depending on a number of factors. Until the early nineties, India supplied Bangladesh with rice, sugar, salt, onion, cows and several other consumer goods, while Bangladesh supplied electronic goods brought from the West that were not legally available in India because of import restrictions. Taking both legal and illegal trade into account, the transactions between the two countries were more or less in balance. According to one estimate, legal trade accounts for something like $ 500 million, while illegal trade accounts for twice or thrice that figure, at $1 to $1.5 billion (Wadhva, 1995, p. 52).

However, with the liberalisation of the Indian economy in 1991 and the relaxation of import control and MNC operation, many of the electronic goods earlier procured from Bangladesh have now become legally available within India. This change has brought about a severe imbalance in cross border trade between the two countries. In 1995-96, Indian official exports to Bangladesh amounted to Rs. 3,470 crores, while its official imports from Bangladesh was only Rs. 280 crores (Government of India, 1997, p. 1). Most probably, unofficial trade is equally unbalanced. Bangladesh is now asking for free access of its goods to the Indian market, on par with Nepal, Bhutan and Maldives, under South Asian Preferential Tariff Agreement (SAPTA) provisions for special tariff concessions to its LDC members (Centre for Policy Research, 1995, p. 12).

Another reason for the above imbalance is the faster rate of liberalisation in Bangladesh, while duties on the Indian side are still relatively higher. Earlier some preferential treatment was given to Bangladesh exports, such as hilsa fish or jamdani saree, under SAPTA. Over the past one year during 1996-97, following mutual visits by the Prime Ministers of the two countries, trade opportunities have expanded, quantitative restrictions removed and tariffs have been reduced, in the case of 202 items from Bangladesh, from the beginning of 1997. A serious effort is now being made to explore further trade opportunities between the two countries, including arrangements for transit and common planning for irrigation, power and transport facilities, along with Nepal and Bhutan.

Joint ventures, for example, in cement, garments, fertiliser and sponge iron industries, to boost the export capability of Bangladesh, are also on the agenda (Centre for Policy Research, ibid., p. 3). Success in such ventures needs to be supported by 'buy-back' arrangements on the part of India. Attempts in the past have not succeeded largely because of the inability or unwillingness of the Indian partners to finance the project entirely and to find a market for its products in India. In the case of a proposed sponge iron plant under joint venture, negotiation has continued for 15 years. Recent attempts have been somewhat more successful and joint ventures being discussed cover a wide range of activities such as composite textile mills, pharmaceuticals, cement mini steel plants, chemicals, machine tools, fish processing, leather goods and assembly plants for automobiles (Dubey, pp. 37-38).

Infrastructure Development

In recent months, a great deal of emphasis has been placed on infrastructure development, in terms of approach roads, truck terminals, railway links, warehouses and other facilities, first in the border trading points and then in other areas, for facilitating trade. A part of the problem lies in the illegality of most trading activities. Trucks queuing up on both sides is a familiar sight, though not formally recognised. Even simple thing such as a Motor Vehicles Agreement, to permit vehicles from one side to move to the other, does not exist. If the ongoing discussion relating to this on this agreement bears fruit, it would be possible for the same truck to carry goods across the border. The restoration of the pre-Independence rail link would also help this process of economic integration. At present, two broad-gauge and three meter-gauge railway lines connect the two countries, but the engines are changed when the train crosses the border. The rail link is absent on the Tripura side. The Inland Water Trade and Transit agreement, since 1972, renewed after every two years, permits the movement of barges along four demarcated water routes. On the Bangladesh side, the development of the Chittagong port and the Mongla port of Khulna should receive high priority.

The following are some of other possibilities which, only now, both countries have begun to give some thought :

Development of Gas Reserves

Both the Titas gas reserve of Bangladesh and some of the gas reserves of Assam remain underutlised and a considerable part of the production is flared, in the absence of important areas of consumption in the vicinity. Possibilities of using such gas for industrial activities in the adjacent areas of the neighbouring country, which would benefit both, have not been explored. At one stage, there were some discussions about the possibility of supplying gas, by way of a pipeline, to the Calcutta area, but the proposal was shelved soon after because of political opposition. One argument against this proposal on the Bangladesh side is that the available reserve is not very large and that it would be better to use it for urea production in Bangladesh and then to export it to India in that form, on the basis of a long term agreement.

Irrigation and Power

A major hurdle has been crossed with the signing of the treaty on the sharing of Ganga water in 1996. The treaty has withstood the lean months of 1997, and has led to propositions of further widening the opportunities of regional water planning. The basins of two of the mightiest rivers of the world — Ganga and Brahmaputra — carry more water than probably any other geographical area in the world except the Amazon and Congo basins. Yet most of the water is allowed to flow into Bay of Bengal and its potential as a major input in agriculture and for power generation remains largely unutilised. In the past, the main constraint facing a proposal for comprehensive planning covering India, Nepal and Bangladesh was political. Bangladesh was apprehensive of a plan that could encourage its economic dependency on India, while India was unwilling to have a tripartite discussion, fearing that the other two parties could conspire against it.

Although a shortsighted attitude as mentioned above has been discarded now, yet one major objection from the Bangladesh side to the proposal for linking Brahmaputra to Ganga-Padma system, to avoid flooding and drought, is the possible eviction of millions to make room for feeder canals. However, if various hurdles to such massive and comprehensive plans can be removed, including environmental concerns and the obstacle of finding the massive capital needed for this purpose, a major share of the demand for irrigation water and power can be met in the entire region. In fact, for Nepal and Bhutan, power can emerge as a major export item that can be effectively transported, by way of interlocking national grids, to Bangladesh and India. The vast areas of Northeast India also remain as a major, equally underutilised, source of irrigation water and power. Using waterways as a cheap, environment-friendly means of transport is another major item on the current agenda.

Border Trade

The 1972 agreement between the two countries allowed for border trade within a 16 kilometre belt for exchanging specific commodities. However, this could not be implemented due to opposition expressed from Bangladesh, on the grounds that adequate checks did not exist and smugglers were taking over. Despite this, smuggling across the border is a fact of life in the frontiers, which distorts economic priorities and vitiates social life. On the other hand, given the nature of the border, and the cultural closeness of the people living on both sides of the border, the monitoring of movement of goods and services has proved to be virtually impossible. During harvesting time in India, the border guards on both sides cooperate, of course, informally and illegally and in exchange of a fee, to allow the daily movement of labourers across the border. Information flows freely, and when a cultural troupe performs music or opera on one side of the border, it is not uncommon for those from the other side to join too. Perhaps, the only option that is feasible and makes sense, is to legalise such trade and make cross border movement of goods, services and also of people free, a point to which we will return later.

Garment and Leather

There are also areas of competition. Bangladesh would be keen to export finished leather goods and cotton garments to India, and, according to one estimate it is possible to raise such exports to a level of $1 billion per year (Centre for Policy

Research, *op. cit.*, p. 4). But such a policy will inevitably lead to serious opposition from Indian domestic garment and shoe industries, which now enjoy some measure of protection from foreign competition, in terms of quantitative barriers.

Garment industry has now emerged as the major industry of Bangladesh, and as the leading item in terms of export earnings after remittances. This industry started with South Korean capital, which in turn were mainly interested in evading MFA quota restrictions for South Korean textile goods. At present, Indian involvement is also quite large as many of the inputs — yarns, fabrics and made ups — are procured from India and thus Indian capital plays an important role as well. This is an important area for joint ventures, with the participation of both Indian and Bangladeshi capital, and for meticulous planning in terms of trade offensive after MFA comes to an end.

Transit Facilities

While efforts are being made to identify goods that can be traded at mutual advantage, such tasks would be easier to accomplish once the transit facilities are expanded in a variety of ways. Rail and road traffic to Northeast Indian states through Bangladesh is one such option that would integrate markets in the region. Chittagong port, rather than Calcutta port, can act as the natural port of Northeast India, thus drastically reducing transport costs of goods produced in the Northeast. Trade between Haldia and other eastern Indian ports and Chittagong, across Bay of Bengal, is another major possibility that remains unexplored.

Such realignment of trade structure in the Northeast would also help mineral (particularly limestone) development in Meghalaya whose mining areas are more accessible from the Bangladesh side. The limestone can then be used for cement production in the nearby areas of Bangladesh. Growing trade between the two countries would bring about a new division of labour between sub-regions in this very large region that would benefit all the participants.

Similar transit facilities, across the Indian territory, for trade between Bangladesh on one hand, and Bhutan and Nepal on the other, had been resisted earlier by myopic Indian diplomats, but things have begun to change now.

Co-operation in Jute

Bangladesh and India being two major jute producing countries of the world, it is possible for them to work out a joint strategy that would help to sustain the demand for jute in the world market, despite the onslaught of paper and polythene bags. Research for diversification of jute-based products and their projection in various markets can be a major task for both the countries.

Political Constraints

Let us now examine some of the major political constraints that inhibit growth. Here we are mainly dealing with those that arise in the context of India-Bangladesh relationship, but their main lessons apply to the entire subcontinent.

Sharing of Ganga Water

This was the main stumbling block in normalising relations between the two countries. Near the Bihar-West Bengal border, Ganga has been divided into two main channels — Padma (mainly flowing through Bangladesh) and Bhagirathi (through India-West Bengal). Since the partition of the country in 1947, two major developments have taken place. First, the peasants of both Bangladesh and India have come to value water for irrigating a second crop. The former has created a large demand for irrigation water in Bangladesh, while a more intensive utilisation of Ganga water in the upper reaches has drastically reduced the amount of water available at the point of bifurcation of the river at Rajmahal.

Secondly, the construction of the Farakka barrage has diverted part of the water towards Calcutta, in order to save its port from silting and to reduce salinity in the drinking water available in Calcutta. As a consequence, the peasants of Bangladesh felt that they were being denied their legitimate share of water from a common river source. Some of the parties, who cultivate anti-Indian feelings for securing political support and votes, also made use of this issue to block any progress in talks — on trade, transit and other issues of mutual interest.

Thus, when the governments changed in both countries in 1996, the first thing the new governments had to do was to find a solution to this highly sensitive issue — to find water for the peasant in Bangladesh while not causing any serious damage to the Calcutta port.

In the negotiations, led by Inder Gujral, the then Foreign Minister of India who latter became the Prime Minister, the Chief Minister of West Bengal, Jyoti Basu, was also involved. The experts found that the problem was serious only during the lean period of 5 to 8 weeks, while during the rest of the year, enough water flowed to satisfy the needs of both. A formula for sharing water, alternating the proportions every two weeks, was worked out for this period, which was then formalised in a new treaty.

While the opposition in Bangladesh was far from satisfaction, the people were satisfied. In India too, sections of Congress and BJP, two major parties in the country, described the treaty as a sell out, but the popular response was positive. Though the weather conditions during the lean weeks in 1997 were worse than these were reported to be in the past two decades, whatever water was available was shared according to the formula, as supervised by a joint commission. Success on this highly sensitive issue has opened the door for wider economic and political co-operation.

Boundary Demarcation and Enclaves

Many of the problems created by the partition of the country in 1947 have remained unresolved. The boundary of the two countries was drawn by Lord Radcliffe, who never visited Bengal. Sitting in his comfortable bungalow in Delhi, he consulted census data and ordnance survey maps and drew a line with his pencil through these. The lines divided villages and even family houses and left many enclaves on both sides, which are still surrounded by the territory of the other country. Further the demarcation of the boundary was not completed in certain areas. Exchange of enclaves was a possible solution, but the political will was missing. On each issue there is a tendency among some parties to whip up popular sentiment and to resist any transfer. Even the data on the list of enclaves and the disputed boundaries are missing.

Separatist Movements

A major area of conflict relates to the use of Bangladesh territory as a sanctuary by divisive and separatist movements — mainly among Nagas and tribal groups of Tripura — where they receive training, from where they launch offensives and to where they retreat after such an offensive. To counter this, the Indian government also patronised one or two dissident groups in Bangladesh. With the improvement in the bilateral political environment, the militant groups in Northeast India are no longer finding Bangladesh as a safe sanctuary and some of them have transferred their bases to Thailand and Bhutan.

Illegal Migration

Another sensitive issue is migration of Bangladeshis across the border. The Bharatiya Janata Party (BJP), a righwing Hindu chauvinist party, takes the view that such migration is changing the religious mix of the population in West Bengal and other states to the disadvantage of the Hindu majority. Data from the Home Department does not substantiate such a claim. It is seen that the majority of those arrested for illegally crossing the border are muslims, while the majority of those, coming on visa but then overstaying and disappearing, are Hindus. Whether the former cancels out the latter, or alters the religious mix can not be established.

It is, however, indisputable that migration does take place, whether legal or not, whether Hindus or Muslims, and this is confirmed by a much higher than average rate of growth in the population in the border areas. More important, perhaps, is the regular participation of the workforce from Bangladesh in the field during harvesting time, who come illegally but return after work.

Free and Unrestricted Flow

One possible approach for coming to grips with the problems of insurgency and illegal migration of work force is to tighten border patrol, erect fences and monitor movements of people from the sky. This is highly expensive and may not work when people on both sides are not culturally distinct and are not hostile to each other. The most obvious alternative is to allow free movement of goods, services, animals and people across the border within the framework of a properly structured South Asian Common market. Legalisation of those movements would immediately eliminate smuggling and other criminal activities. The vast expansion of trade that would follow would benefit both countries and might even reduce the flow of those goods and services that are not desirable.

The countries of South Asia need to learn one important lesson from the experience with common market in Europe. Once Italy was one of the poorest countries of Europe, whose labourers were employed in low wage activities in Germany and other European countries. But, presently it is enjoying a level of living that is higher than that of UK, thanks to its active participation in common market. If the experience in Italy is of any guide, flow of migrants from Bangladesh will very likely reduce, as its domestic economy becomes stronger. From this point of view too, India has a vested interest in the economic well being of Bangladesh, through joint participation in a common market.

Implications for Defence and Development

Such a common market would also have major implications for defence expenditure and development. Defence is a sacred cow in all the major countries in South Asia and no opposition would dare to question defence expenditure. Skirmishes on the border help to strengthen the ruling parties and classes as the other differences get sunk and popular attention is diverted from the fundamental issues of food, employment, housing, inequality and social repression. Countries compete in an unholy arms race — with tanks, aircrafts, and missiles and to develop nuclear capability — which only benefits the world armament industry located in the rich countries and the corrupt domestic politicians who stash away their kickbacks of defence contracts in number of accounts in Switzerland. High defence expenditure, which accounts for a major share of GDP, diverts resources away from sectors such as health, education or food, which are deprived of their legitimate share, and keep the people in abject poverty. In contrast, an economically integrated South Asia, with mutually dependent countries, would take away the rationale for aggressive posturing and armament race, thus helping to devote more resources to development.

Implications for National Integration

No less important would be its implications for national integration, in India, Pakistan and Sri Lanka in particular. The growing economic ties would reduce the use of the territory of a hostile neighbour as sanctuary for divisive and separatist forces, while economic development of backward areas would deflate the rationale for such separatist activities. In India's case, improvements in transit facilities would bring the Northeast and its people nearer the heartland and would, therefore, facilitate economic, cultural and political interactions.

5. Conclusions

The main conclusions are as follows :

(a) that world trade is far from free and competitive, and, within the framework laid down by WTO, there is little chance for economic development of the LDCs without their coming together as a regional block and collectively demanding a renegotiation of the world trade structure.

(b) that SAFTA can take advantage of the loophole in GATT and WTO agreements that permits discriminatory tariff within a regional economic block, and can follow the examples of EEC, NAFTA and other regional blocks to boost the trade of its members.

(c) that immense possibilities exist for expansion of trade within South Asia, which would also have important positive national and international, political, social and economic implications.

REFERENCES

Avery, William P. (ed.), *World Agriculture and the GATT*, Lynne Rienner Publishers, Boulder and London, 1993.

Bhagwati, Jagdish, *Political Economy and International Economics*, edited by Douglas A Irwin, MIT Press, Cambridge, Mass, 1991.

Centre for Policy Research, New Delhi and Centre for Policy Dialogue, Dhaka, Indo-Bangladesh Dialogue, *Economic and Trade Cooperation*, 1995.

Cohn, Theodore H., *The changing role of the United States in the global agricultural trade regime.*, Chapter 2, pp. 17-38, in Avery (ed.).

Deardorff, Alan V (1), *Economic Perspectives on Antidumping Law,* pp. 135-154, Chapter 6, in Stern (ed.).

Deardorff, Alan V (2), *Should patents be extended to all developing countries?*, pp. 435-448, Chapter 15, in Stern (ed.).

Development Committee, *The Uruguay Round : A Preliminary Assessment,* Washington, 48th Meeting, Report No 33, 1994, pp. 71-96.

Dubey, Muchkund, *Indo-Bangladesh Economic Relations*, in Centre for Policy Research, *et al.,* pp. 29-49.

ECALC (UN Economic Commission for Latin America and the Caribbean), *Policies to Improve Linkages with the Global Economy*, Santiago , Chile, 1994.

Government of India, *Indo-Bangladeshi Trade*, New Delhi, 1997 (unpublished note).

Hoekman, Bernard M., *Trade Offs, Coalitions, and National Interests* : Developing Country Options in MTN, pp. 473-501, Chapter 17, in Stern (ed.).

Hopkins, Raymond F., *Developing Countries in the Uruguay Round : Bargaining Under Uncertainty and Inequality*, Ch. 7, pp. 143-63, in Avery (ed.).

Jackson , John H., *Safeguards and Adjustment Policies,* pp. 183-232, Chapter 8, in Stern (ed.).

Krueger, Anne O., 1990, *Perspectives on Trade and Development*, Harvester Wheatsheaf, New York, 1990.

Lele, Jayant and Kwasi Ofori-Yeboah (eds.), *Unravelling the Asian Miracle : Explorations in Development Strategies, Geopolitics and Regionalism*, Dartmouth, Aldershot, 1996.

Lesser, William H., *Equitable Patent Protection In the Developing World — issues and approaches*, Eubios Ethics Institute, Christchurch (NZ) & Tsukuba (Japan), 1991.

Low, Patrick, *Trading Free — the GATT and the US trade policy,* A twentieth Century fund book, New York, 1995.

OECD, *Technology and The Economy — the key relationships*, The technology/ Economy Programme, Paris, 1992.

Okuda, Kazuhiko, *Japan's Perception of NAFTA*, pp. 171-183, in Lele and Ofori-Yeboah (eds.).

Plant, Roger, Labour Standards and Structural Adjustment, ILO, Geneva, 1994.

Schott, Jeffrey J., *The Global Trade Negotiations : What Can Be Achieved*?, Institute of International Economics, Washington DC, 1990.

Stern, Robert M. (ed.), *The Multilateral Trading System : Analysis and Options for change*, Harvester — Wheatsheaf, New York, 1993.

Wadhva, Charan, *Bangladeshi and Indian Perspectives and Consensus*, in Centre for Policy Research, *et. al.*, pp. 50-72.

Watkins, Kevin, *Fixing the Rules, North South Issues in International Trade and GATT Uruguay Round*, Catholic Institute for International Relations, London, 1992.

PART II

ECONOMIC LIBERALISATION AND INSTITUTIONAL REFORMS : COUNTRY STUDIES

4

Institutional Development for Political and Economic Stability in Bangladesh*

AKHTAR HOSSAIN

Bangladesh's Economy Poised to Take-Off

The Bangladesh economy is in transition. After remaining largely stagnant over decades, this economy has been growing moderately at a rate of about 4.5 per cent per annum since the mid-1970s. Although such an economic growth rate is respectable from an historical viewpoint, it is not high enough to make a rapid transformation of the poverty-ridden society, especially when its population of more than 120 million has been growing at a

*This is a revised and shortened version of a paper presented at the Conference on Bangladesh : Governance and Economic Development at the Australian Centre for South Asian Studies in Melbourne during 22-23 March 1997. It draws some materials from Hossain (1996), Chowdhury and Hossain (1996), and Hossain and Rashid (1996).

rate of about 2 per cent per annum[1]. In fact, despite significant economic and social progress since Independence (Hossain, 1996; Hossain and Rashid, 1996), the Bangladesh society remains traditional at the core (Kochanek, 1993; Novak, 1993).

Starting with central planning for economic development under the so-called 'socialist paradigm' during the early years of Independence (1972-1975) (Islam, 1977), Bangladesh has been moving toward a market-oriented approach to economic growth and development. This has, however, been a slow and tortuous process. The successive political regimes since independence, despite having different colours, have followed macro-economic policies which can be roughly characterised as 'macro-economic populism and/or macroeconomic elitism'.[2] Both are featured by large government budget deficits financed primarily from the Central Bank (Bangladesh Bank), the nationalised commercial banks, and foreign aid and loans, bailing out of sick industries (public enterprises) in the name of social responsibility of protecting jobs, providing subsidised bank loans to dubious entrepreneurs, and granting real wage claims of workers in excess of productivity gains. All these have created a culture of complacency among both the business managers and the policy-makers and are the perfect recipes for self-propagating dynamics of inflation, low economic growth, and external imbalance. For an apparently 'resource-poor' country like Bangladesh, this simply means the perpetuation of massive poverty, economic and social inequality, and political instability.

---

1. See Appendix Table 1 for a summary of macro-economic performance indicators for the period 1973-1996.
2. The concept of macro-economic populism has been popularised by Dornbusch and Edwards (1990) in the context of Latin America. This concept can be used for Bangladesh in a broad sense to emphasise the economic and political costs of expansionary monetary and fiscal policies. The concept of macro-economic elitism refers to a phenomenon in which the military-civilian governments having seized power through undemocratic means attempt to legitimise it by buying support of political elites from both the left and right through an all-compassing state-patronage system that breeds macro-economic indiscipline and promotes rent-seeking activity.

Changes are afoot. Facing major macroeconomic imbalances throughout the 1970s and 1980s, Bangladesh has received structural-adjustment loans under conditionality from both the IMF and the World Bank. As part of market-oriented development strategy, the structural adjustment programs have somewhat succeeded in both reducing inflation and trade deficits since the late 1980s and sustaining economic growth at the rate of about 4 per cent per annum. These macro-economic developments have been accompanied by some structural change in the economy, led by enhanced resource mobilisation, buoyant non-traditional exports supported by high growth of ready-to-wear garments, and a near self-sufficiency in food production (Hossain, 1996; Hossain and Chowdhury, 1996).

All these have led many commentators to suggest that the Bangladesh economy is poised to move to a growth path of around 7 to 9 per cent per annum (World Bank, 1994; ADB, 1994). Until now, this has not happened for at least two main reasons. First, a slow pace of structural reforms in key areas, such as public administration, education system and both labour and financial markets, and secondly, persistent political instability.

Bangladesh : State of Development

To begin with, Bangladesh appears to suffer from a developmental disadvantage; that is, except for natural gas and the potential for oil, it does not have other exploitable natural resources. However, it is debatable whether the absence of natural resources is a hindrance to economic development. The recent development literature suggests that the availability of natural resources does not necessarily give an advantage to a developing country in its pursuit of economic development. In contrary, the lack of natural resources may be a blessing in disguise as it may induce a country to pursue such a development strategy which is compatible with its comparative advantage in the production and exporting of, say, labour-intensive manufacturing products. Some East and South East Asian countries can be cited as case examples. Bangladesh has an easily trainable and low cost labour force, which can be productively employed for the production of standardised manufacturing products for exports.

Along with other factors, what has prevented this country from translating its poverty into prosperity is the absence of pro-growth economic policies and institutions/organisations (economic and political). For example, it does not have a strong bureaucracy or economic ministry[3] that can design and implement the kind of economic policies that promote saving, investment and economic growth. Both the political and labour organisations are anti-growth to say the least. In short, in the absence of a 'visionary, competent political leadership', there is no clear economic direction of the country.

Most macro-economic indicators also do not predict a bright economic future for the country. The rates of saving and investment remain relatively low and most investments are inefficient. The government's efforts for mobilisation of domestic resources have been limited and the country remains heavily dependent on foreign aid and workers' remittances as investable funds. Even though there has been considerable increase in food production since Independence, the growth rate of agricultural productivity is negligible. The industrial labour force is inefficient and over-politicised and hence there is chronic industrial unrest. The financial system is underdeveloped, inefficient, and in distress. The higher education system is in a moribund state. According to Novak (1993), Bangladesh's universities are a political training ground and are a national disgrace. The literacy indicators also do not show much improvement in human resource development. The adult literacy rate is less than 40 per cent, for example. Whatever human capital exists remains underutilised or is directed towards unproductive rent-seeking activities. Many skilled

3. In Bangladesh, the Ministry of Finance is the powerful organ of the administration in the sense of its command over development resources. However, it does not have much responsibility for designing and implementing development policies, which are assigned to the Planning Commission that enjoys a lowly status in the administrative hierarchy. One result of it is that the government can bypass the recommendations of the Planning Commission for reasons of political expediency.

professionals are leaving the country to avail themselves of overseas employment opportunities. Corruption has spread in every sphere of life. Along with it, time-adjusted ethical and moral standards in the society are in a decline The public administration system is in decay and most government officials have become thoroughly corrupt. In short, the country is becoming ungovernable (Sobhan, 1993). All these suggest that although initial endowments/conditions in Bangladesh are favourable to economic growth, most of its sociopolitical and economic institutions/ organisations remain anti-growth.

The next Section will review the political developments in Bangladesh since its Independence and argue for institutional development for political stability.

Dynamics of Bangladesh's Politics

One litmus test of institutionalisation of democratic order is the ability of the incumbent government to transfer power to its successor in accordance with constitutional provisions. Such a transfer of power is yet to take place in Bangladesh. Both the elections of 1991 and 1996 have taken place under unusual circumstances. The 1991 elections were held after the overthrow of the Ershad government through an urban-based, middle class uprising, while the 1996 elections were held after more than two years of political chaos. Although the elections of 1991 under a non-party care-taker government was acceptable to both the Awami League and the BNP as both were then in opposition but could not trust the Election Commission under any political party in power, the idea of overseeing the June 1996 elections by a non-party caretaker government was accepted by the then ruling BNP only under political coercion of both the opposition political parties and their newly found allies, the civil bureaucracy.[4] So

4. Although the bureaucracy's withdrawal of support from the BNP government was apparently to force it to resolve the political stalemate, its switching of support to the opposition had the aim of preserving entrenched power in the forthcoming government. Note that the bureaucracy did the same thing during the last stage of the Ershad regime (Ahmed 1995).

the transfer of the state power from the ruling party to its successor on both occasions did not take place in a congenial atmosphere.

The BNP appears to have accepted the transfer of power to its arch rival after the 1996 election, but it was not unqualified and without reservation (Kamaluddin, 1996). There is yet to be a test for the proposed modus operandi (elections under a non-party caretaker government) of future Parliamentary elections in the country. The revealed behaviour of both the Awami League and the BNP suggests that they remain in confrontational mode.

Therefore, what kind of political strategy will the BNP adopt to remove the Awami League from power remains a matter of speculation. In fact, the BNP's 'continuing boycott of the Parliament' has created uncertainty in regard to its future behaviour and raises an obvious question : Is the taking over the reigns of state power by the Awami League the beginning of an end of political instability or is it the beginning of the replay of political drama that was staged by the then opposition political parties to overthrow the Khaleda government?

Besides these two political parties, there is a third contender of state power — the military. Although it cannot claim political power as per Constitution, it has some 'legitimate claim' to be a defender of the country in any event of internal chaos or external invasion/aggression. The past experiences of both Pakistan and Bangladesh suggest that once a military government is able to impose its rule on any excuse, it gets whatever recognition it may need from home and abroad without much difficulties. Although the legitimacy of such a military rule remains shaky, the personality of the 'strong-man' in question can make a lot of difference to the success or failure of such a regime. For example, in the personality-based politics in Bangladesh, while Zia has created a political legacy as opposed to that of Sheikh Mujib, Ershad has created a 'political nuisance' and is counting his days in politics. (Note that both Zia and Ershad were at the helm of power as military rulers and the latter ruled the country for 9 years compared with 5 years by the former.)

The theme of this section is that although there has been systematic political polarisation in this country since the late 1970s. it may not necessarily lead to political stability unless there are cooperation between the Awami League and the BNP out of mutual interests. Sustained high economic growth is also crucial to break the feudal patron-client political culture that leads to political instability.

Political Polarisation

There appears to be a political consensus that Bangladesh should have a democratic political system. The question is how to create a strong multi-party parliamentary democracy. This country has a large number of political parties, four of them dominate the national politics. They are the Awami League, the BNP, the Jatiya Party and the Jamaat-e-Islami.[5] The key issue is whether a multi-party parliamentary system is inherently unstable. Here follows an elaboration of a proposition : that, given that there has been systematic political polarisation around two major political parties — the Awami League and the BNP, they can establish a stable two-party political system provided that they cooperate with each other with respect to their political conduct both inside and outside the Parliament.

Bangladesh's politics remains unstable, but it is not unpredictable. The Parliamentary election results since 1970, especially for 1991 and 1996 (Appendix, Table 2), reveal that there has been a tendency for convergence of the Awami League and the BNP in terms of policies and ideologies.[6] It appears that

---

5. This is not unexpected because, as Duverger (1955) suggests, if free and fair elections are held at regular intervals, the natural tendency of politics is to exhibit dual characteristics.

6. The Jamaat-e-Islami has lost the most from the 1996 election. The Jatiya Party is on notice and has already divided into two factions. If elections are held on a regular basis and power is transferred in accordance with constitutional provisions, the Jatiya Party's support is likely to be diminished to insignificant size. The possibility of a merger between the BNP and the Jatiya Party at some stage in the future cannot also be eliminated (Baxter and Rahman, 1991). How quickly this may happen would depend on the rapidity at which the BNP gains its credibility and

these parties have moved toward each other since the overthrow of the Ershad government in 1990. Facing an intense competition from each other, they have shown a tendency to move toward the centre of political spectrum. An implication of it is that, if these parties cooperate with each other, they can dominate the national politics and their locational stability at the centre could reduce the danger of military intervention. Over time, if free and fair elections are held on a regular interval, these parties are likely to converge in policies and ideologies. Second, given the predominant position of these parties, the ideologically-oriented smaller parties of the left and right will not be in a position to muster enough votes to generate political instability, which is often predicted in coalition governments under multi-party systems with a distinct polymodal distribution of voters (Downs, 1957).

While these are positive developments, there are built-in constraints to political development in Bangladesh along democratic lines. Given the underdeveloped nature of economic structure, Bangladesh's politics has feudal patron-client elements. The present political instability is essentially the outcome of an autocratic political culture, nurtured by hereditary leaders and their sycophants.

Underdevelopment and Political Feudalism

Democracy is incompatible with any brand of political fanaticism. Bangladesh society is not fanatical in religious sense. However, while political competition is the building block of

---

Ershad loses his control over the party. With the collapse of communism in the former Soviet Union and Eastern Europe and, having long been seen as close allies of the Awami League on most political issues, the pro-Soviet communist parties have lost their separate identity, credibility, and political support. Likewise, the establishment of close relationship between US and China and the spread of Indian hegemonism have led the pro-Beijing political parties to practically converse with the BNP and the Jatiya Party. (See Maniruzzaman (1980) for a detailed discussion on factionalism and disintegration of left-leaning parties in Bangladesh.) Given the present state of Bangladesh's politics, it appears that the left-wing parties are unlikely to gain much support in the near future to force their inclusion in any coalition government led by the Awami League or the BNP because the electoral structure is based on plurality rather than proportional.

democracy, political rivalries in this country have fanatical elements that undermine the essence of democracy. As Novak (1993 : 50) writes :

> To a Bangladeshi, politics is what alcohol or sports are to most of the rest of the world... Bangladesh's political rivalries are as fierce as those Scottish clans; the attendant violence reaches Mafia levels, and the depth of passion matches that of religious faith. ... Bangladeshis do not disagree with one another; they hate.

Despite some sociocultural and political transformation, Bangladesh's society remains traditional at the core. Although poverty does not seem to be the major cause of political instability, the root cause of it can be traced to the patron-client elements in an underdeveloped society. As Kochanek (1993 : 332-333) writes :

> Traditional Bangladeshi society is dominated by a network of patron-client relationships. This patron-client system is based on a hierarchically structured, complex maze of mutual obligations and personal ties. The very strength of this vertically structured patron-client network inhibits the development of larger corporate entities. The attitudes and values of patron-client behavior extend beyond the village to all areas of urban society and politics. The personal ties and mutual obligations of the patron-client system contribute to the highly personalized, factionalized character of patrimonial politics in Bangladesh. They are reinforced by a strong sense of individualism, low levels of trust, and a lack of commitment to abstract objectives and ideology.

Political fanaticism is essentially a reflection of feudal character of a traditional society where most people are uneducated, socially backward and politically ill-informed and possess unsophisticated character traits, including feudal or tribal rivalry. The shifting political support of the people from one party/leader to another also have cultural roots. As Kochanek, Novak and others have indicated, the contemporary Bangladesh's politics has a resonance of rural feudalism in its character, intensity and ferocity. Jahan (1980) has shown that most political leaders in Bangladesh are drawn from middle class with rural or semi-urban social background. They behave as if they are feudal landlords/patrons and demand blind-loyalty from their tenants/ clients in exchange for protection and/or patronage. Jealousy, suspicion and mistrust are other hallmarks of poverty and they distort all social, economic and political interaction (Novak, 1993).

From this perspective, the national politics has all the elements of rural power, culture and political structure. This raises a fundamental question whether a stable democratic political system could be developed in an underdeveloped society. Any ritualistic elections cannot establish a true form of democracy. Given that loyalty is absolute in a feudal society, even competitive elections fought on trivial issues, which mobilises and polarises the masses vertically along the feudal lines, merely generate passion as political leaders and their supporters carry with them some of their raw feudal character traits. The division of political support along feudal lines has a manifestation : that most people do not care much about the niceties of democracy, unless it is interpreted in such a way that it affects them economically and socially. Political elites having realising it use different symbols at different times for political mobilisation. The masses respond to the calls of a charismatic leader even if they behave in a contradictory fashion when looked at from an historical perspective. Past events show that political wind in Bangladesh changes rapidly and with it, the mass-support shifts from democracy to autocracy, left to the right, and/or one personality to the other. Such an unstable state of politics is a reflection of underdeveloped or unsettled political beliefs of the masses; they can be twisted through misinformation and outright distortion or may be carried away with any political bandwagon.

If democracy does not thrive in a feudal society, what is the alternative? Is an authoritarian rule inevitable? Kochanek (1993) argues that as Bangladesh's politics has been evolved through mass mobilisation over the past few decades, although authoritarianism remains the core of its politics, any absolute authoritarian rule is not tenable.

If democracy does not have deep roots and absolute authoritarianism is not tenable, then what does the present political system represent? It is neither a democracy nor an autocracy but a hotch-potch system combining the worst elements of the two. Will high economic growth make any difference to political culture? This point is taken up here.

Economic Growth and Political Development

The common presumption is that the growth of economy along the capitalistic lines will promote democracy in the Third World, but there is no certainty in it (Lisbet, 1959; Moore, 1966). It is not mere rise in per capita income rather changes in class and social structure caused by industrialisation and urbanisation which are most consequential for democracy (Huber, *et al.*, 1993). This leads to a logical conclusion that, unless there is such economic development which brings changes in the social and class structure, Bangladesh's politics will remain unstable because the rules of national politics could remain akin to feudal norms and rules that regulate the rural society, politics and economics. This implies that elections and competitive politics do not necessarily establish a democratic system as any ritualistic democratic political events may not remove deep-rooted anti-democratic social and cultural traits ingrained in the minds of political participants in any traditional society. From this perspective, the Bangladesh society is not different. As indicated earlier, one should not overestimate the deepness of democratic roots in Bangladesh's culture and society. The ideal of democracy remains essentially an urban, educated middle-class import from the West. The ordinary people who live at the margin of society are familiar with traditional vices and virtues and are somewhat politically inert. They often exhibit extreme reaction to actual or perceived unfavourable economic and political events. Given that loyalty is absolute in any feudal society, competitive politics, which mobilises and polarises the masses vertically along feudal lines, can generate passion as political leaders and their supporters carry with them some of their raw, feudal character traits.

While economic development does not necessarily lead to the establishment of liberal democracy, one cannot ignore the influences of economic factors on sociopolitical and cultural beliefs and attitudes. The underdeveloped political belief system is expected to change with economic transformation in response to sustained economic growth along the capitalist lines. With economic prosperity, the common people will have access to modern education and political information which could help them in developing their political beliefs. This may give consistency in their political behaviour and weaken their fanatical instincts. In general, the reaction of well-informed masses to political issues is likely to be measured, balanced and less fanatical. Such a behaviour would keep the political temperature well below the boiling point, despite any provocation by, and misinformation of, agitation-mongers.

Economic growth will have another major impact on politics. As political chaos or instability poses a threat to the propertied class, the latter may try to capture political power to maintain political stability and to consolidate economic gains. Although the capitalist class was wary of extending suffrage to workers in the 19th century Europe, the bourgeoisie of advanced capitalist societies of the West now support democratic institutions as the alternatives represent a threat to their material interests (Huber, *et al.*, 1993). This may also happen in Bangladesh. If fact, political power has already started to shift toward the business class (Hossain, 1996). With further economic progress, they will consolidate political power to protect their economic interests.

Despite the positive impact of economic development on political development, one has to keep in mind that political cultures and structures may not alter rapidly in response to economic change. Kohli (1986) points out that authoritarian values and structures, for example, are not readily transformed by the spread of education or of the rise of the middle class. However, even if such changes are incremental, this does not mean that it is unimportant and this goal should not be pursued vigorously. In essence, economic development is a key factor for political development. As Bardhan (1993) points out, if the rate of economic development in a democracy is too slow to meet the ever-widening circle of democratic awareness and raised expectations among the people, the resulting demand overload may short-circuit rudimentary institutions of political mediation, ultimately endangering the survival of democracy.

Institutions and Macro-economic Stability

While the above discussion puts emphasis on development of institutions for political stability, there should be development of economic institutions and organisations to both sustain macro-economic stability and improve policy-making. Sound economic policies do matter for economic growth and development. Such policies should have well-defined goals, such as prosperity, equity, and stability. Stability can be seen as a means of achieving prosperity, although Dornbusch (1993a : 3) points out that 'people psychologically value stability and continuity *per se*'.

In general, good economic policies are the end product of well thought-out policymaking process under well-defined guidelines. This calls for the establishment of an institutional setting which defines the character of economy and forms the foundation of society. In the debate between free market and state planning, the market economy has been in ascendancy since the break up of the former Soviet Union. However, as a free market economy has certain weaknesses, Dornbusch (1993a : 4) argues for what he calls a 'social market economy' in which individual self-interest remains the driving force but market outcomes in terms of individual income and wealth are mitigated by policies that enhance equality. According to him, the following features may broadly define the basic institutional setting for the establishment of a social market economy :

The right to own property is acknowledged by the culture and protected by a well-functioning system.

Competition — both within and across borders — is accepted as the basic rule in markets. Competition is enforced by allowing entry into all and any markets, by vigorously opposing monopolisation, and by opening the economy to world trade. Competition makes the most of resources.

Equity is a distinct social objective and need not emerge from the operation of competitive markets. The government promotes equity through a tax system that strikes a balance between equity and efficiency, and above all, by investing in education and health, which are key determinants of economic advance.

Government action needs to be bound by institutions so that there is less need for individuals to assume a defensive posture against possible governmental action.

Within such an institutional setting, the authorities should follow certain broad guidelines and principles (Harberger, 1984, Dornbusch, 1993b) that define the thrust of economic policies, such that

- avoid large and persistent budget deficits;
- maintain monetary discipline;
- make the tax system simple such that it is easy to administer and is more neutral and less distorting;
- do not overvalue the real exchange rate;
- take advantage of international trade and make it as free as possible;
- make the borderlines between public and private sector activity clear and well-defined;
- make necessary quick adjustments to external and internal shocks and
- create government credibility to make policy effective.

In a modern democratic society, three key institutions — the bureaucracy, the central bank, and the Parliament — are directly or indirectly involved in the process of policymaking. An independent and apolitical judiciary — a creation of Parliament — is another institution which either monitors or complements the actions of the institutions specified earlier. Provided that these institutions jointly and individually perform their proper roles, they can provide a necessary check and balance to policy initiatives of politicians and make them compatible with the basic institutional setting and policy guidelines as suggested earlier.

The conclusion and policy implications are obvious — in the presence of imperfect political climate and market imperfections, there is a need for building institutions that would minimise both market and government failures. The main sources of market failures include monopoly imperfections, externalities, public goods, imperfect/asymmetric information, and transaction costs. In addition, it is often held that the market system does not typically produce a 'fair' distribution of income, implying a biased income distribution in favour of the rich. One can identify at least four sources of government failures — (a) lack of administrative capacity, (b) overzealous government rules and regulations, (c) inefficient political cycles and (d) rent-seeking behaviour.

Most developing countries (including Bangladesh) are not endowed with a large pool of skilled administrators or bureaucrats. In addition, the lack of sufficient training can lead to a limited capacity to interpret and enforce rules and regulations. The situation in Bangladesh was made worse by successive regimes' attempt to corrupt and politicise the bureaucracy. Therefore, the institutional change must start with administrative reform as the creation of a strong administrative capacity is one of the founding blocks of a good state. It is paramount that a meritocratic civil bureaucracy recruited through a highly competitive examination is ensured. This must be boosted with the provision of a high quality training program to enhance the administrative capacity. Administrative rules must be simplified and objectives of such rules be made clear to reduce the scope for corruption. Also the government departments must have clear demarcation of functions and should not have both social and economic objectives, which are often conflicting. This will enhance accountability and transparency.

Any administrative reform must be supplemented by the legal system reform. Once the property rights are clearly defined and enforced by an independent judiciary, the area where government interventions are genuinely required becomes limited. The government should intervene only when there is a clearly defined market failure and concentrate in areas where it has a clear advantage, such as the maintenance of law and order, the enforcement of property rights, and the provision of infrastructure. Where government interventions are necessary, market based instruments (price) should be given priority over quantitative restrictions as a general principle

The political process in Bangladesh is not accountable. Hence, political reforms are necessary to develop an accountable and responsive political system that creates an economically-aware and technically trained political/bureaucratic elite for the management of the economy. Although a development-minded, authoritarian political regime may have certain advantages over democracy in promoting economic growth during the early stages of development, it can breed social and political instability in an underdeveloped society. What is important for development is the relative autonomy or insulation of the state against the ravages of both rent-seeking groups and populist politics by decision-makers : Authoritarianism is neither necessary nor sufficient for such insulation of the state (Bardhan, 1988). A competitive democratic political system under well-defined rules and norms can accommodate the political aspirations of the people. However, it may remain exposed to rent seeking and election populist politics unless the role of the private sector *vis-a-vis* public sector is sufficiently increased in economic activity. If the economy is adequately deregulated and opened up, the scope of patronage by both politicians and bureaucrats in a market-driven economic system will be limited. Politics may then become a relatively less attractive profession in economic sense and the state may be insulated from rent-seeking groups if price distortions are eliminated.

Any political reform should attempt to prevent the emergence of a coalition government or a situation where minority parties hold the balance of power. A coalition government is often found to delay adjustments as it is difficult to achieve agreement among partners on how to stabilise. Therefore, the institution of proportionality may not be conducive to swift fiscal reform when they are needed (Alesina, 1992). If a situation does arise where minor parties hold the balance of power there is a danger of 'war of attrition' as each party waits for the other to concede. This happens as the cost of delay to each party is a private information. This sort of situation can be avoided in two ways. First, the cost of delay must be made explicit. Here lies the importance of an economically literate elite bureaucracy. Second, devise some institutional mechanism whereby the gainers compensate the losers.

Next turn to the crucial issue of macroeconomic performance of the government in the presence of inefficient political cycles which arise from either vote-maximising behaviour of politicians or legitimacy crisis of the regime. An independent central bank with a clear mandate for price stability enhances macroeconomic performance. Therefore, the Bangladesh Bank Order 1972 should be amended to give it a mandate to control inflation only rather than a host of conflicting objectives. This is in line with what has been proposed above in order to enhance accountability and transparency of government departments.

Therefore, the credibility of government's fiscal and monetary policy lies ultimately in the accountability and transparency of the budgetary process. Here lies the importance of an independent fiscal board (IFB). The IFB must have sufficient power to review government expenditure programs and all new initiatives must be cleared by it. The idea of IFB is akin to an independent judiciary. Just as an independent judicial system monitors political interference with institutions for greater political efficiency, an IFB will ensure that the budgetary process is transparent and not influenced by political considerations. The transparency of the budgetary process will enhance efficiency in macro-economic management. IFB is a superior arrangement than a fiscal constitution restricting the government to a balanced budget. Such a constitutionally binding arrangement could be unnecessarily debilitating. IFB should work closely with an independent central bank in order to avoid any co-ordination problem between fiscal and monetary policies.

In a country where politicians have little respect for either Constitution or institutions, and is prone to *Coup'd'etat*, what guarantee is there that the arrangements suggested above would prevail? Here lies the importance of trade and financial liberalisation. The persuance of export-oriented, rather than inward-looking, industrialisation policies can act as an external constraint on the mismanagement of the economy. Large and persistent budget deficits can fuel the expectations of accelerating inflation and create balance of payments and exchange rate crises that lead to an eventual sharp devaluation of domestic currency. The fear of large depreciations of currency may cause massive capital flight, exacerbating the exchange rate crises. Most military dictators try to avoid exchange rate crisis and capital flights as they deepen their legitimacy crisis. Incidentally, macroeconomic stability and economic growth are powerful weapons that legitimise the dictatorial regimes. Trade liberalisation must be supplemented by financial sector development. A well developed financial sector will act as an internal constraint on inflationary financing.

In sum, institutional change, administrative, legal and constitutional reforms along with liberalisation of the economy are essential ingredients for a sustained improvement in macroeconomic performance. In the absence of these, whatever opening there has been of the "window of opportunities" due to the IMF-World Bank initiated structural programs in recent times will shut very soon. The changes suggested here are compatible with a democratic political system.

Summary and Conclusion

The main aim of this Chapter has been to discuss the importance of institutional development for economic and political stability in Bangladesh. It has reviewed the roles of three groups of factors — initial endowments/conditions, economic policies and institutions/organisations — in economic growth in the context of Bangladesh and then has analysed the dynamics of Bangladesh's politics from an historical perspective with a view to determining the requirements of political stability. It is found that although the initial endowments/conditions in Bangladesh are favourable to economic growth, most of its sociopolitical and economic institutions/organisations remain anti-growth. As political instability has become a serious problem for the country, this Chapter has analysed the dynamics of Bangladesh's politics from an historical perspective. It has shown that despite persistent political instability, there has been a systematic political polarisation in this country around two rival political parties — the Awami League and the Bangladesh Nationalist Party. Within the framework of a game theory, it is shown that if these two parties cooperate from the viewpoint of enlightened self-interests, they can establish a stable two-party political system. However, in the absence of democratic traditions within the political parties, they remain in confrontational mode on trivial issues of no national significance. In fact the present non-cooperation between the Awami League and the BNP is the outcome of a political culture where each of these parties intends to monopolise the state power as if the other party does not even have the right to exist. This is a reflection of an attitude of 'born-to-rule' under a dynastic leader — a far cry from the spirit of power — sharing under democracy. This indicates that a political cooperation between the Awami League and the BNP would require the break-up of the hereditary leadership system in both these parties. To put it bluntly, both Sheikh Hasina and Khaleda Zia should not be seen as democratic symbols, they are the obstacles to creation of a democratic system. They have divided the nation, created or perpetuated dynastic myths around two dead leaders and thereby derived legitimacy of what is essentially a feudal rule within a patron-client system. Such a system gives rise to a political culture which promotes suspicion and betrayal, arrogance of power, and intolerance of any political opposition and criticism.

This type of patron-client politics cannot be changed simply by legislation; they require a structural change in both the economy and the society, which in turn will bring a change in the attitude and outlook of the people toward politics. In short, both politicians and the common people must have respect for rules of law, the majority verdict, the opinion of the minority and an adherence to the Constitution (Rizvi, 1994).

While the development of political institutions and the establishment of democratic political organisations are necessary, they by themselves are not sufficient for long-term political stability in an otherwise feudal society of Bangladesh. To break the deep-rooted feudal, patron-client political culture, emphasis should be given on raising economic growth with equity through policy measures that include the development of economic and social institutions and organisations. The conclusion which Bardhan (1988) has reached for India is equally valid for Bangladesh that without high economic growth, the ever-widening circle of democratic awareness and raised economic expectations among the common people would endanger the survival of democracy.

Along with other factors, macroeconomic stability is crucial for sustained economic growth. Three key public institutions that affect macro-economic policy configurations are the bureaucracy, the central bank and the Parliament. Bangladesh needs to improve the performance of these institutions to minimise both market and government failures. Along with such institutions, financial deregulation, opening up the economy, introduction of a flexible exchange rate system and labour market reforms are crucial for improving macro-economic policymaking. It is expected that simultaneous development of economic, social, and political institutions and the establishment of democratic political organisations would create a mechanism for Kuznetsian modern economic growth to take place.

However, building of both economic and political institutions need time and efforts. In this transitional phase, the people's participation in the political process and the government's accountability to the people are crucial. In a traditional society, one cannot expect the return of good governance simply because of a change of power through democratic means. Constitutional forms do not guarantee good governance. At the least, the people should have the expectation and/or tradition of good governance. Good governance over a long period sets a high standard of public behaviour which cannot easily be broken even when a government is changed through unconstitutional means. Likewise a long period of bad governance sets a low standard of public behaviour and diminishes the chances of establishing better government even when the government is changed through electoral processes (Lewis, 1955). In so far as Bangladesh is concerned, as Zafaruliah (1996) finds, the prevailing cultural norms and bureaucratic and political institutions are not compatible with the values attributed to good governance.

APPENDIX

TABLE 1

Bangladesh : Main macro-economic indicators, 1972-1996

	72/73-74/75	75/76-80/81	81/82-84/85	85/86-89/90	90/91-94/95	1996
Real GDP Growth (%)	5.1	5.5	3.6	4.1	4.3	4.7
Per- Capita Real GDP Growth	-0.4	1.7	1.5	2.2	2.1	2.5
Inflation rate (%)	41.9	9.5	11.7	9.8	4.5	4.1
Gross domestic saving (% of GDP)	0	2.2	2.0	2.8	6.2	7.8
Gross domestic investment (% of GDP)	6.7	10.5	14.9	12.7	13.0	17.0
Resource gap (% of GDP)	-6.7	-8.5	-12.9	-9.9	-6.8	-
Trade deficit (% of GDP)	-5.9	-10.8	-12.5	-9.9	-6.6	-8.5
Current account deficit (% of GDP)	-2.6	-5.0	-4.1	-3.0	0.5	-4.0
Debt service (% of total foreign exchange earnings)	9.3	9.2	8.5	11.5	10.0	8.3

Sources : Computed/compiled based on *IMF, IFS Yearbook* (various years) : *Bangladesh Bank, Economic Trends* (various issues); BBS (1993); GOB (1995, 1996).

TABLE 2

Results of Selected* Parliamentary Elections, 1970-1996

	Awami League	BNP	Jatiya Party	Others
Per cent of seats won				
Pakistan**				
The 1970 Parliamentary Election	98.8	-	-	1.2
Bangladesh				
Parliamentary Election : 1973	97.7	-	-	2.3
Parliamentary Election : 1979	13.0	69.0	-	18.0
Parliamentary Election : 1986	25.3	-	51.0	23.7
Parliamentary Election : 1991	31.0[a]	46.7	11.7	10.6
Parliamentary Election : 1996	48.7	38.7	10.7	2.7

TABLE 2 : *continued* . . .

	Awami League	BNP	Jatiya Party	Others
Per cent of votes received[b]				
Pakistan**				
The 1970 general election	72.6	-	-	27.4
Bangladesh				
Parliamentary Election : 1973	73.2	-	-	26.8
Parliamentary Election : 1979	24.6	41.2	-	34.2
Parliamentary Election : 1986	26.2	-	42.3	31.5
Parliamentary Election : 1991	32.6[a]	30.8	11.9	24.7
Parliamentary Election : 1996[c]	37.5	33.3	16.1	13.1

Sources: Computations based on Bangladesh Election Commission Results reported by *Maniruzzaman* (1980); *Haque* and *Hakim* (1993) and *Kochanek* (1997).

Notes for Table 2

*	As the main opposition parties did not participate in the elections, the 1988 and 1996 (February) parliamentary election results are not reported.
**	Out of 162 national assembly seats allocated to Bangladesh.
	Means that either the Party did not exist at the time of this election or boycotted the election.
a	Bangladesh Krishak Sramik Awami League (BKSAL) included.
b	Percent of voters : 1973 = 54.9 per cent, 1979 = 54.9 per cent, 1986 = 60.3 per cent; 1991 = 55.4 per cent and 73.2 per cent.
c	This voter distribution is based on first-round of voting and is not adjusted for changes in voter distribution following re-polling later in 27 constituencies due to electoral irregularities.
n.a.	Not available.

Ideological orientation of major political parties

Awami League	Secularism; 'Bengali nationalism'; committed to large public sector; friendly relations with India.
BNP	'Bangladeshi' 'nationalism'; emphasis on the private sector; friendly relations with USA and China.
Jatiya Party	Identical to the BNP.
Jamaat-e-Islami	Islamic fundamentalism; anti-Indianism.

REFERENCES

Ahmed, M. (1995), *Democracy and the Challenge of Development* (Dhaka : University Press Limited).

Alesina, A. (1992), "Political Models of Macroeconomic Policy and Fiscal Reform", *Policy Research Working Paper No. WPS 970* (Washington, D.C. : World Bank).

Asian Development Bank (ADB) (1994), *Bangladesh : Stimulating Investment and Growth* (Manila : ADB).

Bangladesh Bank (BB) (various years), *Economic Trends* (Dhaka : Bangladesh Bank).

BBS (1993), *Twenty Years of National Accounting of Bangladesh* (Dhaka : Bangladesh Bureau of Statistics).

Bardhan, P. (1988), "Dominant Proprietary Classes and India's Democracy". In Kohli, A. (ed.), *India's Democracy* (Princeton, N.J. : Princeton University Press).

Bardhan, P. (1993), "Symposium on Democracy and Development", *Journal of Economic Perspectives* 7(3) : 45-49.

Baxter, C. and S. Rahman (1991), "Bangladesh Votes-1991", *Asian Survey*, 31(8) : 683-93.

Chowdhury, A. and A. Hossain (1996), "The Political Economy of Macroeconomic Management in Bangladesh", in M. Alauddin and S. Hasan (eds.), *Bangladesh : Economy, the People and Environment* (Brisbane : Department of Economics, University of Queensland).

Dornbusch, R. (1993a), *Stabilization, Debt, and Reform* (New York : Harvester Wheatsheaf).

Dornbusch, R. (1993b), "Introduction", *in Policymaking in the Open Economy* (New York : Oxford University Press).

Dornbusch, R. and S. Edwards (1990), "The Macroeconomics of Populism in Latin America", *Journal of Development Economics* 32 : 247-277.

Downs, A. (1957), *An Economic Theory of Democracy* (New York : Harper and Row).

Duverger, M. (1955), *Political Parties : Their organization and Activity in the Modern State* (translated by Barbara and Robert North) (London : Methuen and Company).

Government of Bangladesh (GOB) (1995), *Bangladesh : Economic Review June 1995* (Dhaka : Ministry of Finance).

Government of Bangladesh (1996), *Bangladesh : Economic Review 1996* (Dhaka : Ministry of Finance).

Hakim, M.A. (1994), "The Mirpur Parliamentary By-Election in Bangladesh", *Asian Survey*, 34(8) : 738-47.

Haque, A.S. and M.A. Hakim (1993), "Elections in Bangladesh : Tools of Legitimacy", *Asian Affairs*, 19(4) : 248-61.

Harberger, A.C. (1984), "Economic Growth and Economic Policy", in World Economic Growth (San Francisco : Institute for Contemporary Studies).

Hossain, A. (1996), Macro-economic Issues and Policies : The Case of Bangladesh (New Delhi : Sage Publications).

Hossain, A. and A. Chowdhury (1998), *International Money and Open Economy Macroeconomics in Developing Countries* (London : Edward Elgar Publishing, in press).

Hossain, A. and S. Rashid (1996), *In Quest of Development : The Political Economy of South Asia* (Dhaka : University Press Limited).

Huber, E., D. Rueschemeyer and J.D. Stephens (1993), "The Impact of Economic Development on Democracy", *Journal of Economic Perspectives* 7(3) : 71-85.

Huff, W.G. (1995), "The Developmental State, Government, and Singapore's Economic Development Since 1960'', *World Development* 23(8) : 1421-1438.

IMF (various years), *International Financial Statistics* (Washington, D.C. : IMF).

Islam, N. (1977), *Development Planning in Bangladesh : A Study in Political Economy* (London : Hurst and Company).

Jahan, R. (1980), *Bangladesh Politics* : Problems and Issues (Dhaka : University Press Limited).

Kamaluddin, S. (1996), "Second Coming : The Awami League Set to Take Power", *Far Eastern Economic Review* (June 27) : 18.

Khan, Z.R. (1994), "Bangladesh in 1993 : Values, Identity, and Development", *Asian Survey* 34(2) : 160-67.

Kochanek, S.A. (1993), *Patron-Client Politics Patron and Business in Bangladesh* (New Delhi : Sage Publications).

Kochanek, S.A. (1997), "Bangladesh in 1996", *Asian Survey* 37(2) : 136-142.

Kohli, A. (1986), "Introduction", in *The State and Development in the Third World* (Princeton : Princeton University Press).

Kohli, A. (1988), "Introduction : Interpreting India's Democracy : A State-Society Framework", in *India's Democracy* (Princeton, NJ : Princeton University Press).

Leipziger, D.M. and V. Thomas (1993), *The Lessons of East Asia* (Washington, D.C. : World Bank).

Lewis, W.A. (1955), *Theory of Economic Growth* (London : Allen and Unwin 1955).

Lisbet, S.M. (1959), "Some Social Requisites of Democracy : Economic Development and Political Legitimacy", *Americal Political Science Review* 53 : 69-105.

Maniruzzaman, T. (1980), *Bangladesh Revolution and Its Aftermath* (Dhaka : Bangladesh Books International).

Maniruzzaman, T. (1992), "The Fall of the Military Dictator : 1991 Elections and the Prospect of Civilian Rule in Bangladesh", *Pacific Affairs* 65(2) : 203-224.

Moore, B. Jr. (1966), *The Social Origins of Dictatorship and Democracy* (Boston : Beacon Press).

Novak, J.J. (1993), *Bangladesh : Reflections on the Water* (Bloomington, Indianapolis : Indiana University Press).

Rizvi, G. (1994), "Democracy, Governance and Civil Society in South Asia", *Pakistan Development Review* 33 : 4(1) : 593-624.

Sobhan, R. (1993), *Bangladesh : Problems of Governance* (New Delhi : Konark Publishers).

World Bank, *The East Asian Miracle* (New York : Oxford University Press, 1993).

World Bank (1994), *Bangladesh : From Stabilization to Growth*, Report No.12724-BD (Washington, D.C. : World Bank).

Zafarullah, H. (1996), "Toward Good Governance in Bangladesh : External Intervention, Bureaucratic Intransigence and Political Inaction", Paper presented at the Seminar on *Bangladesh : People, Economy and Environment*, Department of Economics, University of Queensland, 10 June 1996.

5

Liberalisation and Regional Patterns of Industrialisation : The Indian Experience*

B.S. GHUMAN

The benefits of economic liberalisation are not always evenly distributed across regions. In certain situations, these are confined to select regions. It is argued that as the state vacates space for market forces in the economic decision making sphere, economic benefits have a tendency to concentrate in a few areas having locational advantages. The Indian experience in the field of industry supports this hypothesis, as gains of liberalisation have accrued mainly to select states.

Economic liberalisation in India was introduced during the early eighties. Its pace improved during the mid-eighties. However, the liberalisation policies of the eighties were partial in coverage and ad hoc in approach. It is from mid 1991 onwards that a systematic and comprehensive liberalisation policy was set in motion in India. Economic liberalisation of the 1990s encompasses almost all facets of the Indian economy. However, industrial policy and trade reforms constitute the core of liberalisation.

***Acknowledgement.** I am thankful to Dr. Satya Deva, Prof. of Public Administration (Retd.) and Dr.(Mrs.) D.K. Ghuman, Sr. Lecturer in Geography, Panjab University, Chandigarh for their valuable comments on the earlier drafts.

Earlier, the Nehruvian model of growth adopted during the 1950s and patterned somewhat on the Soviet model, involved strict regulation in most areas of the economy. However, the New Industrial Policy (NIP) of 1991, initiated sweeping measures of deregulation aiming at growth, efficiency and equity through competitiveness. Reforms in the policies relating to five areas, namely, industrial licensing, foreign investment, foreign technology agreements, public enterprises and the Monopolies and Restrictive Trade Practices (MRTP) Act, constitute the NIP, 1991.

The NIP and subsequent reforms have abolished compulsory licensing for all except 16 industries related to security and strategic concerns, social obligations, hazardous chemicals and overriding environmental reasons, and items of elite consumption. This reform has enabled the taking out of the licensing system of about 80 per cent of the industrial sector (Rao, 1996, p. 14). In order to promote foreign investment, a policy of automatic approvals by the Reserve Bank of India, for projects having foreign equity participation upto 51 per cent of equity in 34 high priority industries, has been introduced. For speedy clearance of foreign investment proposals in other industries, in addition to the Secretariat of Industrial Approvals (SIA), a special institution, namely, the Foreign Investment Promotion Board has been set up. With a view to injecting technological dynamism in the industrial sector, the NIP envisaged the provision of automatic approval for technology agreements related to 34 high priority industries upto a lump sum payment of Rs. 10 million, 5 per cent royalty for domestic sales and 8 per cent for exports, subject to a total payment of 8 per cent of sales over a specified period. In the area of public enterprise, four major reforms have been introduced. First, monopoly powers of the state sector have been reduced drastically. Prior to NIP 1991, 17 industries were reserved for the state sector. Their number has, now been reduced to six. Within existing public enterprises, sweeping changes favouring an increasing role of the market are in progress. These include partial disinvestment of government equity in public enterprises; a greater emphasis on performance improvement through a

Memorandum of Understanding (MOU) system; and referring of sick public enterprises to the Board for Industrial and Financial Reconstruction (BIFR) for the formulation of revival/rehabilitation schemes. The MRTP Act has been amended to eliminate the requirement of prior approval of the government for establishment, expansion, diversification and merger. The threshold limit of assets in respect of MRTP and large companies has also been removed. In addition, imports of capital goods have also been liberalised. Further, the industrial location policy has been modified with a view to moderating some of the constraints. These industrial policy initiatives are accompanied by a series of procedural reforms, with the aim to make them transparent and less time consuming.

Other constituents of economic liberalisation include fiscal reforms, foreign exchange control relaxations, foreign trade reforms including convertibility of the rupee on current account, relaxation in price and distribution controls, financial sector reforms, permitting private investors (both domestic and foreign) to invest in the infrastructure sector particularly in the power, telecommunication and road sectors.

The Indian manufacturing sector has gained considerably from economic liberalisation. During the initial years of liberalisation, the industrial sector registered a low and even negative rate of growth owing, in parts, to problems of stabilisation and shifts in the policy regime. However, gradually the sector started responding positively to liberalisation. The rate of growth of the manufacturing sector during 1995-96 was 13 percent. It is very high in the economic history of independent India. Now the question arises whether or not the gains of higher industrial development are evenly distributed across regions.

Regional development has long remained one of the concerns of Indian planning. However, it was only during the Fourth Five Year Plan (1969-74) that the regional parameter was incorporated in the development equation. Following this, a series of programmes were started at national and state levels to mitigate regional disparities (Karandikar, 1991, pp. 9-13). The NIP of 1991 also states that the spread of industrialisation to backward areas of the country will be actively promoted through appropriate incentives, institutions and infrastructure investments (NIP, 1991, p. 175). The policy has adopted the already existing two schemes, namely (i) the Central Government Subsidy Scheme for setting up industries in notified backward areas and (ii) development of growth centres.

A large number of studies have been undertaken to examine issues relating to regional development, both overall and industrial (ASSOCHAM,1996; Dadibhavi, 1991; Das and Barua, 1994; Dholakia, 1983, 1985, 1989, 1994; Goldar and Seth, 1987; PHD Chamber of Commerce and Industry, 1994; Misra, 1991; Nair, 1983; Rao, 1977, 1984; Sarkar, 1989, 1994; Tiwari, 1983). Of these, only two (ASSOCHAM, 1996 and PHD Chamber of Commerce and Industry, 1994) deal with some aspects of liberalisation with regard to States. However, coverage is partial. The objective of this paper is to study in detail the trends in industrial development across states in response to economic liberalisation.

Data And Methodology

The paper is based upon secondary data collected from sources such as the Centre for Monitoring Indian Economy (CMIE), Central Statistical Organisation, Economic Trends Supplements, Economic Surveys, Economic and Statistical Organisations of the States and reports of associations of industries. The impact of liberalisation on industrial development across regions has been captured through three variables : (i) investment on hand in the manufacturing sector[1]; (ii) foreign direct investment and (iii) rate of growth of the manufacturing sector. Suitable techniques such as percentages, the rate of growth, the coefficient of variation, and maps have been used to analyse the data. The analysis of regional patterns of industrialisation which emerged through the application of these techniques, have been supplemented with empirical observations.

1. Every industrial project involving an investment of Rs. 5 crore and above is included in investment on hand.

The behaviour of investment on hand has been studied both for pre-liberalisation and post-liberalisation periods. However, analysis of foreign direct investment is confined to the post-liberalisation period, since statewise data for the earlier periods were not available. Compound rates of growth of the manufacturing sector at constant (1980-81) prices pertaining to the five years of pre-liberalisation phase (1986-87 to 1990-91), have been compared with those of the post-liberalisation phase (1991-92 to 1995-96), to map the emerging trends of industrial development across States during the liberalisation period.

Fifteen major States of the Indian Union have been selected for the study. For one of the States, namely Bihar, estimates of net state domestic product (NSDP) at constant (1980-81) prices relating to the manufacturing sector for the years 1986-87 and 1987-88, were exceptionally low as compared to the estimates of subsequent years. Thus, for Bihar, examination of the pre-liberalisation phase is based upon three year's estimates (1988-89 to 1990-91). Another statistical problem relating to Bihar is the non-availability of the NSDP estimates for the year 1995-96. Thus, the post liberalisation analysis of Bihar is based only upon four years.

Analysis Of Results

In India, the recent liberalisation was initiated during mid 1991. Thus, it is too early to gauge its exact impact on industrial development across regions. The analysis of limited data, however, can be used to map the emerging trends.

(i) Investment on Hand

As far as investment on hand in the manufacturing sector is concerned, various States are competing with each other to attract more and more investment. Most of them have announced their respective new industrial policies in light of NIP, 1991 (Economic Survey, 1996-97, pp. 114-115).

For a comprehensive analysis of investment on hand during pre and post liberalisation periods, states have been grouped into the following regions :

Region I. Investment on hand exceeds 9 per cent.

Region II. Investment on hand varies between 6 and 9 per cent.

Region III. Investment on hand ranges between 3 and 6 per cent.

Region IV. The proportion of investment on hand is below 3 per cent.

Table 1 shows that during the pre-liberalisation period, six States namely Gujarat, Andhra Pradesh, Maharashtra, Madhya Pradesh, Uttar Pradesh and West Bengal constituted Region I, as the share of each State in total investment exceeded 9 per cent. All of these States, barring West Bengal, formed a vast contiguous tract of high investment. The region as a whole accounted for 68 per cent of India's total investment on hand, against a share of 54 per cent of the country's population. Region II encompassed two states — Orissa in the East and Tamil Nadu in the South. Bihar was the only state falling in Region III. Region IV comprised of five states and is scattered in two different blocks : *i.e.*, Karnatka and Kerala forming one contiguous area in the South and the other three *viz.*, Rajasthan, Haryana and Punjab, forming a separate cluster in the North.

During the post liberalisation period, the scenario of investment on hand experienced considerable changes across regions and there is a trend towards concentration. Out of the six states belonging to Region I during pre-liberalisation period, only two states, namely, Gujarat and Maharashtra, have managed to retain their position in this region. Karnatka, Orissa and Tamil Nadu have become the new entrants to Region I. Karnatka has recorded the maximum gain in terms of investment as, during the pre-liberalisation period, it was amongst the bottom states.

Two states (Uttar Pradesh and West Bengal) of Region I of the pre-liberalisation phase, were pushed to Region II during the post liberalisation period. Two other states of the Region I of the pre-liberalisation phase — Andhra Pradesh and Madhya Pradesh, have suffered more on account of investment during the

TABLE 1

State wise Investment on Hand in Manufacturing Sector (Rs. Billion)

State	Pre-Liberalisation (Nov., 1990)	Post Liberalisation (Feb., 1997)
Andhra Pradesh	214.60 (13.54)	238.64 (5.66)
Bihar	90.88 (5.75)	89.70 (2.13)
Gujrat	216.59 (13.70)	711.96 (16.90)
Haryana	24.29 (1.54)	110.45 (2.62)
Himchal Pardesh	—	11.52 (0.27)
Karnatka	45.55 (2.88)	576.53 (13.68)
Kerala	26.82 (1.70)	126.78 (3.01)
Madhya Pradesh	167.96 (10.62)	187.02 (4.44)
Maharashtra	181.19 (11.46)	425.33 (10.10)
Orrisa	140.23 (8.87)	481.24 (11.42)
Punjab	23.88 (1.51)	159.16 (3.78)
Rajasthan	39.66 (2.51)	79.80 (1.89)
Tamil Nadu	100.46 (6.35)	385.10 (6.14)
Uttar Pardesh	155.67 (9.85)	356.99 (8.74)
West Bengal	153.35 (9.70)	272.52 (6.47)
Total	**1581.13**	**4212.74**

Note : Figures in parentheses are percentages.

Source : Centre from Monitoring Indian Economy (1997), *Profiles of States*, Bombay.

post-liberalisation period. Their share has declined sharply to half of their earlier share and as a consequence, these have become part of Region III. Punjab and Kerala have recorded improvements in their share and have shifted from Region IV to Region III. Haryana and Rajasthan have continued to be part of Region IV in the post reform period. Bihar and Himachal Pradesh are other states belonging to Region IV. Bihar earlier belonged to Region III, whereas figures for Himachal Pradesh for the earlier period were not available.

A perusal of change in the regional shift of the pattern of investment on hand during the post-liberalisation period suggests a trend towards concentration of investment (Maps 1 and 2). For example, Region I during the pre-liberalisation period accounted for 68 per cent of total investment, against a share of 54 per cent of the total population. During the post-liberalisation, states falling in Region I continued to claim more than 60 per cent of the share in investment but they contained only 30 per cent of the country's population. During the pre-liberaisation phase, Region I was widely spread consisting of states from North, South, East and West. But after liberalisation all states except one (Orissa) of this region belonged only to Western and Southern India.

A comparison of Region IV reveals that the bottom states have suffered during the liberalisation in investment, though their share of population has remained almost the same. During the pre-liberalisation, this region accounted for one tenth of the total investment of India. Their share declined to 7 per cent during the post-liberalisation period. The population share of the states constituting this Region remained almost constant at 18 per cent during both the periods. A widening of disparity among states, on account of total investment during the post-liberalisation period, is also confirmed by the coefficient of variation (C.V.). The C.V. was 88.85 per cent during the pre-liberalisation phase (1990-91). Its value works out to 107.32 per cent during the post-liberalisation period (1995-96). It is important to note that the C.V. has been increasing constantly since liberalisation. District level analysis of investment in states comprising of Region I also shows concentration of investment in a few belts. For example, in Maharashtra and Gujarat, a larger share of investment was concentrated in a narrow belt of 7 districts, forming a continuous tract from south Gujarat to the Konkan area of Maharashtra, running parallel to the coast. In Gujarat, three Southern districts — Vadodara, Bharuch and Surat account for more than 50 per cent of toal investment on hand. Jamnagar is another district which is attracting investment next to these districts. In most other districts of Gujarat, investment on hand is insignificant. In Maharashtra also, four districts — Thane, Mumbai, Raigarh and Ratnagiri (known as Kokan belt) claim more than 50 per cent of total investment. Other districts that are getting a good response from investors are Chandrapur, Nagpur (both are from Vidarbha region) and Pune (Western Maharashtra). But the whole Marathawada region (consisting of 8 districts) and a large part of Western Maharashtra (about 8 districts) have almost negligible investment on hand (CMIE, December, 1994, pp. vii-viii).

(ii) Foreign Direct Investment (FDI)

The attraction of more and more foreign investment is one of the major aims of the NIP, 1991. Between August 1991 and June 1996, the Indian government approved foreign investment proposals worth Rs. 71.16 billion. Most foreign companies have their Indian offices in Delhi, with a view to having better access to the top bureaucracy and other government/institutional services. About 23 per cent of the approved FDI is confined only to Delhi (Table 2). Figures reported in table 2 are approved FDI proposals. The actual arrival of FDI is far less than approvals. Approximately 23 per cent of the approved FDI actually reaches India (Rao, 1996 p. 21; Economic and Political Weekly, Nov. 23, 1996, pp. 30-36). Keeping this in view, only broad trends have been traced in regard to FDI. The regional break up of FDI reinforces the trend noticed in the case of total investment (also see ASSOCHAM, 1996, p. 18).

Barring one state, FDI has also gone to find its destination in already industrialised states such as Maharashtra, Gujarat, Karnatka and West Bengal. Northern states like Punjab, Haryana,

Rajasthan, Himachal Pradesh, alongwith Kerala in the south have received negligible share of FDI. The remaining states have gained moderately in FDI.

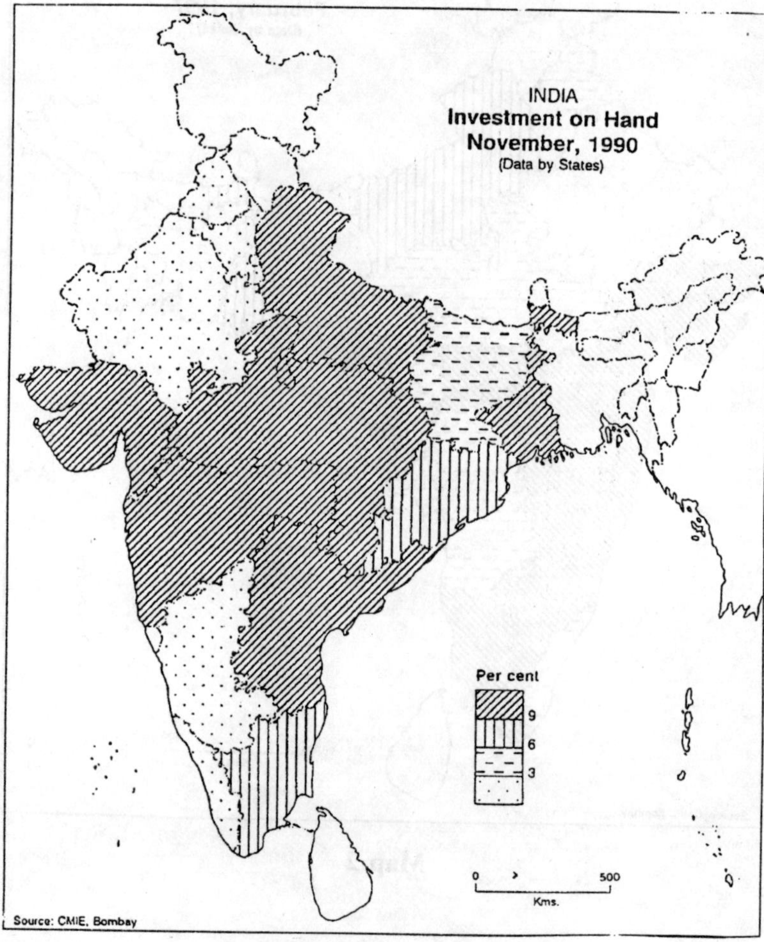

Map 1

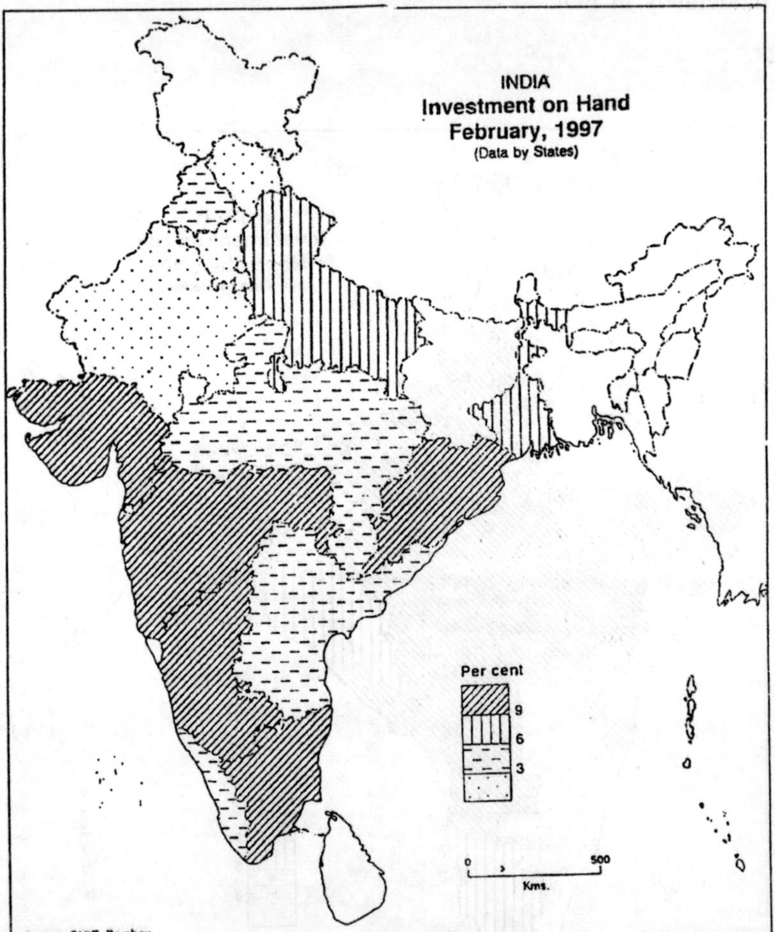
INDIA
Investment on Hand
February, 1997
(Data by States)
Per cent
9
6
3
0
500
Kms.
Source: CMIE, Bombay

Map 2

TABLE 2

Statewise Break-up of Foreign Direct Investment Proposals Approved (August 1991 to June 1996)

State	FDI Amount (Rs. billion)	Per cent to All India
Andhra Pradesh	17.41	2.45
Bihar	1.00	0.14
Gujarat	28.51	4.01
Haryana	6.62	0.93
Himachal Prdesh	3.09	0.43
Karnatka	28.29	3.98
Kerala	1.09	0.15
Madhya Pradesh	10.47	1.47
Maharashtra	105.51	14.83
Orissa	26.54	3.73
Punjab	7.79	1.09
Rajasthan	5.08	0.71
Tamil Nadu	37.00	5.20
Uttar Pardesh	16.87	2.37
West Bengal	42.27	5.94
Delhi	162.20	22.79
Others	211.85	30.00
All India	**711.61**	**100.0**

***Source** : Economic and Political Weekly*, November 23, 1996.

TABLE 3

Statewise Compound Rates of Growth of Manufacturing Sector (Per cent per annum)

State	Pre-Liberalisation (1986/87-1990/91)	Post-Liberalisation (1991/92-1995/96)	Change in Growth Rate (3-2)
1	2	3	4
Andhra Pradesh	4.91	2.03	– 2.88
Bihar	–1.50*	–4.29**	– 2.79
Gujarat	7.20	16.68	9.48
Haryana	8.36	6.54	– 1.82
Himachal Pradesh	17.87	5.67	–12.20
Karnatka	12.32	4.51	– 7.81
Kerala	11.87	6.52	– 5.35
Madhya Pradesh	18.11	10.54	– 7.57
Maharashtra	9.89	11.08	1.19
Orissa	6.61	2.10	– 4.51
Punjab	8.85	9.50	0.85
Rajasthan	9.60	6.94	– 2.66
Tamil Nadu	6.45	9.00	2.55
Uttar Pardesh	6.38	3.31	– 3.07
West Bengal	4.10	4.85	0.75

Notes

* Average rate of growth based upon three years estimates (1988-89 to 1990-91).

** Average rate of growth based upon four year's estimates (1991-92 to 1994-95).

(iii) Regional Patterns of Industrial Growth

During the post-liberalisation period, all states except Bihar have experienced positive rates of growth in the manufacturing sector. However, a comparative analysis of pre and post liberalisation rates of growth clearly indicate that benefits of economic liberalisation are mainly confined to select industrialised states. Northern, Eastern and central parts of India have almost experienced deceleration in industrial growth during the post-liberalisation phase (Map 3).

Out of 15 states, only 5 states recorded a higher rate of growth during the post liberalisation phase. These include Gujarat, Maharashtra, Tamil Nadu, Punjab and West Bengal. Of these, two — Gujarat and Maharashtra — are western States, Tamil Nadu falls in South India, whereas Punjab and West Bengal are respectively from North and East India. Punjab is the only Northern state which has experienced marginal improvement (0.85 per cent points) in its industrial growth during the post-liberalisation phase. However, in Punjab, the rise in the growth rate is partly due to the restoration of peace coinciding with the starting of the liberalisation phase, after a period of widespread violence. Thus, if Punjab is excluded, the beneficiaries of economic liberalisation, namely Maharashtra, Gujarat, Tamil Nadu and West Bengal are already industrialised states. During 1990-91, the share of the manufacturing sector in NSDP (at constant prices) of Maharashtra, Gujarat, Tamil Nadu and West Bengal was respectively 28 per cent, 24 per cent and 18 perc ent. These states were known for their manufacturing orientation even during British rule (Das and Barua, 1994, p. 7). The relative weight (share of manufacturing income of a state in total manufacturing income of the sample states) of these four states works out to 53 per cent. Their share of the country's population is 29 per cent.

Further, out of these four states, three, namely, Maharashtra, Gujarat and Tamil Nadu have emerged as top ranking beneficiaries of economic liberalisation on account of all the three variables, namely, investment on hand, FDI and growth rates.

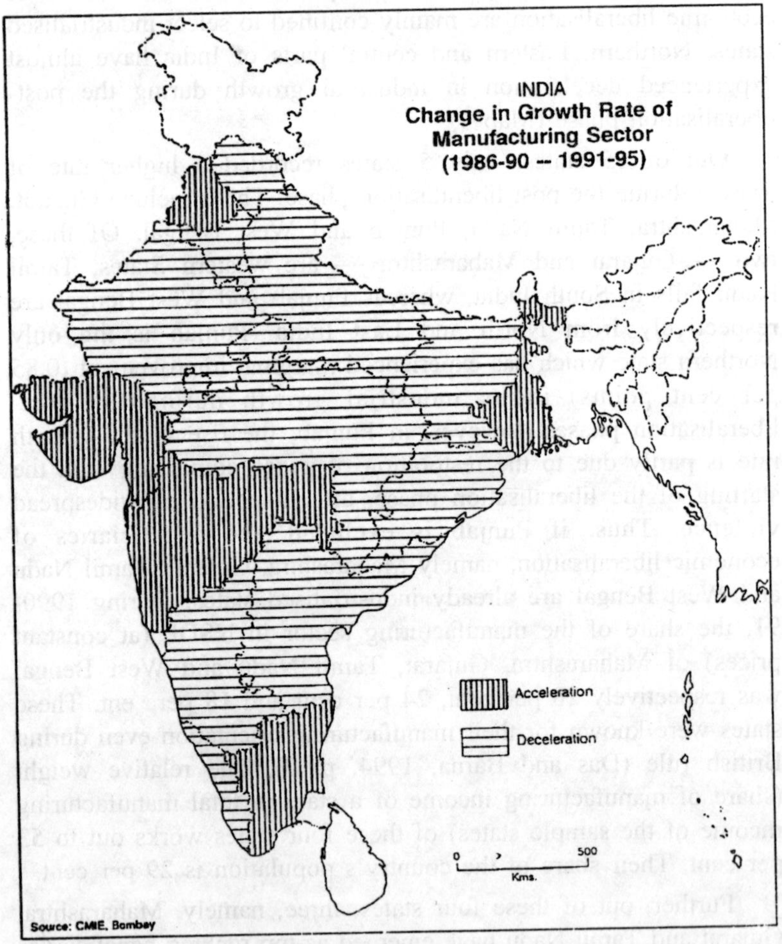
INDIA
Change in Growth Rate of
Manufacturing Sector
(1986-90 -- 1991-95)
Acceleration
Deceleration
0
500
Kms.
Source: CMIE, Bombay

Map 3

Regional Patterns of Investment And Growth Rates

After studying the behaviour of each variable separately, we now propose to analyse them in combination. Since FDI is included in investment, it was decided to combine investment and rates of growth only. The regional patterns of industrialisation which emerge after super imposing investment on growth rates are shown in table 4 and Map 4. The table clearly shows that a group of three states (Gujarat, Maharashtra and Tamil Nadu) has emerged as the top ranking beneficiary of economic liberalisation.

West Bengal, Karnatka and Orissa together are next in the hierarchy of beneficiaries. All these six states have comparative advantages over other states :

- All these states are coastal states and have proximity to ports.
- Barring Orissa, all are industrially advanced states.
- Most of these states are implementing economic reforms vigorously.
- Most of these states are fairly rich in terms of mineral resources.
- Gujarat, Maharashtra and Tamil Nadu have relatively well developed infrastructural facilities. In Orissa, the power sector is being restructured.
- Political stability has emerged as an added quality of all the states.

Equipped with these advantages, the above mentioned six states have cornered most benefits of liberalisation of trade and investment. Being coastal states, these enjoy comparative advantages in terms of better access to the international market. Similarly, most of the investment (more than 50 per cent) has moved towards industries such as refinery, steel, organic chemicals and minerals. The location of this investment is mainly influenced by proximity to mineral resources. Being minerally better off states, these have also benefitted more from additional investment originating from liberalisation.

TABLE 4

Grouping of states by combining investment and growth rates During Post-Liberlisation Period

	Growth Rate	
Investment on Hand	**Accelerated**	**Decelerated**
Very High (Region I)	Gujarat, Maharashtra, Tamil Nadu	Karnatka, Orissa
High (Region II)	West Bengal	Uttar Pradesh
Low (Region III)	Punjab	Andhra Pradesh, Madhya Pardesh, Kerla
Very Low (Region IV)	Nil	Harayana, Rajasthan, Himachal Pradesh, Bihar

The remaining States have either gained moderately or have suffered losses during liberalisation. For example, Punjab has gained moderately during liberalisation, in both the rate of growth and investment. Kerala is another state which has partially gained. All other states have emerged as losers. Barring Andhra Pradesh, all other states are land locked and thus are unable to take advantage of trade liberalisation to the extent of coastal states. It seems that sporadic incidents of violence in some parts of Andhra Pradesh also have adversely affected the investment climate. Most of these states are industrially backward. Only two of them (Madhya Pradesh and Bihar) are rich in mineral resources. Political uncertainty and the threat to law and order, explain partly losses suffered by Uttar Pardesh and Bihar. Losses experienced by Haryana, Uttar Pradesh and Rajasthan suggest that Delhi, as the center of the national market, is losing its strength due to the increasing access of coastal states to the international market. Himachal Pradesh, a hilly state in the extreme north, has its own locational disadvantages.

Conclusion

Gains from economic liberalisation across regions, in certain situations, exhibit a skewed pattern. The Indian experience in the field of industry validates this hypothesis.

In India, it has been found that economic liberalisation has accelerated industrial development. However, the benefits of industrial development are not evenly distributed across states. Two Western states — Gujarat and Maharashtra and one southern state — Tamil Nadu have gained the most from liberalized policy initiatives. The other beneficiaries are West Bengal, Karnataka and Orissa, These states enjoy certain added advantages such as proximity to ports, vigorous implementation of economic reforms, a strong industrial base (except Orissa), greater availability of mineral resources, relatively developed infrastructure in many of them and political stability. The remaining States have either gained moderately or have suffered losses during liberalisation. Most of these states are located in the North.

Thus, in the absence of corrective measures, there is a danger of liberalisation either bypassing some of the states, or even adversely affecting their existing levels of industrialisation. This trend is likely to increase the economic distance among states, which in turn has far reaching political and socio-logical implications in a federal set up like India. The corrective measures can be adopted in the form of a comprehensive regional policy, fully compatible with the new industrial policy.

REFERENCES

Dadibhavi, R.V. (1991), "Growth of Industry and Industrial Infrastructure: An Inter-State Analysis", *Yojana*, Vol. 34, No. 24, Jan., pp. 9-12.

Das, Sandwip Kumar and Alokesh Barua (1994), "Inter-state Disparities : Absence of a Cementing Force", *The Economic Times*, 18 July, 1994.

Dholakia, R.H. (1983), "Inter-state Variations in Economic Growth and State Income Inequality", *Man and Development* Vol. VI (2), June, pp. 43-54.

____________ (1985), *Regional Disparities in Economic Growth in India*, Himalaya Publishing House, Bombay.

____________ (1989), "Regional Aspects of Industrialisation in India", *Economic and Political Weekly* (EPW), 24 (46), Nov. 18, pp. 2563-67.

____________(1994), "Spatial Dimension of Acceleration of Economic Growth in India", *EPW*, Aug., 27 Vol. 29, No. 35 pp. 2303/2309.

Goldar, B and Vijay Seth (1989) , "Spatial Variations in the rate of Industrial Growth in India", *EPW*, Vol. 24 No. 22 pp. 1237-40.

Kalkar, Vijay and V.V.Bhanoji Rao (1996), *India Development Policy Imperatives*, Tata McGraw Hill Publishing Company, New Delhi.

Karandikar, P.D. (1991), "Growth Centre Scheme : Impact on Regional Imbalances in India", *Management in Government*, Vol. XXIII No. 1, pp. 7-41.

Misra, R.N. (1991), "Decentralisation of Industries for Balanced Regional Growth", *Yojana*, Vol. 35, No. 14 and 15 Aug. 15, 67-70.

Nair, K.P.G. (1983), "Inter/state Differentials in India 1970-71 to 1979-80", *Man and Development*, Vol. 6, No. 2 June, pp. 43-54.

New Industrial Policy and Procedure, 1991 (NIP, 1991), A Nabhi Publication, New Delhi.

Parikh, Kirit S. (1997, ed.), *India Development Report*, 1997, Oxford University Press, Delhi.

PHD Chamber of Commerce and Industry (1994), Investment Climate : A Comparative Evaluation of Northern States, New Delhi, *Development Policy Imperatives*, Tata Mc Graw Hill Publishing Company Ltd., New Delhi.

Rao, Hemlata (1977), "Identification of Backward Regions and Trends in Regional Disparities in India", *Artha Vijnana*, Vol. XIX June, pp. 93-112.

____________ (1984), *Regional Disparities and Development in India*, Ashish Publishing House, New Delhi.

Rao, V.V. Bhanoji (1996), *Economic Reforms : The Road Travelled*, in Kelkar and Rao (eds.).

Sarkar, P.C. (1989), "Measurement of Imbalances in Regional Development in India : Graphical Approach", *RBI Occasional Papers*, Vol. 10. No.1

__________ (1994), "Regional Imbalances in Indian Economy over Plan Periods", *EPW*, Vol. 29. No. 11, March, 12, pp. 621-633.

Sen, Anindya, Subarta Sarkar and Rajendra R. Vaidya (1997), "Industry : Coping with New Challenges", in *Parikh* (ed.).

Tiwari, R.T. (1983), "Inter-regional Disparities in Levels of Development : Indian Experience", *Man and Development*, Vol. 6(1), March.

6

Labour Market in the Maldives : The Case for Institutional Reforms

R.N. GHOSH and M.A.B. SIDDIQUE

Introduction

The Republic of the Maldives is a 750 km. long archipelago (from North to South), which comprises 1,190 islands. However, less than 300 islands are actually inhabited, and many of these islands (72) are held by tourist companies on leases from the Government of the Maldives as tourist resorts.

The Maldives follows the practice of quinquennial population census. The census figures of population are as follows :

TABLE 1

Population Census Figures : 1985-95

	1985 (March 29)	1990 (March 2)	1995 (March 25) Preliminary Results
Republic	180,088	213,215	244,644
Males	93,482	109,336	125,052
Females	86,606	103,879	119,592

Source : Ministry of Planning, Human Resources and Environment (1996), *Statistical Year Book of Maldives 1996*, Malé.

The population growth rate in the Maldives is one of the highest in South Asia : 2.75 per cent per annum. The population of the Maldives is expected to double in the next few years. Such increases would be due to a dramatic drop in mortality rates, without a corresponding decline in fertility (the birth rate is high at 46 per 1,000). The problems caused by the rapid population growth are compounded by the small amount of arable land available in the country. There is the additional problem of environmental degradation as evidenced by the loss of vegetation, diminishing supplies of firewood and drinking water, deforestation and the mining of coral and sand for building activities. Nevertheless, the government has yet to develop a comprehensive national population policy and programme.

Malé is the capital of the Republic, and had 62,973 inhabitants (Census 1995), thereby accounting for roughly 25 per cent of the population of the country. The density of population in Malé is very high, but for the country as a whole, population is scattered in over 200 islands (excluding 72 industrial and tourist islands where the Maldivians can stay as long as they are employed but cannot live on a permanent basis). The fact that commutation facilities between islands are not highly developed, and furthermore that commuting by air between distant islands is relatively expensive, have led to the development of a fragmented labour market. For example, demand for labour in one island cannot be easily met by supply from another island. Adverse weather conditions, the relatively high cost of travelling by motorised boats and the abundance of coral reefs are factors which impede labour mobility and have seriously affected the development of a unified national labour market.

Although the Maldives is an Islamic state, divorces are very common in the country. Indeed, the Maldives may have one of the highest divorce rates in the world. On an average, out of 2 marriages, one marriage ends up in divorce. It is, therefore, not uncommon for women to marry and re-marry several times during their reproductive years. As a result, the birth rate tends to be very high in the Maldives. It is, therefore, to be expected that the average annual net addition to the workforce, based on the population growth trends, would be high in the Maldives.

Despite such problems, the Maldives economy has been growing rapidly since 1981. In the 1980s real GDP grew by 11.1 per cent per annum while the annual rate of growth in real GDP per capita was just about 8 per cent. Much of the growth, however, has been concentrated on Malé, the capital of the country and in the surrounding Malé atoll. In the 1990s, the GDP growth rate moderated, and since 1993, the GDP has been growing at an average annual rate of 6.5 per cent.

High growth rates in GDP for over 15 years have made it possible for the Maldivians to have the highest per capita income (US $1,200 in 1996) among the SAARC countries. Much of the economic prosperity, however, is concentrated on the Malé atoll, which is the hub of trade and commerce and tourism in the country.

High growth rates in the 1980s and the early 1990s led to problems of Current Account Deficits (CAD) and inflation. By 1995 the fiscal deficit was running around 21 per cent, and inflation was in double-digit. Under pressure from the IMF, the government of the Maldives was forced to adopt macro-economic stabilisation programmes. Inflation is now down to 5 per cent per annum, and the fiscal deficit has also been brought to manageable limits.

Early Studies

A number of previous studies of the labour market in the Maldives have been made since 1988. The World Bank (1988) Report stands as a benchmark. R T Appleyard (1988) made a careful study of the human resources problem in the Indian Ocean island states. Ian vanden Driesen (1990) was specifically concerned with the problems of labour and the labour market in the Maldives.

Of more recent studies, Mark Wooden's report (1992), prepared on behalf of the National Institute of Labour Studies at Flinders University of South Australia has still considerable relevance to the issues and problems of the labour market in the Maldives. R. Sathiendrakumar and Clem Tisdell (1987, 1988 and 1989) made several interesting studies of tourism and the fishery sector in the Maldives : these studies give insight into some of the problems of the current labour market in the Maldives. R. Sathiendrakumar (1996) continued his earlier studies of the Maldives to highlight the persistence nature of economic problems in the Republic of Maldives due to limited land size, geographic isolation, scattered population, and very limited natural resources and economic opportunities.

The present study is intended to complement the earlier studies of the 1980s and 1990s, the main conclusion emerging is that some of the current problems of the labour market in the Maldives cannot be overcome until the bottlenecks in post-secondary education facilities are eliminated. The excessive dependence of Maldives on expatriate labour is largely due to its poor post-secondary education facilities.

The World Bank (1995) made an exhaustive study of the need for education and skills development in the Maldives and had this to state :

> Education and skills development are critical to any country, but perhaps especially so in the Republic of Maldives, with its rapidly growing population, fragile eco-system, and limited range of economic opportunities. The Maldivian population is very young — close to a third of the population is in school — and demand for education is strong and rising. At the same time, skill shortages are pervasive throughout the economy. Large numbers of expatriates have been employed temporarily to meet these gaps. Maldives need to focus on education to sustain the expansion of its fisheries and sustain the expansion of its fisheries and tourism — based economy, to develop alternative sources of employment, to begin the handover of skilled posts from expatriates to national citizens and to create the awareness needed to slow population growth.

The Labour Market

The potential labour force of a country is the number of people (both sexes) in the age group of 15-64. Many of these people may not be actively looking for jobs (*e.g.*, housewives and students in full time education). In many developing countries, however, children below the age of 15 participate in the workforce in various on-farm and off-farm activities. The actual labour force may, therefore, be greater or smaller than the potential labour force.

At the time of writing this paper (November 1997) the Census figures in the Maldives for the labour force were not available. We have, therefore, to use the earlier 1990 Census figures. According to the 1990 Census, only 49.5 per cent of the Maldivians aged 15 years or above were economically active. Assuming that very few of the older people above the age of 64 actually participate in the labour market, the labour force participation rate was low in the Maldives, as compared with other South Asian countries. (See Table 2 below). When compared with developed countries the labour force participation rate in the Maldives is very low : for example, the rate is 63.5 per cent in Australia (1997), which is comparable to other OECD countries.

TABLE 2

Population of the Republic of Maldives by Activity Status : 1990

	Malé	Atolls	Republic
Total population	55,130	158,085	213,215
Population aged 15 years and over [a]	34,283	78,964	113,247
Employed	17,184	38,360	55,544
Unemployed	254	220	474
Unemployment rate (per cent)	1.5	0.6	0.8
Labour force participation rate (%)	50.9	48.9	49.5

Source : Wooden, Mark (1992), *The Maldivian Labour Market : Issues and Problems,* National Institute of Labour Studies, Flinders University, South Australia.

a. Includes a small number who did not adequately describe their main economic activity. These persons have been excluded from the calculation of labour force participation rates.

A number of considerations emerge from the Population and Housing Census of Maldives (1990). First, an important conclusion is that the labour force participation rate (49.5 per cent) in the Maldives is lower than in many developing countries such as Sri Lanka, Mauritius and French Polynesia, but the Maldivian figure is comparable to other Islamic countries of the region such as Pakistan (49.3 per capita) and Bangladesh (50.3 per cent). An explanation for such phenomenon is to be sought in two different ways : (1) Because of continuing high fertility, the percentage of population below the age of 15 is very high (over 40 per cent in the Maldives in 1990). Such young population is automatically excluded from the definition of the labour force used in the Population and Housing Census of Maldives (1990), although many of these young people are possibly engaged in part, or full-time economic activity, especially in the fisheries sector. (2) Again, in many Islamic countries such as Pakistan and Bangladesh women do not traditionally participate in the workforce but generally perform household chores. Labour force participation by females in the Maldives was only 20.2 per cent (1990) as compared with 43.3 per cent in Mauritius (1989); and 48.5 per cent in French Polynesia (1988).

With an actual workforce of 55,544 (1990) in employment, the Maldives achieved near full employment by 1990, when the unemployment rate for the economy as a whole was reported to be only 0.8 per cent. Clearly the unemployment figures emerging from the Census of 1990 may have underestimated the problem, because of the definitions used. Many persons, particularly women, who were principally engaged in household activity were defined as economically inactive, but not unemployed. Such definition could be misleading, because a significant percentage of economically inactive population might have withdrawn from the labour force because of unavailability of jobs in their home atolls, which were located far away from Malé and the Malé atoll.

Secondly, unemployment figures are also likely to be understated because of under-employment, which is likely to be widely prevalent in the Maldives. In the fishery sector of the

Maldives, it is possible that many men, particularly older men are formally employed but have been reduced to the status of marginal workers.

Third, the reluctance, no doubt due to social and cultural factors, of Maldivian men and women to accept menial and inferior jobs, particularly in the tourist resorts has led to a very tight labour market situation in the hospitality industries, thereby making it necessary for the expatriate labour from Bangladesh and Sri Lanka to fill up the job vacancies in the relatively unskilled sectors of the labour market. As a result, there are about 22,500 expatriates (May 1997) working in the Maldives. We shall of course examine later the problems associated with the presence of a large expatriate workforce in the Maldives.

Occupational Structure

During the period of rapid economic growth in the 1980s and the early 1990s there had been a major occupational shift in the Maldives. Traditionally, the primary sector comprising agriculture, fisheries and coral and sand mining was the main contributor to GDP. In 1977, 45.0 per cent of the employed workforce was in the fishery sector. This declined to 20.6 per cent by 1990. A major reason for this decline was no doubt the adoption of new technology such as motorised fishing boats (Masdhonis) for deep sea or pelagic fishing. Moreover, many women who were earlier employed in the fishery sector, mainly on the job of drying fish for export to Sri Lanka. The emergence of a market for frozen fish and canned fish has now led to a relative decline in the importance of dry fishing. Canned fish is exported to the distant markets of Europe, whereas frozen fish goes to Thailand and other Asian countries. The shift in the fish exports market led to a sharp decline in demand for the services of women, who withdrew from the labour market in the absence of other alternative jobs in their own rural atolls. It is also possible that the attraction of higher paying jobs in Malé and the Malé atoll resulted in the migration of workers, especially men, away from the rural atolls.

The occupational shift in the 1980s was also brought about by the spectacular growth of the tourism sector in the 1980s. From a negligible number in 1975, the total number of tourists arriving in the Maldives reached the impressive figure of 114,554 in 1985 to 279,962 in 1994. Such rapid growth of tourism led to a spurt in construction activity of resorts and hotels, and subsequently a substantial increase in demand for workers in the service sector. Many of the jobs created in the service and construction sector were not suitable for Maldivians either because these needed special skills or because these involved unskilled menial work for which the Maldivians feel no attraction. The gap created between demand and supply was filled up by the expatriates.

The booming Maldivian economy in the 1980s led to a paradoxical labour market situation. The Maldivian women withdrew from the labour markets in the rural atolls, because of the shift in the export market of fish and the decline in the importance of dry fishing. But these women did not go for jobs, which were now available in the booming tourist sector — in holiday resorts, hotels and guest houses, and in construction and trade.

Rapid growth of employment in the public sector between 1985 and 1994, however, created new job opportunities for women, The percentage of women employed in the government sector was only 22 per cent in 1985, but this increased to 29 per cent in 1994, whilst the total number of jobs in the government sector increased from 8,836 (1985) to 18,060 (1994), *i.e.,* an increase of 104 per cent. Women are still in relatively junior government jobs, but their number in senior positions has been rising in more recent years.

An interesting aspect of employment in the Maldives is the high proportion of the workforce who are employed on the "own-account" (Mark Wooden, 1992). In other words, these people are either self-employed or are employed on a sub-contract basis. The Census (1990) recorded 41.8 per cent of the local workforce as "own-account" workers, whereas 45.2 per cent were employees, and the remainder were employers (2.8 per cent), family workers (4.5 per cent), or did not state their employment status (5.7 per cent). "Own-account" workers dominate agriculture, forestry and fishing. But they are also important in "manufacturing", suggesting that there are few large employers but many small businesses dominating the manufacturing sector in the Maldives. (See Table 3 below)

Working on 'own-account' has been sharply declining since 1977, when 85 per cent of the entire workforce (aged 15 years and over) was measured as working on 'own-account'.

TABLE 3

Own-Account Workers by Industry : 1990

Industry	**% of Industry Employment**
Agriculture & Forestry	80.0
Fishing	78.0
Quarrying	63.7
Manufacturing	61.7
Construction	65.3
Wholesale and retail trade	15.5
Electricity, gas and water	8.5
Transport, storage and communications	14.2
Finance and insurance	2.9
Community, social and personal services	14.4
Not stated	37.1

Source : Ministry of Planning and Environment (1990), *Population and Housing Census of Maldives*, Vol. I.

Expatriate Employment

As stated earlier, expatriate employment comprises nearly 28 per cent of the total workforce in the Maldives : Sri Lanka accounts for 49 per cent of all expatriate employment, Bangladesh (19 per cent), India (11 per cent), and workers from Europe account for most of the remainder (13 per cent).

The bulk of expatriates were employed in the private sector (82.4 per cent in 1995), the remainder (17.6 per cent) were employed in the government sector, public sector enterprises and development projects.

Many of the expatriate workers were employed in tourism and tourism-related activities, because of their special skills such as managers, accountants, chefs, engineers, machine operators, etc. But very large numbers were also employed in unskilled occupations such as labourers, peons, domestic servants, and so on. (See Table 4 below) :

TABLE 4

Expatriate Employment by Sector : 1995

	Public and Private sector
Total	18,510
Officials and Managers	257
Professionals	1,490
Technicians and Associate Professionals	1,346
Skilled Agricultural and Fisheries Workers	149
Craft and related trade workers	2,876
Plant and Machine Operators	853
Elementary Occupations	8,994
Others	2,545

Source : Ministry of Planning, Human Resources and Environment (1996), *Statistical Yearbook of Maldives 1996*, Republic of Maldives, Malé.

It should be noted that employment of the local workforce grew by 8.8 per cent between the 1985 and 1990 Census. In comparison, the employment of expatriate workers went up by 324 per cent — although such increase was admittedly from a small base (2,049 in 1985).

Such rapid growth of the expatriate population, particularly in unskilled jobs, might lead to social tensions in a relatively homogeneous society like the Maldives.

Unskilled expatriate workers tend to resent the manner in which they are treated by their employers and by the Maldives Government. First, they have to spend in the range of US $ 500 on the various services provided by the local recruiting agent in India, Bangladesh and Sri Lanka to get jobs in the Maldives. Most of these unskilled workers have to heavily borrow from their relatives, or mortgage and sell their farming land to raise such funds to be able to secure a job in the Maldives. Although the workers have their initial investments reimbursed by most employers at the end of their probation period, which may last up to 6 months, they have no security of stay, as they get only a year's renewable contract, and one year's visa to live in the Maldives. The working visa is seldom extended beyond 2 years, and the workers are forced to return home after the initial 2 year period.

There is still no comprehensive labour legislation in the Maldives to protect workers from the exploitation of their employers (vanden Driesen, 1990), although a legislation is now being drafted and hopefully will be put in place soon. Monthly wages for unskilled expatriate workers vary between US $ 100 and US $ 150, but in the very high cost Maldivian economy, such wages do not allow for comfortable living. In any case, workers have to save to make remittances to their poor relatives at home, thereby forcing them into a low standard living, which few Maldivians would be willingly to accept. Employers provide free accommodation, but as many as 12 workers have to share one room and common facilities. Senior executives and top managers, who are mostly recruited from Europe, the USA and Canada, are generously treated, have luxury apartments, and can earn as much as US $ 3,000 per month.

The Maldivians are likely to have muted contempt for unskilled workers from Sri Lanka and Bangladesh, and guarded jealousy for European expatriates. However, they recognise that the growth of the Maldivian economy might be at stake without the expatriate workers.

A paradox of the Maldivian economy is the wide gap between GNP and GDP (vanden Driesen, 1990) such that GNP falls well short of GDP, and the economy loses substantial funds due to overseas remittances made by foreign workers. The wage-bill of the expatriates is US $ 18 million a year and calculated at the 1985 prices, it represented about 15 per cent of GDP. [GDP = Wealth produced in the Maldives, GNP = income actually accruing to Maldivians].

The Case for Institutional Reforms

It would appear that a number of policy measures involving institutional reforms would be needed to overcome some of the major bottlenecks in the labour market of the Maldives. Some of these are listed below :

(1) A major aspect of the Maldivian labour market is its fragmented character. This is largely because of the geophysical characteristics of the country. The Malé atoll is relatively overdeveloped, and has most of the educational and infrastructure facilities. Shortages of labour are acutely felt in Malé and the Malé atoll, and in the resort islands. But surplus workers especially women in the rural atolls, cannot move to seize the job opportunities elsewhere because of cultural, geographical and family reasons. Most Maldivians live in about 200 islands, but 90 per cent of islands have less than 1,000 inhabitants. The people live in widely scattered islands in small groups, and cannot therefore enjoy developed commutation facilities between islands. Improvement in ferry services between islands is a pre-requisite for better distribution of labour geographically. Private operators are unlikely to provide improved ferry services without guaranteed project. Public sector intervention is, therefore, unavoidable.

(2) A worrying problem in the labour market is the gradual decline of the unorganised sector in which most 'own-account' workers are employed. As the growth of the Maldivian economy continues in the future, there will be

an increasing demand for labour from the organised sector. The unemployment in the unorganised sector may not lead to a situation in which unemployed workers from this sector would seek employment in the modern sectors of the economy. The lack of 'automatic adjustments' in the various sectors of the labour market might lead to a further influx of foreign workers into the Maldives. Suitable institutions for creating jobs in the unorganised sector should be a high priority of the Maldives Government. These institutions should aim at providing credit facilities for new cottage industries in the remote islands.

(3) It seems that a significant percentage of workers in the traditional sectors such as the fisheries sector are underemployed, or are actually "marginal" workers. Institutional reforms are needed to provide underemployed marginal labourers with opportunities for productive employment to ease the shortage of supply of labour. For example, women workers who are now underemployed (if not unemployed) can be given alternative jobs in export-oriented tuna canning facilities.

Here it may be interesting to note that when the world prices for frozen tuna recently collapsed, and a Japanese partner withdrew from a new joint cannery venture with the Government of Maldives, the government did not abandon the project. This project, despite some opposition from World Bank, continued, and efforts were made to integrate the modernisation of a cannery with the development facility for frozen tuna. This decision gave the industry flexibility. The Maldives now has a modern tuna canning complex designed and run to high international standards, producing top quality products for sale under international brand labels.

However, the cannery complex in the Maldives employs very few Maldivians, and is largely run by expatriate workers, especially from Sri Lanka. Government intervention is needed for providing suitable incentives to Maldivian women to seek employment in the modernised fishery sector.

(4) It is necessary to highlight once again the very low participation rate of women in the workforce in Maldives. Early marriages, high birth rates and high rates of divorce do not create a conducive environment for work for women, who spend most of their lives in child-bearing, or child-rearing. Although there is no clear evidence of widespread violence against women, the Maldivian women occupy an inferior status in the household. Lack of economic independence accounts for women's inferiority. In more recent years, women have sought to achieve economic independence by joining the workforce in the public sector mostly in inferior, or junior positions. But the cultural factors still prevent women from taking up jobs in the booming tourist sector and hospitality industries.

Fortunately, however, the Maldivian Government is aware of the need for greater participation by women in the workforce. A Ministry of Women's Affairs and Social Welfare was recently established in order to follow the SAARC plan for development of women. Island committees dealing with women's welfare have been established with funding from the United Nations. There are at present 13 women's centres on islands, which are dedicated to women's affairs, in particular to give women a sense of self-confidence. Such institutional reforms are in the right direction, but much more efforts are to be directed to attract women to join the workforce.

(5) The World Bank (1988, p. 7) report on the Maldives pointed out the difficulty in attracting workers away from their home islands "where 'affluent subsistence' has provided an attractive traditional way of life." Hence, Maldivian workers hate to do menial work which is associated in their perceptions with human degradation. When they do such jobs, they do it with a purpose (such as achieving a definite savings target), and leave their jobs when that purpose is fulfilled. Hence, of course, the labour turn-over rate is very high in the Maldives.

At the same time, the educational facilities in the Maldives are relatively underdeveloped and do not provide adequate opportunities for development of skills for highly skilled jobs. Until 1953 secular education was banned in the Maldives. Facilities for religious education (study of the *Koran*) did exist, but English-medium education started only in 1962. Education began to spread only after 1978, and many new schools were then established. Yet the focus of education today continues to be theoretical rather than practical and vocational training.

Post-secondary education facilities are still very inadequate. There are at present only five post-secondary institutions, or centres in the Maldives. These are :

(i) Institute of Health Sciences,

(ii) Institute of Teacher Education,

(iii) Institute of Hotel and Catering Services,

(iv) Maldives Institute of Technical Education and

(v) Maldives Centre for Management and Administration.

Of these five institutions, only the last two are directly under the Ministry of Planning, Human Resources and Environment and provide for multi-sectoral training.

The post-secondary education facilities in the Maldives are totally inadequate to give places to about 1,700 students who complete secondary education every year. Many Maldivians have, therefore, to go overseas for higher education. There are currently about 110 scholarships for overseas training, and 200 places every year are available at post-secondary institutes in the Maldives. There is, therefore, a wide gap between the availability of higher education facilities and the demand for places.

Without better and more broad-based educational facilities, the dependence of the Maldives on expatriate workers for skilled jobs would likely continue. The Third 3-Year Plan in the Maldives has now identified the need for a University, but University education in itself would not solve the kind of bottlenecks in the labour market now being experienced in the Maldives. A radical re-thinking of the entire institutional structure of the current educational system in the Maldives is urgently called for.

(6) The World Bank (1995), pointed out that the low level of educational attainment of the national workforce has contributed to the employment of under-qualified personnel in Government, where in the past, all post-primary school leavers were bonded to serve a minimum period. The growth of the public sector employment from about 10,000 in 1988 to about 20,000 in 1996 would suggest a tendency towards overstaffing. Many of these public sector employees are to be retrained for private sector jobs. Although major strides have already been made in improving access to primary and lower secondary schools, there are still significant shortfalls in upper secondary and post-secondary facilities. Rapid growth of the school-age population would continue to place more demand on post-secondary education. Expansion and improvement of post-secondary educational facilities would require urgent attention in order to train the Maldivians for the skilled jobs in the private sector and to reduce the dependence upon expatriate workers. The case for an urgent institutional reform of the educational sector does appear to have an overwhelming importance. Surplus staff in the public sector could be released for employment in labour shortage industries, such as tourism.

The institutional responses needed for the current main problems of the labour market in the Maldives are easily identifiable. As long as economic growth remains dependent upon tourism and upon the supply of both skilled and unskilled foreign workers, a steady long-term growth of the economy cannot be taken for granted. The key is to have a domestic labour market in which demand for and supply of labour are generally adjusted internally. On the demand side annual economic growth rates of 6 to 10 per cent would ensure an escalating demand for labour in the growth sectors of the economy. Despite full employment in the Maldives, there is a pool of untapped supply of labour if the female participation rate in the labour force could be increased through institutional measures, such as providing adequate child-care centres for women with young children, and offering suitable work environment for women. In Islamic countries, like the Maldives, women are generally shy of a work environment in which they are not relatively segregated from male workers.

(7) The difficulty in labour adjustment is partly caused by geographical dispersion of the islands, and partly by the lack of skills of the workforce released from the dwindling traditional sector for jobs in the modern growth sectors. Suitable manpower planning, coupled with the provision of adequate vocational and professional training facilities should solve the problem of low skills. However, the enormous costs of higher education would possibly call for funding assistance from other SAARC and developed countries. It is not likely that the cultural factors that discourage women from working on tourist resorts would be overcome easily. So, the dependence on unskilled workers from SAARC countries such as Bangladesh and Sri Lanka would continue in the foreseeable future, but conditions for work for such workers would have to be both controlled and improved by governmental intervention to prevent any large scale discontent among foreign workers.

(8) Geographical dispersion also creates other formidable problems for the Maldivian economy. There is now an overwhelming case for more balanced economic growth - away from Malé. The Malé atoll already suffers from excessive crowding and development. As a result, there is an extreme shortage of housing in Malé, thereby causing very high property prices and scarcities of rental accommodation. Government policy has to be directed to a more balanced development of other atolls, so that these can function as self-contained development centres within the national economy. The Maldivian Government has already identified one island each in eight atolls as regional centres which would develop into 'growth poles' to provide new economic opportunities and services. Success of policy

will be judged by the performance of these growth centres; but in the ultimate analysis, institutional reforms by the Government of Maldives would be the necessary pre-condition for change in the labour market.

REFERENCES

Appleyard, R.T. (1988), "Human Resources" in R.T. Appleyard and R.N. Ghosh (eds.) (1988), *Indian Ocean Islands Development*, National Centre for Development Studies, Australian National University, Canberra.

Asian Regional Team for Employment Promotion [ARTEP] (1988), *Manpower Planning in the Maldives (1987-2000)*, ILO-UNDP Project MDV/86/004, ILO, New Delhi.

Commonwealth Secretariat (1995), *Maldives — Industrial Opportunity Survey — Final Report*, London.

Economic and Social Commission for Asia and the Pacific [ESCAP] (1990), *The Economic Impact of Tourism in Maldives*, United Nations, ESCAP, Bangkok.

Far Eastern Economic Review (1990), "Maldives", *Asia 1990 Yearbook*, pp. 176-79.

Industrial Development Department (1995), *Maldives : Entrepreneurship Development Programme*, EIDD/I/ASP/2, Commonwealth Secretariat, London.

Industrial Development Department (1995), *Maldives : Industrial Opportunity Survey : Final Report*, EIDD/I/ASP/2, Commonwealth Secretariat, London, July.

Institute of Health Sciences (1997), *Prospectus, Malé*.

Maldives Institute of Technical Education (1997), *Prospectus, Malé*.

Maldives News Bureau (1995), *Maldives News Bulletin*, various issues.

Maldives Monetary Authority, *Annual Report* 1995 and *Annual Accounts*, Malé.

Ministry of Planning, Human Resources and Environment (1996), *Statistical Yearbook of Maldives 1996*, Republic of Maldives, Malé.

______ (1994), *National Development Plan 1994-1996*, Republic of Maldives, Malé.

Ministry of Planning and Environment (1997), *Statistical Yearbook of Maldives 1996*, Malé, Republic of Maldives.

______ (1990), *Population and Housing Census of Maldives*, 1990 : Vol I, Population, table p. 21.

Ministry of Education (1995), *Education Master Plan 1996-2005*, Malé, Republic of Maldives.

Ministry of Women's Affairs and Social Welfare (1996), *Directory of Women in Senior Government Positions*, Malé, Republic of Maldives.

______ (1996), *Directory of Women in Senior Government Positions*, Republic of Maldives.

SAARC (1997), "Declaration of the Ninth SAARC Summit", *Ninth SAARC Summit : Head of State or Government : Ninth Meeting*, SAARC/SUMMIT 9/11, Malé, 12-14 May, 1997.

Sathiendrakumar, R (1996), "Problems faced by Indian Ocean Island Economies : The Case of the Maldives", in R. Gabbay, R. Ghosh and M.A.B. Siddique (edited) (1996), *Economics of Small Island Nations*, New Age International, New Delhi.

Sathiendrakumar, R. and Clem Tisdell (1985), "Migration from Traditional Rural Communities and Outside Employment : A Study of Maldivian Fishing Villages", *South East Asian Economic Review,* 8 August, pp. 121-63.

______ (1987), "Tourism and the Development of the Maldives", *Massey Journal of Asian and Pacific Business,* 1 (1), pp. 27-34.

______ (1988a), "Marine Developments and Socio-Economic Conflicts (Internal and External) of the Maldives", Murdoch University, *Economics Programme Working Papers*, No. 12, July.

______ (1988b), "Economic Importance of Tourism for Small Indian Ocean and Pacific Island States" in C.A. Tisdell, C.J. Aislabie and P.J. Staton (eds.), Economic of Tourism : *Case-Study and Analysis*, Institute of Industrial Economics, University of Newcastle, Newcastle.

______ (1989a), "Tourism and the Economic Development of the Maldives" *Annals of Tourism Research*, 16(2), pp. 250-69.

______ (1989b), "Determinants of Relative Wealth in Maldivian Fishing Villages", *Asian Profile*, 17, April, pp. 155-68.

Vanden Driesen, I. H. (1990), "Labour and the Labour Market in the Maldives", in Appleyard, R.T. and R.N. Ghosh (eds.) (1990), *Economic Planning and Performance in Indian Ocean Island States,* National Centre for Development Studies, Australian National University, Canberra.

Wooden, Mark (1992), *The Maldivian Labour Market : Issues and Problems*, National Institute of Labour Studies, Flinders University, South Australia.

The World Bank (1980), The Maldives : *An Introductory Economic Report*, South Asia Regional Office, The World Bank, Washington D.C.

______ (1988), *Staff Appraisal Report : Republic of Maldives*, Education and Training Project, Report No. 7637-MAL, December.

______ (1995), *Staff Appraisal Report : Republic of Maldives*, Second Education and Training Project, Population and Human Resources Division, Report No 13394-MAL.

______ (1997), *World Tables*, DX Data, CD Rom.

Republic of Maldives (1997), *National Development Plan* 1994-1996, Malé.

STATISTICAL APPENDIX

TABLE A1

Tourism Sector Employment : 1995 (as at end December 1995)

Occupation	Total			Local			Foreign		
	Both Sexes	Male	Female	Both Sexes	Male	Female	Both Sexes	Male	Female
Total	12,699	12,292	407	7,159	7,002	157	5,540	5,290	250
Front Office	1,659	1,572	87	1,001	963	38	658	609	49
Public Relations	271	213	58	104	104	-	167	109	58
Food and Beverages	3,402	3,390	12	1,714	1,709	5	1,688	1,681	7
Staff Mess	684	635	49	243	194	49	441	441	-
Power House	468	461	7	291	291	-	177	170	7
Maintenance	2,263	2,263	-	714	714	-	1,549	1,549	-

Contd.

TABLE A1 : *continued*

Occupation	Total			Local			Foreign		
	Both Sexes	Male	Female	Both Sexes	Male	Female	Both Sexes	Male	Female
House keeping	1,637	1,594	43	1,317	1,278	39	320	316	4
Transport	1,359	1,359	-	1,275	1,275	-	84	84	-
Sports	495	388	107	148	146	2	347	242	105
Malé Office	340	315	25	282	260	22	58	55	3
Others	121	102	19	70	68	2	51	34	17

Source **:** Ministry of Planning, Human Resources and Environment (1996), *Statistical Yearbook of Maldives* 1996, Malé, Table VIII-9.

TABLE A2

Expatriate Employment by Sector and Nationality : 1995

Nationality	Public and Private Sector	Public Sector				Private Sector			
		Total	Government	Public Enterprises	Development Projects	Total	Shops and Restaurants	Tourism	Others
All Nationalities	18,510	3,258	2,023	557	678	15,252	6,597	6,574	2,081
Asia	16,988	3,104	1,912	541	651	13,884	6,416	5,437	2,031
Bangladesh	3,313	571	513	54	4	2,742	695	1,869	178
India	4,268	625	413	5	207	3,643	2,160	710	773
Philippines	167	47	40	7	-	120	37	82	1
Sri Lanka	8,785	1,675	873	450	352	7,110	3,429	2,619	1,062
Other Countries	455	186	73	25	88	269	95	157	17

Contd.

TABLE A2 : *continued*

Nationality	Public and Private Sector	Public Sector				Private Sector			
		Total	Government	Public Enterprises	Development Projects	Total	Shops and Restaurants	Tourism	Others
Africa	71	31	30	1	-	40	-	37	3
Egypt	30	28	27	1	-	2	-	2	-
Other Countries	41	3	3	-	-	38	-	35	3
Europe	1,344	88	55	10	23	1,256	142	1,072	42
Austria	47	1	1	-	-	46	-	44	2
France	86	-	-	-	-	86	1	83	2
Germany	246	2	2	-	-	244	7	233	4

Italy	413	-	-	-	-	413	13	399	1
Sweden	40	-	-	-	-	40	2	38	-
Switzerland	127	1	1	-	-	126	8	118	-
UK	133	35	26	2	7	98	33	62	3
Other Countries	252	49	25	8	16	203	78	95	30
America	64	17	14	2	1	47	35	10	2
Canada	35	3	3	-	-	32	28	4	-
U.S.A	23	12	10	1	1	11	7	2	2

Contd.

TABLE A2 : *continued*

Nationality	Public and Private Sector	Public Sector				Private Sector			
		Total	Government	Public Enterprises	Development Projects	Total	Shops and Restaurants	Tourism	Others
Other Countries	6	2	1	.1	-	4	-	4	-
Oceania	43	18	12	3	3	25	4	18	3
Australia	29	8	7	1	-	21	4	14	3
Other Countries	14	10	5	2	3	4	-	4	-

Source : Ministry of Planning, Human Resources and Environment (1996), *Statistical Yearbook of Maldives* 1996, Malé, Table II-15.

TABLE A3

Economic Indicators : 1980-95

	(1)	(2)	(3)	(4)	(5)	(6)	(7)	(8)	(9)	(10)
	%pa	$ US	$ US mill	nc mill	nc mill	nc mill	nc mill	Per cent	Per cent	nc/$ US
1980	23.96	-	25.8	-76.4	45.5	39.3	6.2	21.96	1.87	7.55
1981	23.61	-	38.9	-26.4	71.5	53.3	18.2	10.74	-2.93	7.55
1982	21.95	-	65.1	-19.6	92.0	89.2	2.8	4.92	0.79	7.17
1983	-100.00	-	77.2	-72.8	109.0	90.4	18.6	7.41	10.45	7.05
1984	-	-	82.8	-25.1	128.0	97.4	30.6	-0.42	5.18	7.05
1985	-	-	83.1	-30.6	149.0	112.5	36.5	-0.28	5.38	7.10
1986	-	-	68.7	-83.7	179.0	124.5	54.5	4.46	7.66	7.15
1987	-	430	72.8	19.1	267.0	161.1	105.9	0.13	-2.39	9.22
1988	-	520	71.4	25.6	313.0	193.1	119.9	-0.41	-2.29	8.78
1989	7.22	540	66.8	-42.7	405.0	257.9	147.1	3.49	0.23	9.04
1990	3.63	630	78.0	-170.8	455.0	340.8	114.2	5.48	6.78	9.55

Contd.

TABLE A3 : *continued*

	(1)	(2)	(3)	(4)	(5)	(6)	(7)	(8)	(9)	(10)
	%pa	$ US	$ US mill	nc mill	nc mill	nc mill	nc mill	Per cent	Per cent	nc/$ US
1991	15.00	680	81.2	-238.5	568.0	430.1	137.9	7.35	6.79	10.25
1992	16.52	740	94.9	-356.9	683.0	541.1	141.9	8.28	9.32	10.57
1993	20.15	810	112.3	-412.7	764.0	614.2	149.8	1.63	15.71	10.96
1994	-	890	123.5	-206.6	980.0	691.9	288.1	3.82	3.58	11.59
1995	-	990	154.8	-	-	-	-	-	-	11.77

Source : The World Bank (1997), *World Tables*, DX Data.

Notes : (1) Consumer Price Index : Inflation Rate.

(2) Current GNP per Capita ($ US).

(3) External Debt : Total.

(4) Government Budget : Deficit (-) or Surplus.

(5) Government Budget : Current Revenue.

(6) Government Budget : Current Expenditure.

(7) Government Budget : Current Balance.

(8) Government Budget : Financing from Abroad (% GDP).

(9) Government Budget : Domestic Financing (% GDP).

(10) Exchange Rate Conversion Factor (annual average).

TABLE A4

Labour Force : 1970-95

	Total Labor Force (in '000)	Female Labor Force (Percentage of total)
1970	58.0	37.9
1971	59.6	38.0
1972	61.2	38.0
1973	62.9	38.0
1974	64.6	38.0
1975	66.4	38.0
1976	68.2	38.1
1977	70.1	38.1
1978	72.0	38.1
1979	74.0	38.1
1980	73.9	39.2
1981	75.2	39.5
1982	76.5	39.8
1983	77.9	40.1
1984	79.2	40.4
1985	80.6	40.6
1986	82.0	40.9
1987	83.4	41.2
1988	84.9	41.5
1989	86.3	41.8
1990	87.8	42.1
1991	90.7	42.2
1992	93.7	42.3
1993	96.8	42.3
1994	100.0	42.4
1995	103.3	42.5

Source : The World Bank (1997), *World Tables*, DX Data.

TABLE A5

Gross Domestic Product : 1985-95

	GDP at Market Prices	GDP at 1987 Prices
	nc mill	nc mill
1985	600.3	714.3
1986	691.0	775.6
1987	844.6	844.6
1988	949.1	918.1
1989	1,148.0	1,003.5
1990	1,393.4	1,166.1
1991	1,686.5	1,255.1
1992	2,028.7	1,334.0
1993	2,380.4	1,416.2
1994	2,789.8	1,509.5
1995	3,188.7	1,617.6

Source : The World Bank (1997), *World Tables*, DX Data.

TABLE A6

Student Enrolment in Educational Institutions : 1993-95

Locality	No. of Students		
	1993	1994	1995
Republic			
Total	78,639	83,855	87,878
Government schools	35,138	36,693	39,032
Private schools	35,486	38,761	39,581
Community schools	8,015	8,401	9,265
Malé			
Total	23,177	23,500	24,570
Government schools	12,962	13,226	13,255
Private schools	5,838	5,810	6,368
Community schools	4,377	4,464	4,947
Atolls			
Total	55,462	60,355	63,308
Government schools	22,176	23,467	25,777
Private schools	29,648	32,951	33,213
Community schools	3,638	3,937	4,318

Source : Ministry of Planning, Human Resources and Environment (1996), *Statistical Yearbook of Maldives 1996*, Malé, Table IV-1.

TABLE A7

Number of Educational Institutions : 1992-95

	No. of Institutions			
Locality	**1992**	**1993**	**1994**	**1995**
Republic				
Total	262	265	264	262
Government schools	56	57	57	59
Private schools	28	31	30	29
Community schools	178	177	177	174
Malé				
Total	17	17	17	17
Government schools	9	9	9	9
Private schools	4	4	4	4
Community schools	4	4	4	4
Atolls				
Total	245	248	247	245
Government schools	47	48	48	50
Private schools	24	27	26	25
Community schools	174	173	173	170

Source : Ministry of Planning, Human Resources and Environment (1996), *Statistical Yearbook of Maldives 1996, Malé*, Table IV-2.

TABLE A8

Students Enrolled in Various Educational Institutions by Sex : 1994-95

Locality	1994			1995		
	Both Sexes	Male	Female	Both Sexes	Male	Female
Republic of Maldives	83,855	42,768	41,087	87,878	44,643	43,235
- Malé	23,500	12,393	11,107	24,570	12,639	11,931
- Atolls	60,355	30,375	29,980	63,308	32,004	31,304
Atolls Education Centres	12,867	6,597	6,270	13,613	6,974	6,639
Government Educational Institutions	13,226	6,583	6,643	13,255	6,550	6,705
- Private	4,464	2,624	1,840	4,947	2,709	2,238
- Community	5,810	3,186	2,624	6,368	3,380	2,988
Atolls Primary Schools	6,419	3,220	3,199	6,803	3,479	3,324
Technical Education	158	158	-	155	154	1
Government Schools other than Atoll Education Centres and Atoll Primary Schools	4,770	2,355	2,415	5,361	2,697	2,664

Source : Derived from : Ministry of Planning, Human Resources and Environment (1996), *Statistical Yearbook of Maldives 1996*, Malé, tables IV-3 to IV-7, IV-12, and IV-13.

TABLE A9

Students Enrolled in Primary, Middle and Secondary Schools by Sex : 1995

Institutions	Republic			Malé			Atolls		
	Both Sexes	Male	Female	Both Sexes	Male	Female	Both Sexes	Male	Female
Secondary Enrolment	5,381	2,690	2,691	2,587	1,211	1,376	2,794	1,479	1,315
Middle-School Enrolment	5356	2791	2565	2917	1377	1540	2439	1414	1025
Primary Enrolment	8993	4680	4313	5984	3086	2898	3009	1594	1415

Source : Estimated from Ministry of Planning, Human Resources and Environment (1996), *Statistical Yearbook of Maldives 1996*, Malé, tables IV-9 to IV-11.

7

Economic Development and Institutional Reforms in Nepal : Current Situation and Probable Future Direction

MEENA ACHARYA

Introduction

After the overthrow of the old Panchayat System in 1990, Nepal is passing through a period of political volatility. No single party has working majority in the current parliament. The current coalition government is constituted mainly by United Marxist Leninist (UML) and the Rastriya Prajatantra Party (RPP) — the party of ex-panchas. A major factor of apparent instability in the political system has been the shifting alliances of the RPP members, who number just 19 in the Parliament. UML is trying to appease the RPP and maintain the present coalition at all cost. It, however, faces strong opposition from its cadres for colluding with the leaders from the last Panchayat regime.

External intervention on the part of the neighboring countries and donors is increasing all around, primarily because of the chaos in the political process and volatility of the situation. Given these factors, it is difficult to predict the trend of future events in Nepal. UML has won overwhelming majority in the current local elections. UML has declared that it will try to maintain the current alliance and let the present parliament complete its term.

On the basis of popular feelings among the masses barring some elite groups, UML is likely to win the next election, RPP and NC sharing the opposition seats. But efforts to unseat the UML government by other democratic forces, particularly the Nepali Congress will continue. This forebodes, politically, a volatile situation.

Current instability is rooted in the difficult socio-economic situation that Nepal is passing through. The democratic changes of the early nineties evoked great expectations among the people. The political parties emerging after 30 years of exile and underground existence, however, proved unequal to the task of fulfilling the nation's expectations or people's aspirations (IIDS, 1996).

The elite from the backward ethnic groups and the downtrodden lower caste have seized the democratic opportunities to ventilate their own legitimate grievances. However, their leaders have put improbable demands on political parties and state, with an express objective of advancing their own political ambitions and interests.

The process of liberalisation which was inevitable, no matter what government came to power, has aggravated the economic hardships for the majority of the middle and lower middle classes. The deteriorating terms of trade for agriculture, accelerated erosion of wage earnings due to inflationary pressures, created by both external liberalisation and adjustment of administered prices, have generated disenchantment among the peasants and working class population. The inflow of Indian workers and businesses have created further problems. The superimposition of the market on feudalistic structures have created vast opportunities for graft and profiteering. Income disparities are felt to be increasing.

Religious fundamentalism instigated by various interested foreign and local groups is on the rise — leading to unwarranted religious strife. Political parties, in their shortsightedness are politicising such religious and ethnic divisions.

However, increasing politicisation of the masses, the lower service castes, various backward ethnic groups and lower peasantry, observed since the change of regime in 1990, could be considered a positive factor for change. Rising population pressure on the land and environment, their main source of livelihood, have been eroding their economic status. Various political parties and non-governmental organisations (NGOs), particularly of the left, have been campaigning their causes and raising their expectation and this has led to them increasing politicisation.

Current Economic Situation and Outstanding Policy Issues

Structural Adjustment Programs and Liberalisation of the Economy

Economic stabilisation and economic restructuring programs that had started since the mid 1980s, were perceptibly accelerated during the nineties. These included both demand management and removal of structural rigidities from the economy. On the demand side, the primary aim was to reduce government consumption and contain fiscal deficits. Increased efforts to mobilize a higher level of domestic resources, limit the government's domestic borrowings and to curtail government expenditure through a reduction in subsidies, improvement in performance of public enterprises and their virtual divestment and, a flexible exchange rate system constituted the main hallmarks of demand management policies. Restructuring measures on the supply side included industrial and trade liberalisation, liberalisation of the financial system, tax reforms, besides adoption of a market-oriented flexible exchange rate system. On the whole the economy has irreversibly moved towards a more liberalised and open structure. Impact on various sectors, however, has been mixed.

Industry

Industries were highly protected before the current wave of liberalisation started. With tariff reforms, the removal of additional duties, a downward revision in sales tax on imports, the removal of quantitative restrictions on imports and liberalisation of exchange rate, there has been a drastic cut down in the level of protection in the 1990's. Some of the industries are facing negative protection (like plywood, steel utensils) and some are running at a very low level of protection (like cotton textile, cement, sugar, etc.). Despite the liberalisation of foreign investment policy, the inflow of foreign direct investment has been low, commitment amounting to worth Rs 8.6 billion so far. Actual inflows, according one source (Shakya, 1997), until 1995 amounted to just US $ 8 million, *i.e.*, about Rs. 456 million only. The manufacturing sector has so far been able to provide employment opportunities to a very small number of people and its share in GDP has remained at less than 10 per cent. The industrial base is weak, as is evident from the structure of imports; the figures show that capital goods still constitute only 36-38 per cent of imports.

The private sector is expanding its role, both in savings and investment activities. Liberalisation of the regulatory framework, exchange regime and price controls should provide expanded scope to the private sector. His Majesty's Government (HMG) is inviting private sector participation in the energy, infrastructure, education and health sectors as well. HMG has adopted a two pronged policy of encouraging private sector to expand its activities in urban areas, while itself concentrating in the development of rural and remote areas. This policy will continue during the Ninth Plan period as indicated by the draft Approach Paper. Better relations with India and private sector contacts with Indian businesses directly, have opened up new possibilities for the private sector, more so with the signing of the new Nepal-India Trade Treaty in December 1996. By far, this is the most progressive Treaty from Nepal's standpoint.

A number of agreements were reached between India and Nepal during the visit of the Indian Prime Minister I. K. Gujral to Nepal (June 1997). India and Nepal agreed to prepare a Detailed Project Report on the Panchesware Project by December 1997. This will facilitate Nepal's access to electricity and water from Tanakpur Power Station and Sharada Barrage, as per the provisions incorporated in the Mahakali Treaty, ratified in 1996. It was also agreed that Nepalese parties might negotiate with Indian customers directly on the volume, prices and points of delivery of electricity from Nepal, within the general legal framework prevailing in the two countries. Nepal has been provided with a transit route *via* India to Bangladesh on a six-month trial basis. An air transport agreement provides additional openings to Nepalese airlines, while allowing Indian Airline to pick up passengers on the Kathmandu-Bangkok route.

A review of private sector activities has revealed that the Nepalese private sector is able to exploit market opportunities to a large extent (IIDS, 1994). It, however, is still very weak and unable to compete with the large Indian conglomerates. Its experience so far has been concentrated in trading. The regulatory framework of the past, as also the limitations imposed by the landlocked nature of the country, poorly developed infrastructure facilities in transportation and communication, a small domestic market, which is further fragmented by poor transportation facilities, a poor physical endowment, largely illiterate and uneducated labor force and under developed capital market, have all constrained the growth of the private sector.

Institutional constraints, such as lack of an appropriate legal framework and administrative interventions in the market, have further impeded private sector development in the past. The Government is still to provide appropriate legal acts or regulations for dispute settlements and copyright protection. On the other hand, consumers have very little scope for legal redress against fraud on quality and quantity of services provided. In education and health, this has become a major problem (See IIDS, 1992 and 1994).

With an aggressive structural adjustment program, most of the price interventions have been withdrawn. Subsidies on publicly supplied products and services are withdrawn, except in the field for education and health. The extent of price subsidies on chemical fertilizer has also been lowered.

However, the private sector industries which were established to fulfill the demand for foreign goods of the bordering Indian market, under a different incentive system deriving from the controlled exchange rate, tariff protection and regulatory framework in India and Nepal are facing severe restructuring problems. Liberalization of the Indian economy since the early 1990s has considerably squeezed the profit margin of industries based on third country imports of semi-finished materials. Its impact on Nepal's industrial performance is evident from the slackened growth rate of output of industries covered by the manufacturing survey, from a high of 5.8 per cent per annum between 1981/82-1991/92 to 2.9 per cent annual average in 1992/93, 1993/94 (See Acharya, 1996). The process of liberalization in the industries, unlike in India, has been so drastic and fast that the private sector could not cope smoothly. It is because disinvestment in old industry and transforming them into new capital requires skill, resource, and efficient functioning of the market, all of which are lacking in Nepal.

The index of manufacturing commodities and manufacturing GDP indicate a substantially accelerated rate of industrial growth: which increased from an average of about 8 per cent between 1984/85-1990/91 to 13.6 per cent between 1990/91-1995/96. Part of this acceleration, however, is attributable to revision of the GDP statistics.

Agriculture and Forestry

Although the importance of the non agricultural sector is increasing in the economy, agriculture still occupies the most prominent role as the source of employment for the majority of the population. This sector has always been dominated by individual peasants. But it has suffered because of price interventions and sometimes physical controls on the movement of agricultural products. Fertilizer has been extensively subsidised to boost agricultural production, but lack of rural infrastructure, mismanagement of irrigation facilities and pressure on the natural environment, particularly deforestation, have affected agriculture adversely in the past, leading to declining land productivity. With the process of liberalisation, all kinds of physical controls on movement of agricultural products and price interventions have been withdrawn. Irrigation policies have been redesigned in favour of farmer managed irrigation systems. The policies on forestry have been totally revamped to grant user rights and responsibilities for forest management to the local communities and allowing leasehold forests to the private sector. Problems, however, remain in the subsidy on fertilizer and, management of the fertilizer distribution. Fertilizer is still handled mainly by a parastatal because, given the subsidy in Government distribution, it is not profitable for the private sector to deal in fertilizer.

Infrastructure

In spite of much progress in recent decades, Nepal faces severe infrastructural problems due to its rugged terrain and landlocked position. Its rich hydropower resources have remained unexploited and Nepal faces a severe energy crisis with the lowest per capita consumption of energy in the region. Nepal has opened its energy sector to domestic private and foreign capital. It has concluded an agreement with India in 1996. A number of foreign offers have been received. But these offers are creating apprehension among the Nepalese that they are geared primarily to supplying energy to India without much benefit to Nepal, in the short or long run. There is also strong opposition to such large projects, because it is likely to aggravate the problem of duality and income concentration in the Nepalese economy.

Nepal's transport problems are still enormous, as nearly 77 per cent of the country is constituted by rugged hills and high mountains. The sector is slowly being opened to the private sector. Since the early nineties, private sector participation has been allowed in domestic air transport and communications. Private sector participation in air-transport has quite improved domestic air transport on profitable routes. Private helicopter services are catering to large customers' freight, as well as personal transportation needs to remote areas. Nonetheless, the government has to take full responsibility for providing air access to people of remote areas, at still highly subsidized freight rates. In communication, although the services have improved greatly since the late eighties, there is still quite a gap in demand and supply of telephone lines. The private sector has been invited to participate in this sector also, but the response has been encouraging only for urban areas. The major issue in this sector, therefore, is how to increase the road coverage of the hilly region with minimum construction and maintenance cost and, telecommunication services to less developed areas. Roads are still primarily a public sector responsibility.

Current Foreign Exchange Regime and Foreign Investment

Nepal has two exchange rate regimes, one with the Indian currency and other with other convertible currencies. Nepalese rupee has been fully convertible in relation to Indian rupees and it remains so today. Nepal introduced full convertibility for its currency against convertible currencies in the current account transactions in 1993. Following this, the exchange rate of all convertible currencies is being determined by market forces. Except for items related to public health and national security considerations, all the import items have been put under open general licencing. Controls on foreign exchange have been relaxed for education, medical treatment, trade promotion and travel by Nepali citizen to foreign countries. Foreign exchange received by individuals and corporate through exports and other means can be deposited in Nepal in foreign currency. This can be easily utilised for importing raw materials, foreign travel, foreign training, business promotion and medical treatment.

Foreign investment is allowed in all kinds of industries except in alcohol, cigarettes and bidi, unless production is entirely exported. Foreign investment is not allowed in industries manufacturing arms and ammunitions. Foreigners are allowed to invest up to 25 per cent of individual establishments in the stock markets also. Foreign investment is permitted up to 100 per cent in large and medium industries. However, permission is required for investment in cottage and small-scale industries, which is granted only in cases of transfer of technology.

Several tax concessions are also granted. Guarantee has been granted against nationalisation and in case of dispute, the U.N. Commission for International Trade Law's arbitration is accepted.

To attract foreign direct investment (FDI), the industrial Enterprises Act 1992 and Foreign Investment and Technology Transfer Act 1992, have introduced a one-window policy. These Acts allow repatriation of (i) profit, (ii) the sale proceeds of part or all of the shares, (iii) amortisation/repayment of foreign loans and (iv) amounts received under technology transfer agreements. Besides, compensation against nationalisation can be repatriated in foreign currency. Foreign experts employed in Nepal's enterprises can remit up to 75 per cent of their salaries and perquisites in foreign currency.

Some specified commodities are allowed to be imported from India against convertible currency. Public, and some private industrial enterprises, are allowed to borrow from abroad on a case by case basis. Foreign portfolio investment is allowed in Nepali enterprises up to a ceiling of 25 per cent of the enterprises' total equity.

Selected Macro Economic Indicators

Investment and Savings

The rate of GDP growth has averaged about 5 per cent per annum in the nineties. The agricultural sector has experienced significant fluctuations and affected overall growth adversely. The share of agriculture in GDP is gradually falling. This structural shift in the composition of GDP reflects both weather dependency of agriculture as well as better performance of the non-agricultural sector. The dependence of the overall economy on agricultural performance is somewhat declining. All non-agricultural sectors have increased their share in GDP, but the growth in the service sector is pre-dominating. However, it should also be noted that part of the apparent shift, as compared to the eighties, is due to revision of the GDP statistics to capture a larger proportion of informal sector activities.

The growth impulse generated by large dosages of devaluation in the early 1990s seems to be leveling out and the growth of the non-agricultural sector in the last three years has averaged around 5-6 per cent. Particularly, manufacturing sector growth is still sluggish. This year, the economy seems to be passing through a recession in spite of increased exports. This is reflected in the slackness of stock market transactions, the slackened rate of monetary expansion and a virtual crash in real estate business.

Gross investment, which had fluctuated between 18 to 20 per cent in the second half of the eighties, has averaged at about 20 per cent in the nineties. The domestic savings rate, fluctuating at around 10 per cent between 1980-1990, had picked up in recent years reaching almost 15 per cent in 1993/94. It has, however, come down since 1994/95. Domestic savings are accounted for primarily by the private sector. The contribution of the private sector to total investment averages around 50 per cent level. This reflects the declining role of the government in direct investment due to liberalization. The savings-investment gap, which is accounted for mostly by the government, has been filled by foreign aid and deficit financing in the government sector.

This has led to a rising foreign debt burden on the country, since the proportion of grants in total foreign aid has been declining. Outstanding foreign debt has reached 50 to 51 per cent of GDP. Foreign debt servicing, as a proportion of export earnings, at about 11 per cent, however, is still modest as : (i) bulk of the debt is still to mature, (ii) grant is still flowing in and (iii) most of the loans are concessional.

TABLE 1

Selected Indicators of Performance of the Economy (In per cent to GDP unless stated otherwise)

	1984 /85	1985 /86	1986 /87	1987 /88	1988 /89	1989 /90	1990 /91	1991 /92	1992 /93	1993 /94	1994 /95	1995 /96
Annual Growth Rate												
Real GDP Annual Growth (%)		4.66	1.97	7.03	5.43	4.92	6.44	4.62	3.29	7.90	2.88	6.14
Agricultural GDP (%)		2.70	-0.70	6.56	6.17	5.77	2.15	-1.06	-0.62	7.60	-0.33	5.41
Non Agricultural GDP (%)		6.72	4.66	7.48	4.73	4.11	10.64	9.76	6.47	8.12	5.32	6.66
Share of Agri to GDP (%)	61.40	51.22	50.26	48.94	48.73	49.07	49.46	47.47	44.89	43.19	43.07	41.73
Inflation Rate (CPI change %)	4.1	15.9	13.3	11	6.3	11.5	9.8	21	8.9	8.9	7.6	8.1
GDP deflator	100	114.4	128.9	144.1	160.4	177.6	194.3	231.8	255.9	274.9	293.1	314.7
Agriculture	100	116.1	131.9	148.6	162.1	181.7	195.2	232.1	251.3	268.5	285.6	285.6
Non-agriculture	100	122.7	126.0	139.9	158.7	173.5	193.5	231.5	259.4	279.7	298.5	298.5
Investment	21.86	19.02	20.20	19.81	21.75	18.45	20.83	22.44	23.14	22.41	23.46	24.34
Fixed Capital Formation (GDP %)	20.15	16.92	18.52	17.44	18.36	16.44	18.92	19.58	21.75	21.10	21.91	22.09

Contd.

TABLE 1 : *continued*

	1984 /85	1985 /86	1986 /87	1987 /88	1988 /89	1989 /90	1990 /91	1991 /92	1992 /93	1993 /94	1994 /95	1995 /96
Annual Growth Rate												
Public	7.79	7.01	7.40	7.13	8.85	7.70	7.21	6.91	6.87	6.72	7.33	7.41
Private	12.36	9.91	11.11	10.31	9.51	8.74	11.71	12.67	12.93	14.38	14.58	14.68
Revenue (GDP %)	8.41	8.33	9.36	9.56	8.71	8.98	8.91	9.04	8.84	9.83	11.19	11.16
Deficit (excl. Grants, GDP %)	9.61	9.25	8.67	8.78	11.46	10.04	10.65	8.63	9.19	7.04	6.60	7.46
Export (GDP %)	5.89	5.54	4.70	5.37	4.72	5.00	6.15	9.18	10.09	9.70	8.05	7.95
Trade Deficit (GDP %)	-10.78	-11.28	-12.41	-12.70	-13.54	-12.75	-13.17	-12.22	-12.82	-16.22	-20.98	-22.79
Current A/C Deficit before Grant (GDP %)	-3.97	-4.43	-4.55	-6.01	-7.10	-7.39	-7.89	-6.74	-5.82	-4.03	-5.37	-9.53
BOP deficit (GDP %)	1.86	-1.01	-0.59	-2.96	-0.09	-2.56	-3.43	-2.27	-4.36	-3.33	-0.22	0.42

Note : FR to months of import = (Previous year's imports /12) / Foreign exchange reserve

(i) Export and net income from services

na non availability of data

Source : Calculated from Annex 1.

CHART
Selected Economic Indicators

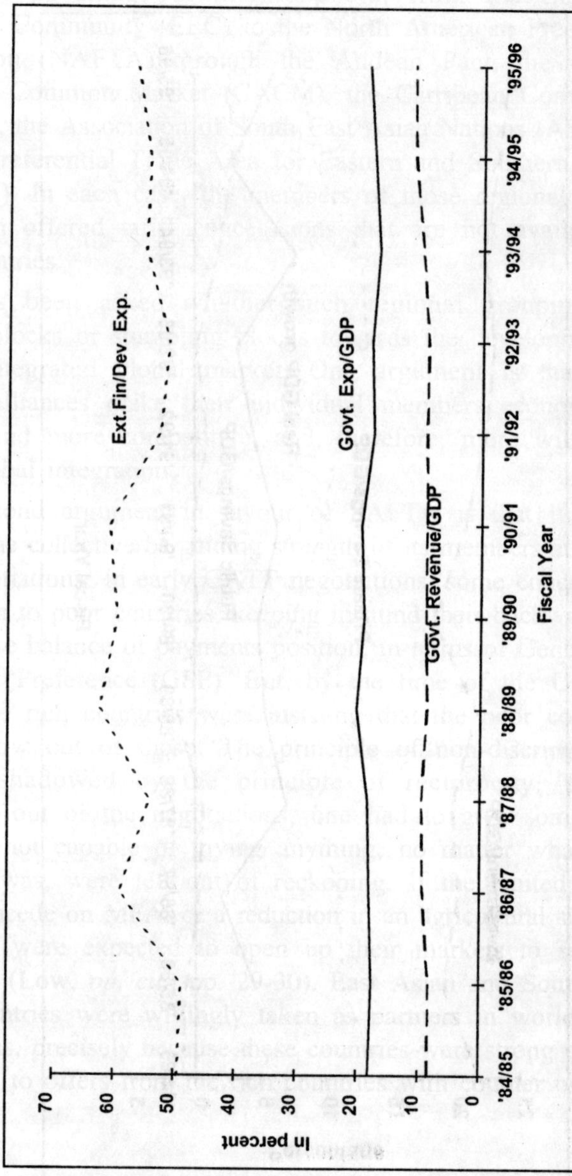

CHART : *continued*

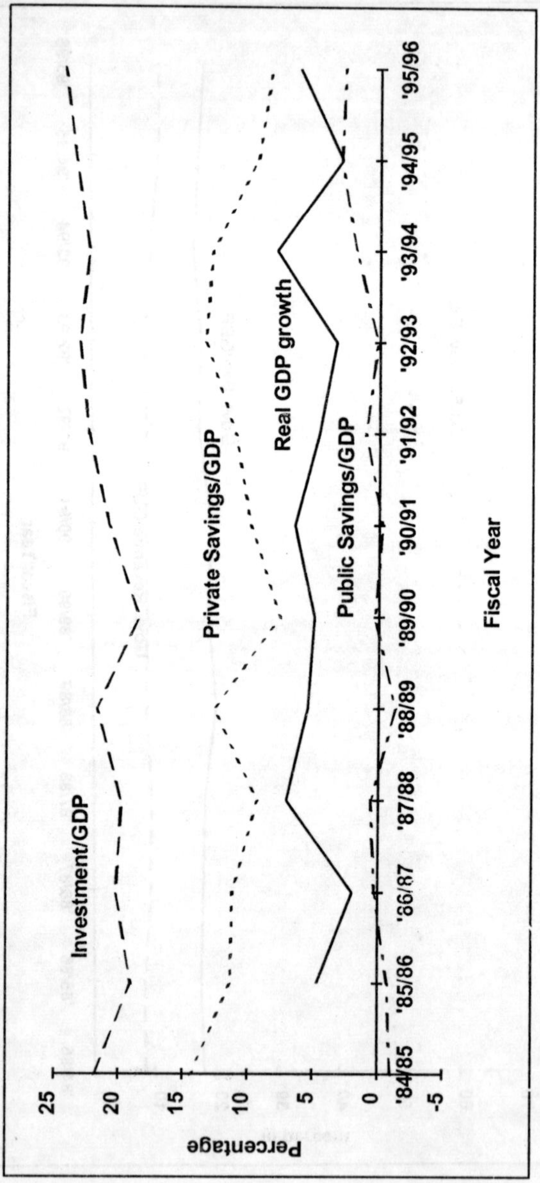

CHART : *continued*

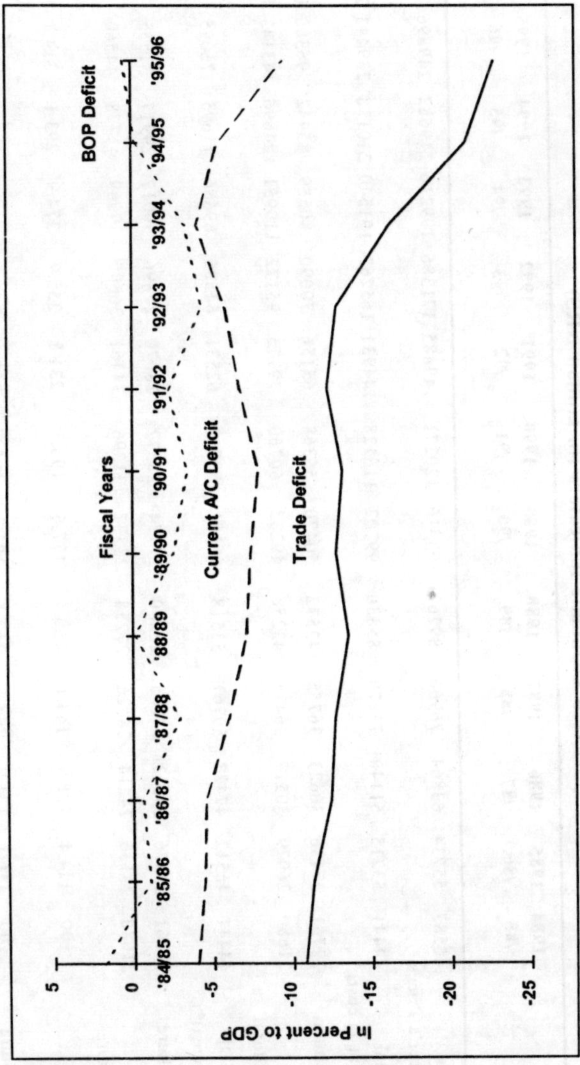

TABLE 2

Selected Economic Indicators (in million NRS)

	1984 /85	1985 /86	1986 /87	1987 /88	1988 /89	1989 /90	1990 /91	1991 /92	1992 /93	1993 /94	1994 /95	1995 /96	1996/ 97 (est.)
1. GDP at Producer's Prices	46587	55734	63864	76906	89269	103416	120371	149485	171386	199216	219582	249896	28427
2. Nominal GDP (at fa.cost)	44441	53215	61140	73170	85830	99702	116128	144931	165262	191540	210138	239443	271461
Agricultural	22761	27136	30623	36755	42572	50470	55368	65156	70090	80589	85442	96300	107405
Non - Agricultural	21680	26079	30517	36415	43258	49232	60760	79775	95172	110951	124696	143143	164056
3. Real GDP (at fa. cost)*	44441	46512	47427	50761	53518	56151	59768	62531	64586	69686	71695	76095	79854
Agriculture	22761	23376	23213	24735	26260	27774	28372	28070	27896	30017	29917	31535	32566
Non-agriculture	21680	23136	24214	26026	27258	28377	31396	34461	36690	39669	41778	44560	47288
4. GDP Deflator	100	114.4	128.9	144.1	160.4	177.6	194.3	231.8	255.9	274.9	293.1	314.7	340
Agriculture	100	116.1	131.9	148.6	162.1	181.7	195.2	232.1	251.3	268.5	285.6	305.4	329.8

Non-agriculture	100	112.7	126	139.9	158.7	173.5	193.5	231.5	259.4	279	298.5	321.2	346.9
5. CPI	104.1	120.6	136.6	151.7	161.3	179.9	197.6	239.1	260.4	283.7	305.4	330.2	
Food & Beverages	101.3	120.1	138.3	155.1	165.9	181.9	200.4	249.2	265.4	289.5	310.7	338.4	
Non-food & Services	109.9	121.7	133.3	145.3	153.7	177.2	193.4	222.4	252.4	274.8	297	316.8	
6. Total Investment	10184	10599	12898	15237	19415	19076	25074	33538	39653	44644	51505	60820	
Fixed Investment	9386	9431	11825	13414	16392	17002	22780	29276	37278	42032	48114	55196	-
Public	3629	3909	4727	5483	7902	7968	8683	10331	11769	13380	16089	18507	
Private	5757	5522	7098	7931	8490	9034	14097	18945	22160	28652	32025	36689	
Change in stock	798	1168	1073	1823	3023	2074	2294	4262	2375	2612	3391	5624	
7. Revenue	3917	4644	5975	7351	7777	9288	10730	13513	15149	19581	24575	28205	
8. Fiscal Deficit (excl. grant)	-4478	-5153	-5538	-6754	-10228	-10381	-12820	-12905	-15749	-14016	-14485	-18476	

Contd.

TABLE 2 : *continued*

	1984/85	1985/86	1986/87	1987/88	1988/89	1989/90	1990/91	1991/92	1992/93	1993/94	1994/95	1995/96	1996/97 (est.)
9. Exports	2746	3086	3003	4127	4211	5170	7403	13726	17286	19316	17680	19875	
A. Trade Balance	-5023	-6286	-7924	-9766	-12086	-13186	-15853	-18261	-21974	-32307	-46060	-56940	
D. Current Account Balance	-1849	-2471	-2904	-4623	-6335	-7644	-9500	-10074	-9972	-8027	-11786	-23824	
H. BOP surplus	866	-563	-377	-2273	-76	-2650	-4132	-3394	-7474	-6632	-480	-1050	

Public sector domestic savings = Revenue - government consumption.

Private sector domestic savings = Gross domestic savings - public savings.

*Real GDP at factor cost 1779/80-1983/84 at '74/75 prices and from 1984/85 - 1996/97 at '84/85 prices).

Blanks signify non availability of data.

Source : *Economic Survey*, 1994/95 and CBS for 1996/97.

The Government Sector and Its Operations

The government sector still accounts for 33 per cent of fixed capital investment in the country. Given the low level of physical and human infrastructure, the government sector's role in the economy will continue in the near future, inspite of liberalisation. One or other party coming to power may not make a difference in this respect. Major problems are still growing deficit and slackness in development activities.

Nepal's attempts at revenue mobilization have not been very encouraging. In spite of annual revisions in tax procedures and series of tax reforms, revenue has remained at 9-11 per cent of GDP, while tax revenue constitutes only about 7-9 per cent of GDP. With rapidly growing total expenditure and sluggish revenue mobilization, the deficit is growing, crossing 7 per cent of GDP in 1995/96. The gap is being filled primarily by foreign and internal loans, as well as deficit financing. Revenue mobilization remains a major problem in the government sector. The introduction of a value added tax shortly is expected to boost tax revenue.

Another major policy option adopted for cutting government expenditure was privatisation of public enterprises and a cut in subsidies. The orientation towards privatisation of public enterprises (PEs) evolved in the 1980s. But the process has accelerated only after 1991, when the government adopted a policy of phased privatisation. Since then, 12 PEs have been privatized and government equity in one has been lowered. Additional PEs, including RNAC, RBB, NBL and NTC, are slated for privatisation by June 1998. The impact of privatization has been mixed in terms of capacity utilisation, labor productivity and profitability levels. In most cases, the employment opportunities have shrunk and product prices have gone up substantially (Rastra Sewak, 1995, Acharya, 1996). Nevertheless, major political parties are agreed that not all PEs need to remain in the public sector. Differences do exist regarding the speed, prioritisation and the process of privatisation.

Smaller items of subsidies have been cut to a large extent. The price of most publicly supplied goods — rice, sugar, edible oil, electricity, water, etc., have been revised upwards to eliminate or reduce subsidies. But the subsidies on fertilizers and interest of credit to small farmers still continue. The fertilizer subsidy is expected to amount almost to Rs. 700 million, even in the current fiscal year 1996/97. The revision of charges on electricity and drinking water is a major political hazard for ruling parties, as it is resisted actively by urban middle class. Petroleum products, particularly diesel and kerosene pricing presents additional problems. Diesel prices have a cascading effect on inflation as Nepal's transportation sector is constituted mainly by roads and aviation.

Debt servicing is eating up a larger and larger proportion of the government budget, consuming about one-third of regular expenditure. Debt servicing has increased very fast in the last decade. However, currently it is accounted for mostly by internal debt servicing. Once the foreign debt servicing catches up, it is bound to affect both the budget and balance of payments adversely. A devaluation/depreciation of the Nepalese Rupees (NRs) adds a direct burden to the budget on account of foreign debt servicing and also impacts adversely on the balance of payment (BOP). External debt servicing is likely to grow to 14-15 per cent of exports of goods and services in the next few years, with foreign direct investment (FDI) in hydropower projects. Without FDI flow to hydropower projects and, with the share of grants in total foreign aid decreasing in the last few years, debt servicing figures are likely to reach 16-17 per cent of the exports of goods and services.

A decelerated rate of development expenditure is another point of concern. Nepal is still far behind other South Asian countries in the development of physical and social infrastructure, with the lowest per head road length and electricity consumption. The literacy rate and life expectancy, as indicators of health status (to be discussed below) are among the lowest in the region (WDR, 1997). The government needs to invest large resources in these sectors, as there is little hope for the private sector or FDI fulfilling the investment requirements, except perhaps in the energy sector. This is because of the small domestic market and, consequently, low profitability for the private sector.

Balance of Payments

Policy reforms in the external sector were the most extensive and fastest among all policy measures undertaken. Starting with a guarded pace of import liberalisation and flexibility in the exchange rate policy since the mid-eighties, Nepal attained full convertibility on the current account in March 1993 and set free the exchange rate of NRs *vis-a-vis* convertible currencies. The tariff and sales tax on imports were reduced substantially.

Nepal's BOP situation, however, is still characterized by rapidly increasing current account deficits (after grants), reaching a high of 9.5 per cent of GDP in 1995/96 and a precarious BOP position, which largely depends on external financing. The current account deficit, as a proportion of GDP, is increasing rather than decreasing. Export growth has remained moderate, barring the immediate post devaluation period. Third country (other than India) trade, concentrated on carpets and garments, has suffered because of the situation in the international market. Nepal has to compete with India in woolen carpets and with India and Bangladesh in garments. Trade liberalisation has not substantially changed the structure of imports, as more than two-fifths of imports are still constituted by manufacturing goods. Finally, the overall BOP situation has remained manageable only because of a high level of foreign aid and, very recently, miscellaneous private capital inflows.

Poverty and Living Standards

Real per capita income in Nepal has been estimated to have grown by about 2.4 per cent per annum during 1985-1995 (WDR, 1997). Neverthless, poverty is perceived to be increasing by various sections in the society, as the employment scenario is still bleak. Some amount of the relative shift in the production structure has not resulted in a corresponding shift in employment.

Agriculture still employs 81 per cent of the labor force. This asymmetry in production and employment suggests growing rural poverty and, increased skewedness in urban income distribution. From a socio-economic standpoint this is a burning issue.

Nepal faces a dual problem of unemployment and unavailability of skilled and semi-skilled human power in modern sectors. The inflow of foreign skilled and semi-skilled manpower has hindered the growth of such workers supply (see ILO, 1997). Moreover, the feudalistic value system which puts a low status on physical labour, has hindered middle class youths from joining the skilled/semi-skilled work force. This has led to increasing economic difficulties among the majority of middle class people who own small plots of land. The lower middle class situation is worse. The rural service class, which depended on local demand from higher classes in the villages, has suffered the most because of the deteriorating situation of the middle class and onslaught of imported cheap goods (*e.g.*, plastic buckets) on their products. According to a recent survey (CBS, 1996), poverty in Nepal has increased in the eighties. Currently about 45 per cent of the people are estimated to have incomes less than necessary to meet their minimum needs of calorie, clothing, shelter, primary health care and primary education (Approach Paper to Ninth Plan). Earlier estimates hovered around 40-42 per cent.

Although the impact of liberalization on GDP growth has been positive in general (see, NEFAS, 1996, Pyakuryel 1995, Bajracharya and Sharma, 1995), there has been only a marginal improvement in real wage rates in general between 1985-1995. According to available indicators, agricultural wages seem to have slumped in real terms (Acharya, 1996). The poor and middle class seem to have gained somewhat because of the higher agricultural growth rates and the increased labor absorption by the manufacturing sector during the 1980s. They seem to be losing during the 1990s. Dampening agricultural growth rates, deteriorating terms of trade between agriculture and non-agricultural sectors, decreasing labor intensity of production, declining employment opportunities in the public sector, increased competition from foreign labor and increasing prices of the basic necessities such as, food, education, health facilities and housing in the 1990s have affected them adversely.

Economic Policies : A Prognostication

Nepali Congress (NC) and UML, the two prominent political parties are expected to influence the course of events in Nepal in the next decade. It is, therefore, important to analyze their attitude to economic management of the country in the next few paragraphs.

As far as economic policies are concerned, in principle UML is unlikely to make a major departure from previous N.C. governments. Whatever differences, if any, will be in the speed and quality of implementation, as well as pace and sequencing of economic reforms. The present government has shown its commitment to liberalisation, by allowing a substantial increase (even unwarranted for increase) in petroleum products and cooking gas prices recently, in spite of criticisms by all parties including UML.

Agricultural growth will be given a boost by both the NC and UML government, as both have declared acceptance of the Agricultural Prospective Plan (APP). The Ninth Plan Approach paper has accepted agriculture as the leading sector of the economy. APP is geared to rural infrastructure building, including rural road and irrigation facilities and provision of adequate improved inputs and chemical fertilizers. Decentralisation and people's participation are viewed as the main tools of management in this growth process, indicating towards a increased flow of resources to rural areas.

In industry, UML appears to be much more activist than NC. To NC, the free play of market forces would result in the most appropriate industrialization of Nepal. Whereas, UML considers that Nepal has the potential to industrialise and it must. To them, if some industry has the prospective global/regional competitive edge in the medium to future term, then the state should nurture that industry through fiscal means. Further, much emphasis has been placed on assistance to small and cottage industries in the Ninth Plan Approach Paper.

The infrastructure — mainly energy, roads and communications are still in government sectors. The Ninth plan approach paper is committed to further liberalisation of this sector. In spite of some liberalisation and opening of the sectors to the private sector, the issue of exploitation of hydropower resources has been greatly politicised. The need for Indian cooperation is realized by all parties, but suspicion of Indian dominance and concern for environment and local population, have tended to slow down the commissioning of large projects. How fast these confusions can be resolved and a meaningful cooperation with neighboring countries can be initiated is not clear. The recent agreement with India on electricity exports by private parties is a positive initiative in this context.

On the fiscal front there is consensus, in principle, among all three major political parties. They all agree on the need for lower fiscal deficit, higher mobilisation of internal revenue, containing the growth of regular expenditure and the implementation of VAT. The current government has already announced that VAT will be implemented from the current fiscal year in a few selected areas.

The problems in external sector-rising imports, export-import deficit and BOP dependence on external funding are likely to continue. The current account deficit, as a proportion of GDP, is likely to rise further from the current 7.5 per cent as inflow of foreign grants are likely to decline further. The external debt problem is likely to exacerbate, as the proportion of grants continues to decline and debts start maturing.

Whosoever comes to power, poverty eradication and employment generation will remain major goals. Major objectives of the Ninth Plan, which is set within the context of a 20 year Perspective Plan, are poverty eradication and employment generation. This approach paper had been primarily formulated by the previous Planning Commission and hence, all parties including NC seem to be committed to the goals of poverty alleviation. This will be achieved by liberalization of the economy and special emphasis on human development, agricultural growth and infrastructure building. The thrust and the content of economic reform will continue. The difference among the parties will be reflected in the speed and quality of implementation and their sequencing. The Ninth Plan Approach paper aims at an annual growth rate of 6.5 per cent. This, however, will be difficult to achieve in view of the unfolding political scenario of instability.

The volatility of political situation is likely to affect the government policy making and investment activities adversely, as political leaders are likely to concentrate on power politics rather than on developmental issues. The bureaucracy is likely to be further paralysed. This will slow down the decision making process, aggravating the infrastructural problems in the country. Slowdown in the government decision making process is likely to affect private investment adversely.

On the positive side, the politicisation of rural masses has increased the mobilisation of the rural population by NGOs for developmental work and grievance settlement, may lead to demand of greater transparency and accountability in the use of resources at the grassroots level. Since both major political parties adhere to the philosophy of liberalisation and since donors play a decisive role in Nepal's economic management issues, there is a little chance of the liberalization process getting reversed. APP and decentralisation, which command a national consensus, will speed up the flow of resources to rural areas.

A national consensus exists for expanding the scope of cooperation within the South Asian Association for Regional Cooperation (SAARC) and joining the World Trade Organization (WTO). Nepal's access to port facilities and market is increasing with better relations with India and opening up of the transit route to overseas *via* Bangladesh. The ideas of a SAARC Growth Quadrangle, and South Asian Free Trade Area (SAFTA), are moving ahead. The growth quadrangle will include Nepal, Bangladesh, Bhutan and India.

The real GDP growth, which averaged around 5 per cent in the first half of 90s is likely to continue. Inflationary pressures will remain moderate at 7-9 per cent annual rate, as in India, or accelerate to some extent. Government savings, revenue mobilization and government expenditure will continue to hover around the 1990-1997 rate, as the Government decision making process is not likely to improve. Debt servicing pressure on the government budget is likely to increase.

Growth impulses are expected to derive primarily from the private sector and the diversion of resources to rural areas following Agricultural Prospective Plan, decentralization and rural infrastructure building. Private sector activities may pick up as a long term impact of liberalization starts to materialise. Further, the opening up of the Indian market and improvement in the transit facilities for Nepal (following the Gujral Doctrine) are likely to improve conditions for growth of manufacturing sector. Tourism will be boosted further with the opening up of new areas.

REFERENCES

Acharya, Meena (1996), *Politico-Economic Situation and Development Programming in Nepal*, submitted to IDV, DGIS, Ministry of Foreign Affairs, Netherlands.

APROSC, ADB/M, MOA/HMG (1994), Agricultural Perspective Plan, Kathmandu.

Bajracharya, P. and Sharma, S. (1995), *Impact of Economic Liberalization in Nepal*, IIDS.

Bhattachan, Krishna Bahadur (1996), *Decentralization in Socio-Culturally Plural Nepalese Society* (*Ibid.*)

Central Bureau of Statistics (1995), *Population Monograph of Nepal*, Kathmandu.

Central Bureau of Statistics (1996), *Nepal Living Standard Survey*, 1995/96.

Josse, M.R. (1997), Gujaral Doctrine revisited - Gleanning from the Indian Media *The Rising Nepal*, June 25, 1997.

HMG (1995), "Economic Survey Fiscal Year 1995/96", Ministry of Finance, July 1996.

HMG (1997), The Approach Paper to Ninth Plan (Nepali), National Planning Commission.

HMG (1997), The Ordinance on Local Polls, April 1997.

IIDS (1992), "An Overview of the Private Sector in Nepal", Kathmandu.

IIDS (1994), "A Strategy For Rural Service Delivery," *Rural Service Delivery Review Phase I and II* ,Vols. I and II Kathmandu.

IIDS (1996), A need for Strengthening Democratic Process within the Political Parties (Nepali). Paper presented to the Seminar organized by IIDS on the similar topic, Kathmandu, 1996.

ILO/UNDP (1997), Nepal : An Employment Strategy (Draft Report), Kathmandu.

NEFAS (1996), *Structural Adjustment Program in Nepal; Impact on Workers*, ed. Dahal N.R. and Shrestha A. P.

Pyakuryal B. (1995), *Impact of Economic Liberalization in Nepal*, University of Maryland, USA.

Rastra Sewak (1995), *Privatization of Public Enterprises in Nepal, Lessons of Experience*, Vol. 1 (3).

Shakya, Bijendra M. (1997), One Window but Closed Doors, *The Rising Nepal*, June 26, 1997.

The World Bank (1997), Human Development Report.

8

Economic Reforms and Prospects for Growth in Pakistan

AMIR MAHMOOD

1. Introduction

Pakistan embarked on a program of economic and institutional reforms in the 1980s with a view to achieve a new equilibrium at a higher growth path. The economic liberalisation process accelerated in the late 1980s, when Pakistan entered into a Structural Adjustment Facility (SAF) arrangement with the IMF. Since 1988, successive Pakistani governments have been perusing an economic and institutional reform process that emphasises the need for an accelerated industrialisation drive, an export-led growth strategy, higher productivity growth and an improvement in national competitiveness to accomplish higher standards of living.

So far, the economic and institutional reforms in Pakistan have failed to generate the conditions necessary to acquire rapid economic growth and higher living standards. The purpose of this study is to provide a critical assessment of Pakistan's reform experience and to outline the necessary conditions and challenges that need to be addressed if the country is to achieve a sustainable rate of economic growth.

The paper is divided into four Sections. Section 2 provides an assessment of the World Bank/IMF sponsored Structural Adjustment Program that was implemented from 1988 to 1991.

During 1992-96, Pakistan did not receive any financial assistance from the above institutions to support its reform process. However, the governments that came into power during this phase adhered to the broad objectives set out in the IMF/World Bank reform agenda. Section 3 provides a brief overview of the instruments of economic and institutional reforms during the non-program years and assesses the outcomes. Faced with an acute economic crisis and a desire to foster the process of economic and institutional reform, the Muslim League government, which was elected in February 1997, had no choice but to incorporate the World Bank//IMF proposed structural reforms into its reform agenda. Section 4 outlines the salient features of the recent reform process in Pakistan and provides a critical assessment of Pakistan's potential for sustainable economic growth in the presence of its structural weaknesses and prevailing social, economic and political environment. Section 5 presents policy conclusions drawn from this study.

2. Economic Reforms in Pakistan : The Program Years (1988-91)

The First Bhutto Government (1988-1990) entered into a Structural Adjustment Facility (SAF) arrangement with the IMF to implement the structural adjustment program of economic reform through (a) adopting an export oriented growth strategy; (b) flexible exchange rates; (c) privatization; (d) deregulation; (e) import liberalization; (f) removal of subsidies with an expansion of the tax base; (g) provision of free market conditions; (h) tight monetary policy aiming to restrict demand; (i) tariff rationalization; (j) industrial incentives; (k) expenditure control; (l) measures to foster savings, investment and non-debt creating capital inflows and (m) removal of price and distributional control for agriculture inputs. The structural adjustment reforms aimed at improving the balance of payment position while maintaining the growth momentum.

The overall impact of these economic and institutional reforms on key macroeconomic indicators, such as, balance of payment, inflation, growth, saving and investment, real consumption levels, fiscal deficit and debt performance, is summarised in table 1[1].

As table 1 indicates, the 1988 structural reform package produced mixed results. On the balance of payments front, there was no improvement. Similarly, there was no headway in terms of a reduction in the ratio of the fiscal deficit to GNP, resulting in the current account deficit moving in the same direction. The demand management policies, prescribed by the IMF reform package, while successful in lowering the rate of consumer price increases, caused real GDP growth to decline.

TABLE 1

Economic Reforms in Pakistan : 1988-91

Economic Indicator	Improvement	Deterioration
Current Account Deficit		X
Inflation	X	
GDP Growth		X
Savings	X	
Investment	X	
Real Consumption		X
Fiscal Deficit	X	
Debt Services		X

Note : X = Improvement or Deterioration.

Source : Table 1-9., Mahmood (1995).

The results insinuate that the demand management policies along with financial sector reform succeeded in increasing the growth in the savings ratio. The policies to restrain demand, while successful in improving the saving performance caused real consumption to decline in the longer-run. The structural adjustment program had considered private investment as an

1. For a detailed explanation on the assessment methology and an evaluation of the IMF/World Bank reform process in Pakistan, see Mahmood (1995).

engine of growth, and one of the principal goals of this program was to encourage domestic as well as foreign investment in the country through various incentives and policy actions. The result shows that the broad features of this adjustment package, such as privatization, deregulation, and liberalization of the domestic economy had a positive impact on investment. In the case of external debt performance, the debt service ratio showed some signs of improvement. This result, however, was not unexpected, as one of the key functions of the IMF reform package in developing countries has been to ensure better debt management.

3. Economic Reforms and Outcomes : The Non-Program Years (1992-96)

Although Pakistan did not receive funds under the structural adjustment program during 1992-96, the country still followed the IMF/World Bank development doctrine. Successive elected, as well as caretaker, governments that came into power introduced various economic and institutional reforms to : (i) achieve a higher rate of economic growth; (ii) improve savings and investments; (iii) increase resource mobilisation and (iv) accelerate industrialisation.

The principal building blocks of these reforms were : privatization, deregulation, liberalization and macroeconomic stability. The key objectives of privatisation, deregulation and liberalisation were to :

(a) eliminate the rigid economic environment that acts as a constraint to economic growth.

(b) reduce trade and tariff barriers (*i.e.*, to encourage competition and boost exports).

(c) improve national productivity.

(d) accelerate the pace of industrialisation.

(e) liberalize the financial sector (*i.e.*, to boost private sector investment).

(f) improve efficiency of government business enterprises and

(g) increase the efficiency and productivity of the private sector through deregulation.

Knowing that privatisation is necessary but not a sufficient condition to improve productivity and efficiency, the government opened up industries, such as, commercial banking; power generation, telecommunications, airlines, shipping, road construction and port operations, for the private sector. Similarly, to encourage foreign direct investment (FDI) , the government took the following actions :

(a) with the exception of few industries, no prior approval is required to undertake FDI,

(b) foreigners were allowed to control 100 percent of equity in a business venture,

(c) with the exception of a few industries (*i.e.*, banks, insurance firms, and airlines), no prior permission is required to remit the dividends,

(d) increased access to domestic borrowing by the foreign banks,

(e) elimination of control on the operation of foreign currency accounts by foreign firms and individuals, etc.

In the foreign trade sector, the leading feature of the trade policy reforms was to liberalise imports to increase the capacity utilisation of domestic industries using imported inputs and to boost exports. The long-term objective of these policy reforms was to switch from being the inward-looking and import substituting to becoming an outward-looking export oriented economy. To this effect, the government reduced the maximum import duty from 125 per cent to 90 per cent and eliminated the public sector monopoly on the export of rice and cotton (Government of Pakistan : 1996). These trade policy measures were reinforced through industry policy initiatives to accelerate the pace of industrialisation. These initiatives included, tax holidays for new industrial ventures, removal of regulatory control and a drop in import duties on imported plant and machinery.

The performance of the Pakistan economy during this politically unstable period, which witnessed six governments, was lackluster. By the end of 1996, when President Leghari dismissed Prime Minister Benazir Bhutto and her government, the country was facing a serious economic crisis. The major elements of this crisis were: slow economic growth (3.1 per cent), high inflation (11.5 per cent), widening trade (5.7 per cent of GDP) and current account deficits (7.07 per cent of GDP), low levels of investment (18.4 per cent of GNP) and national savings (12 per cent of GNP), rapidly increasing budget deficit (6.3 per cent of GDP), depleting foreign exchange reserves (US $ 514 Million), a growing debt service ratio (3.6 per cent of GDP) and a sever financial problem. The extent of this economic crisis can be judged from the fact that when the new government came into power it requested Pakistani nationals living abroad to make foreign exchange deposits to help the country to meet its external debt obligations. Given the rate of GDP growth was similar to the population growth, per capita income remained stagnant. The growth rate of large-scale manufacturing recorded a negative growth rate of 1.4 per cent, whereas the agriculture sector grew at a rate of less than one per cent in 1996 (Government of Pakistan : 1997).

Apart from the above dismal outcomes, the economic reforms in Pakistan have also been unsuccessful to bring about a structural change in the economy, a pre-requisite for industrialisation. The share of the agriculture sector in employment and value added remained stagnant. For example, the sectoral share of agriculture in GDP declined marginally from 25.7 per cent in 1988 to 24.2 per cent in 1996. In the case of manufacturing, the sectoral share increased slightly from 18.1 per cent to 18.4 per cent during the above period. For the services sector, these figures were 49.1 per cent and 49.4 per cent respectively (Appendix 1). The country also failed to diversify its exports and performed poorly in penetrating into the high growth markets of Southeast and East Asia.

4. Recent Economic Reforms and Pakistan's Growth Prospects

Confronting severe economic crisis, the Muslim League government that came into power in February 1997 introduced wide ranging economic and institutional reforms to steer the country away from insolvency and to lay foundations for sustainable economic growth. The recent broad-based economic and institutional reform package stresses the importance of rapid economic growth with macroeconomic stability. It is envisaged that these reforms will accelerate the pace of industrialisation, leading to rising exports, higher productivity growth, and an improvement in competitiveness. The 1997 economic reforms constitute measures to revive the agriculture and manufacturing sectors, tariff and tax reductions, financial sector reforms, expenditure controls to reduce the budget deficit and lower government bank borrowing.

Given the importance of the agriculture sector in the economy, the Muslim League government announced a major agriculture policy package to boost the productivity of this sector and to reduce the country's dependence on food imports. The salient features of this package which targeted better returns to farmers through higher support prices for their crops were, relief in prices of some agricultural inputs, provision and recovery of agricultural credit, and improvement in irrigation and drainage facilities

As a part of the financial reforms of 1994, the State Bank of Pakistan was given autonomous status. As a result of recent reforms in this sector, the Bank now has complete independence to conduct monetary policy and is responsible for the smooth functioning of the entire financial sector and prudential supervision. The Bank has the responsibility to ensure consistency among various macro-economic targets, such as, economic growth, inflation, budget deficit, monetary expansion, and balance of payments.

Realising the complementary role of direct foreign investment in the growth process, the government has relaxed foreign exchange controls to encourage foreign capital inflow. Foreign investors are allowed to participate in local projects on a 100 per cent equity basis and are allowed full repatriation of capital and dividend payments. Similarly, the import duty on machinery and equipment has been abolished or reduced for foreign firms. To encourage domestic as well as foreign investment the new government has expanded the scope of privatization by including the power sector, financial institutions, infrastructure, roads, oil and gas sector, and public utilities.

To reduce the growth of the budget deficit, various initiatives have been taken to curb expenditure and to raise tax revenue. Specifically, the government has taken steps to reduce tax rate, increase the tax elasticity, simplify the tax structure and to shift the emphasis from tariff and export taxes to domestic taxes, eliminate tax exemptions and tax evasion, improve tax administration, increase user charges that reflect cost of provision, remove subsidies, introduce agricultural income tax, and to introduce a Goods and Services Tax.

In the past, the process of economic and institutional reforms in Pakistan has had a little success in generating conditions for sustainable economic growth and higher living standards. In the context of present reforms, the growth prospects depends on Pakistan's ability to improve performance of the agriculture and manufacturing sectors, boost the level of investment and savings, control the rate of inflation, reduce the unsustainable high levels of fiscal deficit, improve the performance of the banking sector, and to contain the growing current account deficit. Macroeconomic stability, political certainty, good governance, investment on human resources, and economic liberalisation can provide a conducive environment for the country to improve national competitiveness and achieve a higher rate of economic growth that is sustainable.

While adherence to the ongoing economic reform process is necessary, the success of these reforms, however, depends on the extent to which the government addresses the following challenges as it enters the next century.

Challenges Ahead

The Agricultural Sector

Like other developing countries, the main impetus to Pakistan's economic growth comes from the agricultural sector. The agricultural sector contributes 24 per cent to GDP and absorbs 47 per cent of the country's labor force (Appendix 1 and 2). Given that over 80 per cent of Pakistan's exports are agriculture based, Pakistan's export performance is sensitively linked with the performance in agricultural sector. Historically, the agricultural sector has been an engine of economic growth in Pakistan. In the 1980s, this sector grew at an annul rate of 5.5 per cent, contributing to over 6 per cent of GDP growth. The recent growth record of the agricultural sector has been far from impressive. During 1988-96, the agricultural sector grew at an average rate of 4 per cent (Appendix 2). This has led to poor GDP growth, widening current account deficit, a slow down in manufacturing activity, deterioration in the balance of payments, and rising inflation. As there exists a limited scope to bring more area under cultivation, the performance of this sector depends, among other things, on raising its productivity. During 1988-1996, the index of agriculture production grew at a modest annual rate of 3.31 per cent per annum (Appendix 3). Among other factors, a key element of the poor performance of agricultural production has been the slow labour productivity growth of an annual rate 2 per cent during the period 1988-1994 (APO : 1996). There exists a wide gap between potential and realized productivity growth of the agricultural sector. Under stable macroeconomic conditions, investment in rural infrastructure, efficient use of existing infrastructure, timely provision of agricultural inputs including credit, improvement in the effectiveness of research and development efforts, maintenance of price stability, and a provision of conducive environments that provide incentives for technological adoption and diffusion, are the necessary conditions for achieving higher productivity growth in agriculture.

The Manufacturing Sector

Among other determinants, Pakistan's growth potential relies on the performance of its manufacturing sector. This sector employs over 10 per cent of the labor force and its contribution in GDP is around 18 per cent. During 1988-96, the manufacturing sector grew at an annual average rate of 5 per cent, with small-scale industries outperforming the large scale-manufacturing sector (Appendix 1 and 3). Since 1994, the performance of large-scale manufacturing has suffered seriously, with the large-scale sector growing at an annual average rate of only 0.89 per cent (Government of Pakistan : 1997). The poor performance of this sub-sector can be attributed to its inability to adjust in the face of economic liberalisation, ethnic and sectarian violence, political instability, breakdown of the law and order situation in Karachi, poor and inadequate public infrastructure and the multiplicity of taxes. Apart from the above reasons, low investment rates and productivity slowdown have constrained the performance of both large and small-scale manufacturing.

Unlike the dynamic economies of Asia which have witnessed a profound structural change, the reform process failed to bring a similar change in Pakistan where the share of manufacturing in GDP grew at a dismal annual average rate of 0.5 per cent during the period 1988-1996 (Appendix 1). To achieve rapid and sustainable economic growth, the manufacturing sector has to play a much more dynamic role. Apart from providing macro-economic and political stability, a sustained manufacturing growth will depend on the level and productivity of private investment and on the provision and efficiency of complementary public infrastructure.

Investment

An important reason for the slow manufacturing growth in Pakistan has been the disappointingly low rate of gross fixed investment which, as a percentage of GNP, has recorded an average growth rate of less than 0.2 per cent during 1988-1996. A breakdown of gross fixed investment shows that during this period where private sector investment, as a percentage of GNP, grew at an annual average rate of 1.6 per cent, investment in public capital, as a percentage of GNP, exhibited a negative growth of 1.2 per cent (Appendix 4). It is highly unlikely that Pakistan can achieve a higher level of economic growth without raising its level of investment. Here, the level as well as the efficiency of the public capital will play an instrumental role in helping the country to attain a higher growth path.

The investment in public infrastructure is one of the key ingredients for growth and competitiveness. In recent times, there has been a realization that economic infrastructure or public capital is an important factor in the growth process. It is now widely agreed that the efficiency and productivity of private capital depends on the provision of well-maintained and efficient public infrastructure, such as, roads, electricity, telecommunication and waste disposal. By the same token a slowdown in the infrastructure investment has adverse repercussions for productivity growth [(Ratner : 1983); Aschauer : 1993); (Holtz-Eakin : 1988, 1992); Munnell (1990, 1992), Fernald (1993); Rafael Flores de Frutos and Alferdo Pereira (1993); Lynde and Richmond (1993), and Swaroop (1994)]. A decline in public infrastructure investment has been attributed to a drop in productivity leading to falling private profits and investment. The interaction between productive private capital and infrastructure investment, therefore, is important to improve competitiveness at all levels. It is crucial to note that investment in the private capital will be productive only if there has been adequate investment in infrastructure involving roads, transportation, communication, water and power systems (Datta-Chaudhuri : 1980). The adequacy of infrastructure coupled with investment in directly productive capital is not a sufficient condition to improve competitiveness. What is required is the adequacy as well as the efficiency of public infrastructure to facilitate private productive investment.

Savings

The financing of a higher level of private as well as public investment demands a major boost in the domestic saving rate.

However, the economic reforms in Pakistan, so far, have yet to succeed to create conditions that are conducive to high rate of savings. In 1996-97, national savings stood at 11.3 per cent of GNP, which was one of the poorest performances in the developing world. Such has been the state of national rate of savings that, as a percentage of GNP, it has recorded a negative growth rate of over 1 per cent during 1988-1997 (Appendix 4).

The poor saving performance has led to reliance on foreign savings which, as a percentage of GNP, has grown at an annual average rate of over 16 per cent during the period under consideration. Given a negative growth rate of national savings, coupled with a heavy reliance on foreign sources, Pakistan's ability to increase the levels of private as well as public sector investment is under considerable doubt, especially when domestic savings are inadequate to support even modest levels of investment. To achieve a rapid and sustainable economic growth, there is need to redouble the efforts for raising public as well private savings by (a) creating an economic environment which is conducive to savings, (b) making the operation of the public sector cost effective and (c) reforming the tax system in order to realize the existing revenue potential in the country.

Budgetary Deficits

Sustainable budgetary deficits are essential to provide helpful environments for rapid economic growth and macroeconomic stability. In general, Pakistan's budgetary performance during the last decade has been disappointing. The fiscal deficit, as a per cent of GDP, remained high and endeavors to bring the deficit within 5 per cent of GDP have been fruitless due to a narrow tax base and government's inability to control expenditures. In 1996, direct tax revenue constituted only 3.7 per cent of GDP, whereas the same figure for indirect taxes stood at 10.4 per cent of GDP (Appendix 5). Although the absolute level of direct tax revenue remained low, the structural reform process has beginning to have an impact on the composition of total tax revenue. During 1988-1996, the direct tax revenue, as a per cent of GDP, grew at an annual average rate of 9.8 per cent at a time when indirect tax revenues were falling at an annual average rate of 1.7 per cent (Appendix 5). While the absolute levels of government expenditures remained high, the structural reforms have succeeded in reversing their growth trend, which is reflected by a negative annual average growth of 1.3 per cent during 1988-1996.

Pakistan's push for achieving a higher growth rate with economic stability depends on the outcome of its efforts in expanding the tax base while improving tax elasticity, reducing the comlexicities of the tax regime, and improving the tax administration while minimizing tax evasion. Similarly, there is an urgency to increase the level of non-tax revenue such as user charges for public utilities, which in most cases do not recover their operational costs. By the same token, public utilities need to eliminate inefficiencies to lower the burden of subsidies.

A reformed tax system along with an efficient public sector can provide a major breakthrough in lowering the budget deficit by raising tax revenue and controlling the government expenditures. The structural reforms have, so far, failed to reduce the budget deficit to a manageable level resulting in rising internal as well as external deficit. The servicing of the mounting foreign debt has limited the country's ability to finance the development needs of the society.

Inflation

Controlling price pressures has been the corner stone of the economic reforms in Pakistan. However, expansionary fiscal and monetary policies, successive devaluation, higher utility charges, an increase in indirect taxes, and adverse supply shocks confronted by both the agricultural and manufacturing sectors, have led to double digit inflation during 1993-1997, which, on average, has risen at an annual rate of over 8 per cent per annum during 1988-97. The success of the reform process to a large extent depends on the government's ability to achieve and maintain a non-inflationary growth path.

Exports

Export-led growth has been the cornerstone of the economic strategy of successive Pakistani governments. A major thrust of structural and institutional reforms in Pakistan has been to increase the world market share through export competitiveness and to narrow the current account deficit. During 1988-96, exports grew at an annual average rate of 9 per cent, while, on average, the terms of trade remained in Pakistan's favour, with unit prices of exports rising faster than that of imports (Appendix 6). This has been a healthy aspect of Pakistan's export performances given the dampening effect of successive devaluation on export prices. In the context of foreign trade, Pakistan's major challenges remained its narrow export base, major reliance on the agricultural sector, and its failure to penetrate into the high growth economies of East and Southeast Asia.

An analysis of the 1996-97 export structure shows that 68 per cent of the export earnings were from manufactured goods, followed by semi-manufactured (21 per cent) and primary goods (11 per cent) (Government of Pakistan : 1997). A disaggregate analysis of exports, however, shows that most of these exports are low-skilled agro-based goods that are subject to sharp price fluctuations. Although the manufactured goods sector is a dominant player in the country's foreign trade regime, its growth performance has been less than satisfactory. While total exports, during 1988-96, have risen at an annual average rate of 9 per cent, the same figure for manufactured goods is 4 per cent (Appendix 6).

Among other factors, the slow growth of manufactured goods' exports is due to the lack of diversification, leading to a to low export-elasticity. Compounding the negative effects of a lack of commodity diversification is the failure to diversify exports geographically. The Pakistani exporters failed to penetrate into high growth ASEAN economies. The share of exports destined to ASEAN countries, which grew at an annual average rate of less than 1 per cent, remained below 6 per cent during 1988-96

(Government of Pakistan : 1997). A slow growth of exports and a rising import bill resulted in a mounting trade deficit that grew at an annual average rate of over 9 per cent during 1988-1996. Among other factors, the growing trade deficit has been one of the key factors in widening the current account deficit that, as a percentage of GDP, grew at an annual rate of over 21 per cent during this period (Appendix 6). In view of the significant widening of the current account deficit, Pakistan faces a major challenge in its pursuit to strengthen the balance of payments position.

Debt

Widening trade and budget deficits, with low levels of domestic savings, have resulted in a heavy reliance on external borrowing. With an annual average growth rate of 6.7 per cent, the level of external debt (disbursed) has risen from US $ 14,190 million in 1988-89 to US $ 23,016 million in 1996-97 (Appendix 8). To service the external debt of this magnitude has been a major limiting factor in the country's drive for sustainable economic growth. In 1996-97, debt services stood at US $ 2,309, representing 23 per cent of exports receipts 16 per cent of foreign exchange earnings, and 3.6 per cent of GDP (Appendix 9). Under present conditions, where the debt servicing is growing at an average annual rate of 8.5 per cent (Appendix 8), the mounting debt problem will have severe growth implications for the country unless there are efforts to create conditions conducive to increase national savings, exports, and foreign direct investment. Among other factors, Pakistan's prospects for rapid growth depends on its ability to overcome the worsening of the balance of payments problem, caused by the slow growth of exports, rising import bill, a widening budget deficit, and low levels of national savings. Consequently, heavy reliance on foreign borrowing have resulted in mounting national debt servicing of which have compounded the country's balance of payments problems.

Human Resource Development and Economic Growth: The Missing Link

Pakistan's failure in the past to maintain its growth momentum can be attributed to its poor record on human resource development. Pakistani experience shows that where growth can take place without uplifting human lives, sustaining such a growth over a longer haul requires a strong commitment and intervention to substantially improve the level of human development. At present, Pakistan is among the most populous countries in the world with a population of 133 million in 1993. At the present population growth rate of 3 per cent per annum, Pakistan's population is growing much faster than the South-Asian average of 2.3 per annum (Human Development in South Asia : 1997). A population momentum of this magnitude has grave implications for Pakistan, where per capita income growth is stagnant, natural resources are limited, total factor productivity growth is low, saving and investment efforts are inadequate, there is a downward pressure on wages due to growing Labor supply, and the level of human development which is exceptionally low.

The level of human development in Pakistan is characterized by a low life expectancy of 62 years; an infant mortality rate of 95 (while the comparable figure for South-Asian countries stands at 82); a lack of provision of basic facilities where 67 per cent of the population is without access to sanitation and 50 per cent of the population without access to safe drinking water; health facilities which are available to only 55 per cent of the population; high adult illiteracy rate of 64 per cent with mean years of schooling standing at 1.9 years; and a low primary school enrolment ratio with 47 per cent of the children dropping out before completing their primary education.

While the overall situation of human resource development in Pakistan is disappointing, gender disparities are shocking. Within South Asia, Pakistan ranks lowest in most of the gender-related human development indicators. The following table illustrates the gender disparity profile of Pakistan.

TABLE 2

Gender Disparities Profile

Gender Disparity Variables	Pakistan (as % of male)	South Asia-Weighted Average (as % of male)
Female Population	93	94
Adult Female Literacy	47	55
Female Primary School Enrolment	61	79
Female 1st, 2nd, and 3rd Level Gross Enrolment Ratio	49	72
Mean Years of Schooling	23	33
Female Life Expectancy	103	100
Earned Income Share	23	32
Economic Activity Rate (age 15+)	16	36

Source : Human Development in South Asia 1997 : 1997.

Among other factors, Pakistan's poor performance in various social sectors also indicates the ignorance of successive governments towards the importance of the investment in human resources in achieving sustainable growth. Pakistan spends only 2.7 per cent of GNP on education and a mere 1.8 per cent of GNP on health (Human Development in South Asia 1997 : 1997). For the emergence of an economically sustainable economy the development of human capital is as important as an emphasis on the quantity as well as the quality of physical capital. As, an effective and efficient use of physical capital, among other things, to a large extent depends on the quality of the human capital. In the past, efforts to improve the level of human resource development in Pakistan have been hampered by major stumbling blocks, such as, a skewed income distribution; ineffective land reforms; reliance on indirect rather than direct taxes; heavy defense spending with the ratio of military expenditures to education and health standing at 125 (Human Development in South Asia 1997 : 1997), and a heavy debt burden. This paper contends that human capital formation is a pre-requisite to achieve a higher factor productivity growth contributing to a sustained economic growth.

5. Conclusions

The objective of the economic and institutional reform process in Pakistan has been to achieve a new equilibrium at a higher growth path, while at the same time uplifting the living standards of the people. Apart from some indigenous initiatives, successive Pakistani governments have been implementing the institutional and economic reforms prescribed by the international financial and development institutions. The outcome of this ongoing reform process has been far from encouraging. The country remains in a state of deep macroeconomic instability, experiencing slow economic growth, high inflation, widening current account deficits, low levels of savings and investment, rapidly increasing budget deficit, a rapidly depleting foreign exchange reserves, and a mounting burden of debt servicing.

This study emphasizes the necessity of macroeconomic stability and acknowledges the role of economic and institutional reforms to achieve this end. However, these reforms, which focus on achieving macroeconomic stability, like in the past, will not generate the conditions conducive to achieve a sustainable rapid economic growth with an improvement in standard of living. The ongoing reform process needs to be complemented by a stable political climate, good governance, investment in the public infrastructure, improved ethnic and sectarian harmony, improvement in law and order, eradication of institutional corruption, and a shift from defense spending to investment on human resources. The above scenario has the potential to provide a conducive environment for the country to improve national competitiveness or productivity. It is the productivity performance that results in rapid and sustainable economic growth and rising standards of living, which should be the main economic objective of a country.

APPENDIX 1

Sectoral Shares in GDP (Real)

Year	Agriculture	Mining & Manu.	Construction	Electricity/Gas	Commodity (Total)	Services (Total)
1985/86	27.3	17.2	4.1	2.4	51	49
1986/87	26.6	17.5	4.4	2.5	51	49
1987/88	25.7	18.1	4.3	2.8	50.9	49.1
1988/89	26.2	17.9	4.2	3	51.3	48.7
1989/90	25.8	18.1	4.1	3.3	51.4	48.6
1990/91	25.7	18.3	4.1	3.5	51.5	48.5
1991/92	26.1	18.3	4.1	3.5	52	48
1992/93	24.2	18.8	4.2	3.7	50.9	49.1
1993/94	24.3	19	4.1	3.6	51.1	49
1994/95	24.6	18.7	4	3.9	51.2	48.8
1995/96	24.8	18.6	3.9	3.8	51.2	48.9
1996/97	24.2	18.4	3.9	4.1	50.6	49.4

Source : Government of Pakistan : 1997.

APPENDIX 2

GDP Growth (Constant facotor Cost)

Year	GDP	Agriculture	Manufacturing	Commodities	Services
1988/89	4.81	6.87	3.96	5.77	3.81
1989/90	4.58	3.03	5.72	4.69	4.48
1990/91	5.57	4.96	6.25	5.91	5.21
1991/92	7.71	9.5	8.05	8.61	6.76
1992/93	2.27	-5.29	5.35	0.09	4.63
1993/94	4.54	5.23	5.48	4.87	4.2
1994/95	5.24	6.57	3.6	5.66	4.8
1995/96	4.58	5.27	4.4	4.43	4.75
1996/97	3.07	0.7	1.78	2.04	4.14
Average	4.71	4.09	4.95	4.67	4.75

Source : Government of Pakistan : 1997.

Distribution of Employed Labour Force By Major Industries

Year	Agriculture	Mining & Manu.	Construction	Electricity/ Gas	Transport	Trade	Other
1985/86	50.56	13.84	5.6	0.69	5.2	11.54	12.57
1986/87	54.01	13.4	5.24	0.52	4.42	11.4	11.01
1987/88	49.24	14.23	6.01	0.73	5.25	12.05	12.5
1988/89	51.15	12.84	6.38	0.59	4.89	11.93	12.22
1989/90	51.15	12.84	6.38	0.59	4.89	11.93	12.22
1990/91	51.15	12.84	6.38	0.59	4.89	11.93	12.22
1991/92	47.45	12.38	6.62	0.83	5.24	13.24	15.22
1992/93	48.27	12.53	6.33	0.79	5.51	13.1	13.48
1993/94	47.55	11	6.93	0.84	5.52	13.32	14.84
1994/95	50.04	10.12	6.5	0.87	4.95	12.78	14.75
1995/96	46.79	10.5	7.21	0.82	5.07	14.5	15.12
1996/97	46.79	10.5	7.21	0.82	5.07	14.5	15.12

Source : Government of Pakistan : 1997.

APPENDIX 3

Index of Agiculture and Manufacturing Production (1998-81=100)

Year	Agriculture	%Change (all crops)	Manufacturing (Value)	%Change
1988/89	134		183.4	
1989/90	134	0	192.1	4.74
1990/91	142	5.97	202.5	5.41
1991/92	161	13.38	218.5	7.90
1992/93	141	-12.42	227.5	4.12
1993/94	143	1.42	237.2	4.26
1994/95	152	6.29	238.3	0.46
1995/96	165	8.55	246.5	3.44
Average		3.31		4.34

Source : Government of Pakistan : 1997.

APPENDIX 4

Investment and Savings (As % of GNP)
(Current MP)

Year	Total I	% Change	Public I	% Change	Private I	% Change	National S	% Change	Foreign S	% Change
1988-89	18.25		8.65		8.04		13.59		4.66	
1989-90	18.15	-0.55	8.01	-7.40	8.58	6.72	13.61	0.15	4.54	-2.58
1990-91	18.52	2.04	8.27	3.25	8.73	1.75	13.86	1.84	4.66	2.64
1991-92	19.94	7.67	8.7	5.20	9.71	11.23	16.9	21.93	3.04	-34.76
1992-93	20.55	3.06	9.02	3.68	9.97	2.68	13.47	-20.30	7.08	132.89
1993-94	19.37	-5.74	8.28	-8.20	9.54	-4.31	15.61	15.89	3.76	-46.89
1994-95	18.27	-5.68	8.18	-1.21	8.61	-9.75	14.23	-8.84	4.04	7.45
1995-96	18.68	2.24	8.1	-0.98	8.96	4.07	11.58	-18.62	7.1	75.74
1996-97	18.38	-1.61	7.77	-4.07	9.04	0.89	11.35	-1.99	7.03	-0.99
Av. Growth		0.18		-1.21		1.66		-1.24		16.69

APPENDIX 5A

Overall Budgetary Position (As % of GDP)

Year	Deficit	%Change	Total Exp.	%Change	Total Rev.	%Change	Tax.Rev.	%Change
1987-88	8.5		26.7		17.3		13.8	
1988-89	7.4	-12.9	26.1	-2.2	18	4.0	14.3	3.6
1989-90	6.5	-12.2	25.9	-0.8	18.6	3.3	14	-2.1
1990-91	8.7	33.8	25.6	-1.2	16.1	-13.4	12.7	-9.3
1991-92	7.4	-14.9	26.5	3.5	17.9	11.2	13.6	7.1
1992-93	8	8.1	26	-1.9	17.9	0.0	13.3	-2.2
1993-94	5.9	-26.3	23.2	-10.8	17.3	-3.4	13.3	0.0
1994-95	5.6	-5.1	22.8	-1.7	16.9	-2.3	13.7	3.0
1995-96	6.3	12.5	23.9	4.8	17.5	3.6	14.1	2.9
Av. Growth		-2.1		-1.3		0.4		0.4

Source : Government of Pakistan : 1997.

APPENDIX 5B

Overall Budgetary Position (As % of GDP)

Year	Non-tax Rev.	%Change	Dir.Tax Rev.	%Change	In.Tax.Rev.	%Change
1987-88	3.5		1.8		12	
1988-89	3.7	5.7	1.9	5.6	12.4	3.3
1989-90	4.6	24.3	1.8	-5.3	12.1	-2.4
1990-91	3.4	-26.1	2	11.1	10.7	-11.6
1991-92	4.3	26.5	2.5	25.0	11.1	3.7
1992-93	4.6	7.0	2.8	12.0	10.5	-5.4
1993-94	4	-13.0	2.8	0.0	10.3	-1.9
1994-95	3.2	-20.0	3.3	17.9	10.3	0.0
1995-96	2.9	-9.4	3.7	12.1	10.4	1.0
Av. Growth		-0.6		9.8		-1.7

Source : Government of Pakistan : 1997.

APPENDIX 6

Annual Changes in GDP Deflator

Year	GDP Deflator	% Change
1987-88	9.61	
1988-89	8.59	-10.61
1989-90	6.45	-24.91
1990-91	13.07	102.64
1991-92	10.07	-22.95
1992-93	8.67	-13.90
1993-94	12.86	48.33
1994-95	14.16	10.11
1995-96	10.3	-27.26
1996-97	11.5	11.65
Av. Growth		8.12

Source : Government of Pakistan : 1997.

APPENDIX 7

Balance of Payments (US $ Million)

Year	Export	%Change	Import	%Change	Trade Balance	%Change	Current Account	% Change
1988/89	4634		-7207		-2573		-1934	
1989/90	4926	6.30	-7411	2.83	-2485	-3.42	-1891	-2.22
1990/91	5902	19.81	-8385	13.14	-2483	-0.08	-2171	14.81
1991/92	6762	14.57	-8998	7.31	-2236	-9.95	-1346	-38.00
1992/93	6782	0.30	-10049	11.68	-3267	46.11	-3688	174.00
1993/94	6685	-1.43	-8685	-13.57	-2000	-38.78	-1965	-46.72
1994/95	7759	16.07	-10296	18.55	-2537	26.85	-2484	26.41
1995/96	8311	7.11	-12015	16.70	-3704	46.00	-4575	84.18
Av. Growth		8.96		8.09		9.53		30.35

Source : Government of Pakistan : 1997.

Components of Balance of Payments (As % of GDP)

Year	Export	%Change	Import	%Change	Trade Balance	%Change	Current Account	% Change
1988/89	11.64		17.56		5.92		4.83	
1989/90	12.41	6.62	17.38	-1.03	4.96	-16.22	4.74	-1.86
1990/91	13.47	8.54	16.74	-3.68	3.27	-34.07	4.77	0.63
1991/92	14.16	5.12	18.97	13.32	4.82	47.40	2.76	-42.14
1992/93	13.18	-6.92	19.24	1.42	6.05	25.52	7.14	158.70
1993/94	13.05	-0.99	16.42	-14.66	3.38	-44.13	3.77	-47.20
1994/95	13.34	2.22	17.04	3.78	3.7	9.47	4.07	7.96
1995/96	13.46	0.90	18.25	7.10	4.79	29.46	7.07	73.71
Av. Growth		2.21		0.89		2.49		21.40

Source : Government of Pakistan : 1997.

Unit Value Indicies and Terms of Trade

Year	Exports	%Change	Imports	%Change	TOT	%Change	Ex. Rate	%Change
1988/89	167.99		187.54		89.58		19.22	
1989/90	192.93	14.85	215	14.64	89.73	0.17	22.42	16.69
1990/91	197.05	2.14	252.79	17.58	77.95	-13.13	24.84	10.80
1991/92	209.59	6.36	253.34	0.22	82.73	6.13	25.96	4.49
1992/93	214.93	2.55	266.72	5.28	80.58	-2.60	30.16	16.19
1993/94	243.75	13.41	297.14	11.41	82.03	1.80	30.85	2.28
1994/95	308.48	26.56	348.38	17.24	88.55	7.95	33.57	8.81
1995/96	347.63	12.69	384.44	10.35	90.43	2.12	33.13	-1.29
Av. Growth		11.22		10.96		0.35		8.28

Source : Government of Pakistan : 1997.

APPENDIX 8

Pakistan's External Debt (US $ million)

Year	Debt (Disbursed)	% Change	Service (Interest)	% Change	Service (Total)	% Change
1987-88	12,913		426		1,117	
1988-89	14,190	9.9	440	3.3	1125	0.7
1989-90	15,094	6.4	491	11.6	1232	9.5
1990-91	15,471	2.5	534	8.8	1316	6.8
1991-92	17,361	12.2	592	10.9	1513	15.0
1992-93	19,044	9.7	649	9.6	1648	8.9
1993-94	20,117	5.6	668	2.9	1746	5.9
1994-95	22,117	9.9	748	12.0	2042	17.0
1995-96	22,275	0.7	790	5.6	2136	4.6
1996-97	23,016	3.3	735	-7.0	2309	8.1
Av. Growth		6.7		6.4		8.5

Source : Government of Pakistan : 1997.

APPENDIX 9

Debt Servicing (As % of GDP)

Year	Export Recepits	% Change	Forex Earnings	% Change	GDP	% Change
1987-88	25.1		14.7		2.9	
1988-89	24.1	-3.98	14.4	-2.04	2.8	-3.45
1989-90	24.9	3.32	14.4	0.00	3.1	10.71
1990-91	21.5	-13.65	13.7	-4.86	2.9	-6.45
1991-92	21.9	1.86	13.4	-2.19	3.1	6.90
1992-93	24.2	10.50	15.3	14.18	3.2	3.23
1993-94	25.7	6.20	16.2	5.88	3.3	3.12
1994-95	25.1	-2.33	16.5	1.85	3.4	3.03
1995-96	24.5	-2.39	16.7	1.21	3.3	-2.94
1996-97	23.2	-5.31	16.1	-3.59	3.6	9.09
Av. Growth		-0.64		1.16		2.58

Source : Government of Pakistan : 1997.

APPENDIX 10

Economic Classification of Exports

Year	PC	%Change	SM	%Change	MG	%Change
1988/89	33		19		48	
1989/90	20	-39.39	24	26.32	56	16.67
1990/91	19	-5.00	24	0.00	57	1.79
1991/92	19	0.00	21	-12.50	60	5.26
1992/93	15	-21.05	21	0.00	64	6.67
1993/94	10	-33.33	24	14.29	66	3.13
1994/95	11	10.00	25	4.17	64	-3.03
1995/96	16	45.45	22	-12.00	62	-3.13
Av. Growth		-6.19		2.90		3.90741464

Source : Government of Pakistan : 1997.

Note :

PC = Primary Commodities

SM = Semi-manufactures

MG = Manufactured Goods

REFERENCES

Aschauer, D.A. (1993), "Genuine Economic Returns to Infrastructure Investment", *Policy Studies Journal*, 21, 380-90.

Datta-Chaudhuri, Mrinal (1980), "Infrastructure and Location" in John Coday, Helen Huges and David Wall (eds.), *Policies for Industrial Progress in Developing Countries*, New York : Oxford University Press.

Fernald, J. (1993), "How Productive is Infrastructure? Distinguishing Reality and Illusion with a Panel of U.S. Industries," *Federal Reserve Board Discussion Paper*, August.

Government of Pakistan (1997), *Economic Survey 1996-97*, Islamabad : Finance Division, Economic Adviser's Wing.

Government of Pakistan (1997), *Economic Survey 1995-96*, Islamabad : Finance Division, Economic Adviser's Wing.

Holtz-Eakin, D. (1988), "Private Output, Government Capital and the Infrastructure Capital", *Discussion Paper*, No. 394, Columbia University, May.

Holtz-Eakin, D. (1992), "Public Sector Capital and the Productivity Puzzel", *National Bureau of Economic Research Working Paper*, No. 4144.

Lynde, C., and Richmond, J. (1993), "Public Capital and Total Factor Productivity", *International Economic Review*, Vol. 34, No. 2, May, 401-414.

Mahmood, Amir (1996), "Economic Liberalization and Structural Reforms : An Assessment of the Pakistani Experience", in Ghosh, R.N., Melotte, Y.M., and Siddique, M.A.B. (eds.), *Economic Development and Change*, New Delhi : New Age International Publishers.

Munnell, A.H. (1990), "Why has Productivity Growth Declined? Productivity and Public Investment," *New England Economic Review*, Jan./Feb., 3-22.

Munnell, A.H. (1992), "Infrastructure Investment and Economic Growth", *Journal of Economic Perspectives*, Fall, 6(4), 189-98.

Pradhan, Sanjay, Swaroop and Vinaya (1993), "Public Spending and Adjustment", *Finance and Development*, Vol. 30, September, pp. 28-31.

Ratner, J.B. (1983), "Government Capital and the Production Functions for U.S. Private Output," *Economics Letters*, 13, 213-217.

Swaroop, Vinaya (1994), "The Public Finance of Infrastructure : Issues and Options", *World Development*, Vol. 22, No. 12, pp. 1909-1919.

Haq, M. (1997), *Human Development in South Asia*, Karachi : Oxford University Press.

9

Market-oriented Policy Reforms and Industrial Restructuring in Sri Lanka

PREMA-CHANDRA ATHUKORALA

Introduction

The post-war debate on trade and industrial policy reforms in developing countries (DCs) is far from settled. While there is a growing consensus in the economic profession that old style interventionist import-substitution policies have "misfired", there is no agreement on the appropriate way forward. The mainstream policy advocacy, in the neo-classical tradition of development economics, sees the removal of government in direct production activities and shifts toward market forces as the appropriate strategy for achieving rapid, robust and equitable growth (Bhagwati, 1993, Krueger, 1997, Little 1982). The economists of structuralist persuasion are, however, less sanguine about the desirability of such market oriented reforms. Based on the widespread failure of market-oriented policy reforms in many developing countries, they argue for activist and selective public policies tailored to the circumstances of each individual country, while eschewing indiscriminate state intervention (Helleiner, 1993, Rodrik, 1992). Apart from stressing the potential adverse effects in the short-run if weak domestic industry is exposed to foreign competition, the structuralists draw upon the conventional economic arguments for selective intervention, on grounds of learning by doing and dynamic economies of scale achievable in the context of a protected domestic market. Mainstream economists counter the structuralist critique by arguing that reforms failed in many developing countries not because of an inherent deficiency of the market paradigm, but because of the partial and half-hearted nature of the reform process.

This paper aims to contribute to this debate through a case study of Sri Lanka. Sri Lanka has experienced a series of changes in its trade regime since attaining Independence from British colonial rule in 1948. During the first decade after Independence, it continued with a liberal trade regime, until growing balance of payments problems induced a policy shift towards protectionist import substitution policies. By the mid-1970s, the Sri Lankan economy had become one of the most inward-oriented and regulated outside the group of centrally-planned economies, characterised by stringent trade and exchange controls and pervasive state interventions in all areas of economic activity. In 1977, Sri Lanka responded to the dismal economic outcome of this policy stance by a sharp change in policy direction and embarked on an extensive economic liberalisation process, becoming the first country in the South Asian region to do so. Despite major macroeconomic problems, political turmoil and government changes, market-oriented reforms have been sustained and broadened over almost two decades so that Sri Lanka today stands out as one of the most open economies in the developing world. This basic policy orientation looks set to continue in the foreseeable future. Indeed, the most dramatic change in the Sri Lankan political landscape in recent years has been the convergence in broad economic policies among the major political parties and groupings; achieving greater openness and liberalisation is now a bipartisan policy in Sri Lanka. Given the decisive policy shift in 1977 and policy continuity during the ensuing years, Sri Lanka appears to provide a valuable laboratory for the study of the impact of foreign trade policy regimes in a developing economy.

The structure of the paper is as follows. In the next Section, we trace the evolution of trade and industry policy in Sri Lanka since independence, followed by a discussion of the key elements of the market-oriented reforms initiated in 1977. Then we examine the industrialisation experience since 1977 in historical context, placing emphasis on aspects such as patterns of industrial growth, export orientation, and factor productivity growth. This is followed by an in-depth analysis of the response of foreign investors to the significant trade-cum-investment liberalisation reforms and the pivotal role played by export-oriented foreign direct investment (EOFDI) in transforming a classical, primary commodity-dependent economy into a 'new exporting country' (NEC). The final Section summarises the main findings of the study and draws policy inferences. A key theme running through the paper is the importance of the concomitant liberalisation of both trade and investment policy regimes in determining the outcome of liberalisation reforms in small trade dependent countries like Sri Lanka. We also draw attention to the need for supportive macroeconomic policies if trade liberalisation was to achieve its full growth impact.

Policy Context

Policy Trends Since Independence

During the first decade after Independence in 1948, Sri Lanka continued as an open trading nation with only relatively minor trade or exchange rate restrictions and liberal domestic policies. From the late 1950s, a combination of change in political leadership and balance of payments difficulties led to the adoption of a state-led import substitution (IS) industrialisation strategy. Trade restrictions, which were introduced in the late 1950s to keep the negative trade balance under control, soon turned out to be the key instrument in the hands of the national planners in directing private sector activities in line with (perceived) national priorities. Following a hesitant and mild liberalisation attempt during 1968-70, the period from 1970 to 1977 was marked by further direct government intervention in the economy, under the guise of creating a 'socialist society'. By the mid-1970s, these policy shifts had transformed the Sri Lankan economy into one of the most highly regulated, inward oriented, statist economies outside the communist block (Fitter, 1973, Cuthbertson and Athukorala 1991, Rajapatirana 1988).

The policy makers in Sri Lanka, like their counterparts in other developing countries, expected the growth of IS industries to reduce the heavy dependence of the economy on imports. The reality was quite different, however. While consumer goods imports were reduced substantially, this was achieved at the expense of increased reliance on imported capital goods and raw materials, resulting, contrary to expectation, in an even more rigid dependence on imports. Given these structural features, the growth dynamism of the newly established industrial sector tended to show a close functional relationship with the fortunes of the traditional export industries. Thus, unanticipated import curtailments brought about by foreign exchange scarcity, turned out to be the main constraint on industrial expansion from the late 1960s. Moreover, the 'inefficiency slipover effects' of the state-owned enterprises (SOEs), involved in intermediate good production on private sector end-user industries, were quite substantial, particularly since import compression policies were implemented with a distinct bias towards SOEs in the allocation of foreign exchange (Athukorala and Jayasuriya, 1993). In most developing countries, the rapid expansion of domestic industry continued until the "easy" import-substitution opportunities (*i.e.,* meeting domestic demand in textiles, footwear, some food processing and other light labour intensive activities) were used up. It was only then that the cost of additional investment in new IS activities began to rise and growth slowed down (Krueger, 1992, 43-4). However, in Sri Lanka, a limit was set on the growth of industry by the balance of payments constraint well before the completion of the easy IS phase.

General dissatisfaction with stagnant economic growth, deterioration in the provision of social services, rising unemployment, shortages and widespread rationing of consumer goods, together with the opposition to increasing authoritarianism in the political arena, set the stage for a change in the political regime. At the general elections of July 1977, the centre-right United National Party (UNP) scored a sweeping victory on a platform of opening up the economy and revitalising the private sector. The first round of reforms carried out during 1977-79 included significant trade liberalisation, revamping foreign investment approval and monitoring process with new incentives for investors, significant interest rate reform and opening of the banking sector to foreign banks, limits on public sector participation in the economy and exchange rate realignment.

The extent of 'outside influence' on the 1977 policy shift towards economic liberalisation remains a debatable issue. From time to time, newspapers interpreted the policies as a positioning for receipt of Western aid and contended that in 1977, the IMF and World Bank became Sri Lanka's 'new masters'. There is little doubt that following the policy reforms foreign aid to Sri Lanka from Western countries increased significantly and the presence of the IMF, World Bank and other international agencies in the policy scene became prominent. However, one judgement commonly made by the Sri Lankan government officials and some economic observers is that, given the dismal economic record of the closed-economy era, even a re-elected centre-left government would have embarked on a similar reform process. Indeed, there was considerable discussion within government circles during the immediate pre-election years on the liberalisation of the trade and foreign investment regimes.[1]

The impact of 1977 policy reforms on economic growth was dramatic; the average annual GDP growth rate more than doubled from 2.9 per cent during 1970-77 to 6 per cent between 1978-83. However, this growth surge could not be maintained in the subsequent period, primarily because of a collapse of political stability : from 1984 onwards Sri Lanka has been subjected to a

1. For further discussion on this issue see Cuthbertson and Athukorala, 1993, Chapter 5.

secessionist war in the Northern and the Eastern provinces, while a radical youth uprising gripped the rest of the country in the late 1980s. In this volatile climate, there was little room for attempts to complete the unfinished agenda of economic liberalisation.

Political instability resulted in severe economic dislocation, and a sharp escalation of defense expenditures, which, in turn, led to widening fiscal deficits, growing macroeconomic problems and the erosion of international competitiveness of the tradable sectors. Apart form continued fiscal expansion triggered by the civil war, the drying up of official capital inflows (with the completion of aid-funded public sector investment projects) also contributed to major macro-economic imbalances. By the end of 1988, official foreign exchange reserves had fallen to the equivalent of 6 week's imports, while the service payments on external debt had risen to 28 per cent of export earnings. Average annual GDP growth during 1984-89 was only 2.6 per cent. In this context, the government, under pressure from the Bretton Woods institutions, agreed in June 1989 to implement a 'second wave' liberalisation-cum-adjustment package. The programme basically aimed to arrest the deteriorating external payments position and control inflationary pressures by bringing down the fiscal deficit and moderating the rate of monetary expansion. The policy package included an ambitious privatisation program, further tariff cuts and simplification of the tariff structure, removing exchange controls on current account transactions, commitment to a policy of flexible exchange rate management, and initiatives to cut the fiscal deficit.

After 17 years in government, the UNP lost power at the 1994 General Elections to the People's Alliance (PA), a loose coalition of the Sri Lanka Freedom Party (SLFP), which ruled the country during most of the closed-economy era and a number of other left-wing parties and a splinter groups from the UNP. The election result was largely determined by the growing disenchantment with the trend towards authoritarian methods of rule and a culture of 'crony capitalism', the continuing civil war, political violence and rampant corruption. In fact, during the election campaign, it became clear that an unprecedented consensus had emerged across all mainstream political groups over the superiority of market-oriented polices pursued since 1977 and the need for continuation of pro-market, liberal economic policies to achieve economic development.

There was speculation at the time of the election that if the PA came to power, it would decelerate, if not reverse, the liberalisation process. But, the actual course of policy under the new government has been quite the opposite. The liberalization process, particularly in the privatization area has, if anything, accelerated under the new regime. The inaugural policy statement of the new government has provided assurance that economic policy will in general be market friendly and the private sector will be considered the principal engine of growth (Government of Sri Lanka, 1995a). The new government is committed to reducing progressively and harmonising tariffs towards a single rate of 10 per cent over the medium term (Government of Sri Lanka, 1995).

With this background we now discuss in detail the key elements of the trade and foreign investment policy in Sri Lanka as they have evolved since 1977.

Trade Policy

Trade policy reform was the key element of the economic liberalisation policy package introduced in 1977. In November 1977, quantitative restrictions (QRs) on imports, which were near universal, were supplanted by a revised system of tariff, retaining only 280 items under license. This far reaching change was accompanied by the removal of most price controls on domestic trade. While many of the tariff changes involved a gazetted increase in the rate, the tariffication typically involved a sharp reduction in the degree of protection provided previously by the stringent QR regime. Further, in practice, the retention of some items under license has proved not to constitute a significant protective barrier, except for items involving health and security considerations; generally licenses have been issued freely. There is evidence that in the process of subsequent fine-tuning of tariff rates, a few items whose free importation had a "damaging" impact on SOEs, were returned to the licensing list. There have also been some moderate revenue oriented across-the-board duty increases in some years. These limitations, notwithstanding, and despite the fact that the pace of trade reforms slackened until a new stimulus was given with the second wave of liberalisation a decade later, there has been no major reversal of the reforms. Indeed, subsequent trade policy initiatives have reinforced the role of tariffs as the central instrument regulating Sri Lanka's merchandise trade. The tariff regime has also become less distortionary during successive rounds of reforms. It currently relies on a three-pronged structure with rates of 10, 20, and 35 per cent. In 1994, the simple (unweighted) average across 6050 tariff items, was in the order of 20 per cent and the ratio of actual duty revenue to imports was even lower (about 11 per cent)[2] (WTO 1995, p. 35).

A wide range of export promotion schemes, including an all-encompassing duty rebate scheme with flexible operational procedures, direct cash subsidies, manufacturing-in-bond, provision of equity and working capital to firms with export potential, and various measures aimed at product and market development, was introduced under a newly established Export Development Board. Steps were also taken to streamline and improve fiscal incentives for export production at successive stages, finally limiting tax-holiday concessions only to export ventures.

Foreign Investment Policy

The promotion of foreign investment, particularly in export-oriented manufacturing has been a pivotal element of Sri Lanka's market-oriented policy reforms since 1977. The most important

2. The difference between the gazetted rate and the actual rate may be due to the operation of tariff exemptions and waivers and the deterrent effects of high tariffs on trade in the relevant items.

aspect of the new foreign investment policy was the setting up of the Greater Colombo Economic Commission (GCEC) in 1978 with wide-ranging powers to establish and operate Export Processing Zones (EPZs).[3] The first investment promotion zone, at Katunayake near the Colombo International Airport (henceforth KEPZ), was opened in June 1978. The remarkable success of the KEPZ paved the way for setting up a second EPZ in Biyagama (BEPZ) in 1982 and a third in Koggala (KGEPZ) in June 1991. The investment promotion policy package offered by the GCEC to EPZ investors included allowing complete foreign ownership of investment projects; a tax holiday for up to 10 years with complete tax exemption for remuneration of foreign personnel employed, royalties, and dividends of shareholders during that period; duty exemption for the importation of inputs and assistance with customs clearances; industrial services at subsidised rates and unlimited access to foreign-currency credit at interest rates prevailing in world financial markets (Athukorala, 1995). As an important part of the DFI policy, steps were also taken to enter into Investment Protection Agreements and Double Taxation Relief Agreements with the major investing countries. A guarantee against nationalisation of foreign assets without compensation was provided under the Article 157 of the new Constitution of Sri Lanka adopted in 1978.

While the GCEC program was to act as the major instrument of promoting export oriented investment, many elements of the 1977 policy package also helped to improve the general investment climate in the country for export-oriented production by both local and foreign firms. These elements included the removal of most of quantitative restrictions on import trade, considerable relaxation of controls on capital and profit repatriation, and exchange rate depreciation. In addition, a wide

3. An area of approximately 160 square miles North of Colombo was demarcated for the GCEC. The Foreign Investment Advisory Committee (FIAC) (set up in 1966) was to continue to approve and monitor foreign investment (in both export-oriented and import-substitution projects) outside the GCEC area. In 1991 the two institutions were amalgamated to for the Board of Investment (BOI).

range of schemes pitched at export promotion was introduced under a newly established Export Development Board (EDB). In 1980, the duty rebate scheme (originally introduced in 1964 and revised in 1969) was completely reformulated with a more flexible implementation procedure to cover almost all non-traditional exports which use imported inputs. The coverage of the duty rebate scheme was expanded in 1982 to include sales to EPZs. This revision was intended to provide a inducement to strengthen 'backward linkages' of EPZ activities. A scheme of manufacture-in-bond for exporters importing material for re-exporting as a part of a finished good, a cash grant scheme based on annual export increments and concessionary credit for exporters, were among the other EDB incentives. A five-year tax holiday was introduced in the 1978 Budget Speech for export-orientated companies. With regard to these concessions and incentives, non-GCEC (FIAC-approved) joint-venture firms were treated equally with locally-owned firms.

There was no major change in the policy towards foreign ventures which did not meet the criterion of "full" export orientation. Such projects had to go through the normal approval procedure of FIAC. Majority local ownership continued to be the general rule for approving such projects. However, under the new policy emphasis on export-oriented industrialisation, FIAC was empowered to adopt more liberal ownership criteria (even up to 100 per cent foreign ownership) depending on the export potential of the project.

A new Investment Policy Statement announced in 1990 (as part of the second-wave liberalisation), introduced several important changes to the foreign investment policy framework in line with the increased outward orientation of the economy. These included the abolition of various restrictions on the ownership structures of joint-venture projects outside EPZs, providing free-trade-zone status to export-oriented foreign ventures in all parts of the country (in addition to the area demarcated by the original GCEC Act) and the amalgamation of the activities of FIAC and GCEC under a new Board of Investment (BOI), in order to facilitate and speed up investment approval within a unified policy framework applicable to both import-substituting and export-oriented investors.

Exchange Controls

Despite significant relaxation of restrictions on commodity imports in 1977, the Sri Lanka rupee was not made fully convertible on service account transactions. As part of the second-wave liberalisation in 1990, foreign exchange restrictions on these transactions were removed in successive stages culminating in the abolition of the foreign exchange surrender requirement on export transactions in March 1993. These policy steps made Sri Lanka eligible for Article VIII status of the International Monetary Fund (IMF). Following the 1993 reforms, the black market premium on foreign currency has virtually disappeared and there is now a Singapore-style competitive retail market (with independent foreign exchange dealers competing directly with commercial banks in foreign exchange dealings) for foreign exchange.

The lifting of many restrictions on capital transactions was an important element in the 1977 reform package. The repatriation of proceeds from sales of shares in Sri Lankan companies was permitted without prior approval of the Controller of Exchange, authorised foreign exchange dealers were permitted to approve applications for such remittances. Moreover, foreign investors were allowed by the Controller of Exchange to repatriate their capital contribution in the equity of a company on the sale or liquidation of the investment, after settlement of local liabilities like taxes. The transfer of shares was freely permitted if they did not increase the ratio of non-resident shareholdings originally approved. Despite these noteworthy reforms, the rupee is still not fully convertible on capital account transactions and the prohibition on overseas capital transfers by Sri Lankan citizens have remained intact. As in the past, they are not permitted to invest abroad, to maintain accounts with banks abroad, or to raise capital in foreign markets for domestic investment without prior approval. However, it is important to note that current account convertibility opened up many avenues for capital transfers. In particular, the abolition of the foreign exchange surrender requirement on exporters is tantamount to a de facto relaxation of these restrictions. Sri Lankans who remit investible funds overseas can now do it through exporters!

Privatisation

Privatisation or closure of uneconomical and inefficient SOEs was a key element of the declared policy. The government envisaged that "the public sector will concentrate on essential areas that are not attractive to the private entrepreneur either because the investment involved is too large or because the financial rate of return is not attractive" (Budget Speech, 1978, p. 30). This policy however, lost much of its rigour in the process of implementation; until the 1990s, even privatisations of SOEs were rare. In fact, a number of SOEs were even accorded preferential treatment, including higher tariff protection.

The reluctance to privatise SOEs was certainly not due to any ideological opposition to privatization, nor was it due to any fear of political and industrial resistance from state sector trade unions. The primary reason was that state enterprises provided an effective and ready made vehicle for dispensing political patronage (Jayasuriya and Knight-John, forthcoming). In particular, they could be used to provide employment to those whom the government wanted to reward. This was a factor of paramount political importance given the government's election promises to its supporters, particularly to the youth. On the other hand there was no revenue-based inducement for privatisation, as the budgetary position was amply strengthened by massive concessionary aid flows in the aftermath of the reforms. Sri Lanka, in the early years of the new government, was the recipient of a massive aid flow — the highest level of aid on a per capita basis in the world at the time — as international donor agencies and Western governments flocked to provide financial assistance to this pro-Western, pro-market government. Released from the pressures of fiscal stringency, the government was able to pursue its policy of expanding employment in state enterprises, while ignoring the heavy economic costs of that policy. The role of state enterprises in the economy had been little affected by a decade of liberalization, though the removal of quantitative restrictions on imports weakened their position; indeed, trade liberalisation proceeded at the slowest pace, or was even reversed to a degree, in those sectors where large SOEs were dominant. By the late 1980s, they still accounted for some 40 per cent of value added, even in the manufacturing sector.

The circumstances had changed by the late 1980s, as the fiscal deficit became a major concern. Under the second-wave of liberalisation in 1990 privatisation was given a central role in an effort to redress the massive macroeconomic imbalance in the economy by reducing the fiscal deficit (Kelegama, 1995). The strategy that has been formulated for privatisation calls for majority shareholdings in given SOEs to be divested through the stock market or through open tender to a corporate investor. To make privatisation politically acceptable, 10 percent of shares are given free of charge to employees. Privatisation over the past ten years has encompassed state enterprises producing goods, as well as public utilities supplying services.

Macro-economic Policy and Real Exchange Rate Movements

The designers of the 1977 policy package were aware of the role of complementary macro-economic policy in making market-oriented policy reforms effective. The basic macro-economic requirements for sustained export-oriented growth are a favourable investment climate and the maintenance of a realistic, competitive real exchange rate. Trade liberalization was accompanied by a significant exchange reform and measures to reduce the budget deficit (which had been the major source of macro-economic imbalances and, *via* domestic inflation, pressure on the real exchange rate since the early 1970s). The prevailing dual exchange rate system (introduced in 1968) was abolished, and the new unified rate was placed under a managed float. This resulted in an initial devaluation of almost 80 per cent. The exchange rate was planned to be adjusted daily to reflect changes in foreign exchange market conditions. However, control of domestic cost pressures was essential if the real depreciation achieved through the exchange rate reforms was to be sustainable.[4] This required prudent fiscal policies to ensure that budgetary imbalances did not generate inflationary pressures.

Some of the initial actions of the government were designed to address this issue. In 1978, the food subsidy — an important source of fiscal deficits — was abolished for nearly one-half of the population. Consequently, food subsidy expenditure declined both absolutely and as a share of total government expenditure, falling from 16 per cent in 1977 to a mere 0.2 per cent in 1985. But the focus on fiscal prudence was short lived and government policies soon resulted in the generation of inflationary pressures, resulting in real exchange rate appreciation. As discussed above, the government's attitude to SOEs was a contributory factor; while a few loss making public enterprises were either shifted to the private sector or closed down, most continued to operate despite dismal performance and ongoing dependence on budgetary transfers. These transfers soon outweighed the expenditure reduction resulting from curtailment of food subsidies and aggravated the budget deficit.

But the chief source of macroeconomic instability and pressure on the real exchange rate in the early post-reform period was a massive public sector investment program that included a billion dollar multipurpose irrigation project, a large public housing program and an urban development program (Athukorala and Jayasuriya, 1994). In this context, from about 1979, the Central Bank started using the nominal exchange rate as an "anchor" for inflation control. The Bank intensified its intervention in the foreign exchange market and eventually abandoned (in November

4. In principle, compensating nominal exchange rate depreciations can maintain a constant real exchange rate; in practice, this leads to a vicious cycle of rising inflationary expectations, increasingly large depreciations and accelerating inflation leadimg to macro-economic crises.

1982) the practice of determining the exchange rate daily. The real exchange rate tended to appreciate and, when the exchange rate policy ceased to provide a stimulus for exports, the alternative adopted was to strengthen the various financial incentives offered by the EDB. However, this indirect approach largely failed because of severe institutional and financial constraints. After the 1984-89 period, characterised by intense political turmoil which made the general environment strongly unfavourable to economic growth, the adjustment programme implemented during 1989/90 provided a brief period of relative macroeconomic stability, with steps being taken to bring the fiscal deficit under control and to maintain a more realistic exchange rate under a crawling-peg system. However, a spending spree related to the elections in 1994, followed by a massive surge in defence expenditures (which had increased to 7 per cent of GDP in 1996) placed major constraints on sound fiscal management, and made it extremely difficult to maintain a conducive environment for investment and growth.[5] Thus, it appears reasonable to conclude that, with the exception of relatively short periods, the economy did not have the benefit of supportive macroeconomic policies to complement the trade reforms in the post-1977 period.

A series of estimated real exchange rate indices are presented in table 1 to shed light on the cumulative effect of economic liberalisation and the developments in the macroeconomic front for the relative incentives for manufacturing production. The procedure commonly adopted in compiling a real exchange index is to develop a trade-weighted index of trading partners' nominal exchange rates (the 'nominal effective exchange rate') and then to adjust this with a (similarly trade weighted) index of relative prices between trading partner countries and the given country. The common practice (followed by the IMF and Central banks in many countries including the Central Bank of Sri Lanka) is to

5. An additional source of upward pressure on the real exchange rate came from a surge in private capital flows in the 1991-94 period.

use consumer price indices (CPIs) to measure both foreign and domestic price levels. Given the fact that the CPI is a weighted average prices of both tradables and non-tradables, this practice can lead to inaccuracy in the measurement of competitiveness in a country undergoing trade liberalisation. A country undergoing trade liberalisation generally experiences slower increases, or even reductions, in traded consumer good prices relative to prices of non-traded goods, and the CPI is likely to understate the cost pressures. We constructed standard CPI-based real exchange rate indices, as well as alternative indices which use the wholesale price index (WPI) in place of the CPI to measure relative prices. As the WPI typically does not capture movements in non-tradable prices, the WPI based indices certainly underestimate cost pressures even more than the CPI, but they can be interpreted as indicators of the relative profitability of selling in the home market over exporting ('the home market bias').[6] The indices were constructed separately for import, export and total trade.[7]

All indices reported in the table clearly point to the deterioration in relative profitability of production of manufactured goods, for both domestic and export markets during the period of massive fiscal expansion in the first half of the 1980s. Since about the late 1980s, the relative profitability of production for export began to improve, thanks to both nominal exchange rate depreciation and favourable world prices. However, the relative profitability of production for the home market continued to deteriorate. The rate of nominal exchange rate depreciation has not been adequate to compensate for the price-lowering effects of further liberalisation of quantitative restrictions and tariff cuts in the 1990s.

---

6. For a more detailed discussion of these measures, see Athukorala and Jayasuriya (1996).

7. Note that in our calculations, the nominal exchange rate has been defined as 'the domestic currency price of foreign currency'. Thus, an increase (decrease) in the index imply real depreciation (appreciation) or improvement (deterioration in) international competitiveness.

Commitment to a policy of flexible exchange rate management, in order to restore international competitiveness, was a key element of the 1989 reform package. Reflecting the new policy, the Sri Lankan rupee depreciated *vis a vis* the US dollar, the intervention currency, by 17.4 per cent in 1989 (based on an end-of-year comparison). Following this substantial nominal devaluation, the Central Bank has continued to adjust the exchange rate daily, taking into account developments in the foreign exchange market. A comparison of the two indices for each trade category clearly supports our proposition that non-tradables inflation has been the major negative influence on the international competitiveness of tradable production in Sri Lanka.[8] However, no matter what indicator is used, the overall picture with respect to the behaviour of the real exchange rate during the period since 1989 is remarkably similar: There was a rapid deterioration in competitiveness in 1990 and 1991, followed by a significant recovery in competitiveness. Almost all real exchange rate indices had surpassed the 1989 level by 1995. The rate of nominal exchange rate depreciation under the managed-floating exchange regime in these years, has more than compensated for the negative effects of the overall macro-economic policies which have fuelled domestic inflation. In other words, the Central Bank has pursued a sufficiently flexible exchange rate policy stance recently to improve the international competitiveness of the traded goods sector. This inference is of course consistent with the our earlier observations about the nature of the Central Bank's intervention in the foreign exchange market. In sum, liberalisation reforms since 1977 included a significant opening of the Sri Lankan economy to foreign trade and investment. However, the macro-economic environment was generally not conducive to the full realisation of the potential gains from liberalisation and constrained domestic investments in the manufacturing sector.

8. Note that non-tradeables have a higher weight in CPI, which has been rising faster than the WPI.

Industrial Growth and Adjustment

Growth Trends

The average annual growth rate of manufacturing[9], which dropped from about 6 per cent during 1965-69 to a mere 3 per cent in 1970-76, significantly recovered following the 1977 reforms (Table 2). Despite higher growth by historical standards, the share of manufacturing value added in total GDP remained more or less unchanged, at around 10 per cent until the mid 1980s. This was mostly a reflection of the superior growth performance of non-tradeable sectors — construction, transport, utilities, trade and other services sectors — propelled by the public sector investment boom. Thus, the impact of real exchange rate appreciation caused by macroeconomic factors is clearly seen in the sectoral growth patterns. However, since the late-1980s, the pattern has changed; in most years, manufacturing growth has surpassed that of other sectors. As a result, the manufacturing share in GDP increased from 10 per cent in early 1980 to 16 per cent by the mid-1990s.

The major immediate cause of manufacturing output growth in the liberalised economy was the free availability of imported inputs and capital goods. In particular, the availability of intermediate inputs contributed to output growth through greater capacity utilisation (Table 2). However, output has continued to expand at an increasing rate even after the capacity utilisation reached an average stable rate of about 70 per cent by the late 1980s. Quite apart from greater input usage, the growth of factor productivity seems to have played a significant role with some time lag.

The results of a simple growth accounting procedure, undertaken to decompose manufacturing output growth in to the relative contributions of factor accumulation and total factor

9. Manufacturing is defined in this paper to cover all production activities which come under item 3 of the International Standard Industry Classification (ISIC).

productivity (TFP) growth, are reported in table 3. The estimates clearly point to the adverse productivity implications of the increased restrictiveness in the trade regime between 1966 and 1974. Between 1974 and 1981, output growth emanated predominantly from factor accumulation, rather than from TFP growth, reflecting the normal adjustment lag in private sector response to new incentives. There was, however, a significant improvement in TFP growth between 1981 and 1993. Out of total output growth between these two years, almost 25 per cent came from TFP growth.

Structural Change

At the time of market oriented policy reforms, SOEs accounted for over 60 per cent of manufacturing output and 50 per cent of total manufacturing employment. This public sector dominance continued virtually unchanged until about the mid-1980s (Table 4). Since then, the position of SOEs has been significantly eroded in the face of rapid output growth in private manufacturing ventures. The share of SOEs in total manufacturing output in 1991 was 20.5, down from over 45 per cent in 1985. As noted, during the controlled era, "inefficiency slipover effects" of SOEs involved in intermediate and capital-good industries on private sector end-user industries were quite substantial, particularly since import compression policies were implemented with a distinct bias towards SOEs in the allocation of foreign exchange. The elimination of this source of inefficiency slipover, through import liberalisation, may have been a factor in improving factor productivity in private- sector industries.

Table 4 presents data on the sectoral composition of private-sector industrial production and employment. It is evident that the response to the new policy environment has exhibited a rather contrasting pattern across various sectors. Interestingly, export-oriented sectors — wearing apparel, footwear, rubber goods and leather goods — indicate impressive growth performance. The only import-substitution sectors which have experienced some increases in output shares are food and beverages.

Relatively more capital intensive industries, such as machinery, transport equipment and industrial chemicals, figure prominently among declining sectors. However, interestingly, output contraction in the liberalised economy has not been limited to capital and technology intensive product sectors only. Many domestic-resource-based import substituting sectors have experienced significant output contraction. At least part of the explanation may lie in changes to the overall incentive structure faced by manufacturing industries as reflected in the real exchange rate measures; these industries are likely to have been hard hit by domestic cost pressures and competitive imports.

The overall export orientation of manufacturing, as measured by the "export coefficient" (the ratio of exports to gross manufacturing output) has tended to increase since the mid 1985. The export coefficient in 1994 was 63, compared to a mere 3 per cent in the mid 1970s (Table 2). Using input-output tables for 1981 and 1991 (prepared by the Sri Lankan Ministry of Finance and Planning), we estimated the relative contribution of domestic demand expansion, import substitution and export expansion to the expansion of total manufacturing output between these two years. The results suggest that export expansion was the most important source of growth (72 per cent), followed by domestic demand expansion (45 per cent), with import substitution registering a negative (-17 per cent) contribution.

Foreign Direct Investment and Manufactured Export Expansion

The export structure of Sri Lanka, as it evolved during the colonial era, was characterised by an extremely heavy reliance on a limited range of primary commodities. By the time of the 1977 policy reform, the share of manufacturers (excluding petroleum products) in total merchandise exports was only 4 per cent (Table 6). Since then, manufactured exports have emerged as the most dynamic element in the export structure. Exports of manufactures grew (in current US $ terms) at an annual compound rate of 32 per cent during 1978-95 and, by the mid-1990s, their share in total merchandise exports was over 70 per cent. During 1980-92, Sri Lanka was among the top five low-income countries in terms of both the average annual growth in earnings from manufactured exports and the increase in manufacturing share in total merchandise exports (UNCTAD, 1994).

Consistent with the early outward orientation experience of most countries, manufactured exports from Sri Lanka initially showed a strong reliance on standard labour intensive consumer goods (Table 7), with the garment industry being dominant. However, since the late 1980s, there has been a noticeable increase in export earnings in other labour intensive product areas such as, electronics (included under the commodity category of "machinery"), leather goods, footwear, toys and plastic products, diamond cutting and jewellery, as well as resource-based products (*e.g.*, tea, rubber and coconut fibre).

Foreign direct investment (FDI) has undoubtedly been the engine of manufactured export growth over the past two decades. During 1967-77, a total of 82 foreign manufacturing firms were set up in Sri Lanka. Of these, only 12 were export-oriented ventures (garments 9; gem cutting 2; ceramic-ware 1; wall-tiles 1) (Athukorala, 1995). In contrast, during 1978-95 the Board of Investment (BOI)[10] signed contracts under the Section 17 of the BOI Law (Special Incentive Scheme for export-oriented firms) for setting up 1136 firms of which 835 had foreign capital participation. Of these 875 contracted 'foreign projects', 368 were in commercial operation, 104 under construction and 20 awaiting production by the end of 1995. (Henceforth, these firms are referred to as Special Incentive Scheme firms, or SIS firms for short.) Projects approved by the FIAC (and BOI since late 1993) under the Inland Revenue and Tax Related Laws (General Incentive Scheme) ("GIS firms") during this period numbered 670. Over 350 of these projects were in operation by the end of 1995. The impressive response of foreign investors to the market oriented reforms gradually waned from the mid-1980s, even

10. Formerly the Greater Colombo Economic Commission, GCEC.

though FDI inflows continued to remain at high levels compared to the pre-1977 period. A surge in investor interest emerged again from 1989 onwards. While the second-wave liberalisation reforms set the stage, the surge in FDI was also aided by the new internationalisation move by manufacturers in Japan and the Newly Industrialised Countries (NIEs) in East Asia (in particular Korea) in response to massive exchange rate appreciations and domestic wage increases.[11]

Data on the relative contribution of foreign firms to manufactured exports are given in table 8. There is a close correlation between the growth of manufactured exports and the share of foreign firms in these exports. The share of foreign firms in total exports of manufactures increased from 24 per cent in 1977 to over 80 per cent in the mid-1990s. The contribution of foreign firms to the total increment in manufactured exports has increased from 46 per cent between 1978 and 1985 to 85 per cent between 1985 and 1995. Apart from the 'direct' contribution captured in this data, there is evidence that the presence of foreign firms generates significant positive slipover effects on the export success of local export producing firms (Athukorala, 1995). The dominance of foreign firms in the expansion of manufactured export growth may be partly attributable to the fact that domestic investors have been restricted in their access to capital by the relative underdevelopment of domestic capital markets and restrictions on their access to foreign capital; however, the major importance of foreign market linkages and other types of firm-specific capital that confer established foreign firms advantages in exploiting market potential, cannot be underestimated.

The emerging export pattern of manufactured exports from Sri Lanka is characterised by a high degree of import intensity and, therefore, limited linkages with the rest of the economy. The average import content of total manufactured exports is as

11. Figures reported in this paragraph are based on (unpublished) official records of FIAC, GCEC and BOI.

high as 70 per cent (Athukorala and Bandara, 1989, Table 1). In addition, allowance has to be made for other leakages related to the operation of foreign firms such as profit remittances, salaries of expatriates and payments of interest on foreign loans.[12] Some commentators have interpreted the high import intensity of export-oriented industries to be an intrinsic feature of export-led industrialisation through neutral incentives and argued for an activist economic policy stance to shift exports towards products with a higher proportion of domestic value added (*e.g.*, Adhikari, 1993, Wignaraja, 1994). Obviously, the higher the net foreign exchange component in a given volume of exports, the greater would be the benefit to the economy from EOFDI. However, for reasons given below, placing too much emphasis on 'per unit net foreign exchange earning,' as a performance criterion, can lead to wrong policy prescriptions.

Firstly, a country's principal objective in export expansion is to generate the largest possible volume of net foreign exchange earnings, not to maximise net foreign exchange earnings per unit of exports. In this respect, what is more relevant is the market potential which determines the total volume of exports. Labour intensive manufactured goods that are made to local specifications using local raw material in developing countries account for only a small and shrinking share of manufactured exports from developing countries. Success in increasing the volume of net foreign exchange earnings, therefore, depends crucially on the country's ability to enter the fast-growing markets for made-to-order manufactured goods and component production and assembly within vertically integrated production systems, which are typically more import intensive (Keesing and Lall, 1992, Athukorala and Santosa, 1997).

---

12. According to estimates by Ramanayake (1984), such leakages amount to almost half of the per percentage of domestic value added (gross exports-value of imported inputs). Thus, the net foreign exchange component embodied in gross export earning could not be more than 15 per cent. This is in fact the composite payment for local labour (about 10 per cent), local raw materials (3 per cent) and payments for services 3 per cent).

Secondly, unlike import-substituting firms, the performance of export-oriented ventures is not subject to the "foreign exchange constraint" (which was a dominant consideration in industry policy under the import-substitution strategy) In the case of export-oriented foreign firms in labour intensive industries, they create no drain on indigenous investment funds or other scarce resources. In the worst case scenario, the total net foreign exchange earning would be equivalent to the payments to local labour. Third, the rapid growth of gross export earnings per se, can be considered an important policy objective yielding considerable national benefits. Entering international markets in manufactures is normally considered a challenging task; therefore, export growth (in gross terms) is widely used as an indicator of efficiency and competitiveness of the domestic manufacturing sector. Thus, rapid export growth has a signaling effect for the attraction of more EOFDI and the mobilisation of foreign loanable funds at competitive rates.

Forging linkages is essentially a time-dependent process linked to quality improvement in domestic input-production industries. Producing what is sought in competitive international markets, in contrast to producing import substituting products for a shortage-ridden supplier's market, calls for a vector of imported inputs meeting exacting quality requirements and specifications. Substitution of inferior locally produced inputs for higher quality imported inputs may lead to significant market losses, and the cost involved in correcting the defects at a further stage may be prohibitive (Keesing and Lall, 1992). Hence, it is often unrealistic to expect export producers to source many inputs from local suppliers at the formative stage of export-oriented industrialisation. There is evidence that the net foreign exchange earning component in the garment industry has recorded a modest increase in recent years. Until the mid-1980s, local purchases by export producers were limited only to packaging material. More recently, local procurement of yarn by the garment industry has begun to increase following enhanced efficiency of the local textile industry with privatisation and the entry of some foreign firms.

Finally, it is important to note that inappropriate macroeconomic policies can constrain the development of backward linkages; the existence of an overvalued real exchange rate during much of the study period would have provided an implicit subsidy for the users of imported inputs (Little *et al.*, Ch. 8). This view is supported by the fact that high import dependence and low value added is not limited to export oriented industries only. Disaggregated data from the Survey of Manufacturing Industries suggests that this has been a common phenomenon across all sectors.

Employment

Total employment in "organised" manufacturing was over 350 thousand in 1993, up from around 150 thousand in the early 1980s (Table 9). This increase has predominantly come from the private sector. The public sector share in total employment declined throughout the post-reform period. It was about 16 per cent in 1993, down from 44 per cent in 1981. Foreign direct investment has played a pivotal role in private-sector employment expansion. Total local employment (*i.e.*, total employment net of expatriates) in firms established under the approval of the Board of Investment (BOI) (formerly the Greater Colombo Economic Commission, GCEC) increased continuously from 10,538 to 145775 between 1980 and 1995. Over 95 per cent of these employment opportunities are in the manufacturing sector and the contribution of foreign firms is about 87 per cent.[13] There is no time series data on employment in non-GCEC foreign firms. According to periodic sample surveys conducted by the FIAC, total employment in non-GCEC projects approved after 1977 increased from about 2,500 in 1978 to about 50,000 by 1988. Roughly, about 50 per cent of these employment opportunities are in export-oriented manufacturing, with the balance coming from import-substituting manufacturing (25 per cent), tourism and

13. Data on employment in GCEC firms reported here are from, Central Bank, *Annual Report* (various issues).

other services (12 per cent) and agriculture and animal husbandry (FIAC 1988). These figures taken together suggest an increase in the share of export-oriented foreign firms in 'formal' manufacturing in the country, from about 10 per cent in the early 1980s to over 50 per cent by the early 1990s.

The sectoral composition of manufacturing employment has undergone significant change over the past two decades (Table 4). Export oriented manufacturing industries — wearing apparel (322), footwear (324), rubber goods (355), plastic products (356) and other manufacturing (Jewelry, sport goods, toys) (390) — have recorded significant gains in employment share. In 1993, the wearing apparel industry alone accounted for over 46 per cent of total manufacturing employment, up from 29 per cent in 1988. The changing sectoral composition of employment clearly suggests that future expansion of manufacturing employment depends crucially on the country's ability to maintain (and improve upon) international competitiveness of domestic manufacturing, which in turn hinges on productivity improvement. Reflecting the rapid expansion of export oriented labour-intensive product sectors (mostly garments, shoes, sport goods and various assembly activities) the share of female workers in total manufacturing employment increased from 32 per cent in the early 1980s to over 60 per cent by the mid-1990s[14].

Concluding Remarks

The market-oriented policy reforms initiated in 1977 have led to far-reaching changes in the structure and performance of the manufacturing sector in the Sri Lankan economy. With the gradual erosion of the dominant role of SOEs, the private sector has been largely responsible for the recent output growth in manufacturing in recent years. The manufacturing sector has become increasingly more export-oriented, and is no longer reliant on the fortunes of the traditional primary export industries to obtain required imported inputs. Despite some output disruption

14. The data reported in this paragraph are from United Nations, *Statistical Yearbook* (various issues).

in the immediate aftermath of the removal of trade restrictions, the sector has turned in an improved performance in terms of output, productivity and employment, confounding the predictions of pessimists who expected trade liberalisation to set in a process of deindustrialisation.

The Sri Lankan experience highlights the complementary role of investment liberalisation for exploiting the potential gains from trade liberalisation. Internationalisation of production through FDI participation has been central to the rapid integration of developing countries in the global manufactured goods trade system. In this context, there is limited room for a small developing economy to enter manufactured goods trade solely through local entrepreneurial initiatives. Foreign investment not only provides the initial stimulus for rapid expansion in exports and the associated increase in employment, but is also a vehicle for the forging of links between local firms and international markets.

To capture the full benefits of both trade and investment liberalisation for industrial and broader economic growth, a supporting set of macroeconomic policies and an attractive investment climate are required. In the case of Sri Lanka, these ingredients have been missing for much of the post-reform period, though there were brief favourable periods, such as the 1990-94 period, when the underlying capacity for rapid manufacturing, export and GDP growth could be glimpsed. On the other hand, there can be little doubt that the resilience of the economy in recent years, in the face of traumatic and debilitating shocks, is due in large part to the greater flexibility provided by an open trade regime. In essence, the industrialisation and growth process in this context can be understood as one where trade liberalisation increases the potential return to investments which capitalises on a country's comparative advantage, while liberalisation of foreign investments permits international firms to be attracted, which have the capacity to take advantage of such profit opportunities. The early 1990s can probably be seen as the period in which these forces were permitted to operate most freely. Unfortunately, the upsurge in political instability and its impact on both macro-economic and country-risk perceptions, has tended to abort the investment flow which was starting to make a strong impact on growth and employment.

REFERENCES

Adhikari, Romesh (1993), "Policy Reforms and Export Performance in Sri Lanka: Some Observations", in R. Adhikari, C. Kirkpatrick and J. Weiss (eds.), *Industrial and Trade Policy Reforms and Experience in Developing Countries, Manchester*: Manchester University Press, 186-97.

Athukorala, Prema-Chandra (1986), "The Impact of 1977 Policy reforms on Domestic Industry", *Upanathi : Journal of the Sri Lanka Association of Economists*, 1(1).

Athukorala, Prema-Chandra (1995), "Foreign Direct Investment and Manufacturing for Export in a New Exporting country : The Case of Sri Lanka", *World Economy*, 18(4), 543-64.

Athukorala, Prema-Chandra and Jayatilaka S. Bandara (1989), "Growth of manufactured Exports, Primary Commodity Dependence and Net Export Earnings : Sri Lanka", *World Development*, 17(6) : 897-904.

Athukorala, Prema-Chandra and Sisira Jayasuriya (1994), *Macro-economic Policies, Crises and Growth in Sri Lanka, 1969-90*, Washington D.C. : World Bank.

Athukorala, Prema-Chandra and Sisira Jayasuriya (1996), *Macro-economic Policies and Export Competitiveness in Sri Lanka*, Report Prepared for the National Development Council of Sri Lanka, Colombo.

Athukorala, Prema-Chandra and Bambang H. Santosa (1997), 'Gains from Indonesian Export Growth : Do Linkages Matter?", *Bulletin of Indonesian Economic Studies*, 33(2), 73-95.

Bhagwati, Jagdish (1993), "Free Trade : Old and New Challenges", *Economic Journal*, 104(423) : 231-246.

Central Bank of Sri Lanka (1996), *Annual Report-1995*, Colombo.

Cuthbertson, A.G. and P. Athukorala (1990), "Sri Lanka", Part 3 in D. Papageorgiou, M. Michaely and A. M. Choksi eds. *Liberalizing Foreign Trade : Indonesia, Pakistan and Sri Lanka*, Oxford : Basil Blackwell, 287-414.

Dornbusch, Rudiger (1992), "The Case for Trade Liberalisation in Developing Countries", *Journal of Economic Perspectives*, 6(1) : 69-87.

Helleiner, Gerald K. (1994), "Introduction" in Gerald K Helleiner ed. *Trade Policy and Industrialisation in Turbulent Times*, London : Routledge.

Fitter, John (1973), "Ceylon on the Road to Long Term Decline", *Intereconomics*, January, 25-27.

Foreign Investment Advisory Committee (FIAC) (1988), *Survey of the Projects Approved by the Foreign Investment Advisory Committee* : 1987-June 1988, Colombo : Ministry of Finance and Planning.

Jayasuriya, Sisira and Malathy Knight-John (forthcoming), "Liberalization and Privatization : Telecommunications Reforms in Sri Lanka", Macdonald, Stuart, Gary Madden and Martin Salamon (eds.), *Telecommunications and Economic Development*, Amsterdam : Elsevier Science B.V.

Kelegama, Saman (1995), "The Impact of Privatization on Distributional Equity : The Case of Sri Lanka", in V.V. Ramanadhan (ed.), *Privatization and Equity,* London : Routledge, 143-80.

Keesing, Donald B. and Sanjaya Lall (1992), "Marketing of manufactured Exports from developing Countries : Learning Sequences and Public Support", in Helleiner, Gerald K. ed. (1992), *Trade Policy, Industrialisation, and Development : New Perspectives*, Oxford: Clarendon Press, pp. 176-93.

Krueger, Anne O. (1992), *Economic policy Reforms in Developing Countries*, Oxford : Basil Blackwell.

Krueger, A.O. (1997) "Trade Policy and Economic Development : How We Learn", *American Economic Review*, 87(1), 1-22.

Little, Ian M.D. (1982) *Economic Development : Theory, Policy and International Relations*, New York : Basic Books.

Little, Ian M.D., Richard N. Cooper, W. Max Corden and Sarath Rajapatirana (1993), *Boom, Crisis, and Adjustment : The Macro-economic Experience of Developing Countries,* Oxford : Oxford University Press.

Meller, Patricio (1995), "Chilean Export Growth, 1970-90 : An Assessment", in Gerald K. Helleiner (ed.), *Manufacturing for Export in the Developing World : Problems and Policies*, London : Routledge.

Ministry of Finance and Planning (1994), Report of the Presidential Commission on Tariffs and Trade-1994, Colombo.

Ministry of Industries and Scientific Affairs (1975), Field Survey of Manufacturing Industry (reference year 1994), Colombo.

Olson, R.S. (1977), "Expropriation and International Economic Coercion : Ceylon and the 'West' 1961-65", *Journal of Developing Areas*, 11(2), 205-26.

Riedel, James (1993), "Vietnam : On the Trail of the Tigers", *World Economy*, 16(4), 401-423.

Rodrik, Dani (1992), "The Limits of Trade Policy Reforms in Developing Countries", *Journal of Economic Perspectives*, 6(1) : 87-106.

Rajapatirana, Sarath (1988), Foreign Trade and Economic Development : Sri Lanka's Experience", *World Development*, 16(10), 1143-1157.

Snodgrass, Donald R (1966), *Sri Lanka : An Export Economy in Transition*, Homewood, Ill : Richard D. Irvin.

Thomas, Vinod, John Nash and Associates (1991), *Best Practices in Trade Policy Reforms*, New York : Oxford University Press.

UNCTAD (1995), *Trade and Development Report-1995, Geneva.*

Wignaraja, Ganeshan (1994), "Outward-oriented Trade Policy and Industrial Performance in Sri Lanka, 1977-92, *Contemporary Asia,* 3(3), 203-15.

World Bank (1995), Sri Lanka : Nonplantation Crop Sector Policy Alternatives, Agriculture and Natural resource Division, South Asia region, Washington D.C.; World Bank (mimeo)

World Trade Organisation (WTO) (1995), *Sri Lanka Trade Policy Review*, Geneva : WTO.

TABLE 1

Real Exchange Rate Indices (1990 = 100) : Exports, Imports and Total Trade, 1975-1995

	RERTX1	RERTX2	RERTM1	RERTM2	RERTT1	RERTT2
1975	39.41	48.76	47.97	59.35	44.42	54.97
1976	46.21	53.50	55.83	64.64	51.59	59.73
1977	53.93	52.24	66.18	64.09	61.06	59.14
1978	94.1	88.42	117.62	110.5	107.92	101.24
1979	94.5	89.57	116.9	110.8	107.36	101.76
1980	90.00	80.48	109.36	97.79	102.55	91.70
1981	91.73	82.79	109.08	98.44	103.71	93.60
1982	89.64	84.95	103.06	97.67	99.00	93.82
1983	89.30	77.19	102.32	88.44	98.54	85.17
1984	82.95	65.45	91.78	72.42	88.68	69.97
1985	88.41	84.91	92.38	88.73	90.91	87.31
1986	92.76	99.19	95.81	102.46	94.62	101.19
1987	98.21	99.73	101.24	102.8	99.71	101.25
1988	98.57	96.86	103.67	101.87	101.30	99.55
1989	101.07	101.58	106.47	107.01	104.19	104.72
1990	100.00	100.00	100.00	100.00	100.00	100.00
1991	95.82	98.46	95.48	98.10	96.01	98.65
1992	95.48	100.55	95.70	100.78	96.25	101.36
1993	95.36	104.25	98.19	107.34	97.92	107.05
1994	93.81	105.92	97.78	110.4	97.57	110.16
1995	97.01	110.81	104.84	119.77	103.62	118.37

RERTX1 = Real exchange rate for total non-oil exports with CPI to measure both foreign and domestic prices.

RERTX2 = Real exchange rate for total non-oil exports with CPI to measure foreign price and WPI to measure domestic prices.

RERTM1 = Real exchange rate for total non-oil imports with CPI to measure both foreign and domestic prices.

RERTM2 = Real exchange rate for total non-oil imports with CPI to measure foreign price and WPI to measure domestic prices.

RERTT1 = Real exchange rate for total non-oil trade with CPI to measure both foreign and domestic prices.

RERTT2 = Real exchange rate for total non-oil trade with CPI to measure foreign price and WPI to measure domestic prices.

Source : Compiled using data from Central Bank, Annual Report (various issues).

TABLE 2

Key Indicators of Manufacturing Sector Performance, 1965-95[1]

	Manufacturing value added : Share of GDP	Growth (%)	Export growth (%)[3]	Capacity utilisation (%)	Export-gross output ratio (%)[4]	Value add Output ratio (%)
1965-69[2]	8.3	8.6	n.a.	-	-	48.2
1970-76[2]	11.6	3.9	10.2	53	3.1	50.1
1977	11.4	0.8	15.2	60	5.7	38.4
1978	11.5	9.9	16.2	70	12.6	35.1
1979	11.3	4.7	27.3	72	21.2	31.9
1980	11.2	4.4	35.3	73	21.4	26.7
1981	11.1	4.5	36.2	74	27.3	26.2
1982	11.4	7.8	23.4	76	28.4	26.1
1983	11.1	2.2	27.2	74	28.1	28.1
1984	12.0	13.8	8.2	75	34.9	31.2
1985	11.8	3.7	4.5	74	33.2	34.5
1986	12.5	10.5	4.3	78	36.9	38.6

1987	13.2	7.5	5.2	79	39.1	38.1
1988	13.7	6.1	3.7	78	40.6	38.9
1989	14.2	5.3	6.0	79	40.7	37.1
1990	14.6	9.7	29.2	81	45.5	35.7
1991	14.8	9.1	13.9	83	47.2	36.6
1992	15.3	12.3	37.6	82	53.3	37.0
1993	15.2	10.8	19.6	83	58.3	36.5
1994	15.4	9.1	8.1	84	54.3	36.2
1995	15.8	9.2	2.9	84	55.3	36.8

Notes :

1. Capacity utilisation, export output ratio and value added-output ratio (the last 3 columns) relates to 'organised' manufacturing only. Others are economy-wide indicators.
2. Annual average.
3. In current SDR terms.
4. In calculating this ratio, FOB export values been adjusted to producer-price basis using trade and transport cost margins from the Input-Output Table-1981 (Ministry of Finance and Planning).

Source : Complied from Central Bank, *Review of the Economy and Annual Report* (various issues).

TABLE 3

Relative Contribution of Growth of Factor Inputs and Total Factor Productivity Growth to Output Growth in Private Sector Manufacturing*

	G_o	G_L	G_K	G_M	S_L*G_L	S_K*G_K	S_M*G_M	TFPG
Total Manufacturing								
1966-74	0.78	3.34	-4.25	8.24	0.45	-1.29	4.61	-2.99
1977-81	3.98	1.68	10.55	2.59	0.18	3.00	1.58	-0.78
1981-88	13.99	7.89	9.93	15.36	0.63	3.64	8.49	1.22
1988-93	25.91	14.23	11.07	21.12	1.09	4.25	11.40	9.17
1981-93	18.96	10.53	10.41	17.76	0.90	3.72	9.87	4.47

1966-74	1.45	2.56	-6.83	7.68	0.33	-2.06	4.36	-1.18
1977-81	2.07	-2.69	11.50	0.04	-0.25	3.74	0.02	-1.44
1981-88	15.15	8.39	10.91	15.78	0.55	4.62	8.05	1.92
1988-93	20.66	10.94	9.64	18.14	0.57	4.08	9.50	6.50
1981-93	17.44	9.45	10.38	16.76	0.68	4.35	8.65	3.76

Notes :

* Estimated using the formula : $TFPG = G_O - S_L G_L - S_K G_K - S_M G_M$ where, TFPG is total factor productivity growth, G_O, G_L, G_K, G_M denotes annual compound growth of output, labour, stock of capital and intermediate input between the two given years; and S_L , S_K and S_M denote the average value shares of labour, capital and material in output.

Source and Method : For details on data source and methodology see Athukorala, P. and S. Rajapathirana (forthcoming), *Economic Liberalisation and Industrial Restructuring : A late Comer's Story*, Washington. D.C : World Bank.

TABLE 4

Contribution of State Industrial Enterprises to Manufacturing Vaue Added by Industry Groups, 1970-1994

(Selected years) (%)

ISIC	Product name	1970	1974	1981	1988	1994
31	Food beverages and tobacco	23.7	41.9	41.9	44.4	17.3
32	Textiles, clothing and leather goods	11.0	37.1	72.1	38.9	0.7
33	Wood and wood products	72.7	92.2	92.2	74.3	46.3
34	Paper and paper products	43.0	69.3	65.7	44.6	37.5
35	Chemical, rubber and plastic	45.6	70.1	42.7	27.7	2.7
36	None-metallic mineral products	72.0	82.4	87.0	60.2	24.8
Metal	products, machinery and transport equipment	87.0	91.2	45.7	31.1	14.6
3	Total manufacturing	29.6	65.7	63.5	41.9	5.1

Source : Athukorala (1986), table 6 (for 1970 and 1974) and Department of Census and Statistics, *Annual Survey of Industries*, 1981, 1989 (reference year 1988), and computer tapes of *Annual Survey of Industries* 1994 (reference year 1993).

TABLE 5

Sectoral Composition of Output and Employment in Private Sector Manufacturing*, 1974, 1981 and 1993

(Percentages)

ISIC Code	Industry	Production			Employment		
		1974	1981	1993	1974	1981	1993
311-12	Food	7.01	8.08	15.75	5.74	5.35	11.14
313	Beverages	2.59	1.43	2.07	2.64	1.12	0.86
314	Tobacco	23.65	19.01	11.62	2.11	2.59	3.21
321	Textile	15.82	8.89	8.41	25.22	23.96	12.27
322	Clothing	5.35	21.64	25.27	11.34	29.31	46.70
323	Leather goods	0.74	0.46	1.17	0.77	0.44	1.38
324	Footwear	1.86	1.19	2.18	2.39	1.24	2.25
331	Wood products	0.20	0.25	0.15	0.41	0.67	0.64
332	Furniture	0.16	0.18	0.12	0.54	0.87	0.43

Contd.

TABLE 5 : *continued*

ISIC Code	Industry	Production			Employment		
		1974	1981	1993	1974	1981	1993
341	Paper and paper products	3.08	1.32	1.01	3.32	1.38	0.65
342	Printing	0.01	1.21	0.99	—	1.65	1.87
351	Industrial chemicals	1.63	0.86	0.98	0.62	0.50	0.82
352	Other chemicals	9.40	10.84	6.85	5.85	5.63	2.95
355	Rubber goods	2.68	6.61	5.55	4.12	6.06	5.55
356	Plastic goods	2.66	3.03	1.88	2.18	2.76	3.25
361	Pottery	0.03	0.85	0.64	0.10	0.99	1.25
361	Glass	0.84	0.92	0.13	2.09	0.77	0.19
369	Non-met. mineral products	0.25	0.55	2.47	2.56	1.43	1.56
371-72	Basic metal products	0.46	0.51	0.52	0.88	0.23	0.17

381	Fabricated metal products	4.49	2.80	1.02	6.93	3.71	1.18
382	Machinery	5.66	1.45	2.12	10.40	2.38	1.41
383	Electrical machinery	6.04	4.04	1.57	4.04	2.65	1.85
384	Transport equipment	2.17	0.63	2.20	3.91	1.17	2.40
390	Other manufacturing#	0.73	1.47	5.31	0.88	2.05	10.97
3	Total manufacturing	100	100	100	100	100	100

Notes :

* Excluding petroleum refining.

— Zero or negligible.

Jewellery, sport goods, toys etc.

Source : As for table 3.

TABLE 6

Manufactured Exports : Composition, Growth and Share in Total Exports, 1965-1995 (%)

ISIC Category	Composition*							Growth#
	1965/66	1969/70	1976/77	1979/80	1984/85	1989/90	1994/95	1978-95
Food manufactures	6.50	17.98	37.07	16.04	6.21	3.91	3.33	7.89
Fish products	5.39	15.52	33.23	13.83	5.34	2.72	2.26	6.03
Textiles	3.82	2.74	4.19	2.45	2.85	2.84	4.77	24.40
Clothing	3.17	18.97	39.37	71.92	75.16	64.61	60.28	19.73
Footwear	0.53	3.50	1.90	0.38	1.44	1.04	1.69	25.82
Pottery and ceramics	0.00	0.15	7.83	2.62	0.89	1.03	1.11	15.07
Non-metalic mineral products	23.65	8.49	2.58	14.41	8.21	19.36	8.49	22.23
Cut-and-polished diamond	0.00	0.00	0.00	0.01	0.20	1.10	0.62	23.46
Non-electrical machinery	0.52	0.00	1.96	1.29	1.17	1.03	1.29	20.39
Electrical machinery	1.64	0.79	0.65	0.30	0.43	0.71	1.62	30.01

Other manufacturing	11.26	5.09	2.86	1.81	3.68	3.74	6.54	20.38
Travel goods	0.00	0.00	0.14	0.04	0.05	0.06	1.52	40.08
Toys and sport goods	0.00	0.00	0.13	0.21	0.37	0.14	1.79	27.29
Jewelry	10.51	3.38	1.31	0.47	0.37	0.47	0.98	25.17
Total manufactured exports	100	100	100	100	100	100	100	
US $ million	3545	4922	29651	125298	381058	832270	2372716	20.21
Manufacturing share in total merchandise exports	0.90	1.48	4.58	12.25	27.21	47.96	67.65	

* Two-year averages.

\# Annual compound growth rate (in nominal US $) estimated by fitting a logarithmic trend line. All growth rates are statistically significant at the one per cent level.

Source : Compiled from UN trade data (Series d) tables held in the *International Economic Data Bank*, Australian national University.

TABLE 7

Industry Profile of Export-oriented Foreign Investment Projects : 1978-1995*

	No. of firms	Total Planned investment US $ mn.	FDI share in total planned investment (%)
Horticulture	10	6.0	1.2
Manufacturing	303	464.9	95.0
Food Products	15	10.8	2.2
Beverages and Tobacco	3	2.5	0.5
Textiles	18	91.7	18.8
Wearing apparel	63	67.5	13.8
Leather goods	7	4.3	0.9
Footwear	6	5.2	1.1
Wood Products	10	2.4	0.5
Paper and Paper Products	3	3.6	0.7

Printing	2	2.6	0.5
Rubber Products	16	51.6	10.6
PVC Products	22	18.2	3.7
Plastic products	6	3.6	0.7
Non-metallic mineral products	10	13.6	2.8
Fabricated Metal Products	10	29.8	6.1
Electronics and electrical goods	19	40.6	8.3
Transport equipment	3	1.9	0.4
Toys (except wooden toys)	9	7.5	1.5
Coir Products	8	4.1	0.8
Jewelry and Lapidary	24	19.7	4.0

Contd.

TABLE 7 : *continued*

	No. of firms	Total Planned investment US $ mn.	FDI share in total planned investment (%)
Fishing Gear and Accessories	3	0.5	0.1
Other manufactures	14	10.8	2.2
Services	56	96.4	19.7
Total	369	489.1	100.0

Note : *Projects in commercial operation as at 31 December 1995.

Source : Compiled using official records of the Board of Investment, Sri Lanka.

TABLE 8

Foreign Firms' Contribution to Manufactured Export Expansion, 1976-1995
(Three-year averages)

	Manufactured exports		Foreign firms' contribution to Manufactured exports	
	US $ Millions	Share in total merchandise exports (%)	All foreign firms# (%)	BOI firms (%)
1975-77	24.8	4.0	23.2	...
1978-80	102.7	10.4	30.2	...
1981-83	234.9	22.1	43.7	30.6
1984-86	421.2	31.9	47.4	35.5
1987-89	653.5	44.2	58.2	43.5

Contd.

TABLE 8 : *continued*

	Manufactured exports		Foreign firms' contribution to Manufactured exports	
	US $ Millions	**Share in total merchandise exports (%)**	**All foreign firms# (%)**	**BOI firms (%)**
1990-92	1083.1	56.6	65.8	47.6
1993-95	2282.2	72.2	78.2	49.1

Notes :

\# Combined export share of GCEC and Non-GCEC foreign firms.

... Not applicable.

Source : Athukorala (1995) (updated to 1995 using the same data sources).

TABLE 9

Employment in Manufacturing

Year	Total employment	Public-sector employment*
1979	160816	
1980	161844	
1981	151549	67201 (44.3)
1983	202100	
1984	212332	70250 (33.0)
1985	210465	
1986	217146	
1987	212223	
1988	219278	72563 (33.1)
1989	243705	
1990	281114	
1993	356950	58030 (16.3)

Note : The share of SOEs in total manufacturing employment is indicated in brackets.

Sources : *Annual Survey on Manufacturing Industries* (for 1978 through 1981), *Annual Survey of Industries* (for 1983 through 1990), and 1993 : data tapes of *Annual Survey of Industries*-1994, all conducted by Department of Census and Statistics. These surveys cover only production units in the formal manufacturing.

PART III

LIBERALISATION EXPERIENCES AND ISSUES : SECTORAL STUDIES

10

Liberalising Bangladesh's External Sector

NASIRUDDIN AHMED

I. Introduction

The last ten years (1986-1995) have seen major changes in Bangladesh's economic policies marking a new phase in her development strategy. These new economic policies aim at reducing the extent of government controls over various aspects of the domestic economy, expanding the role of the private sector along with relying increasingly on market forces to allocate resources, and opening up the economy to trade and foreign investment. These policy reforms were introduced first in December 1980 and then on the economy-wide basis in 1986 along the prescriptions of the Bretton Woods Institutions (BWI) — the World Bank and the International Monetary Fund (IMF) against the backdrop of some major shocks which hit many developing countries including Bangladesh in the early eighties: (i) the global recession of 1979-82, (ii) the increase in real interest rate of foreign loans and (iii) a severe deterioration in the terms of trade along with reduced availability of external aid. This situation seriously eroded Bangladesh's growth prospects and left her with unsustainable external and fiscal deficits. However, the macro-economic policy reforms known as structural adjustment have been undertaken under comprehensive and fairly rigid aid conditionality arrangements.

In keeping with the objective of greater openness and outward orientation, trade liberalisation measures were adopted as part of structural adjustment programme. In fact, significant steps have been taken during the 1990s to liberalise Bangladesh's trade regime in order to solve the problem of persistent trade deficit. However, while structural reforms in such areas as the financial sector, legal reform, infrastructure and energy are difficult and politically sensitive, trade policy reforms, the bulk of which consists of liberalising imports, is perceived to be relatively easy to implement (World Bank, 1996). The primary objective of trade liberalisation policies has been to move towards a liberalised trade regime with flexible exchange rate management. Trade liberalisation is expected to have a positive effect on export and thereby on economic growth by removing anti-export bias and making exports more competitive in international markets. This is done primarily by correcting an overvalued exchange rate and creating incentives for expanding the tradeable sector. By reducing the bias against exports, trade policy reform should be very effective in spurring investment, both domestic and foreign, in export-oriented sectors. Similarly, by reducing the level of quantitative restrictions on imports and permitting increased import of raw materials, intermediate and capital goods, trade liberalisation is likely to contribute to higher economic growth.

The available literature on trade policy reforms in Bangladesh is scanty[1]. The present study will hopefully fill some gaps. This paper reviews trade policy reforms in Bangladesh and attempts to examine the macroeconomic performance of the economy as a result of these reforms in terms of certain indicators.

---

1. Such studies include Mahmood, Rahman and Hasan (1991), Rahman (1992), Khan (1994), Bayes, Hossain and Rahman (1995), the World Bank (1996) and Dutta and Ahmed (1997).

The remainder of the paper is organised as follows. Section II briefly reviews reforms in trade and exchange rate policies in Bangladesh. Some indicators showing the macroeconomic performance of the Bangladesh economy in the context of trade liberalisation are presented in Section III. Concluding remarks and policy implications are given in Section IV.

II. Reforms in Trade and Exchange Rate Policies in Bangladesh

Prior to 1986 Bangladesh was a strongly inward-oriented country meaning that the overall incentive structure strongly favoured production for the domestic market. By combining such indicators as (i) effective rate of protection[2], (ii) use of direct controls like quotas and import-licensing schemes, (iii) use of export incentives and (iv) degree of exchange rate overvaluation, the World Bank (1987) classified 41 developing countries including Bangladesh by trade orientation during 1963-73 and 1973-85. In both the periods Bangladesh was classified as "strongly inward-oriented" country. This is corroborated by the price distortion index derived by Agarwala (1983). Since 1986 Bangladesh undertook the following measures in export promotion and import liberalisation.

Export Promotion Measures

- Doing away with the system of state trading in exports and privatising the same.
- Introducing a number of incentives by the government like export performance benefits, duty drawback system, special bonded warehouse facility etc., as a means of providing access to duty-free import of inputs for exports.
- Introducing back-to back letter of credit method allowing easy financing through supplier credit.

---

2. The level of effective rates of production (ERP) Estimates the level of production to input used as well as to output produced.

- Setting up an Export Promotion Bureau to promote the export of non-traditional items.
- Setting up two export processing zones to provide a secure foothold for direct foreign investment[3].
- Adopting a policy of the frequent exchange rate depreciation in order to prevent overvaluation of the exchange rate.
- Merging the official exchange rate, and a secondary exchange rate which was operative since the mid-1970s.

Import liberalisation

The removal of quantitative restrictions on imports has been accompanied by a gradual lowering of tariff rates. Average

TABLE 1

Trends in Nominal Protection in Import Trade, 1990/91 to 1995/96 (Percentage of assessed value)

Indicators	Pre-reform (1990/91)	Post-reform (1995/96)
Average (unweighted) nominal tariff rate (%)	88.6	24.6
Imported-weighted average (%)	42.1	21.0
Dispersion of tariff rate (%)	59.0	72.7
Tariff range (%) (Low-High)	2.25-508.5	7.5-50
Quantitative restrictions	39.5	10.0

Sources : World Bank 1996; Dean *et al.*, 1994.

Note : Quantitative restrictions in post-reform period relate to 1993/94.

3. Total investment in these two zones is US $168 million; share of 1994/95 exports is 20 per cent; 43 (67.19 per cent) out of 64 operating projects are wholly foreign-owned; total employment is 32,747 of whom about 80 per cent are women (World Bank, 1996).

nominal protection, measured as the average of all import duties and protective taxes, has fallen from 89 per cent in 1990/91 to 25 per cent in 1995/96. However, nominal protection, as measured by import-weighted average protection rates, has declined since 1990/91 but by much less (21 percentage points) than the decline in unweighted average protection rates (64 percentage points). The range of tariffs was reduced from 2.25 per cent-508.5 per cent to 7.5 per cent -50 per cent (apart from a few luxury items). However, the dispersion of the unweighted average protection rates, as measured by the coefficient of variation (CV), shows an upward trend from 59 to 73 per cent. This may be attributed to a non-uniform way of reducing tariff rates. Quantitative restrictions were reduced from 39.5 to 10. But tariff escalation remains a problem for the import of manufactured consumer goods with rates on intermediate goods of 50 per cent and on final goods of 100 per cent. In addition, goods deemed "luxury" items, and many consumer goods items still face rates between 150 per cent and 400 per cent. Table 1 presents indicators of import-trade in pre-reform and post-reform period in Bangladesh.

Accompanying Exchange Rate Policy

One of the major goals of trade policy reform is to eliminate the anti-export bias of the past protectionist policies and thus improve the economy's export performance as well as its overall efficiency in resource allocation. A real exchange rate-based trade liberalisation policy helps to achieve a reduction in the anti-export bias. The reason for this is that in the presence of quantitative import restrictions, a (real) devaluation will result in a lower premium accrued to those with import licence allocations, and thus in a reduction in the anti-export bias. Available empirical evidence shows that successful trade liberalisation has been associated with devaluations either at the same time or beforehand (Bhagwati 1978; Krueger 1978; Michaely *et al.*, 1991; Little *et al.*, 1993; Edwards 1993; Corden, 1997).

The choice of an exchange rate regime is one of the most significant macroeconomic policy decisions that any national government must take. This is because exchange rate influences the relative price of locally made goods to foreign ones, thereby affecting the competitiveness in trade. Since mid-1979 Bangladesh adopted a flexible exchange rate policy fixing the value of taka (Bangladesh currency) in terms of a basket of currencies of her major trading partners (Bhuyan and Rashid 1993). Two major devaluations of the official exchange rate took place in 1970s. Although the Bangladesh currency was not devalued as part of the policy reform package, a policy of frequent adjustment of the nominal exchange rate was adopted since 1985 to reflect changes in the currencies of the major trading partners relative to the US dollar (the intervening currency). The primary objective of the frequent exchange rate depreciation was to prevent overvaluation of the exchange rate (Rahman, 1994). Moreover, the merger of the official and the secondary exchange (called the Wage Earners' Scheme) rate took place in January 1992. The shift from a system of multiple exchange rates to a single rate is an act of liberalisation. This is because a system of multiple exchange rate produces black market premium which acts as an implicit tax on trade causing both exports and imports to be below the levels that would have occurred under a unified exchange rate regime (Ahammad, 1995).

III. Trade Liberalisation and Macro-economic Performance in Bangladesh

To appreciate the prospects and problems arising out of the trade liberalisation policies, it may be useful to look at some of the historical trends in terms of merchandise exports, merchandise imports, workers' remittances, real effective exchange rate, government revenue, net foreign assets of the central bank and GDP growth rate.

Trends in Merchandise Exports

The basic premise of trade liberalisation is to allow resources to shift from the non-tradeable to the tradeable sectors of the economy and thus allow the share of the trade sector to rise in relation to GDP. The export orientation is often measured by the ratio of merchandise exports to GDP. Such a measure shows a low export orientation in Bangladesh (Figure 1). However, the contribution of exports to the economy has more than doubled over the years as is indicated by the rise in the ratio of exports to GDP from 4.42 per cent per annum during 1973-75 to 9.07 per cent during 1991-95.

Figure 1 : Export orientation in Bangladesh

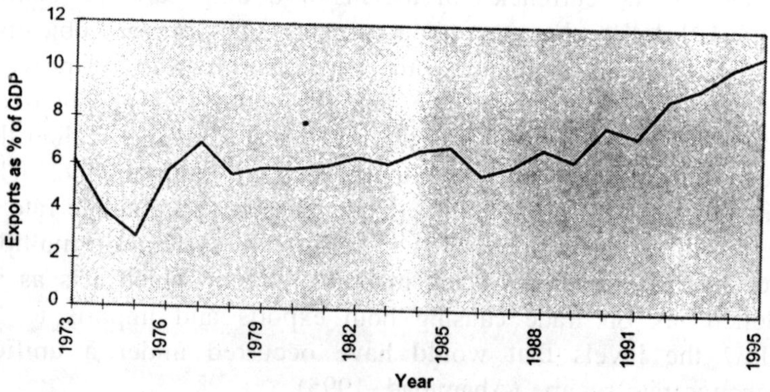

Source : Based on IMF (1997).

There have been two major features of the changes in Bangladesh's export composition : the decline in the relative importance of raw jute and jute manufactures and the increasing share of exports accounted for by readymade garments (RMG). This change in composition of exports away from traditional products and towards non-traditional exports seems to fit with the recipe for export-led growth. Figures 2 (a and b) highlight this information.

Figure 2(a) : Export composition 1982/83

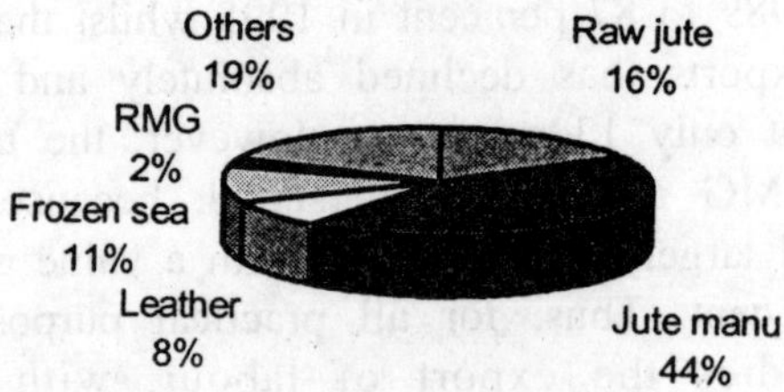

Figure 2(b) : Export composition 1994-95

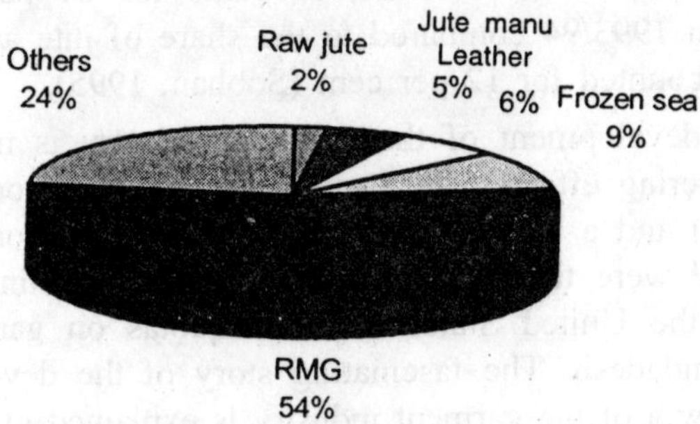

Source : Based on World Bank (1996).

Turning to export performance, growth in export earnings over the last decade has indeed been impressive. Exports in the 1990's have been particularly buoyant, registering a real growth rate of 16 per cent compared to around 5.5 per cent in the 1980s. This export surge has been entirely sustained by non-traditional exports which grew at a rate of 24.8 per cent in the 1990s. Within this category, RMG has come to completely dominate our export growth, though there has been positive growth both in leather and leather products (14.4 per cent), as well as fish and shrimps (12.8 per cent) in the 1990s. The share of non-traditional exports (gross values) has now risen from 31 per cent in 1989 to 87 per cent in 1995 whilst that of traditional jute based exports, has declined absolutely and relatively and now stands at only 13 per cent. However, the trend of export growth of RMG is slightly overstated, because RMG export growth is still largely import-based, with a value addition of less than 30 per cent. Thus, for all practical purposes, the RMG sector embodies the export of labour, with most of the intermediate and capital inputs having to be imported. If we re-estimate export trends in terms of local value added, then the share of non-traditional exports in 1993/94 fell from 84 per cent to 75 per cent. This is still high and reflects again the growth of RMG which, in gross terms, accounts for 61 per cent of all exports in 1993/94 compared to the share of jute and jute goods which accounted for 12 per cent (Sobhan, 1995).

The development of the garment industry is mainly due to the pioneering efforts of a foreign catalyst (Daewoo Corporation of Korea) and a local catalyst (Desh Garments Corporation). So successful were the technology transfer and training efforts that in 1985 the United States imposed quotas on garment exports from Bangladesh. The fascinating story of the development and rapid growth of the garment industry is explained in Rhee (1990).

Apart from this, the rapid growth of the export-oriented RMG sector is facilitated by a number of government incentives which include, inter alia, (i) special bonded warehouse facilities for duty-free imports of inputs, (ii) free import of grey cloth against back-to back letters of credit as a convenient device to bypass both customs and foreign exchange regulations greatly easing the life of our RMG exporters, (iii) corporate tax exemptions for five years, (iv) income tax rebates of up to 100 per cent of export earnings, (v) cash compensation of 5 per cent of FOB value for using local fabrics and (vi) low rate of duty (now zero) on imports of capital machinery for 100 per cent export-oriented units. In addition to the government incentives, (i) quotas under the Multi-Fibre Arrangement (MFA), a world-wide system of managed trade in textiles and clothing, which provide a secure market[4] access to the developed countries for some 60 per cent of our exports[5], (ii) the Generalised System of Preferences (GSP) scheme which has played an important role in enhancing the competitiveness of the Bangladesh's export sector for the last 20 years[6], (iii) buying houses were influential in providing export orders (almost 90 per cent of orders are placed by foreign buying houses operating in Bangladesh) and (iv) the back-to back letter of credit method allowed easy (but expensive) financing through supplier credits (World Bank, 1996).

Trends in Merchandise Imports

The import penetration ratio comes in two flavours, one using the ratio of imports to GDP and the other the ratio of imports to aggregate consumption. The import penetration ratio, measured as the ratio of imports to GDP, is shown in figure 3. It shows a fluctuating trend in import of Bangladesh since 1986 resulting mainly from a low level of investment[7]. This apart, the factors contributing to the decline in the import demand include the gradual depreciation in the value of the Bangladesh currency (taka), and a premium on the secondary exchange market (known as the Wage Earners' market) which was abolished with the unification of the exchange rate market in January 1992.

---

4. It is this sense of market security which has driven both the emergence of a new class of private entrepreneurs as well as the transformation in Bangladesh's external economy.

5. Under the Uruguay Round of the 1993 GATT Accord, MFA would be phased out over a ten-year period beginning July 1, 1995.

6. Under the GSP scheme 27 countries (of which 22 are industrial countries) offer facilities in the form of duty free or lower duty for Bangladesh commodities such as jute and jute goods, frozen food, readymade garments (to a limited extent), ceramic goods, handicrafts, leather, fruits and vegetables etc. However, under the GATT Uruguay Round Accord, the GSP scheme will be phased out in two stages over a period of ten years (Rahman, 1995).

7. The model developed and estimated by Bayes, Hossain and Rahman (1995) on the external sector of the Bangladesh economy, establishes that import growth is a function of investment and GDP growth.

Figure 3 : Import Orientation in Bangladesh

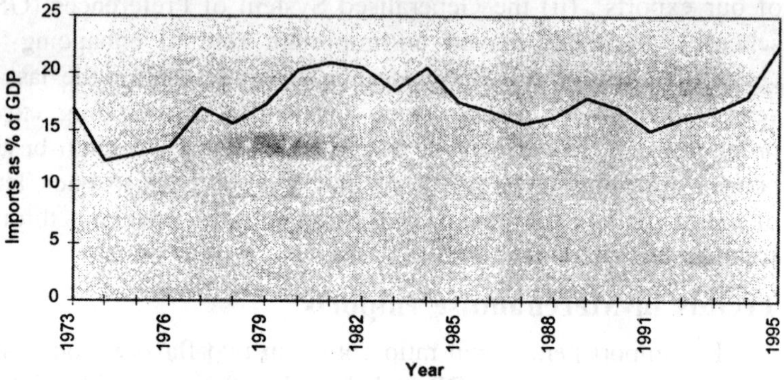

Source : Based on IMF (1997).

However, the ratio of imports to aggregate consumption is a more reliable indicator of a restrictive trade policy than the ratio of imports to GDP since in most developing countries, it is imports of consumption goods that are the most stringently restricted (Andriamananjara and Nash, 1997).

Figure 4 (a and b) presents the composition of import payments of Bangladesh during the periods 1983-86 and 1991-94.

Figure 4(a) : Import composition 1983-86 (%)

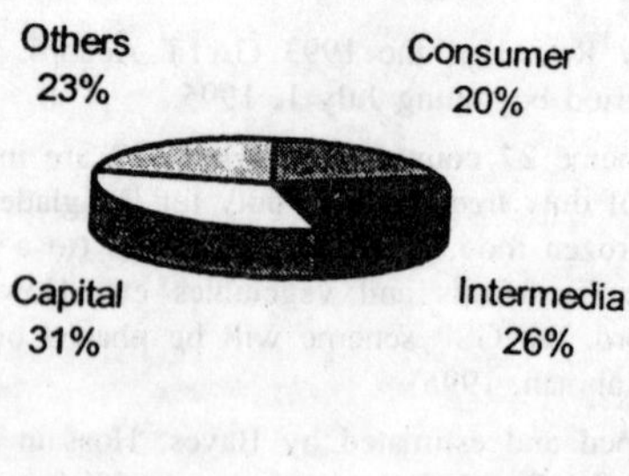

Figure 4(b) : Import composition 1991-94 (%)

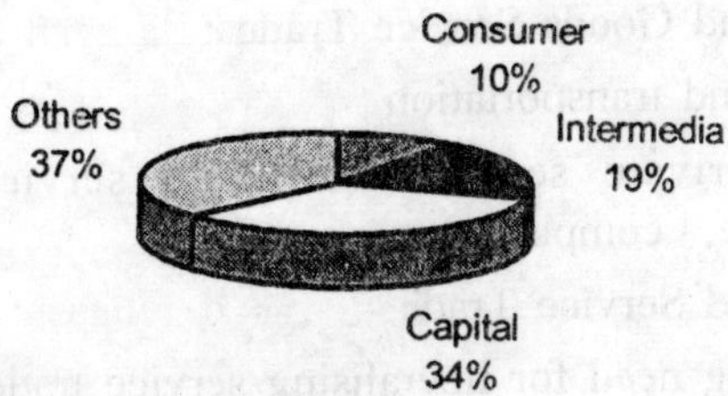

Source : Based on World Bank (1995).

Despite Bangladesh's impressive rate of import liberalisation, there has been no corresponding surge in imports. In the 1990s, real import growth had risen at 5.7 per cent per annum, compared to 1.9 per cent in the previous 5 years. This suggests that a more open economy has indeed had some effect on growth in imports but this is still not sufficient to raise Bangladesh's import/ GDP ratio which hovers around 15/16 per cent. Our weak investment performance has thus kept imports below its expected level and has led to import repression, inspite of the growing liberalisation of the economy. Econometric estimates of an aggregate import-demand function suggest that imports are generally insensitive to relative price changes and that import demand is largely explained by GDP or other indicators relating to general level of economic activity (Dutta and Ahmed, 1997). This reflects the essential and non-competitive nature of Bangladesh's imports.

Trade in Services

The taxonomy of service trade include (Grubel, 1989) :

(i) Factor Service Trade :

- Returns from financial assets, direct investment

- Fees and royalties
- Labour

(ii) People and Goods Service Trade :

- Travel and transportation
- Other private services (business services, banking, insurance, computers)

(iii) Embodied Service Trade

The increasing need for liberalising service trade has resulted in the establishment of a General Agreement on Trade in Services (GATS) in the Uruguay Round held in December 1993. The policy instruments affecting market access for service trade include : (i) quantitative restrictions and similar nonprice-based measures, (ii) charges, taxes and related price-based policies, (iii) administrative practices, technical standards and regulatory regimes and (iv) other government policies including immigration policies affecting market access, production and trade (Hoekman and Sauve, 1995).

In the context of the Bangladesh economy, export of temporary labour to overseas generates significant balance of payments income. Export of contract workers from Bangladesh, particularly to the countries of the Middle-East, has assumed considerable importance during the past two decades. This is because Middle-East migration as a major outlet of overseas employment for Bangladeshi workers emerged after the oil shock of 1973. This oil shock basically promoted employment and remittances, or represented a "conjunction of high oil prices leading to new employment opportunities". The Gulf crisis of 1990-91 precipitated by the invasion of Kuwait by Iraq on August 2, 1990 was a major shock experienced by Asian labour-exporting countries including Bangladesh and migrant workers[8]. Total loss of remittances due to the Gulf crisis was to the tune of US $ 106.5 million (Jahan 1992). Figure 5 shows an increasing trend

8. Kuwait was liberated on February 27, 1991 in a war with Iraq by the Western powers led by USA in collaboration with Arab countries, led by Saudi Arabia.

of Bangladeshi workers' remittances under the Wage Earners' Scheme as per cent of GNP over the period from 1975-76 to 1994-95.

Trends in Real Effective Exchange Rate

One remarkable aspect of Bangladesh's experience of trade liberalisation relates to the movements in the real effective exchange rate (REER)[9]. There is a slowly declining trend in REER for exports (Figure 6) indicating a small depreciation of the domestic currency which is likely to enhance in a limited way the competitiveness of our exports. This is consistent with the fact that the Bangladesh currency (taka) was depreciated about 20 per cent between 1984/85 and 1987/88 (UNCTAD, 1989). Between 1991 and 1994 there was a net depreciation of the REER of about 12 per cent which, with lower inflation, improved external competitiveness (Shand and Ali, 1997). However, even with trade liberalisation, the REER for imports is still considerably higher than that for exports (by about 25-30 per cent), indicating the anti-export bias of the trade regime. Compared to Bangladesh, some of the South Asian countries have experienced a much larger depreciation of the real exchange rate of their currencies[10]. The explanation for the above behaviour of real effective exchange rate seems to lie in a sluggish growth of import demand resulting from low levels of investment and economic activity, along with a relatively buoyant export performance (Mahmud, 1995).

---

9. The REER has been calculated using Bahmani-Oskooee (1995) method. In constructing REER, we have selected nine major export trading partners of Bangladesh, which include USA, UK, Canada, Japan, France, Germany, Belgium, Italy and the Netherlands. REERs are constructed in a manner that an upward movement reflects a real appreciation and a downward movement, a depreciation of domestic currency.

10. According to one estimate, for example, the extent of real devaluation (as measured by the real effective rate for export) between 1985 and 1993 was 40 per cent in Pakistan, 53 per cent in India compared to 18 per cent in Bangladesh (Statistical Appendix in Asian Development Bank (1995).

Figure 5 : Worker' Remittances in Bangladesh

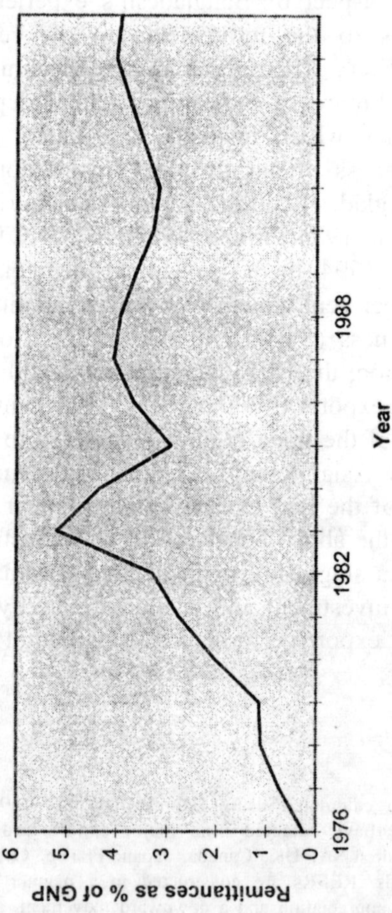

Source : Based on Bangladesh Bank (1996).

Figure 6 : Trends in Real Effective Exchange Rate for Exports

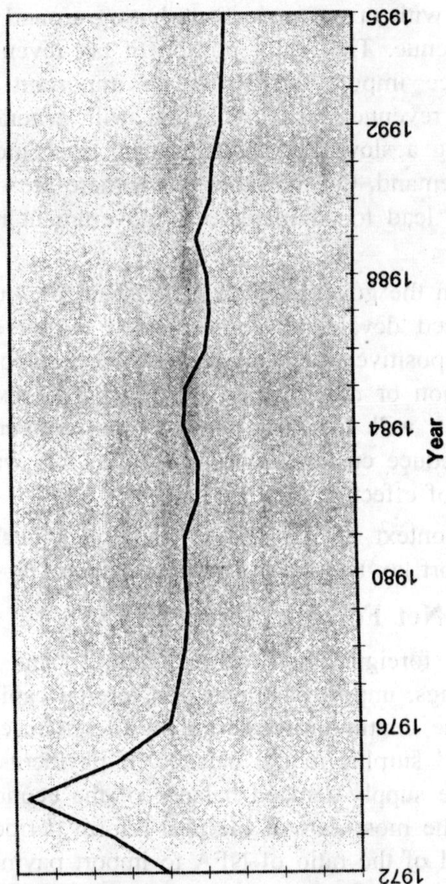

Source : Based on IMF (1996, 1997) using Bahmani-Oskooee (1995) method.

Trends in Government Revenue

In Bangladesh government revenue comes from tax and non-tax sources, with tax revenue contributing around 80 per cent of the total revenue. The major portion of tax revenue comes from import. Since import tariffs are an important component of government revenue, tariff reduction will generate less import tax, assuming a slow reaction and some price inelastic response by import demand. On the other hand, there are different factors which could lead to an increase of government revenue (World Bank, 1979) :

(a) When the government is a net seller of foreign exchange, a compensated devaluation implemented during a trade reform will have a positive effect on the revenue base of import taxes. (b) Elimination or reduction of the number of exemptions from import duties will increase revenues. (c) Lowering very high tariffs can reduce customs evasion, and in this way increase the fiscal share of effective imports.

In the context of Bangladesh we find a declining trend of ratio of import tax to total tax revenue (figure 7).

Trends in Net Foreign Assets (NFA)

The net foreign assets of the central bank are related to export earnings, import payments and foreign capital inflows and outflows. The continuing build-up of foreign reserves represents a "structural" surplus in the balance of payments as well as in the aggregate supply-demand balance of the economy (Mahmud, 1995). For the most part of the post-reform period we notice an upward trend of the ratio of NFA to import payments (figure 8). The level of our foreign exchange reserves in 1995 reached 102.39 billion taka, equivalent to about 5 months' worth of import payments. The corresponding average figure for both low-income and middle-income countries is 3.4 months of import coverage in 1990 (as reported in the World Development Review of the World Bank). This high level of reserves results from the prevailing investment stagnation in the economy which, in turn,

Figure 7 : Import Tax in Bangladesh

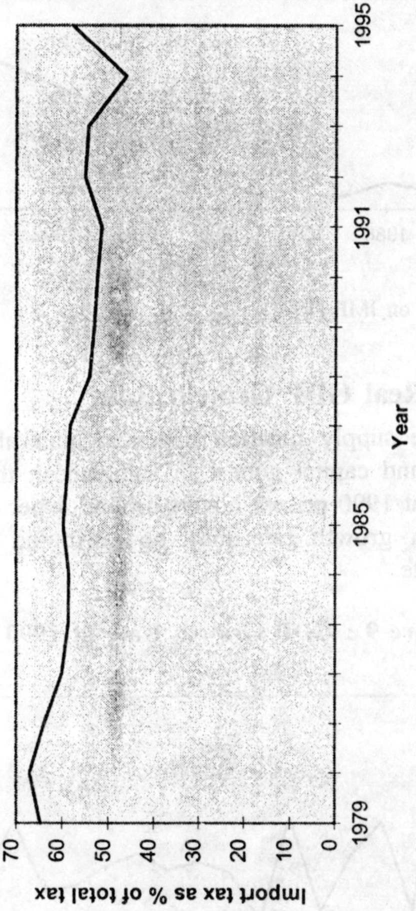

Source : Based on Bangladesh Bank (1996).

has led to import repression, in spite of the growing import liberalisation policies.

Figure 8 : Net Foreign Assets (NFA) of the Central Bank

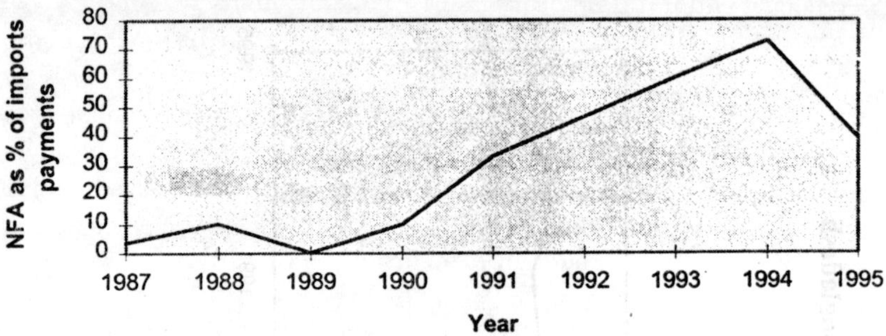

Source : Based on IMF (1997).

Trends in Real GDP Growth Rate

Aggregate supply function depends, inter alia, on imported intermediate and capital goods. In Bangladesh the average GDP growth rate (at 1990 prices) hovers around 4 per cent per annum. This sluggish growth rate may be attributed mainly to low investment rate.

Figure 9 : GDP Growth Rate at 1990 Prices

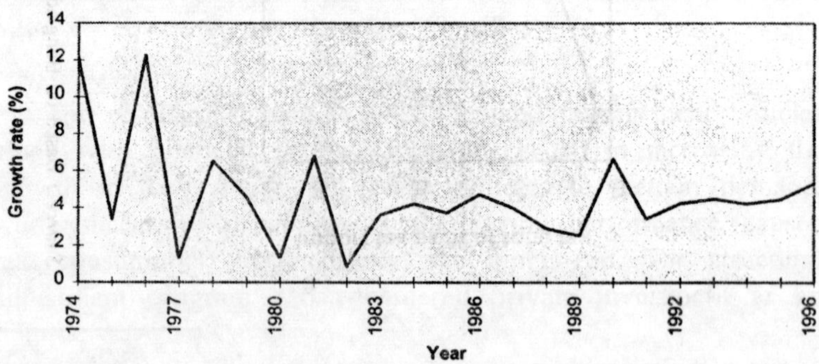

Source : Based on IMF (1997).

IV. Conclusions and Policy Implications

Bangladesh was a strongly inward-looking economy until 1986 when trade liberalisation policies have been adopted as part of structural adjustment programme. However, Bangladesh followed a gradualistic approach in her liberalisation programme. There has been a robust growth in nontraditional exports (readymade garments). Her service trade has expanded substantially as is reflected in sharply increasing trend of workers' remittances. Despite Bangladesh's impressive rate of import liberalisation, import growth has lagged behind because of weak investment performance, a gradual depreciation in the value of the Bangladesh currency, and a premium on the secondary exchange market till 1991. Our weak investment performance has kept imports below its expected level and thus has led to import repression. So a robust level of investment, at around 20 per cent of GDP would have improved import growth and thereby GDP growth rate.

Compared to many other developing countries, Bangladesh has still higher tariff rate which needs to be lowered. Progress is needed in establishing more uniform rates of protection, by compressing the number of tariff rates to reduce dispersion and simplify the trade regime. Quantitative restrictions, especially on textiles, are preventing the development of backward linkages with the readymade garments sector. If these restrictions are removed, protection due to non-tariff barriers will virtually disappear in Bangladesh. This would spur the development of a textile sector that could potentially supply the needs of the readymade garments industry.

Two important provisions under the GATT Uruguay Round Accord with major implications for Bangladesh exports are : (i) the gradual phasing out of the MFA and (ii) the phasing out of GSP. It remains to be seen what the full implications of the GATT conclusion of the Uruguay Round in December 1993. A more liberal trade policy regime over the next decade is likely to present opportunities for greater market access in Europe and North America, but at the same time competition may be intensified as more textile producers seek to take the advantage of the market opportunities. However, in order to face the challenges and avail herself of the opportunities over the next few years, Bangladesh will need to design her strategies and policies with due care and attention to appropriate phasing and sequencing.

REFERENCES

Agarwala, R. (1983), "Price Distortions and Growth in Developing Countries", *World Bank Staff Working Paper # 575*. Washington, D.C. : The World Bank.

Ahammad, Helal (1995), *Foreign Exchange and Trade Policy Issues in a Developing Country* : The Case of Bangladesh. Aldershot : Avebury.

Andriamananjara, Shuby and Nash, John (1997), "Have Trade Policy Reforms Led to Greater Openness in Developing Countries?", *Policy Research Working Paper 1730*. Washington, D.C. : The World Bank.

Bahmani-Oskooee, M. (1995), "Real and Nominal Effective Exchange Rates for 22 LDCs : 1971 : 1 — 1990 : 4", *Applied Economics*, 27(7), 591-604.

Balassa, Bela, and Associates (1971), *The Structure of Protection in Developing Countries*, Baltimore, Md. : Johns Hopkins University Press.

Bangladesh Bank (1996), *Economic Trends*, XXII(10).

Bayes, Abdul, Hossain, M. Ismail and Rahman, Mustafizur (1995), "Trends in the External Sector : Trade and Aid" in Rehman Sobhan (ed.), *Experiences with Economic Reform : A Review of Bangladesh's Development 1995*. Dhaka : Centre for Policy Dialogue and University Press Limited.

Bhuyan, A.R. and Rashid, M.A. (1993), *Trade Regimes and Industrial Growth : A Case Study of Bangladesh*, Dhaka : Bureau of Economic Research, University of Dhaka.

Bhagwati, J.N. (1978), *Foreign Trade Regimes and Economic Development : Anatomy and Consequences of Exchange Control Regimes*. Cambridge, M.A. : Ballinger for the National Bureau of Economic Research.

Corden, W.M. (1997), *Trade Policy and Economic Welfare* (Second Edition), Oxford : Clarendon Press.

Dean, Judith M., Desai, Seema and Riedel, James (1994), "Trade Policy Reform in Developing Countries : A Review of the Evidence", *World Bank Discussion Papers No. 267*, Washington, D.C. : The World Bank.

Dornbusch, R. (1992), "The Case for Trade Liberalisation in Developing Countries", *Journal of Economic Perspectives*, 6 (1992) : 69-86.

Dutta, Dilip and Ahmed, Nasiruddin (1997), "An Aggregate Import Demand Function for Bangladesh : A Cointegration Approach", Working Paper # 97-03, Department of Economics, The University of Sydney.

Edwards, Sebastian (1993), "Openness, Trade Liberalization and Growth in Developing Countries", *Journal of Economic Literature*, XXXI (3) : 1358-93.

Gruebel, Herbert G. (1989), *Liberalisation of Trade in Services : A Taxonomy and Discussion of Issues*, Singapore : Institute of Southeast Asian Studies.

Hoekman, Bernard and Sauve, Pierre (1994), "Liberalising Trade in Services", *World Bank Discussion Papers No. 243*. Washington, D. C. : The World Bank.

International Monetary Fund (1997), *International Financial Statistics on CD-ROM*.

International Monetary Fund (1996), *Direction of Trade Statistics Yearbook 1996*.

Jahan, Selim (1993), "Impact of the Gulf Crisis on the Bangladesh economy", in Piyasiri Wickramasekara (ed.), *The Gulf Crisis and South Asia : Studies on the Economic Impact*, New Delhi : Asian Regional Team for Employment Promotion (ARTEP).

Joshi, Vijay and Little, I.M. D. (1996), *India's Economic Reforms 1991-2001*, Delhi : Oxford University Press.

Khan, Farida C. (1994), "Import Liberalization in a Developing Country with Import Intensive Industry : The Case of Bangladesh", *International Economic Journal*, 8(1), Spring 1994.

Krueger, Anne O. (1978), *Foreign Trade Regimes and Economic Development : Liberalization Attempts and Consequences*, Cambridge, M.A. : Ballinger for the National Bureau of Economic Research.

Krueger, Anne O. (1997), "Trade Policy and Economic Development : How We Learn", *The American Economic Review*, 87(1) : 1-22.

Little, I.M.D., Cooper, Richard N., Corden, W.M. and Rajapatirana, S. (1993), *Boom, Crisis and Adjustment : The Macro-economic Experience of Developing Countries*, Oxford : Oxford University Press for the World Bank.

Mahmood, Raisal Awal, Rahman, Sultan Hafeez and Hasan, Mohammad Nazmul (1991), "Slow Response of Trade and Industry to Import Policy Changes", *Research Report No. 125*, Dhaka : Bangladesh Institute of Development Studies.

Mahmud, W. *et al.* (1991), *Report of the Task Forces on Bangladesh Development Strategies for the 1990's* (Vol. one : Macro-economic Policies), Dhaka : University Press Limited.

Michaely, M., Papageorgiou, D. and Choksi, A. M. (eds.) (1991), *Liberalising Foreign Trade : Lessons of Experience in the Developing World*, Oxford : Basil Blackwell.

Rahman, Sultan Hafeez (1992), "Structural Adjustment and Macroeconomic Performance in Bangladesh in the 1980s", *The Bangladesh Development Studies*, XX (2&3) : 89-125.

Rahman, Sultan Hafeez (1994), "Trade and Industrialisation in Bangladesh : An Assessment", in G. K. Helleiner (ed.), *Trade Policy and Industrialisation in Turbulent Times*, London and New York : Routledge : 259-91.

Rhee, Yung Whee (1990), "The Catalyst Model of Development : Lessons from Bangladesh's Success with Garment Exports", *World Development*, 18 (2) : 333-46.

Roy, D. (1993), "Impact of Incentives on Export Performance of Bangladesh : A Preliminary Assessment, *The Bangladesh Development Studies*, XXI (2) : 25-44.

Sattar, Zaidi (1997), "Non-traditional Exports and Economic Performance : Review and Empirical Evidence" in M.G. Quibria (ed.), *The Bangladesh Economy in Transition*. Delhi : Oxford University Press, 143-79.

Shand, R. and Alauddin, M. (1997), *Economic Profiles in South Asia* : Bangladesh, Canberra : Australian National University.

Spinanger, Dean (1987), "Will the Multi-fibre Arrangement Keep Bangladesh Humble?", *The World Economy*, 10(1) : 75-84.

Thomas, Vinod, Nash, John and Associates (1991), *Best Practices in Trade Policy Reform*, Oxford : Oxford University Press for the World Bank.

UNCTAD (1989), *Trade and Development Report 1989*, Geneva : UNCTAD.

The World Bank (1987), *World Development Report, 1987*.

The World Bank (1992), *Bangladesh : Selected Issues in External Competitiveness and Economic Efficiency* (Report # 10265-BD).

The World Bank (1995), *Bangladesh : Recent Economic Developments and Priority Reform Agenda for Rapid Growth* (Report # 13875-BD).

The World Bank (1996), Bangladesh : *Trade Policy Reform for Improving the Incentive Regime* (Report # 15900-BD).

11

Economic Reforms and Emerging Financial Scenarios in India

B.B. BHATTACHARYA

Introduction

Economic reform in India was initiated in 1991. It had two objectives : stabilisation and structural adjustment. Stabilisation was necessary to correct macro economic imbalances, such as high inflation, unsustainable fiscal deficit and current account deficit, acute foreign exchange shortage and the balance of payments problem. A structural adjustment programme was initiated with the twin objectives of preventing recurring macro-economic imbalances on the one hand, and acceleration of long-run growth of income and standard of living on the other. Both stabilisation and structural adjustment programmes emphasized liberalisation and globalisation as principal instruments of achieving these goals (Government of India, 1993).

The process of liberalisation of the Indian economy, in some respects, had begun from the mid-eighties, or even before. For instance, import quotas were replaced by tariffs from the early-eighties, personal income tax rates were reduced from the late seventies and licensing for private investment was partially deregulated from the mid seventies. But these measures were essentially rationalisation of controls and regulations. In contrast, the current economic reform is a step towards a free market economy.

In the six years of economic reform, the government has deregulated the economy substantially. The pace of reform has been, however, uneven, both sector-wise and functionally. The external sector has been deregulated far more than the domestic sector. This may be partly due to the necessity of augmenting the foreign exchange stock urgently, which at the time of initiating the reform, was as low as 15 days' worth of imports (Government of India, Economic Survey, 1991-92). Some segments of the domestic sector benefitted from the reform quite substantially, in particular, the private corporate sector. In contrast, the public sector and the financial sector have yet to undergo critical minimum reform.

This paper is concerned with the financial reform in India. Financial reform is a concomitant part of the overall structural reform. Structural reforms in general, and especially in areas such as industry and foreign trade, can succeed only if resources are redeployed towards more efficient producers which are encouraged by the reforms in the real sectors. Reforms in the real and financial sectors, therefore, should complement each other (World Bank, 1991). Any critical evaluation of the reform in the financial sector thus requires an assessment of the pace and success of overall economic reform.

We begin by first evaluating the overall economic reform and performance of the economy during the reform period. Following this, we discuss the rationale of financial reform. The paper also examines critically some constraints in financial reform in India in terms of the global perspective. In particular, we shall discuss the impact of foreign capital inflows. Finally, we reflect on the political economy implications of financial reform.

Overall Reform : A Bird's Eye View

Economic reform in India, as in most developing countries, began with financial support from the International Monetary Fund (IMF) and the World Bank. The broad framework of the reform is, therefore, the IMF-World Bank sponsored Structural

Adjustment Programme (SAP). The design and sequencing of the reform, however, needed some adjustments to suit the Indian economic conditions, including the political economy (Government of India, 1993).

It is well known that the SAP is based on neo-classical growth philosophy (World Bank, 1991). It assumes that public expenditure 'crowds out' private expenditure and that the productivity of private investment is greater than public investment. Competition, it is assumed, promotes efficiency and, thereby, improves productivity of both labour and capital. The SAP stresses both free market and globalisation. Foreign capital not only augments the rate of investment, but also improves technology and management, which are essential to modernise domestic industry (Bhagwati and Srinivasan, 1993).

It is obvious that the implementation of the SAP required a drastic change in the earlier economic regime in India, which highlighted the role of the state and self reliance. In the beginning, the government followed the SAP quite faithfully. But as reforms proceeded, the foreign exchange constraints eased — partly because of the reforms and partly because of some favourable exogenous factors — and consequently, the zeal of the government to implement the remaining parts of the SAP slackened. To a large extent, it was also due to the domestic political opposition to reform.

In a nutshell, the government has so far deregulated private investment in all but a few sensitive sectors (defence, environment and natural resources), withdrawn restrictions on monopoly and big business houses, restricted the scope of new public enterprises only in the core sectors, opened the scope of private investment in many sectors hitherto reserved for the public sector (such as power, telecommunication, and other infrastructures), divested shares of some public enterprises, lowered personal tax rates and abolished tax on dividend income, reduced excise and import duties, delicensed imports of most capital and intermediate goods, and liberalised the inflow of foreign capital, not only in terms of direct investment (FDI) but also portfolio investment.

The government has also initiated some institutional reforms. The rupee is now fully convertible in the current account and partially convertible in the capital account. The government has also announced its intention to consider full convertibility in the next couple of years. The Foreign Exchange Regulation Act (FERA) will now be replaced by the Foreign Exchange Management Act (FEMA). Recently, the government has granted autonomy to select profit making public enterprises, under a scheme known as 'the nine gems' or 'Navratnas.' The Constitution of India has been amended (73rd and 74th) to facilitate decentralisation of both economic and political decisions at the village level.

However, the government has yet to initiate many vital reform measures. For instance, it has not privatised any public enterprise, including those which grossly violated the criteria of either public goods or 'core' industry concept. Many of them are loss making enterprises. Nor has the government closed any 'sick' or unviable public enterprises. The government has referred many of them to the Board of Industrial and Financial Restructuring (BIFR), but is yet to take any concrete step towards either privatisation or closure. The basic problem in many of these enterprises is employment. Pending either privatisation or closure, the government could have at least taken steps to improve efficiency and productivity of labour and management. But even in this respect, the actions initiated are grossly inadequate. The divestment programme is also lopsided. Instead of selling shares of unwarranted enterprises, the government has sold shares in profit making, including natural monopolies core enterprises.

Infrastructure has been another neglected area of reform. The burden of fiscal adjustment has fallen quite heavily on investment in infrastructure. Although infrastructure is now open to the private sector — both domestic and foreign — investment in this sector during the reform period is abysmally poor. The anarchic pricing and subsidy policies, together with institutional failure, discourage private investment in infrastructure.

Employment and wage policy in the public sector is another area where reform has failed to make any dent. The exit policy is debated at length, but as of now cannot be implemented in either the public or private sector. Despite deregulation, bureaucratic controls continue to thwart economic activities, particularly at state and local levels. As a result, corruption and inefficiency continue unabated and have probably increased because of the lack of transparency in financial transactions.

Financial Reform : Agenda and Progress

Financial reform is a concomitant part of overall economic reform. When the reforms began, the financial system in India was not only highly regulated, satisfying most of the conditions of 'financial repression,' but also compartmentalised. As a result, there was disequilibrium between the demand and supply of credit, not only at the aggregate level but also in each segment of the financial system. The organised financial system in India is dominated by state owned financial institutions. Together they mobilise nearly 80 per cent of household financial savings. The picture has not changed very much, even six years after the reform.

In the early phase after nationalisation, the state owned financial institutions promoted overall financial development in various ways. Firstly, they not only mobilised but also promoted household financial savings by extending financial services in all sectors of the economy. Between 1969 (when major commercial banks were nationalised) and 1990, household saving as a ratio to GDP doubled from 10 to 20 per cent. During the same period, the share of financial savings in household savings also went up from 20 to 44 per cent. Secondly, they increased the share of credit to agriculture and other priority sectors, from less than 10 per cent in the pre-nationalisation period to more than 20 per cent. Thirdly, they kept real interest rates low and thereby induced investment, especially in agriculture and small-scale industry.

But, along the way various maladies of financial repression began to assert. First, as the volume of transactions increased, the quality of financial services deteriorated. The absence of any effective competition hastened the deterioration. Secondly, the government started using these institutions as an easy source of financing burgeoning fiscal deficit. With this, the quality of fiscal management began to erode, which in turn had an adverse impact on financial management. Thirdly, a great deal of directed credit was misused. The periodic 'loan mela' and loan waiving by the government eroded the quality of credit appraisal. The share of non-performing assets in total assets of financial institutions increased, and by the late 1980s, the balance sheets of not only co-operative and regional rural banks became negative, many commercial and development banks also suffered the same malady. Proliferation of bank branches and staff increased overhead and compounded the problem further. Finally, the differential interest rates structure increased the cost of credit to the organised sector and the gap between interest rates in the Indian and global markets widened.

Since 1991, the Government of India has appointed a number of Committees and Working Groups to study the behaviour of the Indian financial system and recommend reform measures. The most important of these is the Narasimham Committee (Reserve Bank of India, 1991), which recommended drastic changes in the behaviour of both commercial and development banks. The major recommendations of the Committee were as follows : (a) drastic reductions in both the statutory liquidity ratio (SLR) and the cash reserve ratio (CRR), (b) phased deregulation of administered interest rates, (c) phasing out the directed credit, (d) augmentation of the capital base through public issue of shares and (e) prudential classification of assets and liabilities The Committee also recommended consolidation of rural branches, closure of unviable branches, opening up of banking to the private sector and better monitoring of the financial system through new regulatory agencies. The Malhotra Committee (Government of India, 1993) on insurance sector reform also suggested a wide range of changes, including privatisation and foreign competition.

During the last six years, the government has so far implemented only a few of the major recommendations. Banks are now given greater autonomy to determine the structure of interest rates (although even by March 1997, all interest rates are not yet deregulated). The SLR is now reduced to 25 per cent and the CRR brought down to 10 per cent, still well above the international level. The new asset classification has been introduced, to take effect from 1992-93. Major commercial banks have attained 8 per cent capital adequacy norm — the profit making ones through public issues of share and the loss making ones through government budgetary support. Private banks have begun operations and foreign banks have extended business. Although the degree of competition has increased, it has yet to make any significant impact on the quality and efficiency in financial services.

The government has also not done anything substantial to improve the functioning of cooperative and regional rural banks, most of which are on the verge of bankruptcy. Commercial banks are now permitted to close unviable branches only in urban and metropolitan centres, but not in rural and semi-urban areas. Directed credit continues, although its effective share has declined. There has been no privatisation. Management of state owned financial institutions, which deteriorated over time, has yet to gain full autonomy. Professional management and expertise are rare and confined to only a small segment of the financial system. The work culture continues to be poor. The morals of both senior and junior management officials are badly affected by periodic unearthing of gigantic financial scams. In short, the Indian financial system has yet to attain the level of efficiency required to stand up to international competition and either, because of this, or for other reasons stated above, the government has not yet completely deregulated the financial system.

Growth Performance During the Nineties

The SAP produces desirable results when the market is competitive. The successful implementation of SAP also requires a bureaucracy committed to productivity, efficiency and discipline. However, even if SAP is implemented faithfully, growth and investment rates may initially fall, before accelerating to their potentials. The potentials would vary depending on initial conditions : saving and investment rates, the literacy ratio, development of human capital and skill and other socio-economic and demographic parameters. For these reasons, it was observed that SAP was most successful in East Asia and least successful in Sub-Saharan Africa (World Bank, 1991).

The pre-conditions for SAP in India were neither as bad as in Africa, nor as good as in East Asia. The overall performance of the Indian economy since the reform in 1991 has been, therefore, not as impressive as in East Asia, nor as poor as in Sub-Saharan Africa. The average growth rate of real GDP during the reform period (fiscal 1991-92 through 1995-96) was 5.3 per cent, the same as in the 1980s. But since the growth rate first fell (before it recovered to a high level), the reform is considered beneficial by the government (Government of India, Economic Survey 1996-97). According to the latest official statistics (provisional and advance estimates), the average growth rate of real GDP during 1994-97 may be 6 or even 7 per cent per annum. However, it would be naive and premature to infer any real acceleration in the growth rate from these provisional and advance estimates. Besides, it may be difficult to sustain this in the long-run for two reasons. First, during the reform period there has been no exogenous shock, like a monsoon failure, which had adversely affected GDP growth rate in the past. And second, some key sectors, like agriculture and infrastructure, have probably been over stressed during the reform years. Sustaining the present tempo of growth would require massive investment in these sectors, which is probably not feasible under the present budgetary conditions. The strains are already visible in the current fiscal year.

Like the GDP growth rate, saving and investment rates initially fell, before recovering to their pre-reform levels. If we ignore 1991-92, the first year of reform, when output stagnated and saving and investment rates declined, the average (gross) saving and investment rates during the period 1992-97 turn out to be better than in 1985-90, by 3.3 and 2.2 percentage points respectively (Government of India, Economic Survev, 1996-97). The average growth rate of real GDP during the period 1992-97 at 6.5 per cent, is also higher than 1985-90 at 6.0 per cent. But the incremental capital-output ratio (ICOR), which measures the productivity of capital, turns out to be more or less the same at about 3.8, during both periods. The reform, therefore, has not made any perceptible improvement in the productivity of capital. Furthermore, since the public investment rate (as a ratio to GDP) declined and the private investment rate increased in the post reform period (1992-97), ICOR should have declined, by the basic assumption of SAP. Since it has not happened so far, it implies that the reform has yet to make any significant impact on growth and productivity, or the assumption of SAP needs rethinking, so far as India is concerned.

The supply-side growth thrust has been given a big boost in the Union Budget (1997-98). Tax rates have been slashed drastically in this budget and tax on corporate dividend income is abolished. India is now one of the least taxed nations in the world, with the highest marginal income tax rate brought down to only thirty per cent. The budget provides many additional incentives for private investment, particularly investment in infrastructure. The budget also provides a voluntary disclosure scheme, under which a tax payer can convert black income (unreported for tax purpose) of the past into legal income by paying only 30 per cent tax. This budget would, therefore, test the efficacy of the supply-side growth model in the Indian context and if this budget fails to accelerate industrial and overall growth performance, then it may have serious repercussions.

Stabilization : Success and Failure

The reform aimed at stabilisation mainly through fiscal adjustments. Following SAP, it was assumed that the fiscal deficit was the root cause of both inflation and the current account deficit (Government of India, 1993; Bhagwati and Srinivasan, 1993). In 1991-92, the Centre's gross fiscal deficit was drastically cut down to 5>9 per cent of GDP, from 8.3 per cent in the previous year. But thereafter instead of declining further, it has remained more or less at the same level (6.0 per cent on an average during 1992-97). Between 1990-91 and 1996-97, Central Government consumption expenditure, as a ratio to GDP, declined by only 0.4 percentage points, from 4.2 per cent to 3.8 per cent. In contrast, gross capital formation out of budgetary resources of the Centre declined much more sharply, from 6.5 per cent to 4.9 per cent. Deficits in state government budgets have virtually remained unchanged, in some states even increased. The aggregate public sector borrowing (PSB) has also not declined over the reform years. Presently, it is about 13 per cent of GDP, same as in 1990-91. Since the fiscal deficit (and in particular PSB) failed to decline secularly over the reform period, the government was under pressure to keep state owned financial institutions, who finance these deficits, under its control. Fiscal deficit, therefore, remains the main stumbling block in financial reform.

The average inflation rate during the reform period remained fairly high (about 10 per cent per annum), not merely because of the fiscal deficit and excess money supply, but also because of administered pricing of agricultural products and rupee depreciation. In fact, these factors contributed as much as the money supply to high inflation in India (Bhattacharya, 1995; and Bhattacharya and Kathuria, 1995). Fortunately, however, there was no major exogenous shock during the reform period, such as a bad monsoon or oil price hike, otherwise the inflation rate could have been much higher, as may be seen from some econometric simulation results (Bhattacharya, Barman and Nag, 1994).

On the positive side, the reform improved the current account balance and foreign exchange situation. The current account deficit declined significantly, from 3.2 per cent of GDP in 1990-91 to an average of 1.2 per cent during the next six years (1991-97). The trade balance also improved, but not as much as current balance. The exports/imports ratio improved secularly and by the mid-nineties, exports financed nearly 90 per cent of imports, against 50-60 per cent during the eighties.

It is difficult to assess at this stage how much of the improvement in trade balance is due to productivity change, as envisaged in the reform, and how much is due to the mere devaluation of the rupee. The overall depreciation of the rupee against major foreign currencies was well above 100 per cent by 1996-97. The depreciation of the rupee, together with various other reforms in external transactions, have made a remarkable change in the foreign exchange situation. When the reforms began in the mid-l991, India had a mere $ 2 billion worth of foreign exchange reserves, and it was expected that reform measures might push it to $ 10 billion by March 1996. The target was fulfilled even by March 1994 and currently India has about $ 26 billion worth of foreign exchange reserves.

Initially, foreign exchange was accumulated through external debt. But as the reforms gathered momentum, particularly current account convertibility in 1993, direct foreign investment (FDI) and portfolio capital flows began to predominate over other forms of capital inflows. The most buoyant as well as the most violent component is portfolio capital, which has accounted for as much as $ 13 billion out of $ 24 billion foreign exchange accumulation since 1991. Global flows of FDI and portfolio capital have increased phenomenally during the nineties and yet, India has improved its share in both of these after the reform. However, India's performance even in this respect is well below that of East Asian countries.

The phenomenal rise in foreign exchange reserves has necessitated a restraint on the monetisation of the fiscal deficit. In the pre-reform period, 'seigniorage' accounted for the bulk of monetary expansion. At the end of 1990-91, the Reserve Bank of India (RBI) net credit to the government was almost equal to the total reserve money (monetary base). Since then, reserve money has gone up by Rs. 1,120 billion (up to the end of 1996-97), of which the increase in RBI foreign exchange assets has accounted for as much as Rs. 870 billion and that in RBI net credit to the government, only Rs. 340 billion.

With an exogenous rise in foreign exchange reserves, the government tried to restrain the overall growth of money supply through a tight squeeze on domestic credit expansion, not only to the government but also to the private sector. As a result, the real interest rate increased and since 1995, it has hovered around 10 per cent or above. Since the fiscal deficit continued to remain high, a decrease in the monetisation of the deficit increased the burden of financing the gross fiscal deficit on commercial banks and other state owned financial institutions. In the earlier economic regime, this could have been done through an increase in Statutory Liquidity Ratio (SLR). But since the SAP necessitated a reduction in the SLR (brought down to 25 per cent in 1993, from 38 per cent in the pre-reform period) an increase in government borrowing from banks and financial institutions required an increase in interest rates on government securities, which in turn further increased the real interest rates structure. In 1996-97, the interest rates on government securities ranged between 14 and 19 per cent. It has led to two adverse consequences : firstly, the investment rate and industrial output growth rate have decelerated and secondly, it has increased the inflow of speculative capital from abroad.

The problems could have been partially mitigated if the fiscal deficit and foreign exchange reserves were managed through properly synchronized sterilization and open market operations. The effective implementation of these policies, however, require well developed markets for government securities and foreign exchange assets, both of which are presently missing in India. In the pre-reform period there were no markets for these. The government handled them through fiat. Since 1993 these markets are slowly developing and so far, none of these has attained maturity, let alone attained international norm of efficiency.

Portfolio Investment and the Capital Market

Apart from straining monetary management by the RBI, the inflow of foreign capital has changed the behaviour of the Indian financial system in other ways also. Before 1991, Indian mutual funds and development banks dominated the capital market and set the broad bands of prices of shares and debentures. These institutions not only dictated share prices but also greatly influenced both short and long-run interest rates through their money and capital market operations. Since these financial institutions were almost wholly owned by the Government of India, the government virtually dictated the financial and capital market behaviours.

Since then the situation has changed radically. The changes have occurred partly due to partial deregulation of the financial system, particularly interest rates, but largely due to the inflow of foreign capital. The foreign financial institutions who are now allowed to operate in the Indian financial system, including the stock market, have now become the major players by the sheer size of their funds. The cumulative net investment of foreign financial institutions (FIIs) in the Indian financial market is about $ 3000 billion. As against this, the size of market capitalization in India is only about $ 4000 billion (CMIE Report on Capital Market, 1997). By their sheer size of operations, amidst a low level of floating stocks in India, FIIs have now become 'price makers', pushing Indian financial institutions, including the giant The Unit Trust of India (UTI), to become 'price takers' (Bhattacharya 1997). An upsurge or downswing in portfolio investment now affects not only share prices, but also interest rates on a wide range of financial assets, the exchange rate and even the price of real estate. Since portfolio investment depends on financial conditions, not only in India but also abroad, the ripples in global finance are now felt in Indian markets.

The Indian compánies are now permitted to raise capital in abroad through the Global Depository Receipts (GDR). At present, the permission to issue GDR is given selectively, keeping in view, among other factors, company size and reputation. This in turn has made another structural change. The bigger, and well reputed, companies are permitted to raise capital through GDR. Since the cost of borrowing capital in the Euro-Dollar market is much cheaper than in India — the gap has further widened in recent years — the average borrowing costs of big firms have declined. This has given them a competitive edge over small firms, who rely only on the Indian capital market. Since the big firms' dependence on the Indian capital market has come down, the volume and composition of lending of Indian commercial and development banks have also changed.

With globalisation and even partial deregulation, share prices and interest rates in India have now become far more sensitive to expectations. It appears that the relative importance of fundamental factors has weakened and that of speculative factors has increased since 1991 (Bhattacharya, 1997). This could be partly due to the well known 'bubble effects' and partly due to the imperfection of the financial market in India. However, this is a global phenomenon and consequently, many experts have begun to caution about pre-mature financial integration (World Bank, 1997).

Financial Repression

Ever since Mckinnon (1973) and Shaw (1973) propounded the concept, financial repression has become a key issue in financial reform. Financial repression may take various forms, such as interest rate ceilings, high reserve requirements and directed credit. Both Mckinnon and Shaw argue that financial repression lowers growth and worsens income distribution. Financial liberalisation can, therefore, increase economic growth through higher investment and productivity. The World Bank (1989) also endorsed this view and provided some empirical evidences on this.

Many other studies, however, question such simplistic generalizations (see, Fry, 1995). It is also observed that the degree of financial repression was quite high in many East Asian countries throughout the seventies and eighties. One independent study conducted in the mid-1990s found that policy-related loans still accounted for up to half of all commercial banks' outstanding loans in South Korea, more than a decade after the banking industry was privatised (quoted from a special article on "Banking in Emerging Markets", *The Economist*, 1997).

Financial repression in India became quite extensive after bank nationalization in 1969. Real interest rates on deposits were often negative during the seventies. Even the average real interest rate on deposits during this decade was negative. And yet the saving and investment rate nearly doubled during this decade. In contrast, when the real interest rate increased during the eighties, the saving and investment rates stagnated.

Financial liberalisation also did not always produce desirable results in Africa and Latin America. In fact, many banks collapsed after liberalisation, often due to excessive speculative investment (The Economist, 1997). If real interest rates rise too high, speculative investment crowds out long term productive investment. In East Asia, therefore, the governments maintained a tight check on the financial system, even after deregulation. In a recent article, Soros (1997) strongly advocates a check on speculative financial transactions. He argues that the financial market, by nature, cannot attain stable equilibrium. The stock market in particular is inherently unstable. He questions the *laissez faire* ideologues who argue that the financial breakdown was caused by faulty regulations and not by unstable markets. Even Mckinnon, in a talk in New Delhi in 1994 cautioned against premature financial liberalization in India, particularly with respect to portfolio capital, credit card and foreign exchange.

Since 1991, financial repression in India has decreased. Reserve requirements have come down. Interest rates are deregulated and as a result, real interest rates have increased to very high levels. Directed credit to government has declined. (However, market induced credit to the government has increased.) These changes were introduced gradually over the last 6 years and consequently, their full impact on saving, investment and growth can be assessed only after some time. But the proper assessment of these changes cannot be made until the financial system is given full autonomy.

Emerging Financial Scenarios

Emerging financial scenarios in India would depend on the nature and pace of, not only financial reform, but also on reforms in the real sectors. Financial reform in India has so far concentrated on reducing the degree of financial repressions by deregulating interest rates, lowering reserve ratios etc. But the Indian financial system suffers from, not only policy induced financial repressions, but also from poor management and lack of accountability, transparency and effective regulatory mechanism. Most financial institutions are grossly over staffed with low skills. There are too many unviable branches. These are well documented in Narasimham Committee Report (RBI, 1991) and they continue to a great extent even now (Rangarajan, 1997a and 1997b). As a result, the operational cost of banking services in India is very high, currently about 4.5 per cent of working funds and the profitability ratio is very low, less than 0.5 per cent. Profitability has not changed significantly, even after the introduction of prudential norms of asset classification (Rangarajan, 1997b).

These ratios are very poor in comparison to figures in developed countries (World Bank, 1991 and 1997). In open competition, therefore, the Indian banks and other financial institutions, particularly insurance companies, including the Life Insurance Corporation (LIC), which enjoys a monopoly in life insurance business in India, would lose. Many of them would become bankrupt in a short period. The foreign financial institutions are also technologically superior and, because of their global connection, would be better able to exploit the global financial market to their advantages than the Indian institutions.

The first impact of liberalisation and globalisation would be, therefore, quite adverse on the Indian financial system. Financial liberalisation may also induce speculative investment, as observed in many Latin American countries in the early phase of liberalisation (World Bank, 1997; Fry, 1995; The Economist, 1997). The 'bubble effect' has already been witnessed in India during the bank scam period (1991-92). In the last two years several financial institutions, particularly non-banking financial companies, some of which are newly created, have collapsed, partly due to very high interest rates and partly due to speculative investments. Even foreign commercial banks operating in India have suffered losses during the bank scam.

Even without liberalisation and foreign competition, many Indian financial institutions, not only co-operative and regional rural banks but also big commercial banks, may collapse due to inefficiency and a high ratio of non-performing assets. Recently, a major Indian commercial bank, namely, the Indian Bank, was officially declared bankrupt. There is a fear that many more may follow in coming years.

What the Indian financial system needs, therefore, is not immediate liberalisation, globalisation and privatisation, but better management with greater accountability. Banks should be given autonomy to decide not only the interest rates structure and credit allocation, but also employment and the opening and closing of branches. The subsidy on agricultural and rural credit should be either eliminated or borne directly by the government. The Grameen Bank experience in Bangladesh has shown that there is no need to subsidise credit to unorganised economic activities or even the poor. All these would involve a strong political will, which at the moment appears to be lacking in India. A basic obstacle to this may be the excessive fiscal deficit. As long as the fiscal deficit remains high,the political will to grant autonomy to banks would be low. The so called social subsidy (most of it is perhaps misused) could be another political barrier. Even now, there is very little awareness about its futility. This capital deployed more efficiently can enhance not only overall economic growth, but also fiscal resources for welfare and redistribution. What the Indian financial system needs, therefore, is not mere economic liberalisation, but political decontrol.

Capital account convertibility can change the financial system dramatically. The Government of India is now actively considering this. The recently appointed Tarapore Committee (RBI, 1997) has recommended full convertibility of the rupee over the next 3 years. The Committee has, however, put some pre-conditions before capital account convertibility; some of which, such as a sustainable fiscal deficit at 3.5 per cent of GDP and at 3 per cent inflation rate, may be unattainable in the near future. But the government has already begun to relax capital movement, based on this Committee Report.

There are two pressure groups for capital account convertibility: foreign financial institutions, particularly the mutual funds and the Indians who are holding a substantial amount of deposits in foreign banks, unofficially estimated between $ 200 and $ 500 billion. Presently, there is a huge difference between the interest rates in India and those in developed countries. Full convertibility may, therefore, induce a great deal of capital inflows into India. Similarly, Indians who have smuggled capital abroad earlier and kept in Swiss Banks etc., earning almost a zero interest rate, would also benefit from capital account convertibility and Voluntary Disclosure Scheme.

It is well-known that immediately after capital account convertibility, capital inflows generally exceed outflows. This leads to foreign exchange accumulation, the appreciation of the exchange rate and deterioration in the balance of trade. Policy makers, however, ignore this problem as long as the surplus in the capital account more than compensates the deficit in the current account. But since most of the capital comes as portfolio investment rather than foreign direct investment, as observed in all emerging countries during the nineties (World Bank, 1997), it makes very little impact on growth and the productivity of labour and capital in receiving countries. By its own intrinsic behaviour, portfolio capital is volatile (World Bank, 1997) and consequently, after a while when economic conditions in the receiving countries deteriorates, or even slows down, outflows began to exceed inflows. An adverse current account balance then further adds to foreign exchange problems. The outflows can also exceed inflows, even when economic conditions in foreign markets improve vis-a-vis the domestic economy. With full convertibility, not only foreign capital moves out but domestic capital also flows abroad legally. Finally, it leads to the crush. This is the well-known story of the Mexican debacle, now repeated in some South-East Asian countries, particularly in Thailand. Capital account convertibility should be, therefore, one of the last steps in the design and sequence of economic reforms (Fischer, 1997).

Given this background, it would be unwise to usher capital account convertibility in India at this stage of reform. But despite the bitter experiences elsewhere, if capital account convertibility is introduced in any significant measure, especially with respect to domestic capital, then the Indian financial system may suffer.

Another significant change may occur from financial liberalisation. Hitherto, the Central Government impounded resources from state owned financial institutions through fiat and reallocated them as credits and grants to various states and public enterprises. With liberalisation, the Centre would loose this prerogative. If credit is deregulated, then more endowed and financially better managed states, such as Gujarat, Maharashtra, Punjab and Karnataka would attract more capital and poor and backward states would get very little. Whilst this may introduce more discipline in financial management, its immediate impact would be quite adverse on regional balance. Many sick and loss making public enterprises would also be deprived of credit and may die as a result. This could also pose problems for labour and the political system.

To conclude, the emerging financial scenarios in India appear to be quite fluid, partly because of the deficiencies inherited from the pre-reform period and partly because of the dangers from unbalanced financial liberalisation. The Indian financial system is not yet ready for full-scale globalisation. The successful implementation of structural reform in India necessitates a complete revamping of the financial system and most of it should be done under state ownership of financial institutions. The management of financial institutions should be made free from political control and be given greater autonomy in decision making, regarding not only interest rates but also staffing patterns, branch expansions as well as closures, and the allocation of credit. Financial institutions should be encouraged to compete among themselves. Finally, the regulatory mechanism should be strengthened to assess management responsibility. Short of all these, any pre-mature privatisation and globalisation could produce adverse results.

REFERENCES

Bhattacharya, B.B. (1991), *India's Economic Crisis : Debt Burden and Stabilisation*, B.R. Publishing Corporation, Delhi, 1991.

— (1995), "Stabilisation, Adjustment and Growth in India", Theme paper, 78th Annual Conference of the Indian Economic Association, Chandigarh, December 1995.

— (1997a), "Capital Market Volatility and Investment", *in Banking and Financial Sector Reforms in India*, ed. R. Kapila and U. Kapila, Academic Foundation, New Delhi, 1997

— (1997b), "Sustaining the Economic Reform in India : The Political Economy Constraints", in *Economic Liberalization in India : Implications for Indo-US Relations*, ed. K.J. Azam, Delta Publishing House, Delhi, 1997.

Bhattacharya, B.B., R.B. Barman, and A.K. Nag — (1994), *Stabilisation Policy options! A Macro-Econometric Analysis,* Development Research Group Study, Reserve Bank of India, 1994.

Bhattacharya, B.B. and S. Kathuria (1995), "Dynamics of Inflation in India", paper presented in 31st Annual Conference of the Indian Econometric Society, Pune, 1995.

Bhagwati, J. and T.N. Srinivasan (1993), *India's Economic Reforms*, Government of India, 1993.

The Economist (1997), "Banking in Emerging Markets", Special Article, April 12, 1997, *The Economist*, London, 1997.

Feldstein, Martin (1995), "Global Capital Flows", Invited Article, in *The Economist*, June 24, 1995, London.

Fischer, S. (1997), "Financial System Soundness", *Finance and Development*, March, 1997.

Government of India (1993), *Economic Reforms : Two Years After and the Task Ahead! Discussion Paper*, Government of India, 1993.

Mckinnon, R. (1973), *Money and Capital in Economic Development*, Brookings Institution, Washington D.C., 1993.

— (1988), "Financial Liberalisation in Retrospect : Interest Rate Policies in LDCs", in *The State of Development Economics*, ed. Gustav Ranis and T.P. Schultz, Oxford; Basil Blackwell, 1988.

Rangarajan, C. (1997 a), "Banking Sector Reforms : Rationale and Relevance", Fourth STCOM Silver Jubilee Lecture, 1996, reproduced in *50 Years of Central Banking : Governors Speak*, RBI, 1997.

— (1997 b), "The Financial Sector Reforms : The Indian Experience", *RBI Bulletin*, July 1997.

RBI (1991), *Report of the Committee on Financial System* (Narasimham Committee), RBI, 1991.

RBI (1997), *Report of the Committee on Capital Account convertibility* (Tarapore Committee), RBI, 1997.

Shaw, Edward (1973), *Financial Deepening in Economic Development*, Oxford University Press, New York, 1973.

Soros, George (1997), "The Capitalist Threat", *The Atlantic Monthly*, February, 1997.

World Bank (1989), *The World Development Report*. 1989.

— (1991), *The World Development Report*, 1991.

— (1997), *Private Capital Flows to Developing Countries : The Road to Financial Integration*, A World Bank Policy Research Report, World Bank, 1997.

12

"We are the Slowest Reformers" : Disinvestment of India's State-Owned Enterprises

PETER MAYER

"Dramatic and sudden reform and mass changes creates dislocation and political stresses that cannot be sustainable, and can lead to disasters like Mexico or bigger disasters like Russia. But India does not need that lesson — we are the slowest reformers. So the lesson for India is different. At the early stages you have to worry about the sectors of the population that get hurt, because there is a two-three years adjustment process. You can't have half-measures' Madhav Dhar, M.D. Morgan Stanley Asset Management Inc. (anon, 1996a).

The Bos-Wash Consensus[1]

"Once upon a time", John Williamson tells us, "when the movement toward policy reform in Latin America was first taking off, I made a list of the policy initiatives that were being urged on Latin America by the powers-that-be in Washington. The 'Washington consensus' offers a description of what is agreed about the set of measures that are typically called for in the first stage of policy reform..." (Williamson, 1994 p. 17). The eighth of these contemporary Ten Commandments is this : "State enterprises should be privatized" (Williamson, 1994 p. 27).

1. The research reported in this paper was supported by Study Leave grants from the University of Adelaide.

Since those days when Williamson brought down from the mountain the tablets upon which were inscribed the will and words of the IRBD, a new band of muscular evangelists has formed, intent on spreading the true faith among the heathens. This new church, like others before it, has been assiduous in writing tracts which set out the Good News that it may be preached, if not on every street corner, at least in conferences around the globe. The new Bible Society — successor to that older institution which Carlyle once called "a machine for converting the Heathen" — is of course the World Bank itself.

Over the course of the past decade this informal Society for the Propagation of the Gospel has produced a didactic literature which I am tempted to say has no parallel in English prose since moral stories of an improving sort ceased to be written for children at some point early in the 20th century. Unlike the cautionary tales of an earlier time, these new primers are not being written for children of an impressionable age but rather are aimed at finance ministers and professional economists. These contemporary 'Songs of Experience' are frequently styled as "Lessons", as the following titles show : *The Reform of State-Owned Enterprises : Lessons from World Bank Lending* (Shirley, 1989); *Privatization : The Lessons of Experience* (Kikeri, *et al.*, 1992); *Public Enterprise Reform : Lessons from the Past and Issues for the Future* (Galal, 1991); *Public Enterprise Reform : The Lessons of Experience* (Shirley and Nellis, 1991).[2]

In this paper I want to consider a few specific aspects of this extensive literature and — if I may extend the metaphor one step further — look in somewhat greater detail at the emerging orthodoxy concerning the privatisation of State-Owned Enterprises (SOEs), a catechism which in view of what appear to be its East Coast origins, I propose to christen the 'Bos-Wash Consensus'.

2. See also : (Kikeri, *et al.*, 1994; Leeds, 1991; Mathieu, 1996).

Later in the paper I will consider India's experience of 'disinvestment' of its public sector enterprises (PSUs), seeking to understand why, on the whole, the Indian experience shows such weak correspondence with the Bos-Wash Consensus.

The centrality of crisis

If there is a single proposition which commands near universal agreement, it is that most instances of economic reform, and of the privatisation of SOEs in particular, have their origins in episodes of economic crisis. No crisis, no reform. John Williamson and Stephan Haggard include 'the crisis hypothesis' in their assessment of 12 factors which affect the success of economic reforms as a whole.

> It has often been suggested that policy reforms emerge in response to crisis. Crises have the effect of shocking countries out of traditional policy patterns, disorganizing the interest groups that typically veto policy reform, and generating pressure for politicians to change policies that can be seen to have failed (Williamson and Haggard, 1994, pp. 562-4).

Reviewing 13 case studies of reform, they conclude that many periods of reform were preceded by crisis, some significant instances of liberalisation — including Australia's post 1983 — were not consequential on a crisis. They also note while crisis may initiate reform, the experience of Brazil and Peru shows that consolidation of reform is far from automatic (Williamson and Haggard, 1994 p. 564). Hence, their conclusion that while crisis may open space for debate, it is neither sufficient nor necessary for the initiation of reform (Williamson and Haggard, 1994 p. 565).

Similarly in their review of reforms in eight countries, Robert H. Bates and Anne O. Krueger note that crisis is perhaps the more frequent stimulus to reform...When crisis is the trigger of change, policy changes can come about either because earlier policies are perceived as having failed or because exogenous events...require a policy response (Bates and Krueger, 1993 p. 452). They discern three types of 'crisis triggers' in their case studies : those caused by balance of payments difficulties; accelerating inflation; and the state's loss of economic control. While they recognise that not all reforms have taken place under circumstances of crisis, they do argue that reform always follows inadequate economic performance :

> There is no recorded instance of the beginning of a reform program at a time when economic growth was satisfactory, and when the price level and balance of payments situations were stable (Bates and Krueger, 1993 p. 454).

Once a decision to reform has been made, Bates and Krueger argue that issues of implementation become dominant and argue that it is almost inevitable in these circumstances that power accrues to technocrats. They identify two causes for this transfer of power, the "politicians, dilemma" and "partisan theory". By the former they refer to a solution to open-ended populist politics through the creation of independent agencies outside of direct political control. By the latter they refer to political nature of struggles over distribution of benefits which are occasioned by reform. It is bureaucrats aligned with the beneficiaries of change who institutionalise the changes and secure them from change (Bates, 1994 pp. 465-66; Bates and Krueger, 1993 pp. 30-32).

If Williamson and Haggard place most of their emphasis on the initiation of reform, and Bates and Krueger on the implementation of reforms, Joan Nelson in a brief comment has drawn attention to the significance of the different phases through which reforms pass. The severest challenges do not come in the initial weeks or even the first year. Well after reforms have begun they may face resistance and stall or face serious diversion.

> I suspect that the conventional assumption is wrong : the most difficult political challenges come not initially, but somewhat later in a program, after the first months or year...Initial stabilization and adjustment packages ....are administratively easy, in the sense that they can

> be decided and put into effect by a small circle of senior economic officials. Measures that are usually introduced later, such as financial-sector reforms, and the rationalization or privatization of large state enterprises...are much more complex (Nelson, 1994 p. 474).

As a consequence, reforms must develop strategies for the middle-term as well as the short-term.

Reforming State-Owned Enterprises

Theorising about the specific factors which lead to successful reform in the privatisation of SOEs raises themes similar to those we have already considered. Jose Edgardo Campos and Hadi Salehi Esfahani, for example, in an article which asks "Why and When Do Governments Initiate Public Enterprise Reform?", conclude that episodes of economic difficulty, rather than crisis alone, are associated with many 'reform episodes'. In their study of fifteen countries between 1972 and 1993, they found that almost 80 per cent (19 out of 24) of reform attempts had been preceded by periods in which real gross domestic product per capita was negative. So strong is the association that they suggest that "for most developing countries, economic downturn may be an almost necessary condition for public enterprise reform" (Campos and Esfahani, 1996 p. 469). It is, however, possible to view their evidence in another light. In 60 per cent of the cases they studied (28 out of 47) there was no reform of SOEs. India, for example, had five episodes of economic downturn (1971, 1974, 1976, 1979 and 1991), only the last of which Campos and Esfahani take to have been associated with reform of SOEs (Campos and Esfahani, 1996 Figure 2, p. 470). Treating 1991 as a reform episode seems to have required some elasticity in application of their definitions, since they state earlier that "changes such as the sale of minority shares in a few public enterprises to raise revenue...do not qualify as reform episodes" (Campos and Esfahani, 1996 p. 463); as we shall see shortly, there are a number of critics who believe that the initial divestment of shares in India's SOEs involved no more than the sale of minority holdings to raise revenue.[3]

Another, and in my view more subtly nuanced, account of SOE reform from the World Bank is Philip Keefer's chapter in Mary Shirley and Ahmed Galal's Bureaucrats in Business : the economics and politics of government ownership. Keefer identifies three conditions which must be met for there to be successful SOE reform. The first of these is political desirability : "reform becomes desirable when the benefits to the leadership and its constituencies outweigh the political costs". The change which makes reform desirable may arise from a change in political leadership, or from an economic shock or crisis (Shirley, *et al.*, 1995 pp. 178-79). Where there is a large and politically important SOE sector, an economic shock by itself will not produce change: "there was no instance in our sample where an economic shock alone was large enough to make SOE reform desirable to a government that relied heavily on SOE support" (Shirley, *et al.*, 1995, p. 178)[4].

The second of Keefer's criteria is that "reform must be politically feasible....the leadership must be able to implement reform and....to withstand opposition to reform" (Shirley, *et al.*, 1995, p. 190). He observes that :

> India did not meet the requirements of this condition....There was legislative resistance to SOE reform and a high potential for resistance to reform outside political channels (Shirley, *et al.*, 1995, p. 199).

---

3. The IMF, for example remarks that "the divestment program has had mixed success, in part because the objective of raising revenue has often superseded the objective of improving efficiency" (Chopra , *et al.*, 1995 p. 65).

4. For reasons which are not clearly spelled out, Keefer's study of India stops in 1989. As a result the study concludes : "India did not experience a regime change or coalition realignment. Moreover, neither the governing party nor any other major party in India had a support base that favored SOE reform. An economic crisis might have altered this picture, but India did not experience a sharp economic crisis in the 1980s that would have led any of these constituent groups to reverse their opposition to SOE reform" (Shirley, *et al.*, 1995, p. 184).

Resistance was indicated by high levels of overstaffing in SOEs. The overall average is estimated to be 25-33 per cent and (Shirley, *et al.*, 1995, table 4.2, p. 192). In addition, in the 1980s there was no legislative majority in favour of reform and no compensation program had been created to compensate losers (Shirley, *et al.*, 1995 table 4.3, p. 193).

The last of Keefer's criteria is that of the credibility of reform. To be credible, the promises that the leadership makes to compensate losers and protect investors' property rights must be believable. This is the only criterion which India satisfies :

Countries, such as India and the Philippines, have political systems that make reform both difficult to enact and to overturn....This suggests that reforms in countries with political checks and balances are less vulnerable to reversal (Shirley, *et al.*, 1995, p. 205).

> India enjoys a good reputation among investors....Policy reversals to the detriment of investors have been few....India has a Constitution that imposes significant restraints on the executive branch, making policy reversals less likely (Shirley, *et al.*, 1995, p. 213).

Thus, in Keefer's view, India does not meet the test of readiness for reform of its SOEs. That conclusion may serve for most of the approaches to reform we have considered. Taken broadly, we can see that although the foreign exchange crisis of 1991 may have initiated macro-economic reforms there appears to be a consensus in the literature that the impact of the crisis was insufficient to sustain significant reforms of India's SOEs. What I want to argue in this paper is that, contrary to the received wisdom, lacking all prerequisites, the reform of India's SOEs is just beginning to acquire momentum.

A brief history of India's SOEs

When India secured Independence in 1947 its industrial sector was small and poorly developed. Except in cotton spinning and weaving, its capabilities were marginal and its firms small. The strategy chosen to remedy the deficit left by colonial rule was to create a major state-owned capitalist sector. These government-owned industries would provide India with steel, coal, heavy machinery, petroleum, electrical generators and so forth — the essential industrial infrastructure of a modern economy. In 1951 the central government owned only five enterprises; by 1985 the total of state-owned enterprises (SOEs) had risen to 215; by 1994 the total reached 246. Total investment rose from Rs. 290 million in 1951 to Rs. 426.7 billion in 1985; in 1994 the investment in SOEs reached Rs. 1,643.3 billion (Ministry of Industry, 1995 table 1.1, p. 6). The centrally owned industries were major employers; in 1993-4 they employed over 2 million people (Ministry of Industry, 1995 table 1.29, p. 34). In 1996 they produced 100 per cent of India's petrol and copper, and 60 per cent of the country's steel, zinc and aluminium.

Perhaps a single example will serve to illustrate just how commanding are the heights from which India's SOEs dominate the rest of the economy. In 1996, when the magazine Business India finally began to rank SOEs along with private sector firms, it found the following :

> There are 23 PSUs (Public Sector Undertakings) in the top 100 companies and their combined sales is 1,47,583.04 core or 60 per cent of the sales of the 100 biggest companies in the country. The PSUs earned a cumulative net profit of Rs 11,674.48 crore or 50 per cent of the profits of the top 100 companies. These 23 PSUs own assets equivalent to that of the half of the combined assets of the biggest 100 companies. They have under their command 49 per cent of the market capitalisation of the top 100 companies on the Bombay Stock Exchange (*Business India*, 1996 p. 126).

Despite their central role in a highly protected and regulated economy, India's SOEs have on the whole performed poorly. In 1984-5 there were 113 (or 55 per cent) profitable enterprises and 92 loss-making firms. A decade later the proportions were hardly changed — 120 (or 50 per cent) firms made a profit and 117 made a loss (Ministry of Industry, 1995 table 1.13, pp. 18-19).

The most profitable enterprises were those in the production and distribution of petroleum. A number of state-owned fertiliser corporations, the Delhi Transport Corporation and Indian Airlines made the largest losses (Ministry of Industry, 1995 p. 22). V.M. Dandekar reports that subsidies paid to loss-making SOEs rose from 3 per cent in 1970-71 to around 20 per cent in 1989 (Dandekar, 1992 table 9, p. 59).

In addition to the very large proportion of 'sick' industries, the state owned enterprises have tended to make a relatively weak return on capital employed. In 1993-4, textile companies returned 44 per cent, while the fertiliser and petroleum sectors returned just over 19 per cent; steel returned 5.7 per cent and investments in consumer goods made losses which were 535 per cent of invested capital; the average ratio of gross profits to capital employed was 11.7 (Ministry of Industry, 1995 table 1.19 pp. 24-5). In 1996 Finance Ministry issued a set of guidelines which stated that existing SOE returns on equity were only 1.82 per cent and should be raised to at least 5 per cent (anon, 1996d). Damodaran has argued that if taxes received by government from PSUs are included, then the return to government investment is more nearly 32 per cent (Damodaran, 1996). The overall situation is succinctly summed up in a recent World Bank Country Report :

> The central government is the largest investment banker in the country. It holds equity positions in 240 enterprises in virtually all sectors of the economy. The problem is that the Central Government is not an efficient investment banker. With few exceptions, the dividends it earns on its investment in public enterprises are lower than the interest it pays on its debt (*World Bank*, 1996, p. 56).

Chronology of Reform and Disinvestment in the 1990s

Reform of India's SOEs has been among the 'matters arising' on the national agenda of economic since the mid-1980s. Because of the profound political obstacles which surrounded the issue, action on it was constantly deferred. At least three senior committees were formed in the past 15 years to advise government on what should be done with the SOEs : those headed by L.K. Jha, Arjun Sengupta and V. Krishnamurthy (Nayar, 1992).

The economic crisis of 1991 appeared to make reform of the SOEs an issue which could no longer be deferred. The government's Industrial Policy Statement, issued in July, 1991, soon after the Rao government had come to office, foreshadowed disinvestment of some government-held shares in selected SOEs; this announcement was confirmed in the Budget Speech which announced that up to 20 per cent of government's equity would be sold to mutual funds and institutional investors (Gupta, 1991). By December a list of 31 companies had been selected. This was a mixed portfolio of companies; a quarter were 'very good' firms, almost 40 per cent were 'good' and 35 per cent were 'not so good' (that is, firms with a sound track record but whose net asset value per share was less than Rs. 20) (Ministry of Industry, 1995, p. 185).

This ranking of firms arose from another measure designed to increase both the efficiency of the SOEs and the return to the exchequer. SOEs were required to sign Memoranda of Understanding (MoU) with the government. Originally recommended by the Arjun Sengupta Committee in 1985, MoUs were introduced in 1989-90. Amongst other things, an SOE must indicate in its MoU what its targets and performance criteria are. Annual performance evaluations are made on the basis of which SOEs are placed in categories.[5]

The shares which were to be divested in 1992 were offered as 'lucky dip' packages of assorted shares. Because there was no existing market value of the shares and hence a concern that shares might be offered well below market price (or conversely might be significantly over-priced), and because it had been decided to offer mixed packages of shares, the packages were

5. See (Ministry of Industry, 1995 Chapter 14).

sold to institutional investors. The share sales were largely completed by February, 1992. The full 20 per cent of shares were sold in firms such as Hindustan Petroleum Corporation Ltd. and Bongaigon Refineries and Petrochemicals Limited. At the other extreme, only .27 per cent of shares in Indian Railway Construction Company Limited were sold. The final sales constituted a divestment of 8 per cent of government holdings in the 31 companies; the government received Rs 30, 380 million from the sale (Ministry of Industry, 1995, p. 186).

A second round of divestment was undertaken at the end of 1992. This round involved some new firms, including the giant Steel Authority of India Limited (SAIL), as well as others involved in the first round. This was followed by the divestment of a third tranche in March, 1993 and a fourth a year later. In the latter round, approved foreign institutional investors were also permitted to bid. A total of Rs. 42,034 bn. was raised from these sales (Ministry of Industry, 1995 pp. 187-190). A further round of equity sales in 1995-96 was a failure; only Rs. 3, 570 bn were raised, as against a target of Rs. 70, 000 bn. (anon, 1996b).

The sales attracted considerable criticism. The government was accused of disposing of the people's assets at throw-away prices. An editorial in the Indian Express several years later referred to the share sales as "no more than an any-which-way sale of odd PSU shares for a cash-strapped government" (anon, 1996k). An editorial in the Hindu Business Line commented that the 1995 round of asset sales had been "a total failure" which represented a clear adverse judgement by investors "about the prospects for earnings growth in these companies" (anon, 1995). Another commentator reported the view of a British economist that India's attempts at reforming its SOEs could be the basis of a comedy series which might rival *Yes Minister* (Raghavan, 1996).

A report by the Comptroller and Auditor General of India (CAG) condemned the early rounds of divestment, stating that there had been inadequate preparation and few serious efforts had been made to sell stocks to institutional investors. The CAG also condemned the procedure of clubbing good stocks with bad ones saying that it reduced the value received by the government (Srinivasan, 1996).

In a more sweeping criticism of the post-1991 reforms generally, Balraj Mehta accused Finance Minister Manmohan Singh of having 'picked up the blueprints prepared by the IMF-World Bank combination' :

> The fact is that the structural adjustment as conceived and proposed to be implemented, would unleash the forces of primitive accumulation of capitalism by unbridled exploitation of labour and natural resources by foreign capital and Indian comprador business interests working as junior partners in this process (Mehta, 1991).

With the wisdom of hindsight, some of these criticisms seem misplaced, at least as far as the charge of selling off shares cheaply is concerned. By 1996 a number of SOE shares had fallen considerably in value and as a consequence the market valuation of the corporations was dramatically lower than when the shares were floated. SAIL, for example, which was valued in March, 1994 at Rs. 19929 crore was worth just over half that much (Rs. 10961) two years later (Dey, 1996a). On the other hand, exposure to market evaluation seems to have increased the efficiency of a number of SOEs. A survey of data on SOEs for 1994-95 concludes that about 50 per cent of the [top 100] enterprises [in terms of net sales] had higher year-on-year gross profits to total capital employed ratios in 1994-95 [than the previous year] (Dey, 1996b).

As for the charge that India was forced to dance to the IMF's tune, I was told by an informant close to the decision that the IMF standby agreement was seen as a politically convenient means to implement reforms which the Narasimha Rao government desired in any event. According to this source, serious consideration was given to accepting a second IMF loan, which was not needed for currency stabilisation, on the grounds that it would justify further economic reforms.[6] Another participant was emphatic that "there was no question of IMF pressure.[7]

Interesting interests : the role and position of SCOPE

I would like to consider for a moment a key player in India's reform drama, an interest group which doesn't seem to know what its interests are. It is a commonplace of the literature of contemporary economic reform that bureaucracies and employees of state-owned enterprises are amongst the most important interest groups which resist reform. One of the most unexpected aspects of the saga of Indian divestment has been the leading role played by the Standing Conference of Public Enterprises (SCOPE). SCOPE is the peak body representing India's SOEs. What is interesting and unexpected is the consistency with which in recent years it has pressed for structural reform and a greater role for market-forces in the running of SOEs. In its public rhetoric SCOPE has welcomed economic liberalisation and sought reforms which would allow the public sector to compete on terms of equality in the market. SCOPE's Secretary-General M.A. Hakeem expressed some of these ideas in a commentary published in the Financial Express in 1995 :

> PSEs welcome the liberalisation measures and are prepared to compete with the private sector in India and abroad....It is no longer necessary and valid to enter into a debate on public sector versus private sector. Ownership is not going to be so relevant as professional and independent management of the business....
>
> Unfortunately, the interface between the PSEs and the Government has undergone hardly any change. The boards of PSEs, in many cases are incomplete....instead of being provided with experts who could contribute

6. Interview conducted in New Delhi 7 November, 1996.
7. Interview conducted in New Delhi 26 November, 1996.

> to the business decisions [boards] are loaded with people who are not relevant to the business.
>
> Even though some stray loosening of restrictions has taken place, still formal and informal controls from the respective Ministries do not allow the enterprises to act freely. One of the serious problems which many of the enterprises face today is the flight of the technically competent manpower. This is largely due to inadequate compensation provided by PSEs as they are not free to decide compensation in accordance with the market demand. (Hakeem, 1995).

This excerpt summarises many of SCOPE's concerns : the continued subordination of SOEs to ministries, requirements to be model employers, obligations to locate plants in economically backward areas, the political nature of appointments to boards, and, in an era of rapidly rising salaries in the private sector, the stagnation of executive compensation.[8] SCOPE appears lukewarm on divestment, preferring reforms which raise efficiency and global competitiveness (anon, 1996j).

Having considered the anomaly of an SOE interest group actively to promote public sector reforms, let me turn to another unlikely player.

A year in the life of the Disinvestment Commission

The United Front (UF) government which took power after the 1996 elections adopted a Common Minimum Programme (CMP) as the agenda of the unlikely coalition. Section 13 of the CMP dealt with the 'public sector' :

> Public sector enterprises which are essentially commercial enterprises should conduct their business on commercial lines. They cannot be allowed to dissave; they should show a healthy return on the capital employed. It is widely acknowledged that the

8. Concerning salary levels, see (Hakeem and Ratnam, 1993).

> public sector requires to be reformed and restructured. The United Front government will identify public sector companies that have comparative advantages and will support them in their drive to become global giants. Other profit making and efficient public sector companies will be strengthened and their management professionalised, and participation of workers in the management of these companies will be encouraged. Sick or potentially sick public sector companies will be rehabilitated through a menu of option that may include handing over the management to professional groups or workers' cooperatives.
>
> The question of withdrawing the public sector from non-core and non-strategic areas will be a carefully examined subject, however, to assure the workers and employees of job security or, in the alternative, opportunities for retraining and redeployment. The United Front will establish a Disinvestment Commission to advise the government on these steps. Any decision to disinvest will be taken and implemented in a transparent manner. Revenues generated from such disinvestment will be utilised in two vital areas, health and education, particularly in the poorer and backward districts of the country. A part of such revenues will be earmarked to create an investment fund which will be used to strengthen other public sector enterprises (United Front Government, 1996).

On August 7, 1996 it was announced that the Disinvestment Commission (DC) would be created and that it would be headed by G.V. Ramakrishnan, former Secretary for Petroleum, former Member Planning Commission and former Chairman of the Securities Exchange Board of India (SEBI). The mandate of the Commission was to 'off load' up to three-quarters of the government's holding in 'non-core' and 'non-strategic' (*i.e.*, defence, atomic energy, railways and communications) industries (anon, 1996h). Although the DC was charged with working out both the strategy and tactics for the disinvestment of government holdings in SOEs, the suite of firms whose shares would be sold was to be selected by a Core Group of Secretaries to government (anon, 1996c). Setting up the new Commission and initiating its activities took time. In late September, Ramakrishnan complained publicly that the Core Group had still not referred any cases to the Commission (anon, 1996e) and members of his staff were still not on the payroll. By mid-October a list of 40 SOEs had been approved by the Core Group which included Air India, the Gas Authority of India Limited (GAIL), Steel Authority of India Limited (SAIL), the Oil and Natural Gas Commission (ONGC) and Indian Telephones (Nigam, 1996).

Trade Union concerns were intensified by this development. Their anxieties had repercussions, *via* the Communist Party Marxist, which was a constituent of the United Front government (Nigam, 1996). Ramakrishnan emphasised that no disinvestment would take place until all stake-holders, including the unions, had been consulted.[9] He also expressed a wish to undertake a process of 'book building' to increase the eventual value of enterprises when disinvestment took place (Venkitaramanan, 1996). This position was spelled out in detail in a discussion paper "Disinvestment : Strategy and Issues" which the DC issued in early January (anon, 1997f).

By the time of Republic Day, 1997 there appeared to be little that the DC could show by way of progress. In part this reflected political dissension within the UF government and in part the process of consultation with stakeholders and the examination of the balance sheets of individual firms. Although there were some criticisms in the financial press, the Finance Minister P. Chidambaram professed to be unworried that the budget target of Rs. 50,000 m. from disinvestment could not possibly be achieved (anon, 1997b). Barely a fortnight later,

9. Interview conducted in New Delhi 4 November, 1996. When the consultations were completed in mid-January, the position of the unions was virtually indistinguishable from that of SOE managers (Giriprakas, 1997).

however, DC Chairman Ramakrishna announced that the first recommendations on disinvestment would appear before the end of the month (anon, 1997e). These duly appeared, recommending disinvestment of disinvestment of holdings in three SOEs. In April, a second report was issued listing six more SOEs in which up to three-quarters of government holdings could be sold. By the end of June recommendations had been made for the disinvestment of up to forty-nine per cent of public holdings in nine enterprises.

In early July Cabinet took its first action on the recommendations and approved disinvestment by early 1998 of four enterprises : Gas Authority of India Limited (GAIL), Mahanagar Telephones Nigam Limited (MTNL), Container Corporation of India Limited (Concor) and Indian Oil Corporation (IOC) (anon, 1997a). In mid-August, shortly after the first birthday of the DC — when this account concludes — the government had approved two consortia each composed of three international investment bankers to co-ordinate international offerings of GAIL and MTNL (anon, 1997c).

Even more dramatic was the announcement in early July that the government was to act on its announced programme and designate nine firms (promptly dubbed 'navaratnas') which were to be developed into global concerns. In late July Industry Minister Murasoli Maran announced that the nine designated firms would be made substantially independent of government in their accountability and in their day-to-day operations, though their performance would be monitored by the Department of Public Enterprises. The nine designated firms would have the power to hire and fire, to close down unprofitable units and to enter into joint ventures (anon, 1997d; Dasgupta and Sen, 1997).

It's difficult, before the results are known to give a definitive report card on the Disinvestment Commission at the end of its first year. For what it's worth, my view is that a great deal more was achieved than anyone really expected. Indeed, to go further, the changes which are in train make it plausible to argue that India has entered a phase in which major reforms of its SOE sector will take place.[10] What makes this especially interesting is that this transformation has taken place in the absence of the compulsion of economic crisis and has been undertaken by a fragile coalition government, dependent upon parties of the left unsympathetic to the dilution of public ownership — a government, which all experience would suggest, would have done nothing about SOE reform.

Conclusion

In drawing this paper to a conclusion, I want to consider how this 'reform against the odds' has been possible and to suggest that the 'Bos-Wash' consensus is too narrow to be helpful in the Indian case. I should start by acknowledging that my assessment is far from the conventional wisdom. A Coopers and Lybrand/Business Today survey conducted in early 1996 ranked India's privatisation profile at the bottom of seven countries taken as benchmarks. That survey drew the harsh judgement that "the Rao Administration has frittered away all its early advantages. As a result, most PSUs are in no better shape to be sold off to the private sector than they were five years ago" (anon, 1996g p. 68).

In my assessment the forces which are behind the gathering momentum of SOE reform in India are quite different from those which have prevailed in most of the cases which have formed the basis of the studies by World Bank staffers and others. There are many reasons for the differences : the political and ideological associations of the public sector; the nature of publicly owned assets and how they were acquired, the size of SOEs in relation to domestic capital markets, and so on. One aspect which hasn't been considered in drawing World Bank lessons from the

10. It is, of course, easy to point to what hasn't been done. There are, for example, still loss-making and sick industries which have to be tackled. Even on the sick industries front though, there is a story to be told. The Board for Industrial and Financial Reconstruction appears to be clearing up its backlog, with revival proposals for a number of enterprises and winding-up recommendations made for others (Kumar, 1997). For a glimpse of the dark side of the moon, see (Goswami, 1997).

experience of reform is the possibility that the results may be a statistical artefact arising from the fact that in many instances of crisis, countries have had to turn to the IMF for assistance, which has of course imposed privatisation as a condition.

The first of the forces which I would emphasise is the decision to remove controls on a wide range of industries which was taken by Rajiv Gandhi's government shortly after he came to power in 1985. The principal consequence of that initial act of deregulation was more indirect than direct. Rajiv's attempts to effect SOE reforms, after all, came to nothing (Nayar, 1992). Rather, the impact came *via* the intensified competition and dynamism which was injected into the private sector. One marker of that change was to be seen in the executive job market. Managerial salaries in the private sector rose sharply (Chengappa, *et al.*, 1989). The differentials which were already apparent in 1985 had become stark a decade later. Middle-level managers in 1985 received a bit over twice the salaries of their government and public sector counterparts. By 1995 they received almost four times as much (Baruja and Jhaveri, 1995 p. 57). Between 1995 and 1996 alone the salaries of senior executives rose by 41 per cent (anon, 1966 p. 120). Thus, it is not surprising that competition for managerial talent has been a significant source of pressure for change within the ranks of SOE managers. Indirect example, I think, has been as important as direct competition.

Deregulation and delicensing, especially post-1991 have also made a significant contribution to changing the political climate. Removing the monopoly status of SOEs opened them up to competitive pressures of an unprecedented kind. And not all of them have responded well. Goulding has referred to this aspect of the Indian reform model as 'parallelization', arguing that "it has helped India avoid the pitfalls faced by privatisation programs in other emerging economies. Creation of private-sector employment alternatives allows for the gradual absorption of workers from overstaffed SOEs and lays a foundation for future sell-offs" (Goulding, 1997). I think this is only partially correct;

I have seen little evidence that any workers have been retrenched or that they have been moving to private sector jobs.

Goulding also argues that the system of MoUs was a failure. Here too, I remain to be persuaded. It seems probable to me that the rising pressure on SOE managers to increase the rate of return to their public shareholder was a significant force for change, as were the signals which came from stock markets once disinvestment began to occur. This has been especially true as SOEs have faced the fact that funds for future investment and expansion will have to come either from earnings or from the market. Profits and market valuations have become important yardsticks of performance. They have also highlighted the administrative and regulatory straight jacket in which SOEs are confined.

There are, of course, many other factors which have had an impact on the process of reform in India. What I want to emphasise in conclusion is the contrast between the Boston-Washington consensus which takes as normal and desirable the 'short sharp shock' model of privatisation, *et al.*, Chile and Pakistan. India's disinvestment follows a different model : one I prefer to think of as dialectical. In the latter, inner social dynamics are more important than external conditionalities. I think that Robert Jenkins is at least partially correct when he argues that longer-term changes in Indian society have altered the nature of the political system and thus set the stage for economic liberalisation (Jenkins, 1995). Certainly, it is striking that a national survey conducted on the eve of the 1996 general elections reported only 12 per cent felt that the pace of liberalisation was too fast; 24 per cent said it was 'just right' and 44 per cent said it was 'too slow' (anon, 1996i). Another election eve poll reported that only 18 per cent of voters felt that their standard of living had eroded since 1991; 39 per cent reported no change while 41 per cent said they were better off (anon, 1996f p. 54).

India may be, as Madhav Dhar suggests, the slowest reformer. But the essentially dialectical process which has pushed the reforms of India's SOEs forward holds lessons which indicate that the agenda of change can be the result of autonomous decisions and not the result of distress sales imposed by economic disaster. It also suggests to me that irrespective of which party is in power in the next five years, they will still be subject to slowly mounting pressures to continue the process of change.

REFERENCES

anon, 1966. 'Core Team Compensation', *Business Today*, (22 October-6 November, 1996), pp. 120-141.

anon, 1995, 'Referendum of Sorts', *Hindu Business Line*, 11 November, 1995.

anon, 1996a, 'America is bullish on Indian intent, not on implementation', *Economic Times*, 8 August, 1996.

anon, 1996b, 'Disinvestment Panel for Public Sector', *The Hindu Business Line*, 12 August, 1996.

anon, 1996c, 'Disinvestment Panel Set Up : G.V. Ramakrishna Heads 5-Member Body', *The Hindu Business Line*, 8 August, 1996.

anon, 1996d, 'Guidelines for better expenditure management', *Hindu Business Line*, 18 June, 1996.

anon, 1996e, ''Lackadaisical' core group paralyses disinvestment panel', *Economic Times*, 23 September, 1996.

anon, 1996f, 'Mood of the Nation', *India Today* (30 April, 1996), pp. 52-55.

anon, 1996g, 'Privatisation Paradigms', *Business Today* (22 January-6 February, 1996), pp. 68-81.

anon, 1996h, 'PSU share quota for workers, small investors', *Economic Times*, 8 August, 1996.

anon, 1996i, ''Reforms are too slow'', *Business India*, (8-21 April, 1996), pp. 62-65.

anon, 1996j, 'Revamp public sector before disinvesting, says SCOPE', *Times of India*, 16 November, 1996.

anon, 1996k, 'Shareholder Raj', *Indian Express*, 1 July, 1996.

anon, 1997a, 'Cabinet approves disinvestment in 4 PSUs', *Hindu Business Line*, 6 July, 1997.

anon, 1997b, 'Chidambaram on PSU Disinvestment — 'Govt. Will Mop Up Part of Targeted proceeds'', *Hindu Business Line*, 26 January, 1997.

anon, 1997c, 'Lead Managers for GAIL, MTNL GDR issues okayed', *Hindu Business Line*, 13 August, 1997.

anon, 1997d, 'Packaging the nine gems', *Hindu Business Line*, 28 May, 1997.

anon, 1997e, 'PSU Disinvestment Plan in 3 Weeks', *Hindu Business Line*, 6 February, 1997.

anon, 1997f, 'Restructure PSUs Before Disinvestment : Panel', *Hindu Business Line*, 10 January, 1997.

A. Baruja and N. Jhaveri, 1995, 'Are We Getting Richer?', *Business India*, (17-30 July, 1995), pp. 54-60.

R.H. Bates, 1994, 'Comment' in J. Williamson, *The Political Economy of Policy Reform* (Washington D.C. : Institute for International Economics).

R.H. Bates and A.O. Krueger, 1993, 'Generalizations Arising from the Country Studies' in R.H. Bates and A.O. Krueger, *Political and Economic Interactions in Economic Policy Reform* (Oxford : Basil Blackwell Limited).

Business India, 1996, 'The Business India Super 100', *Business India*, No. 486 (October 21- November 3, 1996), pp. 127-171.

J.E. Campos and H.S. Esfahani, 1996, 'Why and When Do Governments Initiate Public Enterprise Reform?', *World Bank Economic Review*, Vol. 10, No. 3, pp. 451-85.

R. Chengappa, C. Rajghatta, S.N. Vasuki and S.G. Prasad, 1989, 'Job Changers : Hop, hop and Away', *India Today* (15 July, 1989), pp. 48-51. Radical change in employment culture has led to increased job mobility and rising salaries. Describes profiles of types of mobile executives, head-hunting, inducements. Problems in clashes of corporate culture also. Profile, too, of employers.

A. Chopra, W. Chu and O. Fratzscher, 1995, 'Structural Reforms and the Implications for Investment and Growth' in A. Chopra, C. Collyns, R. Hemming, K. Parker, W. Chu and O. Fratzscher, *India : Economic Reform and Growth*, Vol. Occasional paper 134 (Washington, D.C. : International Monetary Fund).

H. Damodaran, 1996, 'How 'fair' are PSU dividend norms?', *Hindu Business Line*, 21 June, 1996.

V.M. Dandekar, 1992, 'Forty Years After Independence' in B. Jalan, *The Indian Economy : Problems and Prospects* (New Delhi : Viking).

A. Dasgupta and S.K. Sen, 1997, 'Multi-Layer Monitoring of Navaratnas Planned', *Hindu Business Line*, 28 July, 1997.

P.K. Dey, 1996a, 'PSU Scripts Slip in Market Ratings', Business Standard, 30 May, 1996.

P.K. Dey, 1996b, 'Public Sector Giants Hold on to Gains during 1994-95', *Business Standard*, 26 November, 1996.

A. Galal, 1991, *Public Enterprise Reform : Lessons from the Past and Issues for the Future* (Washington, D.C. : The World Bank).

K. Giriprakas, 1997, 'Unions Reverse Stand, Want Professionals to Run PSUs', *Business Standard*, 16 January, 1997.

O. Goswami, 1997, 'Spinning a Futile Yarn', *Business India* (19 May-1 June, 1997), pp. 81-84.

A.J. Goulding, 1997, 'Retreating from the Commanding Heights : Privatization in an Indian Context', *Journal of International Affairs*, Vol. 50, No. 2, pp. 581 ff.

D. Gupta, 1991, 'New Economic Strategy — Out to Crush the Permit Raj — I', *Business Standard*, 4 October, 1991.

M.A. Hakeem, 1995, 'Murky Future for PSEs under reform', *Financial Express*, 11 January, 1995.

M.A. Hakeem and V. Ratnam, 1993, 'Parity or Disparity?', *Financial Express*, 15 December, 1993.

R.S. Jenkins, 1995, 'Theorising the Politics of Economic Adjustment : Lessons from the Indian Case', *Journal of Commonwealth and Comparative Studies*, Vol. XXXII, No. 1, pp. 1-24.

S. Kikeri, J. Nellis and M. Shirley, 1992, *Privatization : The Lessons of Experience* (Washington, D.C. : The World Bank).

S. Kikeri, J. Nellis and M. Shirley, 1994, 'Privatisation : Lessons from Market Economies', *The World Bank Research Observer*, Vol. 9, No. 2 (July, 1994), pp. 241-72.

A. Kumar, 1997, 'BIFR Cases Remain on the Decline', Economic Times, 7 January, 1997.

R. Leeds, 1991, 'Privatization Through Public Offerings : Lessons from Two Jamaican Cases' in R. Ramamurti and R. Vernon, *Privatization and Control of State-Owned Enterprises* (Washington : World Bank).

N. Mathieu, 1996, *Industrial Restructuring : World Bank Experience, Future Challenges* (Washington, D.C. : World Bank).

B. Mehta, 1991, 'Other Face of Economic Reforms', *Times of India*, 25 December, 1991.

Ministry of Industry, 1995, *Public Enterprises Survey, 1993-94* (New Delhi : Government of India).

B.R. Nayar, 1992, 'The Politics of Economic Restructuring in India : The Paradox of State Strength and Policy Weakness', *Journal of Commonwealth and Comparative Politics*, Vol. 30, No. 2 (July, 1992), pp. 145-171.

J.M. Nelson, 1994, 'Panel Discussion' in J. Williamson, *The Political Economy of Policy Reform* (Washington, D.C. : Institute for International Economics).

A. Nigam, 1996, 'The Disinvestment Tangle Hots Up', *The Pioneer*, 14 October, 1996.

T.C.A.S. Raghavan, 1996, 'Runnion on the Spot', *Business Standard*, 27 November, 1996.

M. Shirley, 1989, *The Reform of State-Owned Enterprises : Lessons from World Bank Lending* (Washington, D.C. : World Bank).

M. Shirley, A. Galal and P. Keefer, 1995, Bureaucrats in Business : *The Economics and Politics of Government Ownership* (Washington, D.C. : World Bank).

M. Shirley and J. Nellis, 1991, Public Enterprise Reform : *The Lessons of Experience* (Washington, D.C. : The World Bank).

G. Srinivasan, 1996, 'Timing, Pricing Key to Successful Disinvestment', *The Hindu Business Line*, 28 September, 1996.

United Front Government, 1996, 'A Common Approach to Major Policy Matters and a Minimum Programme' (New Delhi).

S. Venkitaramanan, 1996, 'To Divest or Not to Divest', *Economic Times*, 12 November, 1996.

J. Williamson, 1994, 'In Search of a Manual for Technopols', *The Political Economy of Policy Reform* (Washington, D.C. : Institute for International Economics).

J. Williamson and S. Haggard, 1994, 'The Political Conditions for Economic Reform' in J. Williamson, *The Political Economy of Policy Reform* (Washington, D.C. : Institute of International Economics).

World Bank, 1996, *India Country Economic Memorandum : Five Years of Stabilization and Reform : The Challenges Ahead* (Washington, D.C. (?) : World Bank).

13

Liberalisation and Structural Change : Nepalese Manufacturing since the mid 1980s

KISHOR SHARMA*

I. Introduction

Despite growing literature on the consequences of liberalisation, only a few studies have examined the impact on industrial structure[1]. These available studies focus on the experience of middle income developing countries, while studies on low income developing countries or least developed countries (LDCs) are both sparse and lopsided. The experience of the former, however, cannot be generalised to the latter given the lower level of human capital, physical infrastructure and R&D in LDCs. At the same time, doubts that liberalisation will not solve the problems of LDCs remain strong (Rodrik, 1992; Diaz Alejandro and Helleiner, 1982 and Taylor, 1981).

Most liberalisation reforms, introduced under the structural adjustment program (SAP) of the IMF and the policy

*I would like to thank Sisira Jayasuriya, Premachandra Athukorala and Edward Oczkowski for useful suggestions without implicating them in any way.

1. For instance, Aswicahyono, Bird and Hill (1996) for Indonesia, Dijkstra (1996) for Nicaragua, Nordas (1996) for South Africa, Diehl (1995) for Vietnam and Yenturk-Coban (1992) for Turkey.

recommendations of the World Bank (the 'Washington consensus'), include public sector reforms including elimination of fiscal deficit and privatisation of public enterprises, liberalisation of trade and industrial policies, financial sector reform and tight monetary policy. The 'Washington consensus' believes that liberalisation programs lead to structural change and efficiency gains, due to a change in incentive structure and external exposure. However, there is a view that if liberalisation programs are introduced at the stage of development it will show a negative, rather than positive impact (Kawai, 1994). For example, the deregulation of financial market in LDCs may lead to higher interest rates making the cost of investment high. This might discourage new investment and the expansion of existing activities. Measures to control inflation and the fiscal deficit might lead to a fall in government expenditure on infrastructure projects, further lowering supply elasticities. Furthermore, devaluation increases the operational cost which might discourage production (Stein, 1992).

Doubts have also been expressed as to the effectiveness of the liberalisation programs in creating a competitive manufacturing sector in LDCs. Firstly, these countries possess a lower level of physical infrastructure, have a shortage of skilled labour and lack efficient institutions. As a result, manufacturing is characterised by the high cost structure. Unfortunately, in the design of SAP, market failures arising from these factors are not effectively addressed. In fact, pressure to improve the fiscal deficit may lead to the slow growth or even a fall in the infrastructure budget, further lowering the supply elasticities. Secondly, industrialisation is in the early stage of development in LDCs and exports are dominated by processed primary products, that are price and income inelastic. Thus, despite liberalisation, a strong manufacturing sector may not be developed at least in the short-run. Thirdly, since the second hand markets in capital goods are not well developed in LDCs, less efficient sectors may not exit if they are cross-subsidised by affiliates in other sectors. Thus, the transfer of resources from less efficient sectors to more efficient sectors may not take place and the benefits of liberalisation can be easily cancelled (Rodrik, 1992b). Realising these limitations, the 'neo-structuralist consensus' advocates selective expenditure cuts in order to maintain a minimum level of public investment, gradual and selective trade liberalisation and less demand restrictions (Dijkstra, 1996). This is particularly important in economies which are at the early stage of development and have poor infrastructure and a low level of skilled manpower (Mosley, 1993).

In this paper, we shed light on this debate by investigating the experience of Nepalese manufacturing — a country which is categorised as one of the LDCs[2]. More specifically, we examine what happens to output structure and trade orientation when liberalisation programs are pursued in a LDC like Nepal. Will there be any impact on manufacturing productivity? Will the spatial distribution of manufacturing activity change? Nepal provides an excellent case to examine these issues. First, manufacturing is in the early stage of development, contributing less than 7 per cent to GDP. Second, after over three decades of import-substitution (IS) policy, Nepal pursued liberalisation programs from the mid 1980s, although the liberalisation was gradual until the early 1990s. Massive liberalisation took place only when India liberalised its economy in the early 1990s[3]. Third, manufacturing data are available at a reasonable level of disaggregation, which permits examination of the issues at hand.

---

2. According to the World Bank Nepal is a least developed country. A major portion of its national income is derived from agriculture and the manufacturing contributes about 7 per cent to GDP and employs about 4 per cent of the labour force.

3. Due to Nepal's land-locked position and open border with India, Nepal had to delay pursuit of a massive liberalisation until India liberalised its policy environment in the early 1990s. If trade and investment policies in Nepal were more liberal than those in India, massive smuggling would drain Nepal's foreign exchange reserve. If Nepal were to provide generous export incentives, Indian goods would be re-exported. Thus, Nepal had to wait for India to pursue a massive liberalisation.

The paper is organised as follows. Section II outlines a brief overview of the policy environment in the past and recent changes. The impact of liberalisation on the structure of manufacturing is investigated in section III. Section IV concludes the paper with some comments and recommendations.

II. Policy Environment in the Past and Recent Reforms

Nepal has undergone three distinct phases in the evolution of its trade policy during the post-war period, moving from a free trade regime (1923-56) to an increasingly closed, protectionist regime (1956-85) and then towards an open, liberal regime from 1985/86. The import-substitution (IS) policy pursued during 1956-85, created a bias against exports due mainly to overvalued exchange rates and excessive government interventions. Since manufacturing was dominated by IS industries, the small size of the domestic market and frequent shortages of intermediate inputs did not permit efficient utilisation of installed capacity. The net outcome of the IS policy was a slow growth in exports, a rise in imports and huge deficits in the current account and government fiscal operations[4]. Although the early stage of IS policy brought some growth in manufacturing output (Table 1), its share in GDP was stagnated by the mid 1980s and manufactured exports were unable to meet its own import requirements[5].

---

4. Export growth was stagnated (about 5 per cent of real GDP) and the current account deficit rose from less than 1 per cent in the mid 1970s to about 4 per cent of GPD by the mid 1980s. International reserve fell to about less than 4 months worth of imports by the mid 1980s and manufacturing capacity was largely unutilised (about 23 per cent). Meanwhile the government's budget deficit rose from 1 per cent of GDP in the mid 1970s to about 7 per cent by the mid 1980s (Sharma, 1997).

5. Manufactured exports financed less than 10 per cent of its own import needs. Thus, the foreign exchange earnings from other sources, such as primary exports, tourism and remittances, were used to meet its import requirements.

Against this background, under pressure from the IMF, Nepal was forced to liberalise its economy in the mid 1980s. However, due to its land-locked position and open border with India, Nepal pursued a gradual liberalisation mainly by dismantling quantitative restrictions (QRs) and simplifying the industrial licensing regime. Tariffs, including sales tax, excise duties and additional duties, were gradually reduced especially from the late 1980s. Programs of trade liberalisation also included narrowing the dispersion in tariff rates and reductions in the bias against exports. Export procedures were simplified, cash subsidies were offered (between 10-30 per cent of the fob value) to a number of exportable items and manufactured exports enjoyed preferential treatment under the generalised system of preferences (GSP) scheme. The trade weighted nominal rate of protection (NRP) indicates a substantial fall in the level of protection from about 80 per cent by the mid 1980s to about 40 per cent by 1993/94[6].

The program of liberalisation also included reforms in investment policy including foreign investment. Effective from early 1996, foreign investment below US $ 300,000 does not need a license, while a 'one window' sanctioning procedure has been introduced to attract foreign investment. A large number of state-owned enterprises (SOEs) have been privatised or liquidated, foreign banks and finance companies are welcome, and commercial banks are given freedom to set their own interest rates. With the pursuit of the liberalisation program, a large devaluation of the Nepalese rupee took place in the mid 1980s and the early 1990s. Since February 1993, the foreign exchange market has been liberalised for all current account transactions and exchange rates have been determined by market forces. The

---

6. Due to the unavailability of the latest input-output (I-O) table we are unable to estimate the effective rate of protection (ERP). The latest I-O table for Nepal was prepared in 1986/87 when reform was only partially implemented. Thus, input, output coefficient obtained from this table for the recent years may not be accurate because imports of inputs have been substantially liberalised in recent years. In this situation we may not be able to estimate ERP accurately.

Figure 1 : Trade weighted nominal protection[7]

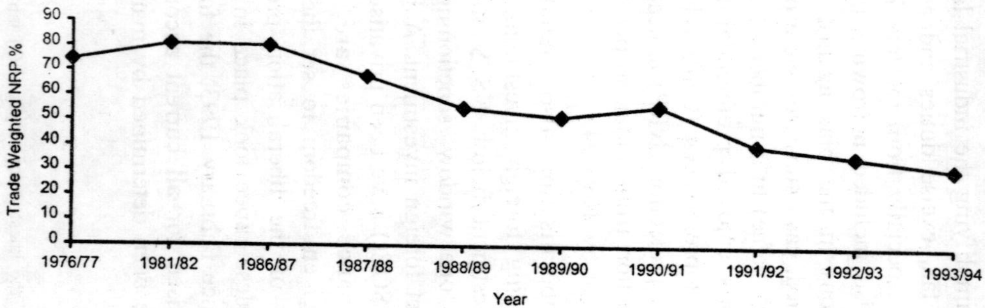

***Source* :** Sharma 1997.

7. According to the Indo-Nepal trade agreements, imports from India are subject to a lower level of restrictions. Thus, they attract basic tariffs only, while imports from the rest of the world are taxed using the basic plus additional tariff. Thus, using the trade share of India and the rest of the world, we obtain a single trade weighted NRP.

Figure 2 : REER Index : 1974-94 (1985=100)

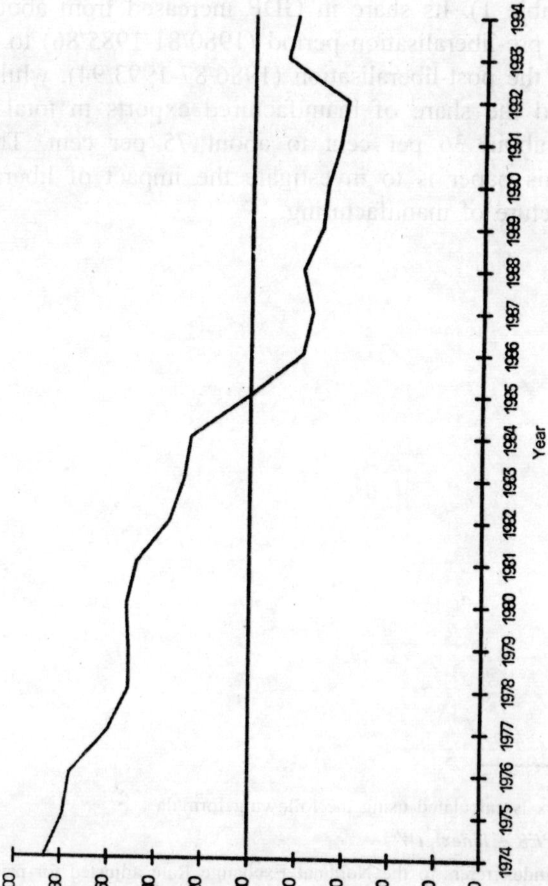

Source : Estimated from data obtained from IMF, 1993 and 1994.

real effective exchange rate (REER) index[8] indicates a real devaluation of the Nepalese rupee from the mid 1980s (figure 2).

The manufacturing sector responded positively to these reforms (Table 1). Its share in GDP increased from about 4 per cent in the pre-liberalisation period (1980/81-1985/86) to about 7 per cent in the post-liberalisation (1986/87-1993/94), while in the same period the share of manufactured exports in total exports rose from about 36 per cent to about 75 per cent. The main focus of this paper is to investigate the impact of liberalisation on the structure of manufacturing.

---

8. REER index is calculated using the following formula :

$REER = \Sigma_i \, (PER - index)_i \, (W_i)$

Where, RER-index refers to the Nominal Exchange Rate adjusted for price changes at home and in the major trading partners and divided by the base year exchange rate. Wi refers to trade weights of major trading partners which is sum to 1. Note that selection of currencies is based on the multilateral trade weights using 1985 trade figures. However, if trade weights have changed significantly, which is unlikely, than this could affect our REER index. The following currencies are included in the REER estimates : Indian rupees, Japanese yen, US dollar, German mark, British pound and Singapore dollar.

TABLE 1

Indicator of manufacturing performance : 1974/75-1993/94

Year	GDP (Rs. Million)	Average annual growth in GDP	Value of Mfg. Output (Rs. Million)	Average annual growth in Mfg. Output	Mfg. as a % of GDP	Mfg. Exports (Rs. Million)	Mfg. Exports % of total Exports
1974/75	16571	-	664	-	4.0	139	15.6
1975/76	17300	4.0	686	3.3	4.0	127	11.0
1976/77	17822	3.0	759	10.6	4.2	157	13.1
1977/78	18607	4.4	749	-1.3	4.0	164	16.6
1978/79	19048	2.4	727	-2.9	3.8	241	21.6
1979/80	18606	-2.3	746	2.6	4.0	275	30.0
1980/81	20158	8.3	774	3.7	3.8	293	24.6
1981/82	20920	3.8	839	8.4	4.0	191	19.0
1982/83	20297	-3.0	878	4.6	4.3	242	35.5
1983/84	22262	9.7	1026	16.8	4.6	361	37.4

Contd.

TABLE 1 : *continued*

Year	GDP (Rs. Million)	Average annual growth in GDP	Value of Mfg. Output (Rs. Million)	Average annual growth in Mfg. Output	Mfg. as a % of GDP	Mfg. Exports (Rs. Million)	Mfg. Exports % of total Exports
1984/85	23630	6.1	1063	3.6	4.5	642	42.8
1985/86	24645	4.3	1281	20.5	5.2	844	56.1
1986/87	26276	6.6	1607	25.4	5.2	722	55.8
1987/88	28802	9.6	1817	13.1	5.3	1038	63.1
1988/89	31914	10.8	1806	-0.6	4.9	1177	76.9
1989/90	34362	7.7	2052	13.6	4.9	1421	82.7
1990/91	36784	7.7	2500	21.8	5.4	1855	79.3
1991/92	37025	0.6	3276	31.0	8.8	2844	81.2
1992/93	39766	7.4	3517	7.3	8.9	3525	84.3
1993/94	43255	8.7	3902	10.9	9.0	3925	88.6

1974/75-1979/80	2.3	-	2.5	4.0	-	17.9
1980/81-1985/86	4.9	-	9.6	4.4	-	35.9
1986/87-1993/94	7.3	-	15.3	6.6	-	74.7

Note : GDP delator (1974/75=100) was used. Period growth rates are average annual.

Sources : GDP and manufacturing output data are from Ministry of Finance (1990/91 and 1994/95). Exports data are from *Nepal Rastra Bank* (various issues).

III. Structure of Manufacturing : Before and After the Liberalisation

In this Section, we examine the effects of a change in incentive structure on the structure of manufacturing output, trade orientation, productivity growth and spatial distribution, using data from Nepalese manufacturing. The selection of these structural variables is guided by analytical considerations and data availability[9]. It should be noted that due to the muti-faced nature of the liberalisation program, it is empirically difficult to isolate the effect of one major component, for example, the impact of trade liberalisation on structural change. Rodrik (1992b) rightly observes that the current terminology of outward-orientation and export promotion strategy lumps together macro-economic policies with trade policy, and credit for positive results is given solely to trade liberalisation. Furthermore, there is an interactive relationship between some of these variables which is difficult to identify. For example, growth in export intensity may be linked with a rise in foreign ownership, while a fall in public sector participation may result in higher productivity growth (Aswicahyono *et al.*, 1996).

Output Structure

The overvalued exchange rates, higher tariffs and QRs during the IS regime appear to have created a bias against exports. As a result, until the early 1980s about 96 per cent of manufacturing output was dominated by IS industries, while the output share of export-oriented (EO) industries was less than 6 per cent[10]. However, the real devaluation of the Nepalese currency and a

---

9. Liberalisation also appears to have an impact on ownership structure, concentration ratio and the size of manufacturing industries. Unavailablity of data, however, does not permit us to examine the effects on these variables.

10. Following Nishimizu and Robinson (1984) industries are classified as either export-oriented industries which export more than 10 per cent of total production, or import-substituting industries which import more than 10 per cent of total domestic supply (imports plus domestic production minus exports).

fall in the level of protection brought about by the liberalisation reforms, have contributed to a rise in the share of exportable output from 13 per cent in the mid 1980s to 28 per cent in 1993/94 (Table 2).

The decomposition of manufacturing output according to the orientation of manufacturing[11] is presented in table 3. It is obvious that since the mid 1980s, the output share of the labour intensive sector has increased from about 12 per cent in the early 1980s to 31 per cent in the mid 1980s and to 41 per cent in 1993/94. This is attributed to the change in incentive structure that encouraged exports of carpets and garments which are labour intensive. The resource intensive sector experienced a fall in output share after the liberalisation program due mainly to the removal of QRs in some industries, like beverage and tobacco, and non-metallic mineral products. The scale intensive sector has shown an impressive growth in output, although its share has fallen in recent years. The output share of the science based sector has been fluctuating, while a new sector producing specialised supplies has emerged following the liberalisation in trade and investment policies.

Trade Orientation

The effects of liberalisation on manufacturing export intensity is clear, while its impact on import penetration is uncertain. It is often argued that liberalisation eliminates the bias against exports and thereby increases export intensity. But liberalisation may increase or decrease import penetration, depending on the

11. Industries are classified into resource intensive, labour intensive, specialised supplier, scale intensive and science based industries using the OECD classification. Resource intensive industries include : food, beverages and tobacco, wood products, petroleum refining, non-metallic mineral products and non-ferrous metal. Labour intensive industries are : textiles, jute manufacturing, carpets, apparel and leather, metal products and other manufacturing. Specialised supplier includes : non-electric machinery, electric machinery, communications equipment and semiconductors, while scale intensive industries are : paper and printing, chemicals excluding drugs, rubber and plastics, iron and steel, ship building, motor vehicles and other transport equipment. Science based industries include : aerospace, computers and office equipment, pharmaceutical and scientific instruments (Nordas, 1996 : 731).

TABLE 2

Decomposition of manufacturing output according to the nature of market-orientation (% share) : 1972/73-1993/94

	1972/73	1976/77	1981/82	1986/87	1987/88	1988/89	1989/90	1990/91	1991/92	1993/94
IS Industries	96.26	99.40	93.78	87.10	86.04	82.48	80.11	75.10	66.90	71.70
EO Industries	3.74	0.60	6.22	12.89	13.96	17.52	19.89	24.90	33.10	28.30
Total	100.0	100.0	100.0	100.0	100.0	100.0	100.0	100.0	100.0	100.0

Source : Estimated from data obtained from *Central Bureau of Statistics* (*CBS*), various issues.

competitiveness of the manufacturing sector. If the sector becomes competitive after the liberalisation programs then the import penetration ratio would fall, otherwise would rise.

We found a rise in export intensity and a fall in import penetration following the liberalisation program in Nepal. Export intensity, defined as export output ratio, sharply rose in the post-liberalisation period, supporting the notion that liberalisation results in higher export intensity. As shown in figure 3, it increased from less than 0.05 by the early 1980s to about 0.20 by 1993/94, probably due to the preferential access to European and American markets under the GSP scheme.

Within EO industries, export intensity is high in carpet, readymade garments, jute products and leather sub-sectors. Since the mid 1980s, their export intensity further increased. Note that higher export intensity in these sub-sectors is not so much due to lower wages, but appears to be due to the incentive available under the GSP scheme. There has been a substantial fall in export intensity in carpets from the early 1990s, mainly due to the boycott of Nepalese carpets in the European and American markets on the grounds that they use child labour. Export intensity in jewellery rose sharply from the early 1990s, due mainly to the liberalisation of silver imports — the major intermediate inputs — and the simplification of export procedures.

As shown in figure 4, import penetration in Nepalese manufacturing fell from 1988/89, although there have been fluctuations from year to year[12]. There are two possible explanations for this. First, liberalisation may have made domestic products competitive, leading to a fall in imports. Second, with the liberalisation in India from the early 1990s, incentives for smuggling imported goods into India have been reduced, leading

12. Import penetration of the *i th* industry in the tth time is defined as :

$$\frac{TM_{it}}{TQ_{it} + TM_{it} - TX_{it}}$$

Where, TM, TQ and TX refer to total value of imports, output and exports respectively (at constant 1992/93 prices).

to a decline in the imports of luxury goods for subsequent (illegal) exports to India[13].

The sectorwise analysis indicates a fall in import penetration in (i) textile, (ii) radio and TV, (iii) electric appliances, (iv) structural metal and (v) leather and leather products from the mid 1980s. With the exception of soft drinks, import penetration is virtually nil or minimal in the highly protected sectors, namely distilled products, beer, cigarettes, plastic products and soap. There have been huge fluctuations in import penetration in food producing sub-sectors, such as vegetable fats, can fruits, confectionery and other food items, which appear to be due mainly to fluctuations in domestic supply. While import penetration in carpet has fallen, it is substantially high in garments, probably due to the increasing reliance on imports of lower quality garments for domestic consumption.

Total factor productivity growth

TFP growth can be estimated either in value added terms or in gross output terms. But there are serious conceptual problems against the former approach[14]. Thus, in this study, productivity growth is estimated using the latter approach in which intermediate inputs are treated as separate factor inputs. This approach becomes important when the objective is to examine the impact of liberalisation on productivity growth, as the availability or scarcity of intermediate inputs has a significant impact on productivity growth. However, it should be noted that TFP growth whether estimated in value added terms or gross output terms, must be treated with caution because it may capture an improvement in capacity utilisation, the effect of work place environment and better quality of inputs.

---

13. Due to an open border between Nepal and India, a substantial portion of unrecorded trade takes place between these two countries. In the past Nepal's trade policy was somewhat liberal than that of India, creating an opportunity for smuggling of third country goods to India.

14. See Nishimizu and Robinson (1984) and Nadiri (1970) for further discussion on this issue.

TABLE 3

Manufacturing output by orientation (% share) : 1972/73-1993/94

	1972/73	1976/77	1981/82	1986/87	1987/88	1988/89	1989/90	1990/91	1991/92	1993/94
Resource intensive	85.19	88.5	82.30	51.51	51.34	45.36	44.53	45.52	42.58	41.31
Labour intensive	12.62	10.56	11.75	30.99	30.69	32.59	35.21	38.48	42.55	41.5
Specialised supplier	-	-	-	1.00	3.16	2.75	2.65	1.69	1.78	2.80
Scale intensive	2.19	0.77	5.21	15.72	14.08	18.71	16.70	13.65	12.44	14.06
Science based	-	0.17	0.23	0.78	0.74	0.59	0.91	0.66	0.65	0.33

Source : Estimated from data obtained from *CBS*, various issues.

Figure 3 : Export intensity of Manufacturing in 1992/93 Constant Prices : 1972/73-1993/94

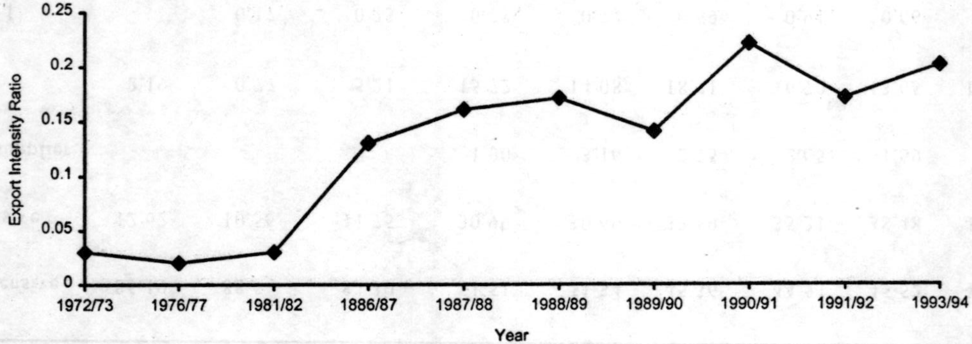

Source : Estimated from data obtained from *CBS* and *Nepal Rastra Bank*, various issues.

Figure 4 : Import Penetration in Manufacturing : 1976/77-1993/94

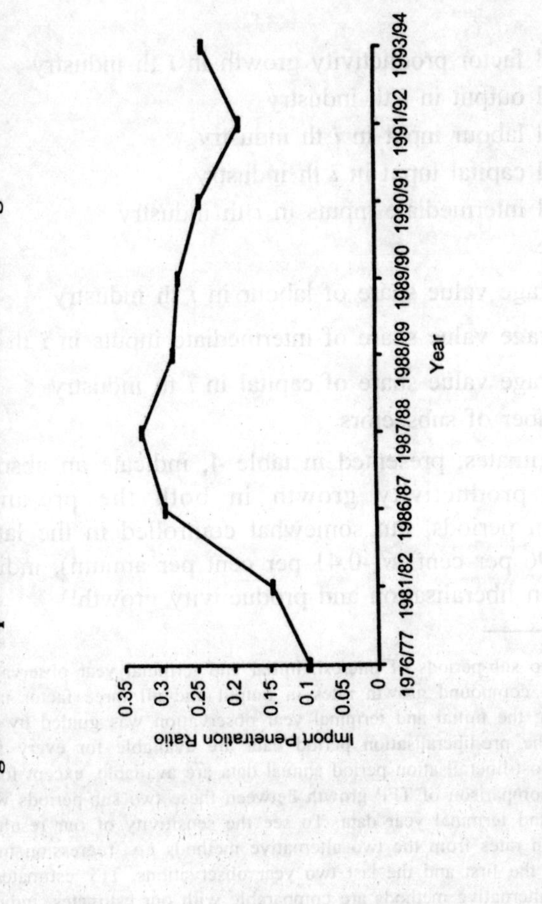

Source : As per Figure 3.

Following Gollop and Jorgenson (1980) TFP growth is defined using the Tornquist index number formula, with :

$$\overset{i}{VT} = \{InY_i(T)-InY_i(T-1)\}-\{\overset{-i}{VL}[InL_i(T)-InL_i(T-1)] + \overset{-i}{VK}[InK_i(T)-InK_i\ (T-1)]+\overset{-i}{VM}[InM_i(T)-InM_i(T-1)]\} \quad (1)$$

$(i = 1, 2.......n)$

where :

$\overset{i}{VT}$ = total factor productivity growth in *i* th industry

Y_i = total output in *i* th industry

L_i = total labour input in *i* th industry

K_i = total capital input in *i* th industry

M_i = total intermediate inputs in *i* th industry

T = time

$\overset{-i}{VL}$ = average value share of labour in *i* th industry

$\overset{-i}{VM}$ = average value share of intermediate inputs in *i* th industry

$\overset{-i}{VK}$ = average value share of capital in *i* th industry

n = number of subsectors

Our estimates, presented in table 4, indicate an absolute fall in overall productivity growth in both the pre-and post-liberalisation periods, but somewhat controlled in the latter sub-period (-0.96 per cent *vs* -0.41 per cent per annum), indicating a link between liberalisation and productivity growth[15].

---

15. For the two sub-periods of interest, initial and terminal year observations were used to obtain compound growth rates in output and all three factor inputs. The choice of using the initial and terminal year observation was guided by the nature of data. For the pre-liberalisation period data are available for every five years, while for the post-liberalisation period annual data are available, except for 1992/93. Thus, for the comparison of TFP growth between these two sub-periods we decided to use initial and terminal year data. To see the sensitivity of our results we also obtained growth rates from the two alternative methods *i.e.*, regression method and the average of the first and the last two year observations. TFP estimates obtained from the two alternative methods are comparable with our estimates, indicating that our results are robust. The most appropriate price indices for TFP growth analysis are the wholesale price indices (WPI). However, in the absence of WPI and the manufacturing GDP deflator in Nepal, the manufacturing price index (1992/93=100) was used, derived from the CPI.

TABLE 4

Growth in output, weighted factor inputs and TFP in the pre-and post-liberalisation periods

	Pre-liberalisation (1972/73-1986/87)			Post-liberalisation (1987/88-1993/94)		
	EO	IS Industries	Total Industries	EO Mfg.	IS Industries	Total Industries Mfg.
Output growth	12.23	0.68	1.72	16.98	8.99	10.83
Weighted material input	5.07	-0.012	0.05	11.86	0.92	7.09
Weighted capital input	3.60	1.29	2.17	10.95	1.06	3.53
Weighted labour input	0.11	0.53	0.46	0.12	0.80	0.62
TFP growth	3.45	-1.13	-0.96	-5.95	6.21	-0.41

Source : Estimated from data obtained from *CBS*, various years.

When the productivity performance of manufacturing industries is decomposed according to the nature of market-orientation, EO industries exhibited better performance than IS industries in the pre-liberalisation period, but not in the post-liberalisation period. Poor productivity in EO industries in the latter period is attributed to the excessive export incentives which did not generate real pressure to improve efficiency, and the shortage of skilled labour resulting from the boom in carpet and garment exports. While productivity performance of IS industries improved from minus 1 per cent to 6 per cent per annum in the post-liberalisation period in response to an increased access to imported inputs, leading to an improvement in capacity utilisation[16]. Among IS industries, productivity growth was higher in the least protected industries in the earlier period, with the exception of distillery and fruit canning, while lower in the highly protected industries including SOEs (see Appendix 1). The productivity performance of the footwear industry, which was privatised in the early 1990s, substantially improved (7 per cent per annum), supporting the notion that privatisation improves productivity performance.

Spatial Distribution

In developing countries, manufacturing industries are concentrated in capital cities and/or relatively developed regions. This is partly due to better infrastructure, relatively higher purchasing power and benefits of agglomeration in capital cities. The tendency to locate in capital cities is further aggravated by an inward-looking policy which requires frequent contact with bureaucrats. However, the need to contact bureaucrats substantially reduces with liberalisation, which might motivate new firms to locate in other regional centres and cities. Since other regional centres and cities might not have well developed infrastructure, new firms may tend to locate in capital cites. Thus, the effect of

16. It should be noted that the level of manufacturing capacity utilisation is still below 50 per cent mainly due to the shortage of electricity supply (Sharma, 1997).

TABLE 5

Spatial distribution of manufacturing industries by region (% of value added) : 1972/73-1993/94

Year	Eastern Dev. Region	Central Dev. Region	Western Dev. Region	Mid-Western Dev. Region	Far-Western Dev. Region
1972/73	28.36	48.26	18.50	2.02	2.78
1976/77	26.76	46.70	15.39	9.19	1.90
1981/82	26.09	49.30	16.38	3.77	4.40
1986/87	18.50	65.68	9.48	4.05	2.57
1987/88	19.65	67.15	7.00	2.72	3.47
1988/89	16.57	71.06	6.54	2.92	2.91
1989/90	15.53	73.11	6.54	2.71	2.08
1993/94	14.26	71.72	9.04	2.83	2.13

Source : Estimated from data from *CBS*, various issues.

liberalisation on the spatial distribution of manufacturing is not clear.

Nepalese experience indicates virtually no change in the spatial distribution of manufacturing industries following the liberalisation program (Table 5). The tendency to locate in a relatively developed region continued even after liberalisation in the policy environment. This can be seen from the rising value added share of the central development region, which is more developed than any other region. The value added shares of the Eastern and Western development regions, which are relatively less developed in comparison with the central development region, have continuously fallen, while there has not been any growth in the value added share of the least developed regions (namely mid-Western and far-Western development regions).

The tendency to locate in the developed region (namely central development region) appears to have increased income disparities between the regions and encouraged internal migration to the major cities, like Kathmandu and Birgunj, making urban congestion and pollution problems worse. Thus, there does not appear to be a link between liberalisation and spatial distribution of industries in a LDC like Nepal. It seems that spatial distribution is sensitive to factors other than liberalisation. These factors may include easy access to the international market, relatively higher incomes and better infrastructure facilities.

IV. Conclusion

In this paper we have examined the effects of liberalisation on the structure of manufacturing, with data from Nepalese manufacturing. Our analysis indicates that despite low supply elasticities due to poor physical infrastructure, lack of efficient institutions and human capital, liberalisation is conducive to structural changes in a LDC like Nepal. Following the liberalisation program, the output share of the labour intensive sector sharply rose and its export intensity increased. However, it appears that growth in export intensity was mainly brought about by the export incentives rather than the actual improvement in competitiveness, as EO industries recorded poor productivity performance in the post-liberalisation period. Although import penetration declined in the post-liberalisation period, it was IS industries that demonstrated better productivity performance, probably due to increased access to imported inputs which improved their capacity utilisation. External competition may also have contributed to enhance efficiency in the IS industries.

We did not find any change in the spatial distribution of industries following the liberalisation programs. The tendency to locate in developed regions continues even after liberalisation, indicating that better infrastructure and an easy access to the international market are more important than the policy environment. However, these results must be interpreted with some caution due to the short period of our data.

APPENDIX 1

TFP Growth in the Pre- and Post-liberalisation Periods at the Four Digit Level

	TFP growth in pre-liberalisation period (%)	TFP growth in post-liberalisation period (%)	Improvement (+) or Fall (-) in TFP growth
Dairy Products	2.2	0.5	-
Canning/preserving Fruits	-24.1	7.0	+
Vegetable Fats	-2.9	7.5	+
Grain Mill Products	-1.1	2.7	+
Bakery Products	-0.5	1.6	+
Sugar	0.1	-0.2	-
Cocoa and Confectionery	2.2	-1.4	-
Mfg. of Food Products, nec	5.5	5.4	-
Animal feeds	-3.6	-1.6	+

Distilleries	0.3	4.9	+
Beer	na	2.3	na
Soft Drinks	na	-3.9	na
Bidi Manufacturing	-0.8	0.3	+
Cigarette Manufacturing	na	0.6	na
Tobacco Manufacturing	na	-3.0	na
Spinning/Weaving and Textile	1.1	-0.1	-
Non-wearing Textile	na	-1.5	na
Knitting Mills	-0.1	3.8	+
Carpet and Rugs	3.8	-5.1	-

Contd.

APPENDIX 1 : *continued*

	TFP growth in pre-liberalisation period (%)	TFP growth in post-liberalisation period (%)	Improvement (+) or Fall (-) in TFP growth
Jute Manufacturing	1.5	-5.3	-
Wearing Apparel except Footwear	11.3	-4.3	-
Leather and Leather Products	na	2.1	na
Footwear Manufacturing	0.3	7.1	+
Saw Mills	0.0	11.1	+
Wood Cork Pro., nec	na	7.8	na
Wooden Furniture	-4.6	-1.6	+
Paper and Paper Products	1.7	7.8	+
Printing	-2.7	-0.1	+
Drug and Medicine	-6.2	0.8	+

Soap	6.7	-4.8	-
Chemical Products, nec	3.8	-9.6	-
Rubber Products	-4.7	1.1	+
Plastic Products	2.5	0.2	-
Structural Clay	-3.2	2.3	+
Cement	11.3	-4.8	-
Non-metallic Mineral Products	na	7.8	na
Iron and Steel	3.0	1.7	-
Metallic Furniture	-2.5	-6.0	-
Structural Metal Products	na	-3.8	na

Contd.

APPENDIX 1 : *continued*

	TFP growth in pre-liberalisation period (%)	TFP growth in post-liberalisation period (%)	Improvement (+) or Fall (-) in TFP growth
Non-mach. Fabricated Metal	0.2	0.8	+
Radio and TV	na	7.2	na
Electric Apparatus	na	6.2	na
Jewellery	-9.4	5.0	+
Other Manufacturing, nec	-5.3	-2.1	+
Manufacturing Total	-1.0	-0.4	+

Source : As per table 4. na = not available.

REFERENCES

Aswicahyono, H.H.K., Bird and H. Hill (1996), 'What Happens to Industrial Structure When Countries Liberalise? Indonesia since the mid 1980s', *Journal of Development Studies*, 32 (3), pp. 340-363.

Centrai Bureau of Statistics (CBS), *Census and Annual survey of Manufacturing Establishments* (various issues), Kathmandu, Nepal.

Diaz-Alejandro, C. and G. Helleiner (1982), Handmaiden in Dress, Washington, D.C. : Overseas Development Council.

Diehl, M. (1995), Structural Change in the Economic Transformation Process : Vietnam 1986-93, *Economic System*, 19(2), pp. 147-182.

Dijck, P. (1990), 'Transforming the Trade and Industrialisation Regime in Developing Countries', in M.P. Van Dijck and H. Secher Marcussen (eds.), *Industrialisation in the third World : The Need for Alternative Strategies*, London : Frank Cass, pp. 9-32.

Dijkstra, A.G. (1996), 'The Impact of Structural Adjustment Programs on Manufacturing: Lessons from Nicaragua', *World Development*, 24 (3), pp. 535-547.

Gollop, F.M. and D.W. Jorgenson (1980), 'U.S. Productivity Growth by Industry, 1947-73' in J.W. Kendrick and B.N. Vaccara eds. *New Development in Productivity Measurement and Analysis*, Chicago University Press, Chicago.

International Monetary Fund (IMF), *International Financial Statistics*, Washington, D.C. (1993 and 1994 issues).

Kawai, H. (1994), 'International Comparative Analysis of Economic Growth : Trade Liberalisation and Productivity Growth', *Developing Economies*, XXXII (4), pp. 373-397.

Krueger, A.O. (1987), *Foreign Trade Regime and Economic Development : Liberalisation Attempts and Consequence*, Cambridge : Ballinger Publishing Company.

Little, I., Scitovsky, T. and Scott, M. (1970), *Industry and Trade in Some Developing Countries A comparative Study*, London : Oxford University Press.

Ministry of Finance, *Economic Survey* (various issues), Kathmandu, Nepal.

Mosley, P. (1993), 'Structural Adjustment : A General Overview, 1980-89', in V. N. Balasubramanyam and Sanjaya Lall (eds.), Current Issues in Development Economics, London: Macmillan.

Nadiri, M.I. (1970), 'Some Approaches to the Theory and Measurement of Total Factor Productivity : A Survey', *Journal of Economic Literature*, 8, pp. 1137-1177.

Nepal Rastra Bank, *Quarterly Economic Bulletin*, (various issues) Kathmandu, Nepal.

Nishimuzi, M. and S. Robinson (1984), 'Trade Policies and Productivity Change in Semi-industrialized Countries', *Journal of Development Economics*, 16, pp. 177-210.

Nordas, H.K.(1996), 'South African Industries — Catching up or Falling Behind?', Journal of Development Studies, 32 (5), pp. 715-733.

Papageorgiou, D., Michaely, M. and Choksi, A. (1991), *Liberalising Foreign Trade*, Vol. 7, Basil Blackwell Ltd.

Rodrik, D. (1992 a), 'The Limits of Trade Policy Reform in Developing Countries', *Journal of Economic Perspectives*, 6, (1), pp. 87-105.

Rodrik, D. (1992 b), 'Closing the Technology Gap : Does Trade Liberalisation Really Help?', in G.K. Helleiner (ed.), *Trade Policy, Industrialisation and Development : New Perspectives*, Oxford : Claredon Press, pp. 155-175.

Rodrik, D. (1992c), 'Conceptual Issues in the Design of Trade Policy for Industrialisation', *World Development*, 20 (3), pp. 309-319.

Sharma, K. (1995), 'Trade and Manufacturing in Nepal', *The Asian Economic Review*, XXXVII (1), pp. 58-86.

Sharma, K. (1997), 'Impact of Policy Reform on Manufacturing Growth in Nepal', *Asian Survey*, XXXVII (6), pp. 550-560.

Stein, H. (1992), 'Deindustrialisation, Adjustment, the World Bank and the IMF in Africa' *World Development*, 20 (1), pp. 83-95.

Taylor, L.J. (1981), 'IS-LM in the Tropics : Diagrammatic of the New Structuralist Macrocritique' in W.R. King and S. Weintraub (eds.), *Economic Stabilisation in Developing Countries*, Washington D.C. : Brooking Institution.

Yenturk-Coban, N. (1992), 'Industrial Strategies, Foreign Trade Regimes and Structural Change in Turkey 1980-88' in Jean-Marc Fontaine (ed.), *Foreign trade reforms and development strategy*, London : Routledge, pp. 274-289.

World Bank (1993), *The East Asian Miracle : Economic Growth Growth and Public Policy*, New York : Oxford University Press.

PART IV

GOVERNMENT PERFORMANCE AND PROSPECTS FOR ADMINISTRATIVE REFORM

14

Good Governance and Administrative Reform : Priorities for India*

BINAYAK RAY

Introduction

Economists, policy analysts and multilateral development agencies agree that economic development and good governance issues are inseparable. The Asian and the Russian economic crises confirm that cronyism, widespread corruption and non-transparent policy setting can trigger economic and political crises of an unmanageable proportion.

*This is a revised version of a paper delivered at the 'South Asian Development in 1997 and Beyond : Its Relevance for Australia' seminar organised by the Centre for South Asian Studies and Department of Economics, University of Sydney, September 1997. The title of the delivered paper was Public Administration in India — Some Issues and Prospects.

Good governance practice means different things to different people. The perception is also different in different countries. Because of these perceived differences it is impractical to provide an all embracive definition of the concept. While examining what contributed most to the rise of East Asian economies, Root (1996) found that the concept of good governance evades definition. However, differences aside, there are certain elements which form its core :

> Governments should be owned by citizens at large and be effective in economic, social and political areas. In other words, factors such as accountability, policy transparency, corruption free administration, rule of law, independent judiciary are considered to contribute to good governance practices (DAC, 1993 : 28-30; World Bank, 1994; DAC, 1995).

While good governance evades definition, notwithstanding some differences in details, the symptoms of poor governance are universal. They are :

- Failure to make a clear separation between public and private interests; hence a tendency to divert public resources for private benefit (leads to the growth of corrupt practices in public life).
- Failure to establish a predictable framework for law and government behaviour conducive to development (encourages arbitrariness in application of rules and laws).
- Excessive rules, regulations, licensing requirements etc., which impede the functioning of markets (encourages corruption and rent seeking; discourage competition).
- Priorities inconsistent with development (resulting in misallocation of resources and narrowly-based or non-transparent decision making).

Singularly none of the above symptoms is considered a sufficient sign of poor governance, but an environment hostile to development is created when they are sufficiently severe and occur together (World Bank, 1992).

Within this context, the results of a national survey in India conducted at the time of the 50th anniversary of India's Independence are startling[1]. The survey found that good governance or civil society related issues remain a major concern of the population at large. The survey finds (don't knows/can't say respondents are proportionately distributed to those who responded) :

- 47 per cent believe that India will disintegrate in 50 years.
- 43 per cent believe that the present law and order situation is worse than under the British.
- 55 per cent believe that politicians are dishonest, compared to 6 per cent believing them to be honest.
- 60 per cent believe that police are dishonest, only 7 per cent believing them to be honest.
- 51 per cent believe that a little over half of their parliamentary representatives are not at all interested in solving the problem of their constituency.
- 34 per cent identify corruption as the biggest evil followed by unemployment (20 per cent) and rising prices (18 per cent).

These responses unequivocally show people's lack of confidence in the political process, politicians, police, administration and generally in those who are in a position of power or authority.

Governance issues are complex, and they need to be examined in their entirety within the context of intra and inter-relationships between the state, government and the community. Furthermore, the government's performance is seen by different sections of the community differently. For example, communities within a

1. *India Today* (1997), 1947-97 Special Issue, New Delhi, *India : State of the Nation*, pp. 42-53.

nation play a collective role to ensure and enhance national interests, and also play an independent role to promote their sectional and individual interests. An understanding of this perspective is essential because the aspirations and roles of each of these individual communities in the development of a nation vary and they influence good governance practices. It is, therefore, necessary to consider administrative reform issues in conjunction with issues such as constitutional, bureaucratic and judicial reform, and political pluralism.

Constitutional Issues

The Indian Constitution drew heavily on the Westminster system (Rustomji, 1997). Events in India and elsewhere confirm that Constitutions based on the European or North American models may not suit the needs of developing countries (Migdal, 1988 : 10-41). Furthermore, a 49 per cent adult illiteracy rate, lack of all-round loyalty to democratic process (Leftwich, 1993 : 605-24) and a failure to create a truly federal system in a diverse society have dented the community's confidence in the Constitution. These have created a feeling of despondency in many sections of Indian society (Kohli, 1992 : 383-7). Balfour's (1936) warning that if a borrowed Constitution fails to correspond with the national temperament, the misfit may have serious results is certainly true for India.

The Constitution framers in their euphoria failed to determine whether borrowed institutions would work in India. Compared to India, China's post-revolutionary Constitution, although based on an imported ideology, used the long-standing Confucian values to ensure that the people accept them. A Chinese scholar (Xin Ren, 1997 : 11) writes 'Mao, no doubt, was a Marxist believer, but he formed his radically revolutionary ideology within the Chinese traditional thinking on power, authority, the ruling and the ruled and the role of law'.

Of many serious constitutional failures, failure to judiciously apply federal government's powers over states by governments of all political persuasion has significantly weakened the inter-government relationship. For example, the power to dismiss elected state governments on questionable grounds was politically manageable when the same political party was in power at both levels. However, when governments are occupied by different political parties it became a political issue (election of a Communist government in the state of Kerala in 1957 which was dismissed by the federal government under questionable circumstances).

This stands counter to the widely recognised and accepted view of political scientists and constitutional experts that federalism and pluralism are two essential principles for organising heterogeneous societies (such as India) into a viable state of political power sharing by reconciling the twin purposes of political unification and diversity (Kidwai, 1997). Although the Supreme Court has put some clarifications on the indiscriminate use of such power, the issue still remains confused (Chaube, 1997), and an ambivalent political leadership has yet to develop a collectively acceptable position on this issue.

Indian states have extremely limited economic power. Their development expenditure is virtually determined by federal institutions such as the Indian Planning Commission. Furthermore, a command economy requiring licenses and permits for even minor economic activities and a powerful federal bureaucracy often unresponsive to community needs have severely restricted states' and communities' capacity to manage their affairs independently (situation has marginally improved since the economic reform measures introduced in 1991).

This has created an environment where a coalition of a small economically powerful elements in society have used the system to feather their own nests rather than working for the greater welfare of the community (Varshney, 1984 : 1511-7). It is no wonder that even after 50 years of Independence and eight Five-Year Plans, 35 per cent of India's population live in abject poverty (World Bank, 1997).

With growing political pressure to address the power imbalance between the centre and the states, the Sarkaria commission was appointed in 1980 to examine the relationship.

Although nearly a decade has passed since the report was submitted in 1988, the federal-state relationship issue remains unresolved. The Commission emphasised the need for healthy political conventions to promote the principle of cooperative federalism, and criticised the abuse of constitutional provisions for political interest (Sarkaria, 1988). The report's emphasis on the need to develop a benchmark in this area has not been acted upon although a decade has passed since the report was published (Brown, 1997 : 22-27).

The Constitution guarantees Fundamental Rights to its citizens, but they are mainly civil, political and legal in nature. None of these rights incorporates economic or social rights for citizens. They are incorporated in the Directive Principles of State Policy which cannot be legally enforced (Mukherjee and Mukherjee, 1995 : 91-9). Without any guarantee of economic and social rights, other rights, no matter how desirable they are, lose importance to ordinary citizens. Even if it is assumed that citizens give high importance to non-economic and social rights, it is difficult to see how these can be legally enforced when the adult illiteracy rate is 49 per cent and when some 25 million cases remain to be arbitrated in Indian courts in 1996 (Ray, 1998).

Political Pluralism

The Congress party's dominating role in the Independence Movement enabled it to gain unprecedented political power in post-independent India. Nehru's unrivalled popularity restricted the growth of an alternative political power. Within this context Kohli's observation that powerful leaders often prove to be the enemies of institutions such as political parties certainly proves to be true in post-independent India (Kohli, 1992 : 402).

During the Independence Movement economic, social and other policy concerns remained subservient to the struggle for Independence, and received little airing within the leadership. All colonial countries have experienced the similar situation. The Ghanaian leader Nkruma's call 'Seek ye first the political kingdom, and all else will follow' was not an exception (Seidman and Seidman, 1994 : 1).

This vacuum enabled self-interested politicians within Congress in post-independent India to use the party for private gains at the community's cost by influencing government policies and their administration. As a result Congress started losing its undisputed mass base of pre-Independence days. Historians such as Brown (1997 : 22-7) rightly observed that amongst many, this was one of the important reasons that in spite of Congress' rhetoric, many of its strong people-focussed policies were generally little more than vote-catching rhetoric.

Congress received an electoral jolt in 1957 when the Communists won the state election in Kerala. Instead of welcoming such political pluralism, Congress found it difficult to accept this loss of power. Despite the constitution framers' categorical assurance that Article 356 would be rarely used to dismiss state governments, the Kerala Government was dismissed by the federal government in 1959 (two years after it was elected) immediately after the Congress chief met the President and demanded state government's dismissal (Noorani, 1984), indirectly confirming its conspiratorial role in this affair.

Notwithstanding its many failures, Congress' electoral success was significantly assisted by the failures of non-Congress parties. Besides their fragmented nature, their leadership could not match the charisma of Nehru or the political guile of his daughter Indira Gandhi. She was a master political tactician in getting people to believe in much of her rhetoric and kept the opposition fighting amongst themselves. Even after she was defeated in the post-emergency election, opposition-led government was very short lived as it was solely focussed on opposing Mrs Gandhi, and not bound by a common program or ideology. Following the coalition government collapse, she proved her political acumen by winning the mid-term election.

Almost all Indian political parties have also failed to observe democratic principles in administering their parties. Post-independent Congress shunned internal democracy by concentrating power in the High Command and focussed on a dynastic leadership. Even as recently as in 1998, following its defeat in the general election, it reverted to a dynastic leadership by replacing an elected president. More specifically, the new leader did not come through any election process and only very recently became a card carrying member of the party. This undemocratic process is widespread as single-issue based parties are promoted by self-appointed leaders of smaller parties. Mushrooming of political parties remains unabated — in the 1998 general election seven national and 34 state or regional Election Commission recognised parties contested the election.[2] In addition, a large number of non-recognised political parties also contested.

Political parties' failures are also reflected in their inability to properly account for their income and expenditure, including their income sources. This has created a fertile environment for corruption by encouraging an unsavoury relationship between the government and self-seeking interested parties. The recent contribution of Indian Rupees 38 million to the Congress Party by overseas companies in an alleged violation of the Foreign Contribution Regulation Act (FCRA) is an example, and the sloppy investigation of this deal was heavily criticised by the Delhi High Court.[3]

Political parties in many circumstances have adopted undemocratic (often illegal) methods to champion their cause. The indiscriminate call for general strikes,[4] inviting citizens to violate the country's laws to demonstrate their opposition to government's policies (known as Satyagraha, championed by Gandhi during the Independence Movement), or defying established rules and practices when it is beneficial to parties are

2. *The Economic Times*, (1998), 17 January, New Delhi.

3. *The Hindustan Times* (1997), 28 November, New Delhi : HC flays Govt. for closing case.

4. The situation in some parts of the country has reached comical proportions. For example, in the state of West Bengal more than 80 per cent of the general bandhs and industrial strikes are observed either on Mondays or Fridays and on occasions proceeding or succeeding public holidays — all political parties took the same position [*The Statesman Weekly* (1998), 15 August, Calcutta] of bandhs and holidays.

examples.[5] These have created a psychology of defiance in an environment when the government is no longer a foreign power, but owned by citizens themselves.

Another major concern is that a relatively small number of powerful people in both urban and rural areas dominate many political parties. This has not helped institutional development, a prerequisite for preventing unscrupulous people or political parties misusing power. For example, Laloo Prasad Yadav, a powerful leader of a disadvantaged socio-economic group, on becoming Chief Minister was in a position to show that his administration would assiduously work for all people, instead of satisfying sectional interests as has been the case with many previous governments. This expectation was short lived as he used the entire administration to advantage his group's political interests. He was not doing anything new except that he was following the same route with more vigour than his predecessors. One political commentator nicely summed up the situation when he wrote 'Some had the class and the style, others did not. But that does not make the former less vulgar than the more obvious, and in a strange kind of way more honest ...'[6]

Similarly, Ms. Mayawati on becoming Chief Minister of the state of Uttar Pradesh presented a budget where almost a quarter of the annual plan-outlay was earmarked for welfare schemes for people belonging to her own class (scheduled caste and tribes).[7] While raising the economic and social status of an underprivileged class is commendable, the question remains whether the state's underlying economic and financial situation justified such huge expenditure for a relatively small section of the community.

---

5. *The Statesman Weekly*, 1998, 11 July, Calcutta : CPI-M refuses to clear out of government bunglow.

6. *The Asian Age* (1997), 2 August, Calcutta : The fault lies in the system, not in Laloo, Mustafa, S.

7. *The Asian Age* (1997), 27 July, Calcutta : Mayawati Budget converts UP into Ambedkar pradesh.

Indian Bureaucracy

On Independence, India essentially maintained its Westminster modelled administrative structure. The British were well served by this model. The mandarin recruitment system recruits people into a career stream through an age-restricted centralised rigorous entrance examination (World Bank, 1997a : 94). Specialised services (*e.g.*, forestry and economic) also follow the same practice. The process is élite focussed and biased towards well-off sections of the community as the system offers little scope for self-made persons or proven professionals and managers to enter the service outside this age-restricted entry system.

In colonial India the bureaucracy maintained its power base within the government when the European collectors left much of the day-to-day management of their districts to the Indian officials, who often manipulated the system to their own advantage and enrichment (Marshall, 1997 : 4-9). By preserving this structure intact the post-Independence government failed to promote organisations capable of meeting the development needs of masses. Even Nehru admitted that one of his major failures was not changing the bureaucratic apparatus after Independence (Subramaniam, 1992 : 24). This failure, as pointed out by Potter (1986), is primarily due to independence fighters who took the reigns of administration after the British left in 1947 underestimating the strength of the bureaucracy.

A recent study found that the Indian bureaucracy does not value leadership qualities of creativity, institution building and tends to indulge in power games, manipulate patronage for personal benefits and shy away from public scrutiny and accountability[8] (Singh and Bhandarkar, 1997). This is not peculiar

---

8. *The Statesman Weekly* (1997), 13 September, Calcutta : Whither Indian Bureaucracy Bhattacharya.

Recently a senior Cabinet Minister and a very distinguished lawyer '... lashed out at senior bureaucrats for maintaining a sinister interest... restricted the recruitment of the Central Vigilance Commissioner to civil servants' reported in *the Statesman Weekly* (1998), 5 September, Calcutta : Bureaucrats misled Cabinet on CVC (Central Vigilance Commissioner) draft, charges Jethmalani.

to India. Independent research confirms that bureaucrats in developing countries often perform in a way that strengthens their own interests and those of the privileged in the society (Davidson, 1992).

The Indian bureaucracy has also failed to perform its routine tasks effectively. For example, it failed to administer the country's tax laws which led to the growth of an enormous black economy. If, indeed, it was doing its job properly why did it fail to unearth the black money in spite of so many Voluntary Income Disclosure Schemes (VIDS)?[9] Even if one assumes that some unavoidable administrative lapses were responsible for these failures, what excuses were there for failing to take the punitive action which successive VIDS promised? Further examples, amongst many, are its failure to forewarn the government of the very serious nature of the 1991 foreign exchange crisis (Bhagwati, 1995) and failure to foresee the importance of geographic patents in the context of the WTO provisions.[10]

In addition, its recruitment policy also has contributed to the decline in its performance standards. Articles 15(4) and 16(4) of the Constitution provide provisions for reservation of posts for Scheduled Castes and Tribes. While social justice requires affirmative action in number of fronts, there is a downside for such actions. The cost of pursuing social policy objectives in perpetuity through preferential employment policy often outweigh the benefits as it causes friction, compromises efficiency and damages the service's integrity. Such policies have been in place since Independence, and yet the Scheduled Caste employees in group A services hold only 10.24 per cent of the positions although they constitute 16.48 per cent of the total population. Schedule Tribe employees constitute only 5.4 per cent of the

9. For a detailed discussion of the Voluntary Income Disclosure Schemes (VIDS), see Bhargava, A(1997), *Taxman*, Taxman Publications Ltd., New Delhi.

10. *The Economic Times* (1998), 18 February, New Delhi : Comment by noted scientist Dr. Swaminathan on the success of an US company in getting a rice grain protected in the name of Basmati.

positions in group A service, although they constitute 8.08 per cent of India's population (Government of India, 1996 : 184-95).

This division creates problems similar to those found in many post-Independent African countries with rapid indigenisation of the bureaucracy. Nigerian scholar Ekeh (1975) found that in post-colonial Africa there were two public realms : a 'primordia' public realm, governed by primordial groupings, ties and sentiments and a colonial-derived 'civic' public-realm. Most educated Africans are members of both these public realms. This duality often precludes impartial and effective application of governments' declared policies and more often than not hinders policy clarity in attaining program objectives.

While social policy objectives often require affirmative action for disadvantaged groups to attain a similar level of socio-economic development as the community at large, it is argued that the best way to raise social and economic conditions is by providing economic and institutional support to build individual and group capacity to compete at par, instead of a negative approach through quotas and reservations. However, because of the entrenched disadvantages when affirmative action is required such provisions should have a sunset clause so that every body feels comfortable that in the medium to long-run all are treated equally. This mechanism will also enable disadvantaged groups to earn their pride, assist self-confidence and increase the authority of the occupant of the position, and any simmering discontent within the bureaucracy will be denied any grounds to flourish.

Another major concern is a lack of separation between the government and the administration. This has provided scope for the bureaucracy to develop an unholy alliance with unscrupulous politicians leading to poor administration, corruption, nepotism, and often to administrative practices falling on the verge of illegality. As a result honest and upright administrators have been harassed for pursuing their duties honestly and truthfully, whereas unscrupulous officers have used the system to further their own career.[11] One way to minimise the scope for such unholy alliance is by clearly defining and separating the functions of government and administration.

Judiciary

The Indian judiciary, in spite of pressures to the contrary, has mainly remained independent.[12] In recent years, prompted by a number of public interest litigation, and concerned at the failure to preserve the constitutional integrity by the executive, the judiciary did not hesitate to take specific administrative action.[13] However, judiciary is also acutely aware of the adverse consequences of such judicial activism.[14]

Overall, there have been lapses in the judicial system as well. A High Court chief Justice was on the verge of being impeached by the Parliament but avoided it by resigning his position; another was forced to resign for indiscretion, and judges

---

11. Universally recognised honest and upright officers such as Biswas (Fodder scam), Madhaban (Bofors, who resigned his post), Bezbaruah (Foreign exchange violation), Mishra (Acting head of the CBI) have experienced extreme difficulties in pursuing their job truthfully. A number of media outlets (particularly print media) have continuously exposed their respective positions as officers in-charge of these politically sensitive cases. For latest development, news items published in *the Statesman Weekly* on 25 July, 1 August and 25 August (1998), Calcutta, are worth reading.

12. Varma, Mr. Justice J.S. (1997), Chief Justice of India, New Delhi, 'I am under too much pressure on Hawla' in a statement at the Court on 14 July before proceedings in the case commenced. This was reported in all major Indian dailies on 15 July.

13. *The Hindu* (1997), 19 December, Chennai : Greater Freedom for CBI to probe graft cases.

A Division Bench of the Supreme Court on 9 September 1998 forced the Government of India to reinstate Mr. M.K. Bezbaruah as Director, Enforcement Directorate, and to cancel earlier order transferring him out of this position. Earlier the Bench censured the government for 'misquoting' and 'completely rewriting' a Supreme Court judgement to justify the transfer of Mr. Bezbaruah from the post of Enforcement Director. *The Statesman Weekly* (1998), 12 September, Calcutta : Bezbaruah to be reinstated.

14. Varma, Mr. Justice J.S. (1997), Chief Justice of India on 26 November, New Delhi : In his key note address at a function organised by the Supreme Court Bar Association to Commemorate 48th Law Day, the day on which the Indian Constitution was born and adopted.

have been found to be corrupt as well. The Executive has manipulated the appointment of judges (the appointment of a Chief Justice during Mrs. Gandhi's emergency rule violating established practice is an example), and a few of the judges are not perceived to be honest and impartial in their judicial role.

The biggest danger is perhaps the number of pending cases in the judicial system. It was estimated that about 25 million cases remained pending in 1996. Such a large number of pending cases denies justice to the majority who do not have the resources to pursue lengthy litigation. In such circumstances only the rich and wealthy can use the judiciary to their advantage.

The rich have also used the system to their own advantage through means such as influencing the direction of investigations or influencing prosecuting agencies to be soft on their submissions before the court[15]. Even though most judges uphold their oath of office, they feel frustrated by serious shortcomings in the system which became clear from a number of recent rulings on major corruption cases[16].

Notwithstanding the judiciary's active role in promoting good governance practices and forcing the executive to perform its duties according to the country's laws and regulations, its role cannot be unlimited for a number of reasons. First, the judiciary is a reactive, not pro-active institution; second, although through its legal interpretations, it sets the scope of individual legislation, in general it deals with past and not future events (Seidman and Seidman, 1994 : 128-9); third, the judiciary neither controls the purse nor possesses executive power — its effectiveness depends upon the willingness and capacity of the executive and legislature to provide resources to perform its tasks properly, a situation which has not changed from when Alexander Hamilton wrote in

15. *The Statesman Weekly* (1998), 31 January, Calcutta. For once, let the law take its course!

16. *The Statesman* (1997, 5 and 18 August, Calcutta : Probe Kesri's son, says HC, and Kesri's monthly income Rs. 1,450; and *The Hindustan Times* (1997), 13 December, New Delhi : HC seeks FCRA probe details against Congress.

1788 that of the three arms of the government, the judiciary was the weakest (Cooke, 1961 : 522-3).

Corruption : A Major Concern In India

Corruption in the public arena is not a new phenomenon, nor unique to India — only the types and causes of corruption vary and differ (Kilgaard, 1997 : 497-510). Existing corrupt practices are mostly a post-war phenomenon, largely created by economic and political circumstances.

While corruption is abhorrent, economic successes of countries like Japan, South Korea and Indonesia influenced many to downplay its impact on policy distortions, program failures and the country's socio-economic fabric. The World Bank, however, argued that in the long-run corruption was destabilising and could adversely impact on countries' economy and stability (World Bank, 1997a : 103). The Asian economic crises triggered by failures in Thailand, South Korea and Indonesia confirm the Bank's position. The economic downturn in Japan is also significantly attributed to corrupt practices in its banking and financial sectors.

Corruption grows and flourishes under variety of circumstances — excessive control and regulations, non-transparent policy setting, poor accountability, institutional weakness, poor salary and limited career opportunities for public officials and the absence of role models in the community. In summary, major causes of corruption are :

- Excessive controls and regulations-encouraging regulators in cohort with politicians to seek rent as people in such an environment always want decisions to favour them.
- Disappearance of transparency in the decision making process.
- Accountability is ignored to suit personal and sectional interests in violation of established rules and practices.
- Failure to properly supervise decisions and actions of subordinate staff either because they are ineffective or

superiors themselves are benefiting from corrupt practices.

- Limited opportunities for government officials for promotion.
- Identified perpetrators of corrupt practices remain unpunished.
- Non-existence of role models with whom the community can identify.

Although corruption in India has been going on for some time, four factors have made the situation critical. First, it now pervades the highest echelons of society at an unprecedented level and they evade retribution by influencing the activities of administration and law enforcement agencies tasked to detect and prosecute perpetrators. Second, many no longer consider corruption morally unacceptable or shameful. Third, non-existence of an effective institutional set-up which could challenge corrupt practitioners at the highest level and finally, the lack of political leadership truly committed to fight corruption.

Since the early 1990s the United Nations, the World Bank, Organisation for Economic Cooperation and Development (OECD), the European Union (EU), Organisation of American States (OAS) and non-government organisations such as Transparency International have combined their efforts to expose corrupt practices in business and administration (United Nations, 1990, 1995; World Development Report, 1997a; Transparency International, 1997). India's high level of corruption is now globally acknowledged, particularly after the publication of the results of the annual business corruption surveys by Transparency International.

Corruption is both a social and law enforcement issue — it primarily reflects a society's values and perceptions. Mistakes are made when governments borrow foreign anti-corruption measures without considering all relevant socio-economic issues. This often results in anti-corruption measures failing to achieve their desired objectives and a loss of faith in the governments' capacity to fight corruption. It is, therefore, imperative that institutional arrangements to fight corruption are only developed after full consideration of all relevant issues.

In recent years a number of countries have attracted global attention for their bold moves to fight corruption. Amongst them are Uganda, Tanzania, Hong Kong, the People's Republic of China and the Australian states of Queensland and New South Wales. While it would be wrong to suggest that they have achieved total success in fighting corruption, it nonetheless is clear that their efforts are bearing fruit.

Lessons from the experiences of these countries are clear — besides competitive economic and transparent government policies, there should be in place an institutional set-up capable of first, creating an environment where there is no scope for corrupt practices to grow and flourish and second, perpetrators of corrupt practices are given exemplary punishment irrespective of their socio-economic status. Within this context institutions' functions should include investigation; policy making — review and revision of methods of work, procedures, laws and practices; advisory; educative and communicating to appropriate authorities, the results of investigation; and prosecutions, as appropriate, through the Director of Public Prosecution.

The foci of these aforementioned countries' anti-corruption strategies are (Conor, 1989; CJC, 1990; ICAC, 1989; Muganda, 1985; Ostergaard, 1986; Ruzindana, 1995 : 191-208; World Bank, 1997a) :

- A fully independent designated agency responsible for fighting corruption answerable either to the Parliament or directly to the head of the state.
- Ensuring such agencies receiving appropriate budgetary and logistic support to carry out their tasks as they were likely to face opposition from powerful quarters of the society.
- Personnel in the anti-corruption agencies recognised for their integrity and commitment to fighting corruption.

- Public officials or senior bureaucrats were treated at par with everybody else in the community by enforcement and prosecuting agencies to ensure communities' trust and respect for their work.
- Continuous research and innovative methods to remove the underlying causes of corruption such as inappropriate economic policies and administrative practices which contribute to the growth of corrupt practice.
- Exemplary punishment when corruption was proved irrespective of the accused's social and political clout.

In summary, the five mantras of anti-corruption drive, following Kilgaard (1997), should be : monopolies must be reduced and carefully regulated; official discretions must be clarified accountability must be enhanced the probability of being caught must increase; and penalties for corruption (both givers and takers) must rise. It is a tall order, but there can be no short cuts when corruption has engulfed society as a whole.

Reform Priorities

It is clear that first, good governance issues cover a wide range of constitutional, administrative, social, cultural and community issues; second, good governance practices cannot be superimposed from outside — these need to be indigenously developed and implemented to ensure success (Lewis, 1995 : 159-60); third, good governance practices and related administrative development must be kept under constant review and finally, a packaged approach is necessary to ensure good governance practices take root in society.

Generally speaking, the Constitution, social structure, economic policies and community traditions largely shape the institutional and administrative structures of a country. However, increasing pressure for national economies to compete globally for economic survival virtually determines government policy focus and priority. Policies in areas such as social, environmental and human rights are also increasingly being determined and influenced by international treaties, covenants and the activities of non-government organisations focussing on specific issues (*e.g.*, Amnesty International's focus on human rights issues).

Within this context, there exists strong grounds for pursuing reform initiatives simultaneously on a number of fronts namely, constitutional, parliamentary, administrative and judicial. In addition, urgent policy initiatives are also required to fight corruption.

Constitutional : The success of Constitutions in promoting constitutional conventions and morality is closely interrelated with the country's administrative structure and the type of Constitution. If the constitutional and administrative form is not of the same nature, it is possible to pervert and violate the spirit of the Constitution by manipulating the form of administration (Noorani, 1989), which has been widespread in India during last few decades.

While individual features of the Indian Constitution are sound, many of them were included without assessing their suitability for Indian conditions. This is not unique to India — it is a colonial legacy and was acknowledged long before colonies started gaining Independence (Balfour, *op. cit.*).

Shortcomings of the Indian Constitution are also apparent as during last 50 years it was amended about 80 times to meet India's contemporary political, social and administrative needs. With such a large number of amendments in such a short period the integrity of the Constitution has been affected resulting in a weakened constitutional structure.

In an environment where coalition governments of convenience dominate the political scene constitutional reform will be difficult, but the issue must be openly and comprehensively addressed and examined to meet the country's needs in the next century. Two important foci, amongst others, have to be first, a clear delineation of functions and responsibilities of three tiers of governments and to create capacities for second and third tier governments to manage their affairs independently within a federal structure, and second, to clearly delineate responsibilities of the government and the administration. A large number of problems experienced during last few decades often originated from an unholy alliance of corrupt politicians and bureaucracy. A clear delineation of their respective roles would substantially reduce such scope.

Parliamentary control : Except for brief periods India has been ruled by Congress Party with absolute majority in both Houses of Parliament. This has resulted in Parliament having very little effective control on the executive. Indian Parliamentary Consultative Committees lack power to effectively supervise the executive — they cannot summon witnesses nor seek evidence under oath, nor can they demand the production of necessary files and documents or examine any official records.

Unless Parliament can exert supremacy over the executive government, good governance practices cannot take root. Parliamentary committees, therefore, need to be remodelled with the power to take evidence under oath from public officials and call for documents, if required. The Executive's privilege of withholding information from the Committees should only be used in extreme circumstances.

Community organisations and individual citizens should also be actively encouraged to take part in Committee proceedings either through written submissions on administrative and legislative matters, or by appearing before the committee when invited. To encourage such participation, decentralised Committee hearings should be encouraged.

Certain senior administrative positions, because of the nature of their responsibilities, remain vulnerable to pressures from politicians and vested interests. To ensure their independence, there exists a strong case for making these positions and functionaries statutory, directly responsible to the Parliament. Suggested positions are : members of the Central Revenue Board; the Election Commission; the Corporate Regulatory Agency; the Human Rights Commission; the independent broadcasting authority; and the crime and corruption control authority (responsible for monitoring, investigating and prosecuting public and elected officials of their corrupt and criminal behaviour), and the Auditor and comptroller General (with wider powers); the Director of Public Prosecution; the Chief Statistician and the Ombudsman (Lokpal).

This will contribute to strengthening important institutions and is likely to bring community's confidence back in the executive and the Parliamentary process because the executive will be forced to become answerable for its activities and people in sensitive areas of administration will be able to perform their tasks unobstructed. Collectively these will assist to create a political environment to promote and facilitate good governance principles.

Administrative : A major failure of the post-independent administration is that its administrative structure virtually remained the same as it was in the colonial days. The administration which Nehru had once denounced as anti-national and requiring drastic reform was maintained by him both in structure of the state itself, despite the universal adult franchise, and in the style of administrative services (Brown, 1997). In spite of many investigations and enquiries, the administration has remained élite focussed and self serving.

The selection process of the Indian Civil Service is very much élite focussed which virtually denies entry of self-made persons to the service. Another important issue is the job reservation policy — in the long run this policy is neither helpful to the disadvantaged community nor in the interest of the service. First, it creates animosity between those who joined the service under open conditions and those who were selected under the reservation criteria. Second, by keeping this division in perpetuity a subculture is preserved which tends to work along similar lines as found in Africa.[17] Finally, the very existence of discriminatory

17. In post-independent African states, with the Africanisation of the civil service most educated Africans were found to be members of 'primordia' public realm, governed by primordial groupings, ties and sentiments and a colonial-derived 'civic' public realm. Most educated Africans are members of both these public realms. This duality often precluded impartial and effective application of governments' declared policies.

policy on caste or tribal basis act against genuine upliftment of the underprivileged class as the system itself perpetuates an 'us and them' mentality. It is argued that a different approach is required for genuine upliftment of the social and economic status of disadvantaged communities.

Last but not least, there exists an urgent need for a thorough examination of the structure of government departments with the objective of drastically reducing the number of positions as well as departments to ensure a modern development-focussed administrative structure. This issue needs to be worked out thoroughly by those who are familiar with Indian society, but have no involvement with the Indian administrative structure directly or indirectly. This will enable them to address the structural issue in a non-emotive and independent way. If overseas experience is of any guide there is scope for bringing down administrative costs by anything from 50 to 70 per cent of the current level. Depending upon the accuracy of various figures, anything from 55 to 90 per cent of state revenues are currently spent to cover administrative costs, leaving hardly any funds for development expenditure. In global terms, general administration costs should not exceed, at most, 20 per cent of government revenue. This would release resources for productive development expenditure including physical and social infrastructure (*e.g.*, health and education). General administration cost for industrialised countries (1988) was 8.2 per cent of total government expenditure, in developing countries (1990) it was 15.3 per cent, in Japan (1992) it was 10.8 per cent and in Singapore (1992) it was 8.0 per cent (Rao, 1988 : 673-94).

Another major concern is the governments' policy to grant pensions at various levels (thus creating future liability) without making appropriate funding provisions. For example, during the 1988/89 to 1996/97 decade combined revenue expenditure of the central and state governments increased by 201 per cent, compared to 235 per cent in administrative expenditure and 284 per cent in pension payments (World Bank, 1997 : 92-3). Funds required for future pension payments, if overseas experience is any guide, will increase exponentially as people's longevity increases. This will have an enormous impact on future government budgets to an unmanageable extent and heavy burden on the future tax-paying work force.

Judicial : Presently, with about 25 million cases to be adjudicated, judicial redress virtually remains beyond the means of ordinary citizens. To ensure that they can afford justice, it is imperative that their cases are heard promptly and at an affordable cost. Whether there exists any scope for conciliatory approaches to resolve certain categories of litigation needs to be explored. The judiciary, the legal profession and the government must collectively address this issue to make people confident in the capacity of the judiciary to deliver justice.

Judicial appointments also remain a controversial issue. Some of the appointments made by government in earlier days did not generate confidence. However, reforms initiated by providing greater power to the Chief Justice of the Supreme Court has also raised concern in recent days, as accusations have been made that a recent Chief Justice did not consult others as required before recommending names to the President for appointment. This has raised concern to such an extent that the President felt obliged to refer the matter to the Supreme Court to decide whether the Chief Justice of India could recommend appointment of judges to the Supreme Court and High Courts without consultation process[18]. There are more than 600 judges in the Supreme Court and High Courts in India. The Chief Justice has constituted a nine-judge Constitution Bench to address this issue. The entire episode, without doubt, reflects badly on the judiciary itself, irrespective of the outcome of the deliberations of the Division Bench. It is interesting to note that one former Supreme Court judge commented at a recent seminar that 'One person, no matter how capable and intelligent, can't shoulder the burden of

18. *The Statesman Weekly* (1998), 1 August, Calcutta. President seeks SC opinion on judges.

appointing more than 600 judges to the Supreme Court and High Courts. Transparency in judicial selections is needed ...'.[19]

As head of the India's judicial system, the Chief Justice is in a very powerful position and the position has the authority and clout to introduce, in consultation with other agencies involved in the delivery and administration of justice, reforms to ensure that everybody has equal opportunity to seek and receive justice through the judicial process. It is very clear that the current delays and exorbitant costs deny many ordinary citizens from obtaining justice. Reforms in the legal system and in the administration of justice must, therefore, be a priority for everyone involved, directly or indirectly, in the delivery of justice.

However, a major constraint in reforming the administration of justice in India is that most of the Chief Justices of the Supreme Court during last five decades have occupied the position for a relatively short period only. This situation is created by the constitutional requirement that no person below the age of 55 can be appointed as a judge in the Supreme Court and judges must vacate office on reaching 65. Except in one or two cases, to date the senior most judge from the bench was appointed Chief Justice — only in a very small number of cases Chief Justices remained in their position for a long enough time to be able to initiate reform and introduce innovation in the delivery of justice. It is, therefore, worth considering whether on appointment the Chief Justice should remain in the office for at least five years or up to the age of 65, whichever is higher. Alternatively, a person who is likely to remain in the position for at least five years should only be appointed in the position. It is interesting to note that the aforementioned former judge has publicly opposed the convention of appointing the Chief Justice on the basis of seniority[20].

---

19. Singh, Mr. Justice Kuldip, (1998), At a seminar; 'The Judiciary in Peril?' at Calcutta on 16 September organised on the occassion of The Statesman Award for Rural Reporting ceremony.

20. *Ibid.*

Conclusion

After 50 years of Independence, India's position *vis-a-vis* other developing countries has not improved in any significant way in terms of overall economic and social development — nearly one third of its population lives below the poverty line, nearly one half of its adult population is illiterate (worse than the sub-Saharan illiteracy rate), violence is widespread and corruption is endemic. This contributes in a gradual loss of faith in the political process to solve community problems and their capacity to meet the social and political aspirations of the people.

India is a Parliamentary Democracy and its administrative structure is based on this. Its administrative structure, in spite of many reform attempts, has virtually remained same as introduced by the British in the 19th century. The British structure was designed to maintain its power in India. Independent India did not change this basic structure. Therefore, it is not surprising that the post-Independent administration failed to meet community's expectations.

The new millennium is pregnant with enormous possibilities triggered by unprecedented technological changes and new global economic and political configurations. In this new environment, national governments are forced by circumstances to be even more aware of the community's concerns, required to give cognisance to regional and global economic issues and more importantly international public opinion. These aspects are closely linked with good governance practices. Administrative reform priorities must be considered in this context. The suggested reform measures will take a long time to be fully effective and bear fruit, but in a rapidly changing world, time is an important element. In view of this, reform initiatives must be introduced systematically and in a timely fashion covering all aspects such as the economic, the constitutional, administrative, the judiciary, social engineering in the form of effective education of the public about civic responsibilities and above all, the importance of a focussed administrative machinery and structure to face the complex issues in the coming millennium.

The task is not and will not be easy — it will require commitment by political parties, national leadership and above all the community. There is no short cut to this process — the task is complex, but not unachievable.

REFERENCES

Balfour, The Earl of (1936), 'Foreword', in Walter Bagehot, *English Constitution*, OUP, London.

Bhagwati, J. (1995), *India in Transition — freeing the economy* (paper back edition), Clarendon Press, New York.

Brown, J. (1997), 'Gandhi and Nehru : frustrated visionaries?', *History Today*, Vol. 47 (9), September, History Today Ltd., London.

Chaube, S.K. (1997), 'President's rule : re-examining Article 356', *The Statesman*, 6 August, Calcutta.

Conor, A.E.W. (1989), 'Anti-corruption legislation : will more and better rules curb widespread corruption?, *East Asian Executive Reports*, January, Washington.

Cooke, J.E. (ed.), (1961), *The Federalist*, No. 78, Wesleyan University Press, Middletown, USA.

CJC (1990), Criminal Justice Commission Queensland Annual Report 1989-90 (1990), Brisbane.

DAC (1993), Draft DAC Orientation Paper on Participatory Development and Good Governance, *OECD*, Paris (unpublished).

____(1995), Participatory Development and Good Governance, *OECD*, Paris.

Davidson, B. (1992), *The Blackman's Burden*, Random House, New York.

Ekeh, P.P. (1975), Colonialism and the two publics in Africa : A theoretical statement, Comparative Studies in Society and History, 17; quoted in May, R.J. in *Des Promesses A La Crise : Economic Politique De La Papousaie-Nouvelle-Guinee, Revue Tiers Monde*, Vol. XXXVIII, No. 149 : 140-56 (English version).

Government of India (1997), *India 1996*, Publication Division, New Delhi.

ICAC (1989), Independent Commission Against Corruption, New South Wales, Annual Report to 30 June 1989 (1989), Sydney.

Kidwai, M.S (1997), Centre is Holding, *The Statesman Weekly*, 13 December, Calcutta. A review article on Rethinking Indian Federalism, edited by Khan, Rasheeduddin.

Kilgaard, A. (1997), Cleaning up and invigorating the civil service; *Public Administration and Development*, Vol. 17 No. 5, Wiley, London.

Kohli, A. (1992), *Democracy and Discontent : India's Growing Crisis in Governability*, Cambridge University Press, Cambridge.

Leftwich, A. (1993), Governance, Democracy and Development in the Third World, *Third World Quarterly*, Vol. 14, No. 3.

Lewis, J.P. (1995), *India's Political Economy — Governance and Reform*, OUP.

Marshall, P. (1997), The Making of the Hybrid Raj, 1700-1857, *History Today*, Vol. 47 (9), September, London.

Migdal, J.S. (1988), *Strong Societies and Weak States : State Society Relations and State Capabilities in the Third World*, Princeton University Press, New Jersey.

Muganda, A.A. (1985), The Corruption Conundrum in Tanzania : Its Limits and Impact; Proceedings of the 7th UN Congress on the Prevention of Crime and Treatment of Offenders, Milan, Italy.

Mukherjee, S. and Mukherjee, I. (1995), *The Constitution of India*, World Press, Calcutta.

Noorani, A.G. (1984), President's Rule in the States, *Indian Express*, 6 February. Also, reprinted in *The Indian Affairs* : The Constitutional Dimension, Konark Publishers, Delhi.

____(1989), The President and the Constitution, *Indian Express,* 18 March, New Delhi. Also, reprinted in the *Indian Affairs* : The Constitutional Dimension, Konark Publishers, Delhi.

Ostergaard, C.S. (1986), Explaining China's recent political corruption, *Corruption and Reform*, Martinus Nijhoff Publishers, Dordrecht.

Potter, D. (1986), *India's Political Administration* 1981-1983, Clarendon Press, Oxford.

Rao, M. Govinda (1998), Accommodating Public Expenditure Policies : the Case of Fast Growing Asian Economies, *World Development* Vol. 26 No. 4, Pergamon, UK.

Ray, B. (1998), Indian Ocean Rim Countries : Policy Challenges for Sustainable Development, *Indian Ocean Centre*, Curtin University, Perth.

Root, H.L. (1996), Small Countries, Big Lessons, *Governance and Rise of East Asia*, OUP, Hong Kong.

Rustomji, K.F. (1997), A 21st Century doctrine, *Hindustan Times*, 10 October, New Delhi.

Ruzindana, A. (1995), 'Combating Corruption in Uganda', in Langseth, P., Katorobo, J., Brette, E. and Muenne, J., (eds.), *Uganda : Landmarks in Rehabilitating a Nation*, Fountain Publishers, Kampala.

Sarkaria, Mr. Justice R.S. (1988), Report of the Commission on Centre-State Relations, Ministry of Finance, Government of India, New Delhi.

Seidman, A. and Seidman, R.B. (1994), *State and Law in the Development Process*, St. Martin Press, New York.

Singh, P. and Bhadarkar, A. (1997), *IAS Profile : Myths and Realities*, Wiley Eastern, New Delhi.

Subramaniam, K.S. (1992), *Political Violence, Social Movements and the State in India*, Institute of Development Studies, University of Sussex, Brighton.

Transparency International (1997), Annual Report, Berlin.

United Nations (1990), Corruption in Government : Report of an Interregional Seminar, 11-15 December 1989, The Hague, Netherlands, New York.

_____(1995), Background paper prepared by the Secretariat on international action against corruption for the Ninth UN Congress on the Prevention of Crime and the Treatment of Offenders, Cairo (A/CONF 169/14).

Varshney, A. (1984), 'Political economy of slow industrial growth in India, *Economic and Political Weekly*, 1 September, Mumbai (Bombay).

World Bank (1994), *Development Practice, Governance : The World Bank's Experience*, Washington, DC.

_____(1992), *Governance and Development*, Washington DC.

_____(1997), *India - Achievements and Challenges in Reducing Poverty*, Washington DC.

India 1997 Economic Update : Sustaining Rapid Growth, Washington DC.

_____ (1997a), *World Development Report : The State in a Changing World*, OUP, New York.

Xin, Ren (1997), *Tradition of the Law and Law of the Tradition*, Greenwood Press, London.